The Politics of Latin American

Liberation Theology

The Washington Institute for Values in Public Policy
The Washington Institute sponsors research that helps provide the information and fresh insights necessary for formulating policy in a democratic society. Founded in 1982, the Institute is an independent, non-profit educational and research organization which examines current and upcoming issues with particular attention to ethical implications.

ADDITIONAL TITLES

The Politics of Latin American

Liberation Theology

The Challenge to U.S. Public Policy

Foreword By
U.S. Senator Dave Durenburger

Edited By
Richard L. Rubenstein and John K. Roth

91-181

Published in the United States by The Washington Institute Press
Suite 300, 1015 18th Street, NW, Washington, D.C. 20036

© 1988 by The Washington Institute for Values in Public Policy

First Printing, August 1988

A Washington Institute Press book

Cover design by Paul Woodward

Library of Congress Cataloging in Publication data

The Politics of Latin American liberation theology : understanding the
challenge to U.S. public policy / edited by Richard L. Rubenstein and
John K. Roth ; foreword by Dave Durenberger.
         p.   cm.
   Bibliography: p.
   Includes index.
   ISBN 0-88702-039-9: $24.95. ISBN 0-88702-040-2 (pbk.): $14.95
   1. Liberation theology. 2. United States—Economic policy—1981-
3. America—Foreign relations—Latin America. 4. Latin America—
Foreign relations—United States. I. Rubenstein, Richard L. II. Roth,
John K.
BT83.57.P643 1988
261.7'09181'2—dc19   88-17260
                                                            CIP

TABLE OF CONTENTS

ACKNOWLEDGMENTS

Work on this book began on March 20–21, 1987, when Richard L. Rubenstein, president of the Washington Institute for Values in Public Policy, convened a planning session in Washington, D.C. Sharing his conviction that the political significance of Latin American liberation theology provided a topic worthy of sustained analysis, John W. Cooper, Dennis P. McCann, John K. Roth, Paul E. Sigmund, and Antonio Ybarra-Rojas joined Rubenstein to lay groundwork for the Washington Institute conference which took up that theme seven months later. *The Politics of Latin American Liberation Theology: Understanding the Challenge to U.S. Public Policy* includes the best fruits of those labors.

In our role as editors, we are grateful not only to the other members of the original planning committee and to all those who contributed papers to the conference and this volume. We have also been fortunate to work with the excellent staff assembled by Neil Albert Salonen, the Washington Institute's executive director. His deputy director, Robert O. Sullivan, Jr., ably coordinated the October conference. With manuscripts in hand, we then turned to Jonathan Slevin, the multitalented director of the Washington Institute Press. Efficiently assisted by Robert J. Rand and Kamlesh Choksey, he ensured that the entire production process went forward in a timely manner and without a hitch.

Two other persons deserve special recognition. We are especially thankful to the Honorable Dave Durenberger, United States senator from Minnesota, for delivering the keynote address at the October conference and for permitting us to use his words as the foreword for *The Politics of Latin American Liberation Theology*. Last, but by no means least, Rebecca Salonen worked tirelessly and cheerfully to copyedit and proofread a complex set of essays. Wherever a need existed, her efforts clarified and focused, corrected and polished these pages. More than any other person, she deserves credit for the good that this book will do.

RICHARD L. RUBENSTEIN

JOHN K. ROTH

NOTES ON THE CONTRIBUTORS

HUMBERTO BELLI is associate professor of sociology at the Franciscan University in Steubenville, Ohio. He is the founder of the Puebla Institute, a Roman Catholic lay organization concerned with religious rights.

Mr. Belli is a native Nicaraguan who was a Marxist and a member of the Sandinista movement before becoming a Christian in 1977. After the Sandinista revolution in 1979, he worked as editorial page editor of the independent daily newspaper, *La Prensa*. Following the imposition of press censorship in 1982, he moved to the United States.

He has published two books in English, *Nicaragua: Christians under Fire* (Puebla Institute, 1984) and *Breaking Faith: The Sandinista Revolution and Its Impact on Freedom and Christian Faith in Nicaragua* (Crossways, 1985).

PHILLIP BERRYMAN is a freelance translator and writer. He worked as a priest in Panama from 1965 to 1973 and as Central America representative for the American Friends Service Committee while living in Guatemala from 1976 to 1980.

He is author of *The Religious Roots of Rebellion: Christians in Central American Revolutions* (Orbis, 1984), *Inside Central America* (Pantheon, 1985), and *Liberation Theology* (Pantheon, 1987). He has translated several books by Latin American theologians.

JOHN W. COOPER is senior research fellow in religion and society studies at the Ethics and Public Policy Center in Washington, D.C. He has served as a researcher at the American Enterprise Institute and was dean for academic affairs and associate professor of philosophy and religion at Bridgewater College in Bridgewater, Virginia.

He is the author of *The Theology of Freedom: The Legacy of Jacques Maritain and Reinhold Niebuhr* (Mercer University Press, 1985) and co-editor of *The Corporation: A Theological Inquiry* (with Michael Novak, American Enterprise Institute, 1981).

DAVE DURENBERGER has served as United States Senator from Minnesota since 1978. In 1987 he completed the maximum eight-year term as a member of the Senate Select Committee on Intelligence, also serving as its chairman for the last two years of his term. Senator Durenberger serves on three other congressional committees with major standing—Environment, Finance, and Governmental Affairs. He is author of *Neither Madmen Nor Messiahs* (Piranha Press, 1984) and *Prescription for Change* (Piranha Press, 1986).

MARC H. ELLIS is associate professor of religion, culture, and society studies at the Maryknoll School of Theology. He is the founder and director of the Institute for Justice and Peace at Maryknoll.

He has lectured internationally and written widely on Jewish and Christian ethics, Holocaust studies, and faith and social justice. His books include *Toward a Jewish Theology of Liberation* (Orbis Books, 1987), *Faithfulness in an Age of Holocaust* (Amity House, 1986), *Peter Maurin: Prophet in the Twentieth Century* (Paulist Press, 1981), and *A Year at the Catholic Worker* (Paulist Press, 1978).

MICHAEL FLEET is associate professor of political science at Marquette University. He has taught in South America at the Universidad Javeriana and the Universidad de Los Andes in Bogotá, Colombia, and at the Universidad de Chile in Santiago, Chile. He is author of *The Rise and Fall of Chilean Christian Democracy* (Princeton University Press, 1985). He is currently working on a book-length study of Christian-Marxist relations in Chile and Peru.

WILLIAM REECE GARRETT is professor of sociology at St. Michael's College. He was editor of *Sociological Analysis* from 1979 to 1982 and was president of the Association for the Sociology of Religion (1985). He is author of *Seasons of Marriage and Family Life* (Holt, Rinehart and Winston, 1982). Professor Garrett has been an ordained Baptist minister since 1961.

W. E. HEWITT is assistant professor of sociology at the University of Lethbridge in Alberta, Canada. In 1984 he attended the University of São Paulo as a special student. He has written widely on basic Christian communities, democracy, and Catholicism in Brazil and on liberation theology.

DENNIS P. McCANN is professor of religious studies and founding director of the Center for the Study of Values in Modern Society at DePaul University. He is author of *New Experiment in Democracy: The Challenge for American Catholicism* (Sheed and Ward, 1987), *Polity and Praxis: A Program for American Practical Theology* (with Charles Strain, Winston Press, 1985), and *Christian Realism and Liberation Theology* (Orbis Books, 1981).

ROLAND ROBERTSON is professor of sociology and religious studies at the University of Pittsburgh, where he is also director of graduate studies in the Department of Sociology. He is president of the Association for the Sociology of Religion and is an elected member of the American Society for the Study of Religion.

He has authored or coauthored a number of books, including *Identity and Authority* (Blackwell, 1980), *Meaning and Change* (New York University Press, 1978), *The Sociological Interpretation of Religion* (Blackwell, 1970), *International Systems and the Modernization of Societies,* (with J. P. Nettl, Basic Books, 1968), and a forthcoming work on globalization and world history.

JOHN K. ROTH is the Russell K. Pitzer Professor of Philosophy at Claremont McKenna College, where he has taught since 1966. A specialist in American studies and in Holocaust studies, he has been a visiting professor at the University of Innsbruck (Austria), Doshisha University (Japan), and Haifa University (Israel).

He has authored or coauthored nine books, including *The Questions of Philosophy* (with Frederick Sontag, Wadsworth, 1988) and *Approaches to Auschwitz: The Holocaust and Its Legacy* (with Richard L. Rubenstein, John Knox Press, 1987). Among his six edited books are *American Ground: Vistas, Visions, and Revisions* (with Robert H. Fossum, Paragon House, 1987) and *Ideology and American Experience: Essays on Theory and Practice in the United States* (with Robert C. Whittemore, Washington Institute Press, 1986).

RICHARD L. RUBENSTEIN is the Robert O. Lawton Distinguished Professor of Religion at Florida State University and president of the Washington Institute for Values in Public Policy. He was the winner of the Portico d'Ottavia literary prize in Rome, 1977, for the Italian translation of *The Religious Imagination* (Bobbs Merrill, 1968). Among his books are *Approaches to Auschwitz: The Holocaust and Its Legacy* (with John K. Roth, John Knox Press, 1987), *The Age of Triage* (Beacon Press, 1984), and *The Cunning of History* (Harper and Row, 1975). He has edited numerous books, including *Spirit Matters: The Worldwide Impact of Religion on Contemporary Politics* (Washington Institute Press, 1987), and *The Dissolving Alliance: The United States and the Future of Europe* (Washington Institute Press, 1987).

PAUL E. SIGMUND is professor of politics at Princeton University, and has also taught at the Catholic University of Chile. He is the author of thirteen books. His most recent books include *St. Thomas Aquinas, On Ethics and Politics* (Norton, 1988), *The Political Economy of Income Distribution in Mexico* (Holmes and Meier, 1984), and *Multinationals in Latin America* (University of Wisconsin Press, 1980).

FREDERICK SONTAG is the Robert C. Denison Professor of Philosophy at Pomona College in Claremont, California. He was a Fulbright regional visiting professor in India, East Asia, and the Pacific areas from 1977 to 1978. He has written widely on philosophy and religious thought; his most recent titles are *The Questions of Philosophy* (with John K. Roth, Wadsworth, 1988) and *The Elements of Philosophy* (Charles Scribner's Sons, 1984).

Liberation Theology: A View from the Senate

Dave Durenberger

As a Catholic, I have followed from the pews the struggle which my church has had over the emergence of liberation theology, particularly in Latin America. But as a businessman who traveled frequently in Central America in the mid-1970s I saw, firsthand, the conditions which liberation theology attempts to address.

The time I spent in Central America—when the political leaders of those countries had names like Anastasio Somoza and Humberto Romero—was an experience which I have recalled many times as a United States Senator. I saw then the inevitability of revolution—the extreme poverty next door to arrogant wealth; the decades of frustrations with little hope for the future; the repressive nature of governments; the death squads; the torture; the ignorance of the real values on which human rights are based.

And everywhere there were children—hungry children, children without adequate health care and education, children without the hope of a job once they reached maturity.

In the summer of 1975 my eldest son, Charlie, had the experience of a lifetime, spending several months living with friends in San Salvador. Much to our surprise, Charlie wrote home—long letters expressing the wonder that only a young boy could feel at seeing the most cruel evidence of poverty, the shacks made of cardboard and tin right next to the most arrogant evidence of wealth. And he wrote of the fearful experience of seeing soldiers armed with machine guns walking the streets of San Salvador.

Because the company I worked for has its international headquarters in San Jose, I traveled most often to Costa Rica. The contrast with the rest of Central America made the expectation of coming revolution all the more clear. Costa Rica's peace-loving, relative prosperity and its open enthusiasm for democracy make today's Costa Rican leadership in the elusive search for peace as natural and expected as it is courageous.

Since I was elected to the Senate, I've been back in Central America several times. And still the images which stick most firmly are those of children—and of the inevitability that they, and their parents, will seek, in some way, a better life.

That's the challenge being faced by the politicians and church leaders as they struggle to adapt centuries-old institutions to meet the needs of today and of the future.

It's very hard for me, based on my religious upbringing—and on my experience before and since I was elected to the Senate—to understand the ignorance and simplicity with which our own government has sought to respond to these challenges throughout our history.

Books like *The Politics of Latin American Liberation Theology* are essential if we are ever to make the kind of contribution to meeting those challenges which we are capable of and which we as a nation have an obligation to make. The contributors have done a superb job of laying out the parameters of the development of liberation theology, of analyzing the framework used by its practitioners, and of exploring the relationship between liberation theology and revolution.

It is clear that liberation theology was developed because existing doctrines and institutions no longer fit with the "situation on the ground." Two events of the early 1960s proved to be crucial stimuli.

First, the Second Vatican Council led to an atmosphere of change and a willingness to explore new ideas and new paths. Vatican II opened a new era as the Catholic church launched a far-reaching reform movement from within. And once the doors of change were opened, Latin American Catholics began to walk through them to examine critically their role and to seek to adapt to the new realities.

Second, the political atmosphere of the 1960s was marked by turmoil and ferment throughout the world. Student movements in the developed nations became increasingly radical. Racial tensions in the United States exploded as the civil rights movement came into being. Civil disobedience—to protest the war in Vietnam or to oppose racial injustice—became widespread. Even the Communist bloc was affected when Soviet tanks crushed the Prague Spring in 1968.

But what was most important in Latin America was an event that opened the decade—the victory of Fidel Castro's revolution in Cuba. This seminal event had repercussions we feel today. In Latin America, it ignited the hopes of revolutionaries who thought the Cuban model could be quickly and easily replicated in their countries. Castro supported a number of guerrilla movements throughout South America, and he sent Che Guevara to the continent as his field officer.

The triumph of Castro sent shock waves throughout the policymaking elite in Washington. Like revolutionaries to the south, policymakers in Washington thought that Castro's revolution was made for export—but where revolutionaries were hopeful, the United States was fearful. Castro's virulent anti-American rhetoric was matched with action. The era of United States neglect was suddenly over; a new, panic atmosphere set in.

We all know what happened. The grandiose Alliance for Progress was launched in 1961 with the triple goals of economic growth, political democratization, and structural social change. While there was reasonable progress on the first goal, there was little on the other two.

And as Castro's efforts to subvert the hemisphere failed, United States interest waned. By 1970, we had learned to live, albeit reluctantly, with totalitarian Cuba. We were absorbed by the unfolding tragedy of Vietnam. But the problems of Latin American underdevelopment did not go away.

While United States policy first focused on and then looked away from Latin America, the Catholic clergy concentrated their efforts on constructing a new role for themselves—one that did not simply acquiesce in repression and poverty with little prospect for change.

At the second plenary meeting of the Latin American Bishops' Conference (CELAM)[1] at Medellín, Colombia, in 1968, this effort resulted in what Philip Berryman has called "the Magna Carta of liberation theology."[2] I need not go into detail about the product of the Medellín meeting; assembled here are recognized experts who can address the subject far better than I.

What is most important from the view of someone concerned with policy is that the bishops stepped into a void. The void was left by corrupt and stagnant elites in Latin America who refused to accept meaningful change, and by United States policymakers who, preoccupied with other regions and other problems, fell back into a cycle of neglect.

The development of liberation theology, spurred on after Medellín, proceeded rapidly in the 1970s. While CELAM as an institution moved away from the more radical positions expressed in 1968, the leading liberation theologians wrote and spoke widely. Their names have been much discussed—Gutiérrez, Segundo, Assmann, Boff.

But the advocates did much more than write; they organized the "Christian base communities" (CEBs). While much of the debate and exposition of liberation theology took place in the rarified atmosphere of Marxist analysis and structural paradigms, it is the base communities where liberation theology is transformed into political action.

In the decade after Medellín, base communities sprang up in many of the poor neighborhoods surrounding the large cities of Latin America. CEBs became foci of action ranging from Bible study to political mobilization, and they often became lightning rods for those who saw any change as a threat. In some cases, CEBs became the link between the church and revolutionary movements.

By the end of the 1970s, the situation in Latin America had changed considerably. Years of pent-up frustrations, of governments without legitimacy, of economic decline, and of political repression made upheaval inevitable, particularly in Central America. In 1979 both Nicaragua and El Salvador underwent social transformation. In Nicaragua, a popular revolution ousted Somoza, after which reform-minded junior officers staged a coup in El Salvador.

In the United States, there was a replay of the reaction to Castro's triumph almost two decades earlier. The victory of the Sandinistas led to a renewed panic cycle; fears of a rapid string of Leninist guerrilla victories became widespread in official Washington once again.

But what made the panic cycle extend beyond Marxist guerrillas to liberation theologians was the role played by Catholic clergy in the Sandinista triumph. As has been extensively discussed, the clergy in Nicaragua played an important role in the ouster of Somoza. It was this role that set off alarm bells in Washington.

There were a few like Ernesto Cardenal, now minister of culture, and Miguel D'Escoto, now minister of foreign affairs, who not only opposed Somoza but actively supported the FSLN. But for the majority of the clergy, and the majority of Nicaraguans, opposition to Somoza did not automatically mean support for the FSLN. Like so many Nicaraguans, the clergy were unprepared for the determination of the Sandinistas to control the key levers of power—the party, the security service, and the army.

Perhaps the best way to illustrate what happened to the clerical opponents of Somoza is by relating a personal discussion I had with Archbishop Roman Arrieta in 1983. Arrieta, then the chairman of the Central American Secretariat of Catholic Bishops, was known as "the Red Bishop" due to his support for anti-Somoza forces. I met with him during a visit to Central America, and he spoke in gentle but critical terms of his "beloved brethren" who flirt with liberation theology. He said that we must never forget that Marxists capitalize on the legitimate grievances of the people and that they will use religion as a "scaffolding" to assist in the creation of a new society. "But," he cautioned me, "remember that after a building is erected, the scaffolding is destroyed. This is what I fear in Nicaragua." Given what has happened in Nicaragua—the persecution of the church, the forced exile of priests, the silencing of Cardinal Bravo, the sham of "the popular church"—I think the fears of Bishop Arrieta were well-founded.

But at the same time the FSLN was consolidating the theft of the revolution, another more promising trend was under way in the Americas—the transition from authoritarian regimes to democratic governments. The most important phenomenon in Latin America in the last ten years is not the "fusion" of Christianity and Marxism, it is the movement toward democracy.

In the last decade, ten Latin American states have taken steps, often dramatically, toward instituting democratic forms of government. In some states, notably Brazil, observers have argued that CEBs played a crucial role in aiding the transition to democracy. And in others still laboring under dictatorships, notably Chile, those of us who support democracy look to the church to play an important role.

What remains is to address the significance of liberation theology from a United States senator's point of view. To do this I would distinguish between the critique—implicit or explicit—of capitalism and the concurrent call to revolution, and the actualization of the "preferential option for the poor" in the base communities.

The Marxist language and the analytical style of the early liberation theologians is both disquieting and, I believe, misplaced. It is disquieting to me because, as a Catholic, when I think of the corruption of man, I think of original sin and not private property. And when I think of important relationships, I think of man's relationship to God and not to the means of production.

The critique of capitalism, blaming the economic system for the social and political ills of Latin America, which is used so extensively by some liberation theologians, is simplistic and dangerously misleading. The call for a revolutionary transformation of the social system may resonate in the abstract, but it ignores the tragic history of Marxist revolution.

While revolutionaries promise the world, they do not deliver. One need only look at Cuba with its people enslaved, its young men fighting Soviet wars in Africa, and its economy in ruins. In the words of the great Mexican writer, Octavio Paz, "The failure of the Castro regime is evident and undeniable.... For years and years, Latin American and many European intellectuals refused to listen to the Cuban exiles, dissidents, and victims of persecution. But it is impossible to hide the truth." [3]

Beyond a failure to look seriously at what revolution hath wrought in our times, to the extent that liberation theologists see capitalism as the problem, they are wrong. The view that capitalism is an unfair or unjust system overlooks the historical record. Liberty is an essential component in social justice—and liberty includes property rights, free economic institutions, and the other key elements of capitalism. Even the "mainstream" United States Catholic church glossed over this distinction in early drafts of its pastoral letter on the economy. [4]

Not only is capitalism not the problem in Latin America, it is an integral part of the solution. Without sustainable economic growth, without an economic infrastructure, without full trading ties with each other and the United States, and without United States investment, Latin America's people will not be better off.

If the critics of capitalism would look seriously at states like Taiwan or South Korea, they would see that development is aided, not hindered, by vibrant free enterprise. Any measure of standard of living reveals that the Asian "Gang of Four" [5] has wisely embraced capitalism as the path toward development. These societies still have a long way to go in terms of political liberty but, as we can see, economic development encourages—even forces—political development. My experience in the relationship between economic and political development is direct; I was in the business of fostering economic advancement in Central America. And I know it works.

Instead of issuing invectives against capitalism and expounding the virtues of revolutionary change, liberation theologians should look at how they can support democratic evolution. The "third way" of democracy offers a path out of the dual traps of dictatorships of the Left and Right.

The recent growth of democracy in Latin America is something that could not have been foreseen fifteen years ago. It is easier to understand how someone could turn to the extreme "solution" of revolution in, say, the Uruguay of 1971; but it is much more difficult to understand a continued denigration of democratic processes in, say, the El Salvador of 1988.

One of the questions posed by Paul Sigmund's paper is, from my perspective, the most relevant for policymakers. It bears repeating: What is the attitude of liberation theologians toward the democratization of Latin America? Although I recognize that the movement is not monolithic, it seems to me that this is the central issue. Are the clergy dedicated to aiding the poor in the CEBs going to channel their efforts to support the evolution of democracy? Just as the original movement was a response to changed circumstances, I hope that its leaders can seize the opportunity and adapt to the new, democratic reality in Latin America.

How much significance does liberation theology have for American security policy? I must admit that, after ten years in the Senate playing an active role in our deliberations on Latin America, I am pessimistic over the chances of a serious consideration of this question. If I have learned anything about how the United States views Latin America, it is that ideology is more important than information.

Recently I have tried to put the Senate on record in support of democracy in various countries. I have had mixed results. I was unable to get a resolution commemorating the efforts of the democratic opposition in Chile to a vote. I succeeded in fashioning a broad coalition in support of a similar resolution on Panama—but only because General Noriega finds his friends in Managua and Havana.

An even more timely example took place when a simple resolution congratulating President Oscar Arias as the recipient of the 1987 Nobel Peace

Prize was held up because some senators did not want to express support for the prospects of peace in Central America. It turned out that only three senators voted against the resolution, but it is revealing that after all the time and treasure we have invested in the region—and after so many Central Americans have been killed or left homeless—we spent a mere twenty minutes discussing the Nobel Peace Prize recipient.

Our policy has been inconsistent, vacillating between panic and neglect. There was tremendous bipartisan support for the Kissinger Commission when it was formed and after it released its findings. But after we learned that the price tag for the Jackson Plan was $6 billion, Congress quickly forgot the key tenet of the commission's findings—the need for an integrated, long-term commitment to Central America.

Many in Congress know little about the region. I remember an incident in 1983 when the Senate went into executive session and a disconcertingly large number of my colleagues had to run to the map in the front of the chamber to locate El Salvador.

Even if more in Congress now know where the countries of Central America are, few understand that each of the countries is unique—in history, society, and tradition. Ignorance of the important role of Spanish and Portuguese colonization is widespread. And understanding of the role of the Catholic church in Latin America, whether supporting or opposing autocracy, is unfortunately quite limited.

For all of these reasons, views of liberation theology in Congress will tend to fit ideological predispositions. This is not merely because Latin America is the arena of debate. In general, religion is a difficult issue for American policymakers to deal with. This is true whether we are discussing Iranian Shi'ites or Nicaraguan Maryknolls.

In addition, there is what can be termed "institutional infirmity" as well. Congress is notoriously short-sighted—and, if anything, it is getting worse. In 1987, we spent four weeks on the authorization bills for the Defense and State Departments, considering over 200 amendments. Every time a senator reads the morning paper, it seems that his staff is already drafting new amendments.

Congress wants to share war powers with the president but it cannot do it "as a Congress." Congress is an amalgam of 535 entrepreneurs put in business by single issues, scientific polling, and media consultants. Party unity and seniority are dead and with them went the major consensus-forming mechanisms. Constitutional advice and consent have been reduced to declarations by most senators in advance of any actual floor debate.

The most important task for us—whether legislators, policymakers, or citizens—is to understand why a religious movement has appeal. Then we can try to anticipate its potential effects. This is, first, a function of raising awareness, and then of shaping intelligent analysis that understands the dynamics of change in the Third World. *The Politics of Latin American Liberation Theology* is so important because it makes real progress toward those objectives.

NOTES

1. CELAM is the acronym from the Spanish title of the conference: Consejo Episcopal Latino Americano.

2. Phillip Berryman, *Liberation Theology: Essential Facts about the Revolutionary Religious Movement in Latin America and Beyond* (Philadelphia: Temple University Press, 1987), pp. 22–24.

3. Octavio Paz, *One Earth, Four or Five Worlds: Reflections on Contemporary History,* trans. Helen R. Lane (New York: Harcourt Brace Jovanovich, 1985), p. 173.

4. The controversy over early drafts of *Economic Justice For All* was widely covered. See, for example, the *New York Times* accounts of November 12, 1984, p. A1; June 15, 1985, p. A46; and especially November 5, 1986, p. A20.

5. The economic success stories of Asia that make up the "Gang of Four" include Taiwan, South Korea, Singapore, and Hong Kong. Recent events indicate that the People's Republic of China, among other Asian nations, is attempting to apply some of the lessons from the Gang of Four's economic progress.

Debt, Dollars, and Development

Richard L. Rubenstein

On Thursday and Friday, October 15 and 16, 1987, as the world's financial markets began their downward plunge toward the stock market crash of October 19, the Washington Institute for Values in Public Policy convened a conference on "The Political Significance of Latin American Liberation Theology" in the city of Washington, D.C. Revised in the light of the discussion that ensued, essays from that multidisciplinary meeting form the contents of this book. In keeping with the Institute's policy of welcoming to its forums responsible opinion, both liberal and conservative, the chapters that follow offer a broad spectrum of views concerning the politics of liberation theology, some critical, others skeptical, and still others sympathetic.

Both the conference and this book, however, reflect a broad consensus concerning the political importance of liberation theology. All the participants and essayists, for example, share the conviction that religiously legitimated values have the power to define political and social objectives as well as to confer legitimacy on political movements and institutions which promise to attain those objectives. This is especially true of Latin American liberation theologians who pursue their vocations in a region in which the Roman Catholic church has long enjoyed something close to a cognitive monopoly in religious affairs.

In his introductory remarks, the president of the Institute stressed the fact that the conference was in no way concerned with evaluating the adequacy of liberation theology as an expression of Christian thought. The conference planning committee was of the opinion that debate on that subject ought to be carried on by committed Christians authorized to speak and teach on behalf of their tradition. The conference had a different mandate. Thus, both it and this book explore the *political significance* of Latin American liberation theology for the domestic and foreign policy of the United States. A number of participants discussed the fact that theologians in Asia, Africa, and the United States have also expressed themselves on the theme of liberation. Nevertheless, the distinctive importance of Latin America to the United States, as well as the growing size and influence of the United States Hispanic population, were deemed sufficient reasons for focusing on Latin America.

RESPONSES TO THE GREAT TRANSFORMATION

As William R. Garrett observes, the substantive preoccupation of the founding fathers of modern social theory has been the "Great Transformation," that is, the economic, political, technological, demographic, social, cultural, and religious transformations of the old feudal-agrarian order which produced the historically unprecedented phenomenon we recognize as the modern world.[1] Put differently, a fundamental preoccupation of social science has been modernization theory. Garrett further observes that social scientists have renewed their interest in modernization theory since the middle years of this century. However, in this latter period the emphasis has no longer been on the *origins* of the modern era but on the question of the developmental strategies which could enable traditional societies to embark upon the process of modernization. Initially, the renewed interest expressed itself in theories of development which sought to identify the stages of economic, political, and social development necessary for successful modernization. In general, those who took this approach believed that the modernization of underdeveloped nations would require replication of the steps taken by the "advanced industrial societies" in their journey to modernity.

Implicit in this approach was the idea that unsuccessful modernization was due to a flaw or flaws in the underdeveloped community, such as an unsuitable religious or cultural ethos or a want of appropriate political or economic resources. Developmental theory tended implicitly to place the onus for failure on the underdeveloped nation, hardly a welcome analysis to Third World intellectuals.

Many Third World intellectuals found Marxist and neo-Marxist theories of underdevelopment far more congenial. These placed the onus for failure on "late capitalist societies" or "societies in the late stages of monopoly capitalism." (The same nations had been identified by developmental theorists as "advanced industrial nations.") The Marxist terminology had ideological overtones which suggested that Latin American underdevelopment was largely caused by the "neo-imperialist" exploitation of North American and European multinational corporations and their Latin American agents.[2] Terms like "late stages of monopoly capitalism" were used to suggest that the imminent collapse of the advanced nations had been temporarily forestalled through a process identified by Andre Gunder Frank as "the development of underdevelopment." According to Frank, North American monopoly capitalism systematically exacerbates the underdevelopment of Latin America by exploiting the region's raw materials for the sake of the metropolitan center, by siphoning off the profits of the underdeveloped nations, and by preventing Latin American nations from developing an independent economy or industrial infrastructure. Frank argues that, far from contributing to Latin American modernization, North American banks and corporations have fostered a condition of "structural underdevelopment."[3] This issue is discussed by William R. Garrett and Roland Robertson in this volume.[4]

If, as Marxist theoreticians claim, capitalist development fosters Third World underdevelopment, the poverty and misery of Latin America's masses will not be overcome by political or economic reforms which leave the present system more or less intact. The negative economic and social consequences of neo-imperialist domination will only be overcome by overthrowing the *system* that fosters underdevelopment. The prescribed therapy is thus revolution. Whether the overturn advocated by liberation theologians is to be violent or nonviolent is a matter of great importance to United States policymakers, as Frederick Sontag suggests.[5]

As is evident from the papers of both those critical and those sympathetic to liberation theology in this volume, liberation theologians have largely accepted the Marxist analysis of Latin America's economic predicament. This in itself is a radical development. As this writer observes in his paper, before the rise of liberation theology, theologians tended to address the problem of modernization as an exercise in *dissonance-reduction.*[6] The fundamental problem of theology, both Christian and Jewish, was the defense of religious tradition in the face of the challenge of the predominantly secular values of the modern era. Put differently, theologians sought to defend their religious traditions in the face of a crisis of plausibility brought about by modern secularizing tendencies.[7] They attempted to demonstrate that modernity, properly understood, was either in harmony or could be reconciled with religious tradition. Other theologians argued that modernity and religious tradition were irreconcilable. They depicted the values of modernity either as a retrogression to paganism or as an atheistic *novum* which had to be contested at all costs.

Insofar as theologians sought to reconcile faith and modernity, their enterprise was essentially apolitical, albeit hardly lacking in political consequences.[8] Theology tended to become overtly political only when the Great Transformation was thought to involve the affirmation of values and institutions irredeemably hostile to traditional religion. Thus, from the time of the French Revolution to the Second Vatican Council, the Roman Catholic church regarded with deep hostility the pluralistic, secular society of contract and acquired status which was the Revolution's sociopolitical legacy. The church favored political parties which sought to contain or negate that legacy. As such, the church could hardly be described as apolitical. The Bolshevik Revolution of 1917 and the subsequent, aborted socialist revolutions in Hungary and Bavaria intensified this tendency. Committed to world revolution, the Bolsheviks were overtly anti-Christian. Perceiving a potentially mortal threat, the Roman Catholic church tended to favor authoritarian and even fascist movements whose programs included militant suppression of communism. Although ostensibly neutral during World War II, the Vatican of Pope Pius XII regarded National Socialist Germany as Europe's ultimate defense against the triumph of atheistic bolshevism in the heart of Christendom. Although the pope was fully informed concerning the wartime behavior of National Socialist Germany by one of the world's most effective intelligence networks, his fear of bolshevism caused him to overlook or remain silent concerning the political crimes of National Socialism.[9]

The right-wing authoritarian politics of pre-Vatican II Catholicism was an understandable response to a militantly antireligious Left. Hence, left-wing liberation theology constitutes a radically new departure in Roman Catholic thought. In his essay, Paul E. Sigmund traces the rise of this new expression of Christian theology and the responses it has elicited both within and without the church. Sigmund especially indentifies Pope John XXIII's call for *aggiornamento* and his socially oriented encyclicals, such as *Pacem in Terris,* as watershed events in which the church finally committed itself to "democracy, human rights, and religious freedom." The commitment was ratified by the Second Vatican Council (1962–65) which, according to Sigmund, "ended the self-imposed isolation of the Catholic church from the modern world,...and formally endorsed democratic government and religious pluralism."[10]

Nevertheless, even when the church was most opposed to Marxist collectivism, it never gave its unqualified endorsement to liberal capitalism. It regarded the latter as fostering socially atomizing, economic egoism. The church's critical stand toward capitalism has recently been restated by Pope John Paul II in his encyclical, *Sollicitudo Rei Socialis (On Social Concern)* issued to commemorate the twentieth anniversary of Pope Paul VI's encyclical, *Populorum Progressio (On the Progress of Peoples).* The pope wrote that "the Church's social doctrine adopts a critical attitude towards both liberal capitalism and Marxist collectivism."[11] His position gives renewed expression to the strong communitarian emphasis in Catholic social thought.

On the other hand, the new encyclical contains an important recognition of the strengths of capitalism in the pope's acknowledgment of the economically productive role of the entrepreneur. The passage deserves to be quoted in its entirety:

> It should be noted that in today's world, among other rights, the right of economic initiative is often suppressed. Yet it is a right which is important not only for the individual but also for the common good. Experience shows us that the denial of this right, or its limitation in the name of an alleged "equality" of everyone in society, diminishes, or in practice absolutely destroys the spirit of initiative, that is to say the creative subjectivity of the citizen. As a consequence, there arises, not so much a true equality as a "levelling down." In place of creative initiative there appears passivity, dependence and submission to the bureaucratic apparatus which, as the only

"ordering" and "decision-making" body—if not also the "owner"—of the entire totality of goods and the means of production, puts everyone in a position of almost absolute dependence, which is similar to the traditional dependence of the worker-proletarian in capitalism.[12]

This passage may prove disquieting to the more overtly pro-socialist liberation theologians.

THE FATE OF "NONPERSONS"

Intellectual and theological movements are not likely to attract a large audience unless they express a widely held concern. Liberation theology expresses such a concern. Liberation theologians have pointed to the fact that the modernization process has had at least as many losers as winners. They have also argued that the strategies of development noted above have yet to overcome the mass poverty and radical social divisions which have increasingly afflicted Latin America since the end of World War II. Pope John Paul II makes a similar point in *Sollicitudo Rei Socialis* when he observes that the hopes for development which were "so lively" at the time of the publication of *Populorum Progressio* (1968) "today appear very far from being realized." Moreover, the situation today is further exacerbated by the phenomena of mass homelessness and unemployment. Concerning contemporary homelessness, the pope writes:

Even the most highly developed peoples present the sad spectacle of individuals and families literally struggling to survive, without a roof over their heads or with a roof so inadequate as to constitute no roof at all.[13]

The pope also points out that the situation has further deteriorated since 1968 as a result of the debt crisis:

Through this mechanism, the means intended for the development of peoples has turned into a brake upon development instead, and in some cases has even aggravated underdevelopment.[14]

The concerns expressed by the pope are precisely those that have moved liberation theologians. Without parting company with orthodox Christian faith, liberation theologians have taken as their distinctive concern one of the most problematic aspects of modernization, the fate of the mass of "nonpersons" who have arisen wherever the rationalization of hygiene, industry, and agriculture have led to *both* a radical population increase *and* a radical decrease in the need for labor-intensive production. The phenomenon has been a crucial feature of Western civilization since the beginning of the modern period. During the eighteenth and nineteenth centuries the resultant social crisis was mitigated by the availability of the New World and Australia as "safety valves" for the vocationally redundant population of the modernizing societies of Europe.[15] In the United States the western frontier served the same function. No such "safety valve" exists today in Latin America. Displaced workers and peasants crowd into the squatter settlements known as *favelas* in Brazil and *barreadas* in Peru. Unfortunately, in most instances urbanization yields no solution to the problem of Latin American population redundancy. Modernization entails the expansion of capital- and knowledge-intensive rather than labor-intensive industries. Skilled labor is often in short supply, but the underclass lacks the training and skills necessary for gainful employment.

Elsewhere this writer has defined a surplus population as one that for any reason can find no viable role in the society in which it is domiciled.[16] Surplus people can also be seen as nonpersons. Full humanity is more a political and an economic than a biological phenomenon. Individuals who belong to no community willing or able to protect their rights may be biologically human, but politically they are nonpersons.[17] As essayist Marc H. Ellis points out, Gustavo Gutiérrez, the dean of liberation theologians, has emphasized liberation theology's concern for Latin America's "nonpersons," the marginalized, superfluous ones who have until recently been the unseen objects of history.[18] How such people are trying to cope with their predicaments is illuminated by the articles in this book that W. E. Hewitt and Michael Fleet have authored.

If, as we hold, full humanity is more a political than a biological fact, liberation theology has the potential of becoming a far more revolutionary force than secular Marxism. Politics is the domain of power. Even when motivated by distorting ideologies, successful revolutionaries ignore a rational calculation of ends and means at their peril. Those who offer no cost-benefit to revolutionaries who have successfully seized power are likely to find themselves regarded as nonpersons whether they are rich or poor. Even if the underclass achieves the status of persons under a Marxist regime, such regimes have demonstrated a capacity to target large numbers of the commercial and professional classes as "objective enemies" and, hence, as nonpersons. These classes are so regarded because their social location and economic interests put them at odds with an ideology that promises them only downward economic and social mobility. This writer is a resident of the state of Florida, which has more than a million Cuban residents, many of whom are well-educated, middle-class professionals and business people. Florida served as a population safety valve for these people when they became or were about to become nonpersons in Castro's Cuba. Had no such safety valve existed, it is very likely that many would have ended up in Cuban *gulags*. If today many of Latin America's poor are nonpersons, under a Marxist regime other classes would be targeted as such.

Religious institutions such as the Roman Catholic church are the only human institutions capable of credibly insisting on the full humanity of all persons regardless of station or economic condition. In the past, religious exclusivism has limited recognition of full humanity to members of one's own religious community. Since Vatican II that limitation is no longer insisted upon by the leadership of the Roman Catholic church. In any event, the overwhelming predominance of the Catholic church in Latin America means that it can insist on the personhood and full human dignity of each and every individual more effectively than any other institution. The credibility of the church as a legitimating institution for the personhood of the poor has been greatly enhanced by encyclicals such as *Sollicitudo Rei Socialis*. When generals and politicians can no longer be trusted, the church remains the one institution deemed worthy as a repository of trust by the vast majority of Latin Americans.

That is one reason the question of liberation theology's attitude toward violence and revolution is so important. In his essay, Phillip Berryman points out that *Economic Justice for All*, the pastoral letter on the economy by the U.S. Catholic bishops, expresses a concern for the poor very much like that of the Latin American liberation theologians. Moreover, the bishops have adopted a critical stance toward United States institutions that would not have been possible forty years ago. Nevertheless, Berryman characterizes the bishops' approach as "reformist" and, in general, compatible with the modern capitalist welfare state. By contrast, the positions taken by both the Latin American bishops and liberation theologians have been far more critical of capitalism.[19] Berryman cites Clodovis and Leonardo Boff, two of Latin America's most important liberation theologians, who criticize the U.S. bishops' analysis for seeing the problems besetting the poor as " 'dysfunctionalities' within a system that is in overall harmony."

Berryman sees Latin American liberation theologians as opting for a distinctly Latin American socialism that will have learned from the shortcomings of existing socialisms in preference to capitalism.[20] By contrast, a number of the other contributors are more skeptical about the possibility of a Latin American "socialism with a human face." Like Berryman, Dennis P. McCann discerns differences between the approach taken by the U.S. Catholic bishops in *Economic Justice for All* and the approach of the Latin American liberation theologians.[21] According to McCann, the U.S. bishops call for "economic rights" as an expansion of political rights, not as in Marxism, where economic rights are seen as a tradeoff with political rights. In addition, McCann argues that an important difference between the U.S. bishops and the Latin Americans lies in the bishops' faith in democratic self-correction and the Latin Americans' faith in Marxist social analysis. As McCann and others fully understand, *the way a social problem is analyzed has a direct bearing on the kind of solution one is likely to offer.* This leads McCann to express his misgivings about the real intentions of the liberation theologians, citing especially evidence found in contributor Humberto Belli's book, *Breaking Faith: The Sandinista Revolution and Its Impact on Freedom and Christian Faith in Nicaragua.*[22] McCann fears that the response of liberation theologians to papal and other criticisms "may simply be a cover-up designed to mislead both sympathizers and critics about the true nature of their hard-core ideological commitments."[23] John K. Roth expresses similar misgivings as he assesses the anti-American tendencies implicitly as well as explicitly stated in the writings of most liberation theologians. It is Roth's opinion that both the aims and the methods of Latin American liberation theology put it on a "collision course" with the United States.[24] John W. Cooper draws a distinction between those liberation theologians who seek "genuine justice, peace, freedom, and prosperity" and those who "reject democracy and just-market economies in favor of Soviet-style communism." The former constitute no threat to the United States; the latter do.[25]

ECONOMICS AND LATIN AMERICAN UNDERDEVELOPMENT

How the future of the politics of Latin American liberation theology unfolds, particularly in relation to the United States, may hinge on two additional issues that are fundamental. Neither has been discussed at much length by liberation theologians despite the fact that both are vital in the problems of Latin American underdevelopment. The first is the rise of Japanese investment and trade in both Latin and North America during the past ten years. If there is any merit to Andre Gunder Frank's "development of underdevelopment" thesis, it would certainly be applicable to Japanese business policies vis-à-vis North America and *mutatis mutandis* Latin America. United States manufacturing know-how is being lost as North American consumer electronics corporations cease to manufacture many of the products they sell and place their corporate logos on products imported from Japan and Korea. For example, one of the most promising areas of future development in consumer electronics is high definition video (HDTV). Hundreds of millions of dollars have been invested in HDTV research by Japan's public television network, NHK, which is counting on Japanese corporations to sell 500,000 HDTV video cassette recorders in the United States between 1990 and 1992. These sets are expected to cost an average of $3,000. American corporations did not begin to manifest a serious interest in HDTV development until 1987. Having come to depend on the Japanese to produce what they are now unable to produce, American corporations stand to lose billions of dollars in future sales and royalties as American workers lose potential employment opportunities when the new technology is marketed.[26]

The same trends are visible in all too many other industries in both the United States and Latin America. It would seem that the Latin Americans are so fixated upon identifying the United States as the source of their problems that they have hardly noticed that the United States is in the process of being displaced by a far more sophisticated economic power. Japanese competition will not be met effectively in either the United States or Latin America as long as attention is focused on what the Japanese did to their trading partners rather than on what the trading partners have done to themselves. In the case of liberation theology's tendency to blame the United States for Latin American underdevelopment, there is more than a little self-defeating self-evasion.

The second, related issue is the role of the policies of the United States Federal Reserve Bank in the Latin American debt crisis. Latin American liberation theologians tend to blame United States multinational corporations for Latin American underdevelopment in spite of the fact that only one percent of the United States domestic and foreign investments is placed in Latin America. Arguably, a better case can be made that the monetary policies of the United States central bank under Chairman Paul Volcker have adversely affected the economies of Latin America. Consider, therefore, the following scenario and its implications for the politics of liberation theology.

The 1970s became a period of unparalleled price inflation in the United States. Although *nominal* interest rates tended to increase during the decade to compensate creditors for the declining value of paper money, *real* interest rates, that is, the price of money minus the rate of inflation, decreased sharply. Creditors were thus net losers as borrowers profited handsomely. Just as it made sense for American families to borrow money with which to purchase tangible assets in the expectation that the debts could be paid off in depreciated currencies, so it made sense for underdeveloped countries like Brazil, Mexico, and Argentina to finance their development by borrowing recycled and depreciating petrodollars at very low real interest rates from America's money center banks.

Sooner or later, America's politically powerful creditors were bound to insist on an end to a cheap money policy which favored debtors over creditors. The turning point came with Jimmy Carter's 1979 appointment of Paul Volcker as chairman of the Federal Reserve system. Volcker made it clear that his first priority was to curtail inflation. By causing interest rates to rise in the autumn of 1979, Volcker hoped to bring inflation to a halt. Instead, the Fed only succeeded in causing an exceedingly painful economic downturn. Individuals and corporations simply took the rising cost of money as yet another element in the rising cost of doing business in an inflationary environment. Volcker responded by raising interest rates to their highest level in this century, as much as 21.5 percent at one point. By December 1982 unemployment in the United States had reached a post-Depression high of 10.8 percent of the work force. Twelve million were unemployed, but the situation was actually worse. For another five million, having given up looking for work entirely, were not even counted among the unemployed. The Fed inflicted monumental injuries on the manufacturing and agricultural sectors of the American economy in order to break the inflationary cycle by creating surpluses of labor, land, commodities, and manufactured goods.

The effect of the Fed's policies on Latin America was disastrous. In 1980 Third World debt totalled about $400 billion, about 40 percent of which was held by United States banks. Eighty percent of the lending was done by twenty-four banks. By raising interest rates to such high levels, the Fed drastically increased the cost of borrowing money for both domestic and foreign borrowers. As noted above, the Fed's policies caused the worst recession since the Depression. As the cost of borrowing increased, Latin America's revenues from its best customer, the United States, decreased. The Latin American debtor nations had no choice but to borrow more money in order to pay the interest on their already outstanding debts.

Moreover, Volcker and his colleagues understood that they were putting Third World borrowers in a squeeze by raising both interest rates and the real value of the money to be repaid while simultaneously weakening the ability of the United States to import the borrowing nations' goods. The debt crisis continues to this day and could conceivably engulf the United States and Latin America in a monumental financial collapse.[27]

The debt situation was further exacerbated by the upward revaluation of the dollar against foreign currencies. More units of foreign money were required to repay dollar-denominated debts than had been received by the foreigners originally. Recently, Lyle Gramley, chief economist of the Mortgage Bankers Association and one of the seven governors of the Federal Reserve system during much of Volcker's tenure, acknowledged that the Fed leaders were aware of the fact that increased interest rates would lead to a higher value for the dollar. In an interview with Peter T. Kilborn of the *New York Times,* Gramley confirmed that Volcker and his colleagues knew that the Fed's tight monetary policy, when combined with unprecedented federal budget deficits, would draw foreign money into the United States causing the dollar to rise in value. The Fed correctly anticipated that domestic wage and price inflation would be constrained by the flood of low-priced imports purchased with overvalued dollars.[28]

High interest rates increased costs to American manufacturers and farmers while the high dollar reduced the competitiveness of American products. Apart from microelectronics and other cutting-edge industries, there was little incentive for United States corporations to modernize their plants or invest heavily in long-term research. Neither American industry nor agriculture has yet recovered from the Fed's "cure" for inflation. According to Gramley and others, the Fed discounted the damage as part of the "pain" necessary to end inflation. However, Gramley acknowledged that the Fed never expected things to get as bad as they did. In his words, "It was the degree with which those things happened that surprised us."[29]

When liberation theologians write of "the development of underdevelopment," they would do well to consider the role of the Federal Reserve Bank in fostering underdevelopment within the United States. Far from being a strategy employed by greedy northern capitalists to exploit less-developed countries, the Fed was engaging in a struggle to end inflation by reducing the purchasing and borrowing power at home and abroad.

In retrospect, many Fed officials who served under Chairman Volcker fault his policies for having been too extreme. However, the Fed's fight against inflation was complicated by the monumental federal budget deficits of the Reagan years. President Reagan entered office with the promise that his administration would balance the federal budget and reduce individual income taxes by 30 percent in three years. As we know, the administration failed to balance the budget, and the United States entered a period of unparalleled federal budget deficits, reaching $200 billion for three years during the eighties.

In his book on the Federal Reserve system, William Greider likens economic policy under Reagan and Volcker to a car with two drivers going in opposite directions.[30] Fiscal policy, the budget deficit, was inflationary; monetary policy, the Fed's high interest rates, was deflationary. America was simply consuming more than it produced. The difference was financed largely by foreigners attracted by the high interest rates. To no avail, Volcker pleaded with Congress to reduce the budget deficits. Committed to holding down inflation, the Fed used its basic tool, high interest rates. Even when nominal interest rates declined the Fed refused to lower the real rates, which were at an all-time high.[31]

The role of the fiscal policies of the Reagan administration and Congress and the monetary policies of the Federal Reserve Bank in creating a decade of crisis of indebtedness and underdevelopment in both the United States and Latin America has received little, if any, serious attention from liberation theologians. This is surprising in view of the fact that liberation theologians pride themselves in having initiated the utilization of the social sciences in contemporary Catholic theology. On reflection, however, this gap should not be surprising. The social science in which most liberation theologians have been trained, both in Europe and at home, is sociology, with a strong bias toward Marxist analysis. The social sciences required for an understanding of the complexities of the debt crisis are economics and economic history.

By virtue of their religious vocation and the cosmic sweep of their subject matter, theologians are subject to the temptation of a certain quest for totality when confronted with the social dimensions of evil. More than any other "science," Marxism responds to that quest. Marx's social theory was a response to the Great Transformation in Europe, the industrial modernization of England, the political modernization in France, and the response to those events in the German lands. When Latin American theologians began to respond to the dire consequences of modernization in their own region, it is not surprising that they turned to that social theory which relentlessly criticizes all existing institutions in the name of total human emancipation and promises the creation of a new society and a new humanity. The religious appeal of Marxist social theory has been succinctly described by philosopher Richard J. Bernstein:

> ...The appeal and power of Marxism is because it speaks to what men so desperately want to believe. Marx fuses themes that have been basic to the entire tradition of Western civilization. Explicitly or implicitly, he tells us that the perennial dream and hope of Western man—that he will achieve freedom, that he will finally overcome the alienation and suffering that have plagued him, that he will achieve complete emancipation—is not only a real historical possibility, but one which is imminent.[32]

Economics as a discipline offers a far less grandiose vision of human affairs. Economics is concerned with the production and distribution of a scarce resource, wealth. It is a far less visionary discipline than dialectical sociology. It deals in tradeoffs and constraints more than with the total solutions and promises of imminent redemption which are so appealing to men and women with a religious vocation. Above all, economics is concerned with the cost of things, including the cost of social revolution.

It is not this writer's intention to suggest that liberation theologians abandon sociology in their efforts to understand and change their society. He does, however, believe that theologians ought to give more serious attention to the discipline of economics. Taken together, economics and sociology can assist us in understanding the problems of contemporary society. By itself, dialectical sociology encourages a messianic response to the acknowledged misery of Latin America, namely, the demand for its revolutionary overturn. Such a demand is bound to fail, leaving in its wake anger, resentment, and the quest for a scapegoat, a role already assigned to the United States.

NOTES

1. See William R. Garrett, "Liberation Theology and Dependency Theory," chap. 8 of this volume.

2. The use of terminology as an ideological weapon is noted by Peter L. Berger, *Pyramids of Sacrifice: Political Ethics and Social Change* (New York: Basic Books, 1974), p. 14. For an overview of theories of imperialism, neo-imperialism and neo-colonialism, see Wolfgang J. Mommsen, *Theories of Imperialism: A Critical Assessment of Various Interpretations of Modern Imperialism,* trans. P. S. Falla (New York: Random House, 1980).

3. Andre Gunder Frank, *Capitalism and Underdevelopment in Latin America: Historical Studies of Chile and Brazil* (New York: Monthly Review Press, 1969), pp. 242–318.

4. See infra, Garrett, and Roland Robertson, "Liberation Theology, Latin America, and Third World Underdevelopment," chap. 5 of this volume.

5. See Frederick Sontag, "Liberation Theology and the Interpretation of Political Violence," chap. 4 of this volume.

6. See Richard L. Rubenstein, "Liberation Theology and the Crisis in Western Theology," chap. 3 of this volume.

7. See Peter Berger, *The Sacred Canopy* (Garden City, N.Y.: Doubleday Anchor Books, 1966).

8. See infra, the discussion of Karl Barth's rejection of nineteenth-century liberal Protestantism's "reconciliation" of Christianity with the culture of pre-World War I imperial Germany in Rubenstein, "Liberation Theology and the Crisis in Western Theology."

9. This subject is covered in detail by Saul Friedlander, *Pius XII and the Third Reich,* trans. Charles Fullman (New York: Alfred A. Knopf, 1966), and Guenther Levy, *The Catholic Church and Nazi Germany* (New York: McGraw-Hill, 1964).

10. See Paul E. Sigmund, "The Development of Liberation Theology: Continuity or Change?" p. 23 of this volume.

11. Quotations from Pope John Paul II, *Solicitudo Rei Socialis* are taken from the text of excerpts published in the *New York Times,* national

edition, February 20, 1988, p. 4. At the time of this writing the full text was not yet available.

12. Pope John Paul II, *Sollicitudo Rei Socialis*.

13. Ibid.

14. Ibid.

15. This subject is discussed in detail in Richard L. Rubenstein, *The Age of Triage: Fear and Hope in an Overcrowded World* (Boston: Beacon Press, 1983). For a study of the use of Australia as a population "safety valve," see Robert Hughes, *The Fatal Shore* (New York: Alfred A. Knopf, 1987).

16. Rubenstein, *The Age of Triage,* p. 1.

17. See Richard L. Rubenstein and John K. Roth, *Approaches to Auschwitz: The Holocaust and Its Legacy* (Atlanta: John Knox Press, 1987), pp. 190–96.

18. See ibid.

19. See Phillip Berryman, "Liberation Theology and the U.S. Bishops' Letters on Nuclear Weapons and on the Economy," chap. 11 of this volume.

20. Phillip Berryman, *Liberation Theology* (New York: Pantheon Books, 1987), pp. 91–93.

21. See Dennis McCann, "Liberating without Being Liberationist: The U.S. Catholic Bishops' Pastoral Letter on the Economy," chap. 12 of this volume.

22. Humberto Belli, *Breaking Faith: The Sandinista Revolution and Its Impact on Freedom and Christian Faith in Nicaragua* (Garden City, Mich.: Puebla Institute, 1985).

23. McCann, "Liberating without Being Liberationist," p. 275.

24. See John K. Roth, "The Great Enemy? How Latin American Liberation Theology Sees the United States and the USSR," chap 10 of this volume.

25. See John W. Cooper, "Liberation Theology, Human Rights, and U.S. Security," chap. 13 of this volume.

26. See Martin Levine, "High Def: Tomorrow's Television...Today?" *Video Review,* March 1988, pp. 28 ff.

27. The role of the Fed in creating the debt crisis is discussed by William Greider, *Secrets of the Temple: How the Federal Reserve Runs the Country* (New York: Simon and Schuster, 1987), pp. 432 ff.

28. Peter T. Kilborn, "Already, a New Look," *New York Times,* Sunday, January 24, 1988, Section 3. p. 25.

29. Ibid.

30. Greider, *Secrets of the Temple,* pp. 351–404.

31. It should be noted that Greider, whose views we follow, does not hold the Fed alone responsible for America's current economic problems. He holds that much of the blame can be placed upon (a) the supply-side economics of the Reagan administration and (b) a Congress which engaged in a bidding war with the president in 1981 to see who could decrease taxes and raise expenses the most, heedless of what such actions would do to the economies of the United States and the Third World. In fairness to the supply-siders, it should be stated that the tax-cutting program was scheduled to go into effect gradually, over a three-year period, whereas the Fed overreacted and tightened interest rates almost immediately. By so doing, the Fed killed whatever long-term benefits the tax cuts promised the economy.

32. Richard J. Bernstein, *Praxis and Action: Contemporary Philosophies of Human Activity* (Philadelphia: University of Pennsylvania Press, 1971), p. 309.

Part I

Liberation Theology and History

1

The Development of Liberation Theology: Continuity or Change?

Paul E. Sigmund

Mention liberation theology to the average educated person, and you are likely to get one of two reactions, either strongly positive or equally strongly negative. To some the emergence of liberation theology demonstrates that at last the Roman Catholic church in Latin America has abandoned its historic alliance with the wealthy classes and taken a position in favor of the poor, as Christ was in favor of the poor. Leading theologians in the United States and in Europe have hailed it as a major new approach to doing theology. Karl Rahner in Austria, Johannes Metz in Germany, and Robert McAfee Brown in the United States have written about it with enthusiasm. In Latin America, where it originated, liberation theology has been praised by the Brazilian Conference of Bishops as "indispensable to the church's activity and to the social commitment of Christians."[1] Its leading proponent, Gustavo Gutiérrez, lectures at major universities, and his book, *A Theology of Liberation*, is an international best seller.[2]

Yet others are not so enthusiastic. Joseph Cardinal Ratzinger, the prefect of the Vatican Congregation for the Doctrine of the Faith, has called it "a fundamental threat to the faith of the Church,"[3] and the body he heads accused the liberation theologians of using "concepts uncritically borrowed from Marxist ideology."[4] In September 1984, Ratzinger summoned a leading Brazilian theologian, Leonardo Boff, to Rome, and after a discussion of his writings ordered him to observe a period of "penitential silence." Leading Colombian churchmen have led the fight against the influence of liberation theology, accusing it of "using instruments that are not specific to the Gospel" and "promoting hate as a system of change."[5] Latin Americans (and since its translation into English, Americans as well) have been able to read in *Fidel and Religion*, Frei Betto's twenty-three hours of interviews with Fidel Castro, of his enthusiasm for the movement and his call for a "strategic and lasting alliance" between Marxists and liberation theologians "to transform the world."[6] And just as Castro's words were published, Pope John Paul II wrote to the Brazilian bishops in April 1986, "We are convinced, we and you, that the theology of liberation is not only timely but useful and necessary. It should constitute a new stage—in close connection with former ones—of theological reflection."[7]

So which is it—an important new way to do theology, or a kind of crypto-Marxism that reduces the Christian message to revolutionary activism? The answer, of course, was given by Pope John Paul II on his way to the Latin American Bishops Conference in Puebla, Mexico, in 1979. "Ah, yes, liberation theology, but *which* liberation theology?" (*New York Times*, January 20, 1979). To sort out what is a complex and evolving current of theological reflection that has now developed a very substantial literature over nearly two decades, it is necessary to examine its history and to identify the various elements which make it up. Some of those elements have been deemphasized and even abandoned, while others have taken a more prominent role. Specifically it is the thesis of this paper that liberation theology includes a core element of commitment to identifying and ameliorating the sources of spiritual and physical oppression of the poor, but that that core element has been applied in different ways over time. What began as a movement that seemed committed to revolution as the way to express what was later called "the preferential option for the poor" also contained from the outset a belief in the importance of *Comunidades Eclesiales de Base* (CEBs) as a way to express and resolve the spiritual and physical needs of the poor. The base communities approach has become more important over time than the earlier strident calls for revolution. The opponents of liberation theology look to the early writings and see them as a call for Marxist-led revolution while its supporters focus on the base com-

munities (there are an estimated 100,000 in Brazil alone) and regard liberation theology as a way to empower the poor. Both elements are present in
the liberationist writings, thus accounting for the ambiguity of the response
to them.

The movement takes its name from the title of a book by Gustavo
Gutiérrez, which was published in Spanish in 1971 and in English two years
later, though its essential elements first appeared in the 1960s. In both Latin
America and the Roman Catholic church, the sixties were a period of ferment and revolution. Early in the decade Pope John XXIII had called the
Second Vatican Council to carry out an *aggiornamento* (updating) of the
Catholic message, and he had published several socially oriented encyclicals, the best known of which was *Pacem in Terris* (1963), which had at
last officially committed the church to the values of democracy, human
rights, and religious freedom.

Vatican II (1962–1965) ended the self-imposed isolation of the Catholic
church from the modern world, opened its thinking to other religious and
philosophical currents, and formally endorsed democratic government and
religious pluralism. (See especially two of the council's final documents,
The Church in the Modern World (Gaudium et Spes), and *The Declaration
on Religious Freedom (Dignitatis Humanae)*.[8] In a way those documents
only recognized changes that had already taken place in contemporary
Catholicism. In Europe and Latin America large Christian Democratic parties had emerged which were committed to democracy, freedom, and the
welfare state; and in Italy, Germany, and Belgium, as well as in Venezuela
and Chile, they were major contenders for power. Those parties had
developed as representatives of Catholic social teachings, articulated in
papal encyclicals such as *Rerum Novarum* (1891) and *Quadragesimo Anno*
(1931) which criticized both the egoism of "liberal capitalism" and the collectivism of "atheistic socialism." However, while the earlier papal writings had proposed a quasi-corporatist political structure which might be
either democratic or authoritarian, the Christian Democrats strongly supported pluralistic democracy, human rights, and a mixed economy.

The Second Vatican Council legitimized philosophical and religious
pluralism, endorsing dialogue not only with other Christians, Jews, and
Moslems, but also with agnostics, atheists, and Marxists. Christian-Marxist dialogues had already been taking place in Europe, but in Latin America
the Roman Catholic church strongly opposed communism—especially in

its Castroite form, which in the wake of the Cuban Revolution had acquired a new appeal for intellectuals and youth. Church-inspired labor, youth, and student groups joined with the Christian Democratic parties to promote democratic reform which would be a viable alternative to the Cuban model of revolution. In the same period the United States government established the Alliance for Progress which was intended to demonstrate that with United States financial support democratic governments could promote reforms in land tenure, taxation, education, and social welfare. These improvements would prove that it was not necessary to resort to revolution to secure social progress. United States and Latin American social scientists wrote about solving the problems of modernization in the Third World by promoting development—especially economic development—which could respond to a perceived "revolution of rising expectations." As millions flocked to Latin America's already overcrowded major cities, economists argued that the promotion of industrialization through import-substitution and economic integration, as well as agricultural development through agrarian reform, would provide the basis for a democratic response to the underdevelopment of the continent.

GUSTAVO GUTIÉRREZ AND THE CRITIQUE OF DEVELOPMENTALISM

Yet by the last half of the sixties it was apparent that the millennium was not about to arrive in Latin America. Military coups in Brazil, Argentina, Peru, and Bolivia and continuing military domination in Central America demonstrated that there was no inevitability about a democratic future for Latin America. The agrarian reform programs bogged down or were emasculated. Latin America's economic integration fell afoul of nationalist economic pressure groups. Latin America did not seem to be approaching the "take-off" which had been promised by the theories of Walt Rostow's *Stages of Economic Growth* early in the decade.[9]

Why not? Some Latin American social scientists argued that Latin America had been kept in a state of underdevelopment because of its *dependencia* on the developed countries in the capitalist world, especially the United States. Students and intellectuals became disillusioned with the possibilities of reformism and argued that a more revolutionary approach along Cuban lines was necessary.

In Catholic-influenced groups, such as the Catholic universities in Lima and Santiago and the International Movement of Catholic Students (MIEC), this led to a rethinking of the developmentalist models of the earlier part of the decade. Much of this rethinking was related to the meeting of the Latin American Bishops Conference (CELAM) to be held at Medellín, Colombia, in 1968. In a preparatory seminar held at Chimbote, Peru, Father Gutiérrez first set out the themes that were to be developed in later papers and books. He was also present at the Medellín meeting and influenced the content of the final documents of the meeting which spoke of the need for the transformation of man in the light of the gospel as "an action of integral human development and liberation,"[10] denounced poverty in Latin America, referring to "a deafening cry from the throats of millions of men asking their pastors for a liberation that reaches them from nowhere else,"[11] and called for the church to give effective "preference to the poorest and most needy sectors."[12] In the most controversial sections of the Medellín documents, the bishops asserted that "the principal guilt for the economic dependence of our countries rests with powers, inspired by uncontrolled desire for gain,"[13] and declared that "in many instances Latin America finds itself faced with a situation of injustice that can be called institutionalized violence."[14]

As Latin American countries became more radicalized at the end of the 1960s (along with, one might note, the United States, France, and many others), the Medellín documents appeared to legitimize a corresponding radicalization of the Catholic intelligentsia. In Chile, for example, the "rebelde" left wing of the Christian Democratic party split off in 1969 to form part of the Allende Popular Unity coalition in the 1970 elections, and they were followed by another split by the Christian Left in 1971. Because of the expansion of air travel, like-minded Catholic and Protestant theologians were able to meet in many parts of the continent, and Gutiérrez took the lead in forming a theologically-based Catholic radicalism which he called "liberation theology."

As articulated in English first in a 1970 article in the Jesuit journal, *Theological Studies*, Gutiérrez argued that for "poor countries, oppressed and dominated, the word 'liberation' is appropriate"[15] rather than development. "Latin America will never get out of its plight except by a profound transformation, a social revolution that will radically change the conditions it lives in at present. Today, a more or less Marxist inspiration prevails among those groups and individuals who are raising the banner of the continent's liberation. And for many in our continent, this liberation will have to pass, sooner or later, through paths of violence."[16] Gutiérrez quoted the Medellín bishops on the "institutionalized violence"[17] in Latin America and related it to the "situation of dependence"[18] and "conditions of neocolonialism"[19] in Latin America. He called for the Latin American church to "break her ties with the present order,"[20] to "denounce the fundamental injustices on which it is based,"[21] and to commit itself to the poor as the bishops at Medellín had done.

In the book that followed the article, Gutiérrez criticized the developmentalism that provides only palliatives that "in the long run actually consolidate an exploitative system."[22] He attacked Christian Democracy for its "naive reformism" and described it as "only a justifying ideology...for the few to keep living off the poverty of the many."[23] Referring to Marx's Eleventh Thesis on Feuerbach ("The philosophers have only *interpreted* the world,... the point, however, is to *change* it") Gutiérrez defined liberation theology as "critical reflection on Christian praxis in the light of the Word."[24] Theology needed "a scientific and structural knowledge of socioeconomic mechanisms and historical dynamics,"[25] and this would come from a recognition of dependence, "the domination exercised by the great capitalist countries, and especially by the most powerful, the United States of America."[26] That domination was a result of the worldwide class struggle "between the oppressed countries and dominant peoples."[27] New solutions, "most frequently of socialist inspiration"[28] were emerging involving a variety of different approaches, a "broad, rich, and intense revolutionary praxis"[29] which sought a "qualitatively different society" and the "building up of a new man."[30] Gutiérrez cited one among those approaches that was to be central to the future development of liberation theology—the literacy programs of the Brazilian educator, Paulo Freire, involving a process of *concientización*, by which the oppressed person becomes aware of his situation and is encouraged to find a language which makes him "less dependent and more free as he commits himself to the transformation and building up of society."[31]

Freire's methods were already being applied in a new movement of renewal within the Brazilian church—the basic Christian communities. These small groups, usually in rural or marginal areas, discussed the application of selected passages of the Bible to their daily lives in ways that the liberation theologians saw as an example of the *praxis* that they were promoting. Along with the structuralist critique of capitalism the basic Christian communities rapidly became a central element of the liberationist social program.

In a later section of the book which was to be quoted often by his opponents, Gutiérrez called for the abolition of the private ownership of capital because it leads to "the exploitation of man by man" and insisted that "the class struggle is a fact and neutrality in this question is not possible." "To love one's enemies presupposes recognizing and accepting that one has class enemies and that it is necessary to combat them."[32]

What his critics do not quote is Gutiérrez's discussion of "a spirituality of liberation" which he was to develop further in the 1980s.[33] This involves a recognition that "conversion to God implies conversion to neighbor in an act of gratuitousness which allows one to encounter others fully, the universal encounter which is the foundation of communion of men among themselves and of men with God," producing a joy and celebration which is "the feast of the Christian Community."[34] However, rather than developing what could have been a fruitful theological exploration, Gutiérrez then returns to themes of the relation of the church to ideology and the class struggle. Biblical references begin for the first time at this point (there are none in chapters 1 to 8), but only in the last chapter is there a meditation on the biblical meaning of poverty.

STRUCTURALIST ANTICAPITALISM, GRASSROOTS COMMUNITIES, AND THE HERMENEUTIC OF PRAXIS

Gutiérrez's discussion of Christian community suggests a problem that was to dog the liberation theologians as their thinking developed—the relation between a conflictural and a cooperative model of society. The liberationists have borrowed from the Left a belief in conflicting interests and structural oppression as an explanation for poverty and oppression. Yet they also share the Christian belief in community and charity. The conflict is partially but not fully resolved through their support of basic Christian communities made up primarily of the poor and underprivileged who are to apply the Bible to the solution of their day-to-day problems through a process of grassroots democracy and participation. From the outset, liberation theology thus has contained both elements—a structuralist anticapitalism and a populist grassroots communitarianism—and the relation and interaction and occasional tension between the two continues as it develops over time. The different implications of the two elements also help to explain the varying reactions to the movement—since those like the Brazilian bishops, who see it primarily as the theoretical support for the basic Christian communities, take a different attitude from that of the members of the Colombian hierarchy, who view it as a justification for Christian participation in the guerrilla movements that have plagued that country for the last three decades.

For the academic theologian, however, what was exciting about liberation theology was its claim to have developed a new way of reading the Gospels—a "hermeneutic of praxis" arising out of the experience of the poor as related to the Bible and to history. The rejection of the abstract intellectualism of the earlier social teachings of the church in favor of direct social involvement by committed Christians came at a time when new alternative approaches were being opened by the assimilation of the changes of the Second Vatican Council and help to account for the rapid development of the movement.

CHRISTIANS FOR SOCIALISM IN CHILE

Another reason for the spread of liberation theology's influence and the increased controversy surrounding it in the early 1970s was the emergence in Chile of what appeared to be an example of the kind of social analysis and transformation described by Gutiérrez and other liberation theologians. In September 1970 Salvador Allende, the candidate of a coalition of Marxist, lay, and Christian Leftist groups, Popular Unity, was elected president of Chile with 36 percent of the popular vote and subsequently confirmed by the Chilean congress. Allende was a Marxist Socialist who was committed to assisting the poor and oppressed and to opposing dependence and American imperialism. A major partner in his coalition was the Chilean Communist party, the largest such party in Latin America outside of Cuba. However, Allende took pains to maintain good relations with the Catholic church, and to appoint members of the Catholic-inspired parties in his coalition to important positions. A year and a half after he came to power, a group of pro-Allende Christians organized a meeting of the "Christians for Socialism" with representation from various Christian Left groups throughout Latin America. The meeting adopted resolutions that were characterized by heavily Marxist rhetoric, and the Chilean bishops finally forbade Chilean Catholics to participate in it. Gutiérrez participated in the meetings, as did others now identified with what had become an emerging theological school in Latin America, and its extremism led other Latin Americans, especially in Colombia, to attack the movement and to take measures to counteract its influence.[35]

THE DEVELOPMENT OF LIBERATION THEOLOGY

One of the more active participants in the meeting in Chile was Hugo Assmann, a Brazilian of German extraction, who wrote a book, later translated as *A Theology for a Nomad Church*, at the time he was living in Chile.[36] It marks the high (or low) point of the lyrical leftism of the liberation theologians, being characterized by overstatements such as that "the concept of 'development' has been shown up for the lie that it is"[37] and a quotation from a Brazilian Protestant, Rubem Alves, "Truth is the name given by the historical community to those actions which were, are, and will be effective for the liberation of man."[38] For Assmann, "commitment to liberation means introducing the class struggle into the Church itself," although "a truly historical reading of the Bible, particularly of the message of Christ, leads to a whole series of radical questions to which Marxism has not paid sufficient attention, of which perhaps the most significant is the Christian affirmation of victory over death, that final alienation to which Marxism can find no satisfactory answer."[39]

Another influential liberation theologian, and the only one to have two studies about his theology written in English, is Juan Luis Segundo, a Uruguayan Jesuit. While his most important contribution is the analysis of the ideological conditioning of theological discourse in *The Liberation of Theology*, the most frequently cited (and attacked) passage in his writings is his definition of socialism as "the political regime in which the ownership of the means of production is removed from individuals and handed over to higher institutions whose concern is the common good."[40] To requests for more details concerning a future socialist society, Segundo replied lamely that to demand that "Latin Americans...put forward a project for a socialist society which will guarantee in advance that the evident defects of known socialist systems will be avoided" was like asking Christ before he cured the sick man to "guarantee that that cure will not be followed by even graver illnesses."[41]

Critics of the liberation theologians often note such vagueness in their discussions of the future socialist society and the absence of explicit criticisms of Marxist states. Yet there is one liberation theologian, José Comblin, a Belgian who has been teaching and writing in Latin America for thirty years, who is quite specific both in his differences with Marxism and in his proposals for a future liberated society. In his best-known work in English, *The Church and the National Security State*,[42] he criticizes the identification of the gospel with any specific party or groups, including specifically the Christians for Socialism; and he argues for a new society based on human needs and Christian charity which differs from the exploitative models of both the Marxists and the theorists of capitalism and modernization. The gospel message is one of liberation from sin.

> Sin is present in everything—in all personal behavior and in all social structures. The very organization of life and society is based on sin and domination.... Liberty is a new kind of common life, a mutual relationship based on equality and cooperation.... Liberty in the nation...depends on the institutions of liberty being established as the structures of national life. There is no liberty without the institutions of liberty (a parliament, congress, or some form of popular representation; constitutions; and courts of justice independent from repressive or military power; etc.).[43]

Although his Belgian background may account for his concern for constitutional restraints, here is at least one well-known liberation theologian who is aware of the connection between the Christian belief in sin and the need for constitutional guarantees, an independent judiciary, and an elected legislature.

Comblin is also highly suspicious of Marxism. "Marxist science is only the ideology of the party, the result of the reduction of any rationality to the voluntarism of the party, a collection of arguments in order to justify the pragmatist decisions of the party.... In practice, the party finds the problem of power more important than the problem of freedom.... The party is supposed to be sufficient to create a new world, but it ends by creating a new power."[44]

One of the best known of the liberation theologians, largely because of his troubles with the Vatican in recent years, is Leonardo Boff, a Brazilian

Franciscan. He studied theology in Germany and wrote a thesis later published in English as *The Church as Sacrament*. His interests in church organization were continued with the publication in 1977 of *Ecclesiogenesis*, which analyzed what he called "the reinvention of the church" in the form of the basic Christian communities in Brazil.[45] He sees these groups as marking a return to the sense of community and the presence of the Holy Spirit that characterized the early church. However, he is careful to emphasize that the communities do not function in opposition to the institutional church but in "permanent co-existence" with it. He argues against a "pyramidal" or hierarchical model of the church, but he accepts the papacy, the bishops, and the priesthood as necessary responses of the Christian community to the need for "union, universality, and bonding with the great witnesses of the apostolic past." They must exercise their functions, however, within the community rather than over it, "integrating duties instead of accumulating them, respecting the various charisms and leading them to the oneness of one and the same body."[46] In the early 1980s Boff made a similar argument in his *Church: Charism and Power* but couched it in such extreme language[47] that it brought down on him the wrath of the Congregation for the Doctrine of the Faith in Rome.

Boff also wrote *Jesus Christ, Liberator*,[48] but the best-known writer applying liberation theology to the life of Christ is Jon Sobrino, a Spanish Jesuit who has been teaching for many years at the Jesuit university in El Salvador. Sobrino's *Christology at the Crossroads* talks about Christian "transforming practice" and political hermeneutics as applied to "the concrete manifestations of politics, bodily life, and the cosmos."[49] For Sobrino an understanding of Jesus' resurrection presupposes an historical consciousness that sees history both as promise and mission. And one must engage in a specific praxis that is nothing else but discipleship (carried out through) "service to the community performed out of love."[50] Sobrino's work represents a more specifically biblical attempt to relate Christianity to the problems of Latin America than the writings earlier in the decade which borrowed so heavily from Marxism and dependency theory. He also attempts to develop the historical approach that the earlier liberation theologians had preached but not practiced. Like Boff, Sobrino also was criticized in the early 1980s by the Vatican for "rereading" the gospel in ways that made it seem a product of historical conditions, subject to constant reinterpretation.

THE CRITICS OF LIBERATION THEOLOGY

By the late 1970s the most important liberation theologians had emerged, and they were beginning to get an international audience because of translations into other languages. (In the case of the United States, liberation theology is identified with Orbis Press, the publication house of the Maryknoll missionary order, which has published over 200 titles in the field, most of them translations from Spanish or Portuguese.) In 1975 a "Theology in the Americas" project, co-sponsored by the U.S. Catholic Conference and the World Council of Churches, brought the Latin American liberation theologians together with their American and Canadian counterparts. The meeting was the occasion for some harsh criticism of the Latin Americans by American feminist and black theologians. They attacked the writings of the Latin American liberation theologians for their lack of concern with racial and sexual oppression in a continent which was built on the exploitation of the Indian and in which machismo was the dominant sexual ethic.[51]

The critics in Latin America were mainly on the Right. Colombia was the principal center of the counterattack, the first step of which was the election of the Archbishop of Medellín (later Cardinal) Alfonso López Trujillo as general secretary of the Latin American Bishops Conference (CELAM) in 1972. Aided by Roger Vekemans, a Belgian Jesuit who had left Chile at the time of the election of Allende, López Trujillo eliminated adherents of liberation theology from positions of influence in the CELAM structure, and both he and Vekemans wrote books and articles against liberation theology. Aside from occasional articles in religious journals in Europe and the United States—the two most notable being Thomas Sanders's attack on liberation theology as "utopian moralism" (*Christianity and Crisis*, September 17, 1973) and the German theologian Jürgen Moltmann's "Open Letter to a Liberation Theologian," arguing that it was nothing more than "seminary Marxism," liberation theology was still not widely discussed outside of Latin America. Two events changed this—the Third General Conference of Latin American Bishops at Puebla, Mexico, in January–February 1979, and the triumph of the Sandinista-led revolt against the Somoza dictatorship in Nicaragua in July of the same year.

THE BATTLE OF PUEBLA

The meeting at Puebla had originally been scheduled for October 1978, the tenth anniversary of the last CELAM General Conference at Medellín. However, the deaths of Pope Paul VI and his successor, John Paul I, and the election of John Paul II led to its postponement. The CELAM staff sent out preliminary papers that were attacked by Gutiérrez and others as insufficiently concerned with the problems of the poor. When none of the well-known liberation theologians was invited to the meeting as expert advisors (*periti*), they secured invitations from individual bishops and held their own meetings and press conferences outside the meeting place of the bishops. The Puebla conference was covered extensively by the world press, which was especially interested in how the new pope would define his position. His opening address was an indication not only of the seriousness with which the pope took the challenge of liberation theology, but also of the influential power of Vekemans's journal, *Tierra Nueva*, which John Paul II had been receiving as cardinal before his election. The pope criticized the politicization of the gospel message, decried the effort to promote a "people's church" in opposition to the institutional church, and called for a "Christian concept of liberation that cannot be reduced simply to the restricted domain of economics, society and culture."[52] During the meeting a leftist newspaper in Mexico published the contents of a cassette dictaphone tape that had been inadvertently given to a journalist by the secretary of Archbishop López Trujillo. It complained of the leftism of the Jesuits and other religious orders in Latin America and urged its recipient to "prepare your bombers for Puebla and get into training before entering the ring for the world match."[53]

The liberation theologians outside the meeting worked tirelessly, criticizing speeches and draft resolutions and replying to attacks on their views. The result was a final document which could only be described as a draw. It condemned the politicization of theology and "a praxis that has recourse to Marxist analysis," but it also was critical of "liberal capitalism" and of the doctrine of the national security state that was used by current military regimes to justify their rule. Most importantly, Puebla made a decisive commitment to "the preferential option for the poor" which was to be almost as controversial in future discussions as Medellín's reference to "institutionalized violence." That commitment was described by the conference as "non-exclusive" in order to defuse criticisms of its possibly partisan or even Marxist (the poor versus the rich) character, but it committed the Latin American church more clearly than in the past to work with the poor as the liberation theologians urged.[54]

The press covered the battle between the pro- and anti-liberation bishops as if it were in fact the prize fight alluded to by López Trujillo. Although the reporters were disappointed that the final outcome was not a decisive victory for one side or the other, they should have known from past meetings that an effort would be made to fashion a consensus document with something for everyone.

NICARAGUA AND THE POPULAR CHURCH

If Puebla began to focus attention on liberation theology, it was Nicaragua which made observers aware of the movement's potential political force. After Vatican II and Medellín, the Central American church had undergone a decisive shift in the direction of involvement for social justice. In 1977 the Salvadoran right-wing death squads even threatened to kill all the members of the Jesuit order if they did not leave the country. In Nicaragua, leading churchmen and women, especially the members of the religious orders, cooperated actively with the Sandinistas in the overthrow of Somoza, and four priests joined the government that they established in 1979. The Nicaraguan bishops wrote a pastoral letter that justified the revolution and, with certain important reservations, initially endorsed the government that followed. While the honeymoon between the Sandinistas and the church hierarchy was of short duration, there were many church activists, particularly the Jesuits and Maryknoll missionaries, who continued to support them and who justified their support in terms of the categories drawn from liberation theology. While church leaders were scandalized by the publication by a government-supported research group of a picture of a guerrilla fighter, gun in hand and arms upraised, superimposed on the crucified Christ, there were others who were ready to support a "popular church" which was committed to the Sandinistas. Fernando Cardenal, a Jesuit, organized the Sandinista literacy campaign, headed their youth organization, and later became minister of education, while his brother, Ernesto, a well-known priest-poet, became minister of culture. As polarization increased in the Nicaraguan church, anti-Sandinista Catholics blamed liberation theology for dividing the church and aiding the Marxists to expand their "totalitarian" control of Nicaragua.[55] When the professors at the Jesuit Central American University in El Salvador also seemed to favor the guerrillas there, and some leading Christian Democrats joined the Left in the civil war, it was liberation theology that was blamed.

As early as June 1981 the priests in the Sandinista government were asked by their bishops to leave their posts, because the bishops regarded these as incompatible with priestly duties. When the priests refused to do so, two of them were forbidden to exercise their priestly functions, another was suspended from the Jesuit order, and a fourth requested laicization. The tension between the pro-Sandinista priests and the Vatican was dramatically illustrated during the pope's visit in March 1983. At that time he was seen on television shaking his finger reprovingly at Ernesto Cardenal, as he knelt to receive the pope's blessing.

When the Reagan administration came to power and made the Central American struggle a central focus of United States foreign policy, explanations for the radicalization of Central America often cited the changes in the Central American church, including the expanding influence of liberation theology. Leading neoconservatives such as Michael Novak attacked it, and Ernest Lefever's Ethics and Public Policy Center published a collection of critical articles.[56] They all quoted the early Gutiérrez on the class struggle and dependency and Segundo's definition of socialism, and they criticized the liberation theologians for attributing all of Latin America's ills to capitalism while at the same time being willing to turn over political power to an undefined socialism which, from their enthusiasm for those governments, seemed likely to bear a strong resemblance to Cuba or Nicaragua. Others in the United States such as Robert McAfee Brown, Rosemary R. Ruether, and the publishers of the National Catholic Reporter expressed strong support and attributed the conservative criticisms to opposition to the efforts of the poor in Latin America to end centuries of exploitation and imperialism—when, in fact, the arguments of the neoconservatives were that the poor would be better served by a free market or mixed economic system than by the statist socialism proposed or implied by the liberationists.

THE VATICAN CONFRONTS LIBERATION THEOLOGY

More directly threatening to Latin American liberation theologians was a series of investigations and public statements ("Instructions") by the Vatican Congregation for the Doctrine of the Faith headed by Cardinal

Ratzinger. Leonardo Boff had already been subject to investigations as to his orthodoxy in 1976 and 1980, but during the 1970s the Vatican had usually been content to leave the matter to the Latin Americans. When Joseph Ratzinger, former archbishop of Munich and a widely published theologian, took over as prefect of the Congregation, the Vatican began to take a greater interest in the subject.

Boff himself initiated action on his writings in 1982 when he sent the congregation his reply to an investigation of his book *Church: Charism and Power* by the archdiocese of Rio de Janeiro, headed by the conservative Eugenio Cardinal Sales. Two years later (the Vatican moves slowly) Cardinal Ratzinger sent Boff a letter criticizing his "ecclesiological relativism" and his "sociological" analysis of the church as an institution engaged in production and consumption.[57] When Ratzinger summoned Boff to Rome for a "conversation" on the subject, the Brazilian basic communities rallied to his defense and were reported to have sent 50,000 letters of support to Rome. Boff arrived in Rome in September 1984, accompanied by two fellow Franciscans, Cardinals Lorscheiter and Arns. In April 1985 it was announced that his religious superiors had been requested to impose on the friar "obsequious silence for a convenient time," meaning that he could not write, preach, or give interviews—but he did not retract his views. Less than a year later, the sentence was lifted, and Boff continues to function as before, writing, teaching, and editing an important Brazilian theological journal.

In April 1983 Ratzinger also sent the Peruvian hierarchy a list of "observations" on the writings of Gustavo Gutiérrez. The Peruvians were divided on whether to take action against Gutiérrez; and in response to the Vatican criticism, Gutiérrez denied that he favored a synthesis of Marxism and Christianity, cited church documents on the existence of class conflict in Latin America, and argued that liberation theology's attempt to make use of the social sciences (not just Marxism) necessarily involved, "a critical perspective in their employment." Gutiérrez cited passages from his original writings that "rejected facile solutions and uncritical positions concerning historical socialism," quoted his favorable reference to the Prague reforms of 1968, and argued that it was not up to theology to propose specific political solutions.[58] The Vatican pressed on, but when the forty-four Peruvian bishops came to Rome as a group in October 1984, they issued a generally worded statement which could not be interpreted as a condemnation of Gutiérrez.[59]

The Peruvian bishops announced their support of the *Instruction on Certain Aspects of the Theology of Liberation*, which had been published by the Congregation for the Doctrine of the Faith in early September. The document had been prepared because of Cardinal Ratzinger's concern with the danger to Catholicism posed by certain versions of the new theology. Ratzinger's concerns had already been known as the result of the publication in Chile and Italy of a private memorandum that Ratzinger had written linking liberation theology with neo-Marxism, the politicization of Christianity, and advocacy of an alternative vision of the structure of the church ("ecclesiology") from that of Catholicism.[60] The memorandum had limited its criticisms to those (unspecified) theologians who had "made the Marxist analysis their own," but as noted earlier, it described them as posing a "fundamental threat to the faith of the Church." The 1984 *Instruction* toned down this wording, speaking of the "risks of deviation, damaging to the faith and Christian living, that are brought about by certain forms of liberation theology which use, in an insufficiently critical manner, concepts borrowed from various currents of marxist thought." (Again neither the Marxist nor liberation writers are specified.) The *Instruction* attacked the liberationists for accepting Marxism's false claim to be "scientific," supporting violence, and politicizing the gospel and the church.[61]

The 1984 *Instruction* promised a second statement on the broader theme of Christian freedom and liberation. Eighteen months later, after what were rumored to have been several revisions at the pope's behest to give it a more positive tone, *The Instruction on Christian Freedom and Liberation* was published in April 1986. While it denounced those who propagate "the myth of revolution," it admitted that armed struggle might be resorted to "as a last resort to put an end to an obvious and prolonged tyranny." The *Instruction* generally took a much more positive approach to liberation theology; it was particularly favorable to the basic Christian communities, "if they really live in unity with the local Church and the universal Church," and to theological reflection developed from particular experience "in the light of the experience of the Church itself." Rather than the controversial term, "option," it endorsed "preferential love for the poor" by the church, and called for a "Christian practice of liberation," based on solidarity (against individualism) and subsidarity, the initiative and responsibility of individuals and intermediate communities (against collectivism).[62]

The second *Instruction* was greeted very favorably by the liberation theologians. Gutiérrez said, "It closes a chapter, a new more positive period is beginning."[63] But what really overjoyed the liberationists was a papal letter sent to the Brazilian hierarchy—who had consistently supported the liberation theologians—which was written following a two-week visit by the Brazilian bishops to Rome in March 1986. In that letter, after reasserting the church's identification with "the poor, the suffering, those without influence, resources and assistance...with a love that is neither exclusive nor excluding but rather, preferential," the pope referred to the two *Instructions* published "with my explicit approval" and endorsed the Brazilian effort to find responses to the problems of poverty and oppression that are "consistent and coherent with the teachings of the Gospel, of the living Tradition, and of the ongoing *Magisterium* [teaching] of the Church. As long as all this is observed we are convinced, we and you, that the theology of liberation is not only timely but useful and necessary.... May God help you to be unceasingly watchful so that correct and necessary theology of liberation can develop in Brazil and in Latin America."[64]

Cardinal Ratzinger is said to have described his efforts in the Congregation for the Doctrine of the Faith as a "restoration" in the church. His critics argue that this means turning the church back to the period of centralization and authoritarianism before the Second Vatican Council. Ratzinger himself prefers to see his goal as curbing extremist tendencies that have emerged since the council, and he points out that he attended the council as an adviser to Cardinal Frings of Munich, who was one of those most active in promoting its reforms. However one interprets the Cardinal's intentions, the result of the Vatican's confrontation with the liberation theologians has not been a repudiation of their theology but its incorporation in modified form into the mainstream of theological discussion. The modifications include an abandonment in practice of its initial emphases on the class struggle, the near-inevitability of violence, and the rejection of "reformism"—all of which were characteristic of the period of lyrical leftism from the late 1960s to the mid-1970s.

The modifications in tone and content are most evident in the recent writings of Gustavo Gutiérrez. In an article on "Theology and the Social Sciences" published in September 1984, which drew on his written replies

to Ratzinger's criticisms, Gutiérrez argued that any use of the social sciences, whether Marxist or not, must be "continually subject to critical examination" that itself is an expression of "authentic rationality and personal
freedom."[65] The use of Marxist concepts in social analysis does not and
should not imply acceptance of atheism or a totalitarian world view.

> These are to be rejected on the basis of our faith, of a humanis-
> tic perspective, and also of sound social analysis.... The con-
> tributions of Marxist analysis should be situated and criticized
> within the framework of the social sciences.... There is no
> question of identifying the preferential option for the poor
> with an ideology or specific political program which is used
> to reinterpret the Gospel.... The universality of Christian love
> is incompatible with the exclusion of persons, although not
> with a preference for some.[66]

Gutiérrez's *We Drink from Our Own Wells* (1984), the title of which is
taken from the spiritual writings of St. Bernard of Clairvaux, is filled with
biblical references, and the class struggle and Marxism are not even mentioned.[67] The main themes of the book are a criticism of individualism and
"spiritualism" and a call for social involvement and awareness of the
spiritual dimensions of bodily existence.

Gutiérrez quotes from Matthew's Gospel, chapter 25 ("I was hungry and
you gave me food to eat, I was thirsty and you gave me drink"), to argue
for "a new approach to the human body" and "concern for the material
needs of the poor."[68] It is true that traces of the old revolutionism remain
when Gutiérrez quotes from letters of Christian guerrilla fighters, but the
basic message of the book is the duty of Christians to take action in community to help the poor.

In another recent book, *The Truth Shall Make You Free*, he again argues
for a critical approach to the analyses of poverty offered by the social sciences (not just Marxism), subjecting them to continual evaluation and
revision. In so doing, he says, we must take account of actual historical experience, including that of "historical socialism," in evaluating the possibilities of liberation; and he quotes with approval the 1986 Vatican
Instruction on Christian Freedom and Liberation: "A liberation which does
not take into account the personal liberty of those who fight for it is already
condemned to failure."[69]

More striking is the transformation of the thinking of Hugo Assmann, often regarded as the most radical of the liberation theologians. In a paper delivered in 1985, Assmann seems now to equate revolution with democracy. Arguing that the radicals are aware "that they must now reestablish their organic relation to the popular majorities which never understood their abstract revolutionism," he asserts that "many of them have begun to understand that democratic values are revolutionary values."[70] While Latin America now is dominated by "an absolutely savage and inhuman form of 'capitalism'...no socialism exists presently or around the corner.... Real revolutionaries have learned to value democratic participation and the authentically popular movements [and] are no longer interested in chaotic social explosions...." Instead of the Manichaean dualism of "certain leftist circles" that engage in "divinization or demonization," it is time to develop "a spirit of openness to negotiate minimal consensus...."[71]

Does this mean that liberation theology has become deradicalized in a way that is parallel to the deradicalization of social democracy in Western Europe? In a way it has, since the emphasis has shifted from conflict to negotiation, from the class struggle to solidarity with the poor. Yet the change is also a recognition that theologians seriously interested in the empowerment of the poor and oppressed should look for ways other than revolution to do so. While the revolutionary fervor of the early seventies has died down, there is still a strong strain of anticapitalism in the liberationist writings. The main emphasis, however, is upon the second theme in liberation theology, learning from and promoting the self-knowledge of the poor.

Once their revolutionism was tempered, it was easier for the liberation theologians to become part of the mainstream of Catholicism, which had always had an anticapitalist strain and from early Christian times had thought of itself—in theory, if not in practice—as a church of the poor. This left only the problem of the liberationist theories of church organization. But even here, because of the organizational reforms associated with the Second Vatican Council, the liberation theologians were not that far out of line with the mainstream. They had never rejected the hierarchy, tending to accept it in theory, although they did deemphasize its importance in relation to the communitarian aspects of Christian tradition. Now they have discovered that the bishops of Brazil, the largest Catholic country in the world, are increasingly favorable to their work, and they have initiated, with the approval of a number of Brazilian bishops and religious superiors, a fifty-volume series of theological expositions that will attempt to develop their theology in greater detail. If past experience and public statements are any indication, the volumes devoted to the structure of the church will argue for the necessity of *both* hierarchy and people rather than for conflictual "popular" versus "institutional" church models.

LIBERATION THEOLOGY AND LIBERALISM

If an outside observer who is not a theologian but a social scientist were permitted to make some suggestions as to topics to be discussed in the new theological series, so as to respond adequately to the criticisms that have been made of the earlier writings, the following questions might be explored:

1) Does theological reflection on the experience of the poor and oppressed always lead to the conclusion that capitalism must be replaced by a socialist system? If not, are there alternatives which combine the efficiency of the market with the equity of the "preferential love for the poor"? If socialism is the alternative, what would an ideal socialist state look like? (Here José Comblin might be asked to develop further the ideas he introduced ten years ago.)

2) What is the relation of private property and liberation? Is the former always to be viewed as an obstacle to liberation, or are there important ways, for instance the small family farm or innovative new business, in which it can contribute to free people from oppression, whether by private interests or public authorities?

3) How can human rights, especially but not only the rights of the poor, be best promoted in the modern state? What is the place of courts, or private groups, and of the media in guaranteeing those rights? Does the dialectical approach that many liberation theologians employ make it conceptually difficult to develop a theory of rights? Does the preference for the poor imply a kind of "affirmative action" that may undermine the ideal of equal treatment under law?

4) What is liberation theology's attitude toward the redemocratization of Latin America? Is it to be rejected as "fraudulent," as it was in the early 1970s? Can the fragile new democracies of Latin America promote participation and greater opportunity for the poor and oppressed, or is total

socialist transformation—all or nothing—the only possibility? If so, what lessons in revolutionary *praxis* in terms of its impact on the well-being of the poor are to be drawn from the failure of the revolutionism of Latin America in the 1960s?

5) What is the "prophetic" role of the theologian? Is it only to remind the people of their moral duties to others, especially to the poor and oppressed? Or are there more specific criticisms, denunciations, and proposals that theologians ought to offer? Does the Bible, in fact, offer a blueprint for the good society? Do not those liberation theologians who believe that it does so run the same risk of identifying a particular ideology with God's purposes in history that was run by the right-wing Catholic integralists and reformist Christian Democrats whom they denounce?

6) Finally, if the cure for the weaknesses and failures of democracy is more democracy, should not the liberation theologians devote their primary energies to the development of a spirituality of socially concerned democracy, whether capitalist of socialist in its economic form, rather than to denunciations of dependency, imperialism, and capitalist exploitation? If those theories are inadequate explanations of poverty and underdevelopment ("the rich are not rich because the poor are poor") should not the very considerable abilities of the liberation theologians now be devoted to the promotion of democratic participation, the protection of human rights, and the satisfaction of basic needs rather than to the sterile revolutionism that characterized their earlier writings?

It took the official Roman Catholic church a century and a half to recognize that democracy and freedom were central elements in the Christian message. As I hope this essay has shown, it has taken only two decades for it to relate that message to human liberation. The secular Left earlier defined liberation either as the overthrow of capitalism and the abolition of private ownership of the means of production (Marx) or as the extension of democracy and equality to all human beings, regardless of sex, race, or social class (Rousseau). Liberation theology will have to chose which it is to represent—grassroots democracy or anticapitalist revolution.

NOTES

1. *New York Times,* December 4, 1986.

2. Gustavo Gutiérrez, *A Theology of Liberation: History, Politics and Salvation,* trans. Sister Caridad Inda and John Eagleson (Maryknoll, N.Y.: Orbis Books, 1973).

3. Joseph Cardinal Ratzinger with Vittorio Messori, *The Ratzinger Report* (San Francisco: Ignatius Press, 1985), p. 175.

4. Congregation for the Doctrine of the Faith, *Instruction on Certain Aspects of the Theology of Liberation* (Rome, 1984), p. 12.

5. *New York Times,* December 1, 1986.

6. Frei Betto, *Fidel and Religion,* trans. Cuban Center for Translation and Interpretation (New York: Simon and Schuster, 1987), pp. 903–1014.

7. *Origins* (Washington, D.C.), May 1986, p. 12.

8. Austin Flannery, ed., *Documents of Vatican II,* rev. ed. (Grand Rapids, Mich.: William B. Eerdmans, 1984).

9. Walt W. Rostow, *The Stages of Economic Growth* (Cambridge: Cambridge University Press, 1960).

10. Second General Conference of Latin American Bishops, *The Church in the Present Day Transformation of Latin America* (Washington, D.C.: U.S. Catholic Conference, 1970), II, 34.

11. Ibid., p. 172.

12. Ibid., p. 175.

13. Ibid., p. 49.

14. Ibid., p. 53.

15. Gustavo Gutiérrez, "Notes for a Theology of Liberation," *Theological Studies* 31 (June 1970): 243–61.

16. Ibid., p. 250.

17. Ibid., p. 251.

18. Ibid., p. 250.

19. Ibid.

20. Ibid., p. 254.

21. Ibid.

22. Gutiérrez, *Theology of Liberation*, p. 110.

23. Ibid., p. 48.

24. Ibid., p. 11.

25. Ibid., p. 49.

26. Ibid., p. 88.

27. Ibid., p. 87.

28. Ibid., p. 90.

29. Ibid.

30. Ibid., p. 91.

31. Cited by Gutiérrez, *Theology of Liberation,* p. 91. See Paolo Freire, *Pedagogy of the Oppressed* (New York: Herder and Herder, 1970).

32. Gutiérrez, *Theology of Liberation,* pp. 275–76.

33. Ibid., pp. 203–208.

34. Ibid., p. 207.

35. For the documents see John Eagleson, ed., *Christians and Socialism* (Maryknoll, N.Y.: Orbis Books, 1975). See also the criticisms of the movement in Teresa Panosa Loero, *Los cristianos por el socialismo* (Santiago: El Mercurio, 1975) and Afonso López Trujillo, *Liberación marxista y liberación cristiana* (Madrid: Biblioteca de Autores Cristianos, 1974).

36. Hugo Assmann, *A Theology for a Nomad Church,* trans. Paul Burns (Maryknoll, N.Y.: Orbis Books, 1976).

37. Ibid., p. 49.

38. Ibid., p. 76.

39. Ibid., pp. 138, 144.

40. Juan Luis Segundo, "Capitalism and Socialism, The Theological Crux," in *The Mystical and Political Dimension of the Christian Faith,* ed. Claude Geffré and Gustavo Gutiérrez (New York: Herder and Herder, 1974), p. 115. *The Liberation of Theology* was trans-

lated by John Drury and published by Orbis Books (Maryknoll, N.Y.), in 1976.

41. Ibid., pp. 120–21.

42. José Comblin, *The Church and the National Security State* (Maryknoll, N.Y.: Orbis Books, 1979).

43. Ibid., pp. 160–61.

44. Ibid., pp. 219–20.

45. Leonardo Boff, *Church: Charism and Power,* trans. John W. Diecksmeier (New York: Crossroads, 1985). See also Boff's *Ecclesiogenesis,* trans. Robert W. Barr (Maryknoll, N.Y.: Orbis Books, 1986), and *Kirche als Sakrament* (Paderborn: Verlag Bonifacius-Druckerei, 1972).

46. Ibid., p. 60; p. 71 in Portuguese edition.

47. For example, "There has been a gradual expropriation of the means of religious production from the Christian people by the clergy." Ibid., p. 112.

48. Leonardo Boff, *Jesus Christ, Liberator,* trans. Patrick Hughes (Maryknoll, N.Y.: Orbis Books, 1978).

49. Jon Sobrino, *Christology at the Crossroads,* trans. John Drury (Maryknoll, N.Y.: Orbis Books, 1978), p. 256.

50. Ibid., pp. 380–81.

51. Sergio Torres and John Eagleson, eds., *Theology in the Americas* (Maryknoll, N.Y.: Orbis Books, 1976).

52. John Eagleson and Philip Scharper, eds., *Puebla and Beyond* (Maryknoll, N.Y.: Orbis Books, 1979), pp. 68–69.

53. Ibid., p. 37.

54. See the criticisms of the movements in Teresa Panoso Loero, *Los cristianos por el socialismo* (Santiago: El Mercurio, 1975) and López Trujillo, *Liberación marxista y liberación cristiana*

55. See, for example, Humberto Belli, *Breaking Faith* (Westchester, Ill.: Crossway Books, 1985).

56. Michael Novak, *The Spirit of Democratic Capitalism* (New York: Simon and Schuster, 1982), ch. XVII, and *Will It Liberate?* (New

York: Paulist Press, 1986) as well as Quentin L. Quade, ed., *The Pope and Revolution* (Washington, D.C.: Ethics and Public Policy Center, 1982).

57. The text of the letter appears in Roberto Jiménez, *Teología de la liberación* (Caracas: CEDIAL, 1986), pp. 597–601 (author's translation).

58. For Ratzinger's observations and Gutiérrez's reply, see Jiménez, pp. 517–559. See also *Misión Abierta* (Madrid) 1 (Feb. 1985): 36–76 (author's translation).

59. *New York Times,* October 10, 1984.

60. The memorandum was originally published in the Italian journal *Treinti Giorni* and is available in Ratzinger with Vittorio Messori, *The Ratzinger Report,* pp. 174–86.

61. Congregation for the Doctrine of the Faith, *Instruction on Certain Aspects of the Theology of Liberation* (Rome, 1984).

62. Congregation for the Doctrine of the Faith, *Instruction on Christian Faith and Liberation,* (Rome, 1986), pp. 41–47.

63. "Responden los teologos de la liberación," *Vida Nueva* (Madrid), September 1986, p. 23 (author's translation).

64. The text of the letter is published in Marcello de C. Azevedo, S.J., *Basic Ecclesial Communities* (Washington, D.C.: Georgetown University Press, 1987), pp. 257–67.

65. Gustavo Gutiérrez, "Teología y las ciencias sociales," *Páginas* (Lima) 11 (September 1984), reprinted in *Cristianismo y Sociedad* (Mexico City) 84 (1985): 53 (author's translation).

66. Ibid., pp. 53, 64 (author's translation).

67. Gustavo Gutiérrez, *We Drink from Our Own Wells,* trans. Matthew O'Connell (Maryknoll, N.Y.: Orbis Books, 1984).

68. Ibid., pp. 102–103.

69. Gustavo Gutiérrez, *La verdad los hara libres* (Lima: CEP, 1986). (Author's translation.)

70. Hugo Assmann, "Democracy and the Debt Crisis," *This World* 14 (Spring/Summer 1986): 93.

71. Ibid.

2

Liberation Theology and the Crisis of Western Society

Marc H. Ellis

For some time now Western intellectuals have been analyzing the crisis of Western society from two major perspectives: as a movement of progress punctuated by the difficult passage of modernity, and as a process of decline where significant areas of life lose their unity and creativity. Both analyses point to the roles of secularization, technology, capitalism, state socialism, and militarism as agents and consequences of this crisis. Depending on one's intellectual perspective, solutions vary from the restoration of a conservative order to revolutionary change, and policymakers dealing with the immediate and the concrete have little time to think of the crisis or possible solutions, at least on the broader scale. However, whether seen through the lens of interrupted progress or significant decline, whether approached through a neoconservative or revolutionary social change methodology, the central facts of our century remain what Hannah Arendt and Richard Rubenstein proclaimed them to be in 1951 and 1975—a century of triage and holocaust.[1]

For Arendt and Rubenstein the crisis of the West has come to a point of culmination in the twentieth century. This prompted Arendt to announce the decline of Western civilization:

The tragedy of our time has been that only the emergence of crimes unknown in quality and proportion and not foreseen by the Ten Commandments made us realize what the mob had known since the beginning of the century: that not only this or that form of government has become antiquated or that certain values and traditions need to be reconsidered, but that the whole of nearly three thousand years of Western civilization, as we have known it in a comparatively uninterrupted stream of tradition, has broken down; the whole structure of Western culture with all its implied beliefs, traditions, standards of judgments, has come toppling down over our heads.[2]

Rubenstein images the horrible possibilities within that decline:

There is always the danger that Metropolis will become Necropolis. The city is by nature antinature, antiphysis, and hence, antilife. The world of the city, *our world,* is the world of human invention and power; it is also the world of artifice, dreams, charades, and the paper promises we call money. But even the richest and most powerful city can only survive as long as the umbilical cord to the countryside is not cut. Whenever men build cities, they take the chance that their nurturing lifeline to the countryside may someday be severed, as indeed it was in wartime Poland. One of the most frightful images of the death of civilization envisages a time when the city, deprived of the countryside's surplus food and bloated by the countryside's surplus people, feeds upon its own ever-diminishing self and finally collapses. The starving inmates of Auschwitz, consuming their own substance until they wasted away into nothingness, may offer a prophetic image of urban civilization at the end of its journey from the countryside to Necropolis. Could it be that as the Jews were among the countryside's first exiles and among the pioneer inhabitants of Metropolis, so too they were among the first citizens of Necropolis, but that, unless current economic, social, and demographic trends are somehow reversed, there will be other citizens of the city of the dead, many others?[3]

Though Arendt and Rubenstein analyzed our century within the context of Western society and mainly through the Jewish experience in Europe as paradigmatic of twentieth-century history, it is clear that the phenomena of triage and holocaust have been visited upon non-Europeans by Europeans in their centuries of power and through exploitation and expropriation of resources and human beings, as well as through disease and war. Since the end of World War II, the base of power has shifted considerably from Europe to North America, the Soviet Union, and China, though the results are in many ways quite similar—suffering of the masses of people and human-induced death (through commission or omission) on a major scale. Of course the new threat combines the exploitation of labor and resources with the threatened extinction of the human species through biological and nuclear warfare.[4]

A major and often misunderstood response to the crisis of Western society is the emergence of liberation theologies around the world. From the outset, it is critical to emphasize the plurality of these movements before addressing the particular strain found in the Americas: for each theology is localized, responding to the history of crisis impinging on a particular region. Therefore, Minjung theology emerging from South Korea is in important ways quite different from the "theology of struggle" found in the Philippines. Though both nations are Asian, differing backgrounds of colonialism and dependency, oriented initially around China/Japan and Spain respectively, thrust their struggles and theology in particular directions. South African liberation theology remains distinct even within the African continent by emphasizing the revolutionary political struggle while liberation theologies in African states that have won independence concentrate more on cultural roots and inculturating the Christian message. From this perspective, Latin American liberation theology (through its local variants, responding to the diversity of the continent) is part of a worldwide theological response to the multifaceted crisis facing a troubled world.[5]

Unfortunately, citing Asian, African, and Latin American theological responses to crisis often allows us to keep "that world" out there. We cannot, however, understand the birth of liberation theologies outside the crisis of Western society: in a real sense liberation theologies were born within that crucible and as a result of it. For example, major elements of Minjung theology and the "theology of struggle" confront the significant economic and military presence of the United States in South Korea and the Philippines and the impact that presence has had on the internal structure of Korean and Filipino society. Too, liberation theologies have developed within the United States and Europe as well, as an attempt to address the crisis of Western society, and have assumed a dialogical role vis-à-vis liberation theologies in the rest of the world. Political theology in Europe and black and feminist theologies in North America are three such liberationist attempts from a First World perspective. If it is true that the crisis of Western society helped give birth to liberation theologies, liberation theologies now address their crisis from both within and outside of the Western world.[6]

THE EMERGENCE OF LATIN AMERICAN THEOLOGY

Latin American liberation theology emerged in the 1960s as a response to at least four levels of crisis: political, economic, cultural, and religious. At the Second General Conference of Latin American Bishops at Medellín, Colombia, in August–September 1968, the situation of Latin America was described as one of injustice and despair that "cried to the heavens." In analyzing injustice, the political, cultural, and religious were linked together.

> Just as Israel of old, the first People (of God), felt the saving presence of God when He delivered them from the oppression of Egypt by the passage through the sea and led them to the promised land, so we also, the new People of God, cannot cease to feel his saving passage in view of "true development, which is the passage for each and all, from conditions of life that are less human, to those that are more human. *Less human*: the material needs of those who are deprived of the minimum living conditions, and the moral needs of those who are mutilated by selfishness. *Less human*: the oppressive structures that come from the abuse of ownership and of power from exploitation of workers or from unjust transactions. *More human*: overcoming misery by the possession of necessities; victory over social calamities; broadening of knowledge; the acquisition of cultural advantages. *More human also*: an increase in respect for the dignity of others;

orientation toward the spirit of poverty; cooperation for the common good; the will for peace. *More human still*: acknowledgement, on man's part, of the supreme values and of God who is their source and term. *More human, finally*, and especially, faith, the gift of God, accepted by men of good will and unity in the charity of Christ, who calls us all to participation, as sons, in the life of the living God who is the father of all men."[7] [Internal quote from Paul VI, *Populorum Progressio*.]

In 1971, just three years after the bishops' statement at Medellín, an extended discussion of the problems facing Latin America and a theology which addressed them was published by Gustavo Gutiérrez, a Peruvian priest, under the title *Teología de la liberación, perspectivas*. Translated into English in 1973 with the title *A Theology of Liberation: History, Politics and Salvation*, this book and its author articulated an important shift in the vision of politics and theology for people living on the underside of Western history, as well as for those within Western society becoming aware of the nightside of their Western inheritance. It is not too much to claim that this book ignited a worldwide revolution in the way Christians understand theology and its relation to social change.[8]

Though diverse and nuanced in its original argument and further developed in later works, especially in *La fuerza histórica de los pobres* (1979; in English translation, *The Power of the Poor in History*, 1983) and *Hablar de Dios desde el sufrimiento del innocente* (1985; in English translation, *On Job: God-Talk and the Suffering of the Innocent*, 1987), several themes are of critical importance from the first: the movement from a model of developmentalism to liberation in the social and political fields; the movement from a Christendom model, albeit updated and modernized, to a liberationist understanding of the Christian message. Involved here is the understanding of sin as individual *and* social and the eschatological promise of Christ as involving the spiritual *and* political, fused but not absorbed—a tension calling a people forward into the struggle for liberation in this world.[9]

Far from distancing himself from the Western world, Gutiérrez argues his political and theological agenda from within the Western framework; indeed, it has been the political and theological failures within this framework, at least in Latin America, which have occasioned the theology of liberation. For Gutiérrez, the developmentalist approach and the ideology of modernization are confronted by the increasing impoverishment and division within Latin American societies; the church's inability to address the social order from a radical faith perspective tends to cast it in an irrelevant and even harmful role for those who struggle for justice. The critique is strong and unsparing: Latin Americans are experiencing in their lives the inability of the Western economic and religious system to deliver the goods it promised.[10]

The dialogue Gutiérrez encourages with political and religious models of change is also distinctly Western. To begin with, he emphasizes the need to use the social sciences to analyze the structures of society, including and especially the forms of injustice. Citing the call of the Second Vatican Council to search out the signs of the times, Gutiérrez utilizes the social sciences to help Christians discern those signs. Along with other methods of analysis, Marxism is cited as providing a "fruitful confrontation" with contemporary theology. For Gutiérrez, it is to a large extent due to Marxism's influence that theological thought, "searching for its own sources, has begun to reflect on the meaning of the transformation of this world and the action of man in history." Thus Marxism's importance as a tool of analysis is superseded by the introspection demanded of the church to rediscover its own radical message of transformation. Still Marxism is only one of the many Western schools of analysis Gutiérrez cites; the philosophical and psychological ideas of Descartes, Hegel, Kant, Freud, and Marcuse are also used to show the development in Western thought of the social and personal elements of liberation which, according to Gutiérrez, liberation theology brings together in a new configuration.[11]

Gutiérrez also explores the history of Roman Catholic theology to provide the backdrop for the changes needed in the Latin American situation. In fact, his book, *A Theology of Liberation,* begins with an analysis of the two classical forms of theology—theology as wisdom, found in the early centuries of the church, and theology as rational knowledge, a concept initiated in the twelfth century. According to Gutiérrez, theology as wisdom was above all monastic, promoting "a spiritual life removed from worldly concerns"; it used Platonic and Neoplatonic categories, stressing a dualistic understanding of the world with, as time went on, the consequent devaluation of earthly life. Theology as rational knowledge established itself as a science, an "intellectual discipline, born of the meeting of faith and reason." Unfortunately, from the thirteenth century on, there was a degradation of this understanding of theology. The demands of rational knowledge, for example, were reduced to systematization and exposition and finally to an ancillary discipline of the magisterium of the church. Gutiérrez sees the task of the contemporary Latin American church to realize the strength within these theologies by discarding the aberrant transformations they have suffered through history.[12]

Theology as critical reflection on praxis is the model of theology which Gutiérrez feels emphasizes the spiritual and rational dimensions of previous theology and responds to the new philosophical and political emphasis on people as masters of their own destiny developed in the West since the Enlightenment. For Gutiérrez, faith in a God who loves us and calls us to the gift of full communion with God and each other is not foreign to the transformation of the world; rather, it leads necessarily to the building up of that brotherhood and sisterhood in history. Hence there is an emerging understanding of orthopraxis, which is not meant to deny the meaning of orthodoxy understood as a proclamation of and reflection on statements considered to be true. As Gutiérrez sees it, the goal is to "balance and even to reject the primacy and almost exclusiveness which doctrine has enjoyed in Christian life and above all to modify the emphasis, often obsessive, upon the attainment of an orthodoxy which is often nothing more than fidelity to an obsolete tradition or a debatable interpretation. In a more positive vein, the intention is to recognize the work and importance of concrete behavior, of deeds, of action, of praxis in the Christian life."[13] Thus Gutiérrez's definition of theological reflection is a criticism of society and the church insofar as they are called and addressed by the Word of God and is a "critical theory, worked out in the light of the Word accepted in faith and inspired by a practical purpose—and therefore indissolubly linked to historical praxis."[14]

At the same time that Gutiérrez investigates the Western political and theological tradition, including the political and theological crisis engendered by it, he also places Latin America and its indigenous peoples in a critical relationship with the West. In fact, this is where Gutiérrez develops the distinctive Latin American flavor of his political and theological outlook. For if Latin America has benefited from Western political and religious thought, it has also been an object of Western domination. Remarkably, it has also retained its own distinctive history, especially among those banished to the underside of history—the "nonpersons" of this world. These nonpersons are the objective reality of the historical crisis in the West, the ones who prompt the challenge to regain the particularity of the Latin American experience.[15]

For Gutiérrez, nonpersons are the ones on the margins, the exploited, the unseen; collectively, they are those absent from history. They are the exploited classes, marginalized ethnic groups, and despised cultures, the ones who are dying before their time. The last years have seen an irruption of these poor in history in Latin America and around the world. The result is a new and difficult language for affluent Westerners to understand. According to Gutiérrez, nonpersons are learning to speak without interpreters; they are rediscovering themselves and making the system feel their disquieting presence. At the same time, they are becoming less and less objects of manipulation and social work mentality and more and more the agents of their own destiny—forgers of a radically different society. Nonpersons are creating a history that no longer focuses on the dominant classes but on those on the underside of history. Thus history is seen from a different perspective: the movement for liberty among the middle classes in the West, for example, seen from beneath has meant new and more refined forms of exploitation of the very poorest in Latin America. For the wretched of the earth, "the attainment of freedom can only be a result of a process of liberation from the spoilation and oppression being carried on in the name of 'modern liberties and democracy.' "[16]

Of course, the irruption of the poor has occurred throughout history, though it is reaching a more profound level today. At certain times the poor have had spokespersons on their behalf. Gutiérrez cites Bartolomé de las Casas, a sixteenth-century Spanish missionary to Latin America, because he inverted the relation of heathen and saved. He pointed out that the Spaniards were placing their own salvation in jeopardy by degrading, exploiting, and murdering the indigenous people of Latin America. Las Casas also had the "prophetic depth" to see the Indians as poor people rather than as heathens. In a letter to the Spanish ruler, Las Casas wrote that if the Indians' conversion to Christianity could not take place without their death and destruction, it would be better "for them never to become Christians." More recently, Gutiérrez sees revolutionary ferment in Mexico, Bolivia, and Guatemala in the 1950s, the socialist revolution in Cuba, and the figures of Camilo Torres and Che Guevara as "symbolizing so many others— anonymous, commited, setting an indelible seal on the Latin American process, raising questions and exerting definitive influence in Christian circles." For Gutiérrez, however, the gathering momentum is seen more and more as the active participation of the poor themselves in becoming aware and articulate about their own world, giving rise to a new person and believer, to a new way of living and theologizing the Christian faith. The process is radicalized and revolutionary because of this participation and Christian articulation rather than in spite of it. As Gutiérrez points out, the irruption of the poor has political and religious significance: "To participate in the process of liberation is already, in a certain sense, a salvific work."[17]

What is the power of the poor in history? According to Gutiérrez, they reverse our perceptions of political, economic, and cultural history. They remind us of the other side of power and affluence. But more, the irruption of the poor seeks a remaking of history—subverting history, turning it around, making it flow backward, not from above but from below. From this viewpoint, the great wrong is to become, or to continue to be, "a 'super-versive,' a bulwark and support of the prevailing domination, someone whose orientation of history begins with the great ones of this world." Sub-versive history is the "locus of a new faith experience, a new spirituality, and a new proclamation of the gospel." Thus the power of the poor in history and in Latin America today is to continue the ancient prophetic tradition of Judeo-Christianity in light of contemporary anguish and possibility; it is to announce the reality of a God who struggles with the poor against domination and oppression.

> What had been a dominated, repressed theology, an under-ground spring working its own way to the surface, today has burst into the sunlight in uncappable geysers. Rivulets have formed, then streams, and now, in the rivers of this theology, we recognize not only the tributaries of the present situation, but waters flowing from the living wellsprings of a historical, concrete past as well. These torrents are thundering straight for the windows of the great ones of this world. They in turn peer out and see all this, only too well. The waters are mount-ing for them. Their time is up. The ill humor, the thinly-veiled contempt—even the occasional condemnations that these movements provoke—are not long for this world. The poor of the earth, in their struggles for liberation, in their faith and hope in the Father, are coming to the realization that, to put it

in the words of Arguedas, "the God of the masters is not the same." Their God is not the God of the poor. For ultimately the dominator is one who does not really believe in the God of the Bible.[18]

LIBERATION THEOLOGY AND THE NORTH AMERICAN CRISIS

For policymakers in North America, it is crucial to understand that while Latin American liberation theology operates within the crisis of Western society and challenges it from the Latin American continent, its insights have deeply penetrated theological and activist circles in North America. That is, Gutiérrez and other liberation theologians have spoken a word that is deeply relevant at home.

By the 1960s, Thomas Merton, a prominent Trappist monk, writer, and poet, and Dorothy Day, a lay social activist and founder of the Catholic Worker Movement, came to understand the future significance of Latin America in the theological landscape of North America. For Merton this was occasioned by his having a number of novices from Latin America, including the Nicaraguan poet, Brother Lawrence, alias Ernesto Cardenal, who would later join the Nicaraguan revolution and become minister of cultural affairs in post-revolutionary Nicaragua. As early as 1957, Merton read one of Cardenal's poems attacking the United Fruit Company and its presence in Central America. At this time Merton himself was recovering his awareness of social issues. Merton and Cardenal's relationship was close enough that on several occasions Merton thought seriously about joining Cardenal in a new monastic enterprise at Solentiname, a Nicaraguan island. In 1965 the Vietnam War was intensifying, and Merton's sense of the crisis in Western civilization almost overwhelmed him. Because of the history of the United States in Latin America, he wondered whether he would not be "too ashamed to be in a Latin American country and to be known as a North American." Ultimately his desire to join Cardenal was turned down by Pope Paul VI. Later Solentiname became famous for resisting the Somoza dictatorship and for producing revolutionary artwork and commentary on the Gospels.[19]

In 1962, Dorothy Day traveled to Cuba and devoted several of her monthly columns in the *Catholic Worker* to the subject of revolution and Christian faith. For her, Castro's "atheistic revolution" was occasioned by the failure of Western Christianity and Western society in general. Though an absolute pacifist, she supported the revolution as the solution to problems such as hunger and illiteracy. Some critics asked whether she had given up her stand on pacifism. Day replied:

> What nonsense. We are as unalterably opposed to armed resistance and armed revolt from the admittedly intolerable conditions all through Latin America as we ever were. In Chile, land is being redistributed and reforms are taking place in many Latin American countries. But how much land, and to whom, and with what means to cultivate it? Is it good land, or waste land, and is the redistribution made in the spirit of Ananias and Sapphira?[20]

Of the revolution she wrote:

> The motive is love of brother, and we are commanded to love our brothers. If religion has so neglected the needs of the poor and of the great mass of workers and permitted them to live in the most horrible destitution while comforting them with the solace of a promise of a life after death when all tears shall be wiped away, then that religion is suspect. Who would believe such Job's comforters? On the other hand, if those professing religion shared the life of the poor and worked to better their lot and risked their lives as revolutionists do, and trade union organizers have done in the past, then there is a ring of truth about the promises of the glory to come.[21]

In 1968, already in her seventies, Day was asked to write a preface to the works of Camilo Torres, the Colombian priest who had joined a guerrilla movement and had been killed. At first glance, this seems to be a mistake: an ardent Catholic pacifist was to comment in a positive way on a priest/freedom fighter killed attempting to ambush an army patrol. Yet the end result was quite striking. One is stunned by the beauty of her words and the insight Day had into a life very different from her own. Nor did she equivocate. A new understanding of faith was being born which we now know as liberation theology. Day wrote:

> This morning as I sat in a church waiting for Mass to begin,
> I was still thinking of Camilo Torres and the ideas for which

he had died. Earlier on that morning I had read over again that thrilling manifesto entitled *Gospel and Revolution,* signed by those sixteen bishops of the Third World....

I began to think of the outward Church, the respectable Church, and the accusation that it is not relevant today. I began to think of all the people I knew who had fallen away from church-going, from the Sacraments. Certainly over the decades I had met people, dedicated people, finding their religion in service, in union activities, in teaching, in emptying themselves. And in revolution.

Revolution has followed revolution in Latin American countries, but new revolutions have emerged which are unlike any other we have seen.

Camilo Torres joined the guerrillas, their life in mountain and jungle, joined their pilgrimage to the people, the campesinos. He broke bread with them, and so truly became the *compañero,* the one who breads bread, the companion.

What would Mass be like in a jungle, in one of the encampments of the republics in Colombia where no priest had been sent as missionary, where the idea of the Church was linked up in the minds of the destitute with the rich, the exploiter?

Suppose a priest like Father Torres looked at his companions sitting around a fire by night, hunted men, but men bringing a gospel of hope to the poor, men who were workers themselves, unlearned men like the twelve apostles. Suppose he picked up bread—in this case tortillas—and after speaking to them of the first communion at the Last Supper, and using the gospel words, broke and gave it to them. Suppose he had wine, as the fugitive priest did in Graham Greene's book *The Power and the Glory.* And suppose he blessed the cup and passed it to them all, for the forgiveness of sin. Would not this be a church, there in the wilderness? Would not this be a Mass? Would not this community of men have communion together just as the two men walking with Christ on the way to Emmaus did, as they sat at the inn and knew Him in the breaking of bread? And could it not be just as casual and as quiet, and yet just as earthshaking?[22]

Day wrote this preface just after the death of Martin Luther King, Jr., and, in an almost prophetic way, she concluded her reflection on Camilo Torres by connecting in the form of prayer the death of Torres and the assassination of King, "Martin Luther King, we ask your prayers that we learn more to overcome ourselves, and to learn the violence we need to impose upon ourselves in overcoming righteous wrath against the oppressor, and so grow in non-violence. Father Camilo Torres, pray for us, that we may have your courage in offering our lives for our brothers. And may God's light shine upon you both, and may you rest in peace."[23]

By 1975, just two years after the English publication of Gutiérrez's seminal work, a group of theologians, policy planners, social scientists, and activists met in Detroit under the banner "Theology in the Americas: 1975." Their task as set forth in the preparatory document was to grapple with the question of how theology is done today, against the backdrop of clashes between networks of domination and forces of liberation, in both domestic and international society. The participants began by asking a suddenly relevant question: What meaning does Latin American liberation theology have for the theology done in the United States?[24]

The preparatory document sets the historical background for the conference as one of crisis—a short history of the growth of the American "empire" in relation to the Third World is followed by an analysis of the severe strains in the empire at present. The future is ominous, with hegemony of United States capital undercut in the international community and upward mobility replaced with downward mobility on the domestic scene. No longer will the United States be seen as the leader of the world or even as a "source of bounty to its own people." Yet the collapse of empire will be anything but smooth; as empire recedes, its international and domestic policies endanger the human family. The conveners of the conference see the United States religious scene as parched desert with the creative font being the voice of the theology of liberation from Latin America. The document section on the religious voice of Latin America concludes: "Interest in the new theology has been stimulated in part by the political exile of many of its practitioners from Latin America. It has also been stimulated by a growing sense that the traditional theologies simply are inadequate foundations for creative and critical grappling with the pervasive crisis of the West." The executive secretary of the organizing committee was Sergio Torres, a Chilean priest exiled after the overthrow of Allende's democratically elected socialist government; and the entire first day of the conference was devoted to speeches and panel discussions by Latin American liberation theologians then hardly known in the United States— Juan Luis Segundo, José Miguez Bonino, Enrique Dussel, Hugo Assmann, and Leonardo Boff. Detained by political events in Peru and arriving at the end of the conference, Gustavo Gutiérrez addressed the final general session.[25]

As the conference met in 1975, two other documents, an article and a book, that extended the analysis of the North American crisis were being circulated. The first attempted to represent a majority group, the latter a minority. Both contained severe indictments of Western society historically and in the present and called for a dialogue between North and South America on the question of liberation.

The first was an article by Elisabeth Schüssler Fiorenza titled "Feminist Theology as a Critical Theology of Liberation." Clearly the title of the article itself showed a debt to Latin American theologians, though its emphasis on patriarchy and sexism was the beginning of a more mature and realistic dialogue. As it promoted new symbols, myths, and lifestyles, feminist theology shared the concerns and goals of liberation theology— though, according to Schüssler Fiorenza, because Christian symbols and thought are deeply embedded in patriarchal traditions and sexist structures, and because women belong to all races, classes, and cultures, its scope is more radical and universal than Latin American liberation theology. In sum, the crisis of the West and the theological demands of the moment were being expanded and particularized. They were also moving beyond geographic boundaries. On the issue of women, male liberationists from Latin America were going to have to listen.[26]

In 1969, James Cone, the most prominent of black theologians, published his first book, *Black Theology and Black Power,* which was followed in 1970 by *A Black Theology of Liberation.* The seminal statement of his theology came in 1975 with the publication of *God of the Oppressed.* Thus we can say that, though developed independently of each other, Latin American liberation theology and black liberation theology, as responses to crisis in their respective continents, also developed simultaneously. Though most liberation theology begins with a political and theological analysis on a macro level, Cone's *God of the Oppressed* brings the reader to an everyday level of experience. His introduction is a description of his upbringing in Bearden, Arkansas, and the lessons he and other blacks learned about white society. He also relates the circumstances of his first venture into black theology well after his seminary training, which concentrated almost exclusively on European theologians. In 1967, teaching in Adrian, Michigan, just seventy miles from riot-torn Detroit, Cone found the "black insurrection" and the white response puzzling and galvanizing. Sensitive whites deplored the riots, though sympathizing with the reason for them. For Cone this was tantamount to saying: "Of course we raped your women, lynched your men, and ghettoized the minds of your children and you have a right to be upset; but there is no reason for you to burn our buildings. If you keep acting like that, we will never give you your freedom." Cone experienced a personal and theological crisis; neither the education of white theologians nor his own prepared them to deal with Watts, Detroit, and Newark. What was needed was a new way of doing theology, one that emerged out of the dialectic of black history and culture, the underside of Western and North American history. His question was similar to that of the Latin Americans: What has the gospel to do with the black struggle for liberation? His situation was also similar: How to articulate the history of his people and their present situation from the underside of Western history and its contemporary crisis? It is not surprising that over the last years Cone's black theology of liberation has had a profound effect on the revolutionary struggle in South Africa and that his current agenda is to deepen the dialogue of black theology and other theologies of liberation around the world, especially through EATWOT, the Ecumenical Association of Third World Theologians.[27]

LIBERATION THEOLOGY
AND THE CALL TO FIDELITY IN THE AMERICAS

The connective links forged among theologies of liberation in the Americas and around the world signal a new understanding of the crisis of Western civilization as a global crisis. At the same time, possibilities of solidarity, heretofore only dimly imagined, come into view. Responding to the crisis of politics and culture, a transformation of theological consciousness is occurring which rivals those previous heraldic intellectual and religious events in Western history, the Reformation and the Enlightenment. Amidst the pain and suffering of the poor and the oppressed, a call of fidelity is being spoken and increasingly heard. Though the examples of Latin American liberation theology, the foresight of Merton and Day, the emerging theology in the Americas, including black theology and feminist theology, hardly exhaust the theological expressions of our day, they point to the future of theological expression vis-à-vis the political and economic structures of society worldwide.

At the root of this shift in theological consciousness is the question of God's presence in the contemporary world and how that presence is understood within the life of society. In a sense all liberation theologies deal with this fundamental question, and their commonality and diversity can be seen within the question of God's presence. For example, Latin American liberation theology and black liberation theology are quite similar on this theme: Christ is with the poor in their struggle for justice. The biblical God is one who chose sides and chooses sides today; those who oppress and see themselves as believers are worshiping a God other than the one found in the Bible. Thus the themes of Exodus, the prophets, and idolatry are critical to both Latin American and black theologies of liberation. The sight of Chilean dictator Pinochet receiving daily communion raises for Latin American liberationists the same questions as were raised for black theologians by Christians who blessed and participated in the slave trade: What God were/are they worshiping?[28]

Yet seeing the nonperson as the ground of theological reflection also introduces other difficult questions of God's presence, including the ancient question of the suffering of the innocent, now seen on a mass scale. After twenty years of liberation theology, this area is increasingly explored, slowly to be sure, but with a depth which is striking. On the one hand, liberation theologies' handling of God's presence is an attempt to integrate the Christian faith and the modern world in a new configuration, and this is of extreme importance to First World theologians. On the other hand, such discussions link together those who were originally conquered by the gospel and the West, charting a different way of being Christian within political and religious empires. While the West discovers the nonpersons of the world it has colonized and controlled, the nonpersons of Latin America discover the nonpersons within the West—or to put in another way, the Third World is discovered both on the periphery of and within the First World.[29]

Gustavo Gutiérrez's latest writings on Job are critical in understanding this dialogue. For Job speaks about the suffering of the innocent and therefore discusses the presence of God from the garbage heap of history.

According to Gutiérrez, once Job rejects the doctrine of retribution in light of his personal experience two major shifts of viewpoint occur. The first happens when Job broadens his initial position and realizes that the real issue is not his individual suffering but the suffering and injustice that mark the lives of the poor. Job's conclusion is to try to "lighten the burden of the poor by helping them and practicing solidarity with them." The second shift comes from God's speeches when Job understands that the world of justice is to be located within the horizon of freedom that is formed by the gratuitousness of God's love. That is, God is not bound by our understanding of justice. For Gutiérrez, Job has discovered two types of language about God—the language of prophecy and the language of contemplation. Of course more than language is at issue. "Talk about God presupposes and, at the same time, leads to a living encounter with God in specific historical circumstances. It requires, therefore, that we discover the features of Christ in the sometimes disfigured faces of the poor of this world. This discovery will not be made apart from concrete gestures of solidarity with our brothers and sisters who are wretched, abandoned, and deprived."[30]

For Gutiérrez, the questions about God are not answered within the book of Job or for those today who struggle for justice in the Americas. "God is a presence," Gutiérrez writes, "that leads amid darkness and pain, a hand that inspires confidence." To be sure, not all ignorance is dispelled; the route, however, is clearly marked. Gutiérrez quotes Luis Espinal, a priest murdered in Bolivia: "Train us, Lord, to fling ourselves upon the impossible, for behind the impossible is your grace and your presence; we cannot fall into emptiness. The future is an enigma, our road is covered by mist, but we want to go on giving ourselves, because you continue hoping amid the night and weeping tears through a thousand human eyes." According to Gutiérrez this is what Job did, and it remains the call today: "He flung himself upon the impossible and into an enigmatic future. And in this effort he met the Lord."[31]

As with his interpretation of Job, throughout his writings Gutiérrez emphasizes the importance of commitment as the path through which critical analysis and faith come alive. This ultimately may be his most trenchant response to the crisis of Western society. With a tradition that has come "toppling down over our heads" and a future which might resemble the "starving inmates of Auschwitz," the tendency is to deny the crisis or to believe in the ameliorative power of the old order. Faced with the enormity of the problems and the void of values articulated by Arendt and Rubenstein, the ability to act in a creative way, the ability to change course individually and communally, becomes more difficult. The problems are complex and multifaceted, but the central necessity, to commit ourselves to the values of community and solidarity, is, for Gutiérrez, the first step.[32]

Gutiérrez, in concert with other theologians in the Americas, raises this question of commitment in terms of fidelity. What does it mean to be faithful in a world of triage and holocaust? Arendt's assessment after her analysis of collapse includes the impotence of religious and humanist traditions to address the central crisis of our day. She writes: "For it means that though we may have many traditions, and know them more intimately than any generation before us, we can fall back upon none, and that, though we are saturated with experience and more competent at integrating it than any century before, we cannot use any of it." But could Arendt anticipate a humanist and religious response emanating from the underside of Western history? Is is possible that those who carried the banners of Western civilization, who conquered the colonies and built the gas chambers, and who conquer and build them today, are now being called to account by the nonpersons of our world? Is the reality not only collapse and void but movements for liberation that announce values and insights which come from a history of oppression and struggle? And, who, at the time of Arendt's writings, ever would have thought that theology would have anything to say to the crisis she outlined?[33]

As Rubenstein points out, the starving inmates of Auschwitz may indeed be our future as they have been part of our past. Still, liberation theologians from Latin America need to grapple with the present. In the conclusion of his book on Job, Gutiérrez, while deploring the Jewish holocaust, states that for Latin Americans the question of how to do theology after Auschwitz is a challenge to speak of the Latin American situation of *Ayacucho,* the Quechuan word for "the corner of the dead."

> Our task here is to find the words with which to talk about God in the midst of the starvation of millions, the humiliation of races regarded as inferior, discrimination against women, especially women who are poor, sytematic social injustice, a persistent high rate of infant mortality, those who simply "disappear" or are deprived of their freedom, the sufferings of people who are struggling for their right to live, the exiles and

> the refugees, terrorism of every kind, and the corpse-filled
> common grave of *Ayacucho*. What we must deal with is not
> the past but, unfortunately, a cruel present and a dark tunnel
> with no apparent end.[34]

Therefore the question for Gutiérrez is how to do theology in the midst of *Ayacucho*. How are we to speak of the God of life when murder on a massive scale endures in the corner of the dead? It is within this question that the crisis of Western society is articulated and a path toward a future beyond collapse and Auschwitz is suggested.

The political implications of Gutiérrez's analysis are profound, especially when the connections among the oppressed in the Americas are factored in. The crisis of Western society, now seen in the light of liberation theology, suggests the need for a new inclusive politics which not only embraces the nonpersons as persons of value and dignity, but sees in their plight and struggle for justice the limitations and hopes of Western civilization. Viewing the situation of the Americas from the perspective of the poor and vulnerable allows movement beyond the polarizing and artificial Cold War construct that has led to paralysis and abstraction from the historical crisis we face. That millions of lives are being violated and lost awakens us to a sense of urgency—a politics on behalf of justice. As Gutiérrez suggests, this politics is already being taken up by the oppressed themselves, whether the powerful recognize this or not. On the one hand, the powerful deny this irruption of the poor at their own peril because they miss the opportunity to exercise power on behalf of others. On the other hand, because the powerful cannot understand the political realities at home or abroad without recognizing this force, they increasingly lose touch with viable foreign relations and risk increasing alienation among significant numbers of American citizens who are either poor themselves or have come to know the world of the poor. At the same time that United States policymakers understand less and less about the Americas, the connecting links from the underside of the Americas increase. What occurs is a confrontational politics founded on diverging understandings and values.

Understanding liberation theologies in the Americas as a constructive attempt to deal with the crisis in the West calls for a creative and imaginative leap for most United States policymakers. By entering into the lives of the dispossessed, one's vision of the world is questioned—even challenged. Yet the world of the poor is the same world as that of the affluent, though the view of the landscape differs. As Gutiérrez points out, this landscape is a political one with theological implications or, to put it another way, theological probing can give rise to a different view of the political challenge. Thus, for American policymakers, theological positions taken by liberation theologians are less important than the values and visions they proclaim in the political realm. The political implications are found in the discovery of these values and visions, which are bequeathed by the underside of history and by those who seek to join in a concerted effort to imagine a future beyond collapse and Auschwitz.

NOTES

1. For their extended analysis of this crisis see Hannah Arendt, *The Origins of Totalitarianism* (New York: Harcourt, Brace, 1951) and Richard Rubenstein, *The Cunning of History: Mass Death and The American Future* (New York: Harper and Row, 1975).

2. Arendt, *Totalitarianism,* p. 434.

3. Rubenstein, *Cunning of History,* p. 95. From this understanding of the twentieth century Rubenstein adopts a "genuinely conservative" position. In some ways this paper represents an acceptance of Rubenstein's analysis of the crisis of the twentieth century while arguing that new progressive politics and theology hold the key to the transformation we both desire.

4. For a devastating critique of the twentieth century and the continuity of mass death, see Gil Elliot, *Twentieth Century Book of the Dead* (New York: Charles Scribner's Sons, 1972).

5. For an interesting overview of the diversity of liberation theologies see Deane William Ferm, *Third World Liberation Theologies: An Introductory Survey* (Maryknoll, N.Y.: Orbis Books, 1986) and *Third World Liberation Theologies: A Reader* (Maryknoll, N.Y.: Orbis Books, 1986).

6. The primary exponent of political theology is Johann Baptist Metz. See his book, *Faith in History and Society: Toward a Practical Fundamental Theology,* trans. David Smith (New York: Seabury Press, 1980). For black theology see James H. Cone, *God of the Oppressed* (New York: Seabury Press, 1975). An extended analysis of feminist theology can be found in Elizabeth Schüssler Fiorenza, *In Memory of Her: A Feminist Theological Reconstruction of Christian Origins* (New York: Crossroads, 1983).

7. Second General Conference of Latin American Bishops, *The Church in the Present-Day Transformation of Latin America in Light of the Council* (Washington, D.C.: National Conference of Bishops, 1979), p. 28.

8. See Gustavo Gutiérrez, *A Theology of Liberation: History, Politics and Salvation,* trans. and ed., Caridad Inda and John Eagleson (Maryknoll, N.Y.: Orbis Books, 1973).

9. Gutiérrez, *Theology of Liberation,* pp. ix–xi. For further developments of Gutiérrez's thoughts see *The Power of the Poor in History,* trans. Robert Barr (Maryknoll, N.Y.: Orbis Books, 1983), and *On Job: God-Talk and the Suffering of the Innocent,* trans. Matthew O'-Connell (Maryknoll, N.Y.: Orbis Books, 1987).

10. Ibid., pp. 24–28, 256.

11. Ibid., pp. 9, 27–32.

12. Ibid., pp. 3–15.

13. Ibid., p. 9.

14. Ibid., p. 11.

15. Though the theme is as yet not fully developed in his writings, Gutiérrez sees Latin America as Western and non-Western. See *Power of the Poor,* pp. 113–17.

16. Gutiérrez, *Power of the Poor,* pp. 193, 190, 186. That Latin American liberation theology begins with the nonperson is the essential difference between it and progressive theology in Europe and North America. Gutiérrez writes: "Progressive theology seeks to answer the questions of the nonbeliever; liberation theology confronts the challenge of the nonperson" (p. 92).

17. Ibid., pp. 72, 190, 195. The Ecumenical Association of Third World Theologians meeting in New Delhi, India, in 1981 defined *irruption* as the dramatic movement of the "exploited classes, marginalized cultures, and humiliated roles. They are bursting from the underside of history into the world long dominated by the West. It is an irruption expressed in revolutionary struggles, political uprisings, and liberation movements." See *Irruption of the Third World: Challenge to Theology,* ed. Virginia Fabella and Sergio Torres (Maryknoll, N.Y.: Orbis Books, 1983), p. xii.

18. Ibid., p. 204.

19. See Michael Mott, *The Seven Mountains of Thomas Merton* (Boston: Houghton Mifflin, 1984), pp. 304, 305, 329, 330, 426, 430. For an insight into what the community at Solentiname ultimately became see Ernesto Cardenal, *The Gospel in Solentiname,* 4 vols., trans. Donald Walsh (Maryknoll, N.Y.: Orbis Books, 1982).

20. Dorothy Day, *On Pilgrimage* (New York: Curtis Publishing Co., 1972), p. 100.

21. Ibid., p. 101.

22. *Camilo Torres: His Life and His Message,* trans. Virginia O'Grady, ed. John Alvarez Garcia and Christian Restrepo Calle, preface by Dorothy Day (Springfield, Ill.: Templegate, 1968), pp. 20–21.

23. Ibid., p. 36.

24. See *Theology in the Americas,* ed. Sergio Torres and John Eagleson (Maryknoll, N.Y.: Orbis Books, 1976), p. 7.

25. Ibid., pp. 10, 13, 273–74.Gutiérrez's address is found on pp. 309–13.

26. Elisabeth Schüssler Fiorenza, "Feminist Theology as a Critical Theology of Liberation," in *Churches in Struggle: Liberation Theologies and Social Change in North America,* ed. William Tabb (New York: Monthly Review Press, 1986), p. 53.

27. James Cone, *God of the Oppressed,* (New York: Seabury Press, 1975), p. 6. Also see his *Black Theology and Black Power* (New York: Seabury Press, 1969), and *A Black Theology of Liberation* (Philadelphia: J. B. Lippencott, 1970). For his analysis of the relation of black theology and the Third World see *For My People: Black Theology and the Black Church* (Maryknoll, N.Y.: Orbis Books, 1984), pp. 140–56.

28. For a discussion of the biblical God see Gutiérrez, *Theology of Liberation,* pp. 154–174, and Cone, *God of the Oppressed,* pp. 62–83.

29. Though this is beyond the scope of this paper, starting theology from the perspective of the nonperson allows a new ecumenical dialogue between Latin American liberationists and the Jewish people. See Marc H. Ellis, *Toward a Jewish Theology of Liberation* (Maryknoll, New York: Orbis Books, 1987), pp. 66–90.

30. Gutiérrez, *On Job,* pp. 16, 17.

31. Ibid., pp. 91–92.

32. For the difficulty and possibility of such a commitment from a North American perspective, see Marc H. Ellis, *Faithfulness in an Age of Holocaust* (New York: Amity House, 1986).

33. Arendt, *Origins of Totalitarianism,* p. 434. Also see Ellis, *Faithfulness,* pp. 49–64, 136–39.

34. Gutiérrez, *Job,* p. 102.

3

Liberation Theology and the Crisis in Western Theology

Richard L. Rubenstein

One of Latin American liberation theology's most distinctive features has been the claim that, in spite of its diversity, it constitutes a radical departure from European and North American theology. According to liberation theologians, North Atlantic theologians have been largely preoccupied with the problem of credibility and "the challenge of the nonbeliever" who is a literate, well-educated product of post-Enlightenment secular society. Not infrequently, the nonbeliever is likely to be a loyal, albeit skeptical, member of the institutional church.[1] Liberation theologians such as Gustavo Gutiérrez argue that such nonbelievers are more likely to question the religious world than "the economic, social, political and cultural world" from which they have benefited and in which they feel more or less at home. By contrast, Gutiérrez and his colleagues have argued that theology must concern itself primarily with the "nonpersons" who exist at the bitter margins of society.[2] According to Gutiérrez the nonperson is he or she "whom the prevailing social order fails to recognize as a person—the poor, the exploited, the ones systematically and legally despoiled of their humanness, the ones who scarcely know that they are persons at all."[3]

Gutiérrez asserts that such people do not question the world of religion. No matter how superfluous to the processes of production they may be, the poor know that the church regards them as children of God and objects of Christ's love. They do, however, question the economic, social, and political order that has allegedly degraded and exploited them and then expelled them to the utter margins of human society. Although few, if any, of Latin America's nonpersons have read Thomas Hobbes, they would instinctively understand how his analysis of human worth applies to their condition. According to Hobbes,

> The Value, or Worth of a man, is as of all other things, his Price; that is to say, so much as would be given for the use of his Power: and therefore is not absolute; but a thing dependent on the need and judgment of another.... And as in other things, so in men, not the seller, but the buyer determines the Price.[4]

When no one is willing to offer a price for the labor of the poor, they become superfluous nonpersons. The poor are hardly likely to question a religious inheritance which alone accords them a measure of nonnegotiable human dignity. Nevertheless, it is my conviction that (a) liberation theologians and their constituency are no less vulnerable than their North Atlantic counterparts to the theological and the sociological problems arising out of the question of religious credibility; and (b) insofar as Latin American societies succeed in demarginalizing the poor, a principal objective of liberation theology, the poor will be threatened with the same loss of traditional values or anomie that currently afflicts much of the North Atlantic educated bourgeoisie, including intellectual professionals in the field of religion. This does not necessarily mean that as the Latin American poor enter the economic mainstream they will experience a radical loss of faith. On the contrary, some may opt for fundamentalism or pentecostalism as a cognitive defense against anomie. Finally, it is my belief that religious issues such as these influence behavior in the public sphere and, hence, have considerable relevance for public policy.

Elsewhere I have argued that a principal function of theology, especially in modern times, has been *dissonance-reduction* and that theologians are intellectual professionals who fulfill that function. Dissonance-reduction is necessary wherever there is a conflict between religious faith and significant disconfirming items of information.[5] There is less need for dis-onance reduction in a traditional society then in a secularized society in which value-neutral, functional rationality, with its cultural, information-al, and ethical challenges to traditional religious belief, becomes the predominant mode of individual and institutional problem-solving.

An important source of value disconfirmation is the modernization process itself.[6] Liberation theologians tend to blame free-market capitalism for the desperate predicament of Latin America's poor. Nevertheless, the marginalization of the poor can more accurately be seen as a consequence of the modernization process. That process has entailed the progressive rationalization of the economy and society, first in the North Atlantic region and eventually throughout the world.[7] Elsewhere I have argued that mod-ernization, whether capitalist or socialist, tends at a certain stage to result in a vast enlargement of the number of people who are superfluous to the processes of primary production in agriculture and industry. This process is currently manifest in Latin America.[8] Moreover, to the extent that a society has become fully rationalized in the formal sense, all values that impede the efficient attainment of that society's practical ends will be rejected in practice although, in the case of religion, often affirmed rhetori-cally. In a fully rationalized economy, impersonal cost-benefit calculations of profit and loss tend to eliminate considerations based upon shared feel-ings of kinship, fraternity, community, or even simple humanity.[9] Unfor-tunately, there is little sympathy for those who have the misfortune of becoming nonpersons.

Once set in motion, such a system is both internally compulsive and destructive of all other systems with which it comes into contact. Failure to conform to the system's rules entails the most severe economic penal-ties. This is especially true of advanced technological societies in which the scale of capital investment is so huge that failure to meet the test of rationality in education, planning, manufacturing, and distribution can result in catastrophic loss.

The overwhelming advantage in power and affluence of rationalized ad-vanced technological societies compels less developed societies to mod-ernize, if only to meet the imperatives of national security. The most successful example of this phenomenon was the nineteenth-century mod-ernization of Japan. When national survival is at risk, even those most fer-vently committed to traditional religious values have little choice but to conform to the value-neutral, market- and performance-oriented norms of the system.

Liberation theologians assert that the poor do not need *theoria,* which ignores or masks their true condition. Instead, they require "a concrete *praxis* of liberation."[10] By liberation *praxis,* theologians such as Gutiérrez mean revolutionary activity whose objective is the abolition of the economic and social injustices and the material exploitation that have transformed the poor into nonpersons. Moreover, just as there are poor persons, there are poor nations who have been rendered dependent as a consequence of neocolonialist exploitation by the rich, capitalist, North Atlantic nations. Because liberation theologians see the condition of the poor as one of oppression and domination, they regard society as essentially beset by class conflict. They see their own task as involving taking sides (a) with the poor against their oppressors and (b) for socialism against capitalism.[11] Gutiérrez has written that liberation theology "insists on a society in which private ownership of the means of production is eliminated, because private ownership of the means of production allows a few to appropriate the fruits of the labor of the many, and generates the division of society into classes, whereupon one class exploits another."[12]

This sounds very much like both Marxist analysis and prognosis, and a number of liberation theologians have acknowledged their intellectual indebtedness to Marxist social theory.[13] Nevertheless, while liberation theologians are far more likely to be allied with Marxist than with conservative political movements, most liberation theologians express some reservations about Marxism that go beyond the obvious conflict over atheism. Gutiérrez, for example, cautions that "Christ's liberation cannot be reduced to political liberation."[14] Still, Gutiérrez rejects the idea that Christ's liberation is wholly otherworldly. On the contrary, Christ's liberation interpenetrates human history even though its completion will occur as history's climax and finale.

The Old Testament account of God as creator and liberator and the New Testament account of God's becoming poor in the person of Jesus Christ form the basic theological paradigm for liberation theology's program of social reconstruction.[15] Liberation theologians stress that the God of the Bible is the God-who-acts-in-history, liberating Israel from slavery and oppression in Egypt. This act became the basis of Israel's faith and constitutes the essential demand for Israel's future and ultimately for the future of all humanity. Truly to know God is to do justice and, according to liberation theologians, it is impossible to do justice without taking sides with those who are the primary objects of injustice, the poor, as God took sides with Israel in Egypt. God is the God of the poor. God rejects those who oppress and exploit the poor no matter how loyal the exploiters may be to religious institutions.

Above all, God so loved the poor that in Jesus Christ he became one of them, taking upon himself the fate of the poor to the bitter end. Liberation theologians argue that as God has taken sides, so should we. In the person of Jesus Christ, he condemned the rich and proclaimed the coming of the kingdom of God, which is to be "a kingdom of justice and liberation, to be established in favor of the poor, the oppressed and the marginalized of history."[16]

Nor are Christians to wait passively for the coming of the kingdom. They are obligated to enter history as *subversives*. According to Gutiérrez, Christianity has largely been white, Western, and allied to the interests of the dominant class. Gutiérrez, who is of Peruvian Indian descent, tells us:

> History must be turned upside-down from the bottom not from the top. What is criminal is not to be *sub*versive, struggling against the capitalist system, but to continue being "*su-per*versive"—bolstering and supporting the prevailing domination. It is in this subversive history that we can have a new faith experience, a new spirituality—a new proclamation of the gospel.[17]

We can thus see that Scripture with its emphasis on the God of history constitutes the theological foundation of liberation theology's socioeconomic program. Nevertheless, liberation theology's reading of biblical texts has the practical effect of legitimating a political alliance between Latin American Christians and Marxists.

In spite of the priority accorded to *praxis* over *theoria* in liberation theology, it is my conviction that any theology, including liberation theology, based upon the doctrine that God acts in history for the salvation of humanity is vulnerable to disconfirmation. Although much has been written concerning the warfare of science and religion in the modern period, the major crisis in modern Western religious thought has been more a consequence of the disconfirming impact of historical events and the discipline of history itself upon religious belief than the conflict between the scientific and religious world views.

Many of the foremost liberation theologians are thoroughly cognizant of the theological problems arising from history and the historico-critical study of Scripture. They are the products of a superb intellectual and theological training whether the bulk of their theological studies was done in Europe or closer to home. Observing that liberation theology is biblical but not literalist or fundamentalist, Phillip Berryman acknowledges that some may regard critical biblical scholarship as a problem for liberation theology. He writes:

> Some may be left with a very basic question: do these theologians really believe all this? After all, they have studied in European universities, they can read several languages, they are familiar with the complexities of Marxism. Do they ever wonder—late at night, perhaps—whether this is not after all simply a kind of language game?

Berryman's response to his own rhetorical question is instructive:

> Certainly, in their own lifetimes most of these theologians have seen their own understanding of Christianity undergo change. Their belief may be less literal than it was twenty-five or thirty years ago. Nevertheless, I think their answer might be that their faith has been deepened and validated by their experience with poor people.... The firmness of faith comes not from particular concepts—even those of liberation theology or the Bible itself—but from commitment to a certain kind of life, exemplified in Jesus Christ and lived today by many ordinary men and women in Latin America. In the commitment of their brothers and sisters, theologians find their own faith fortified and validated.[18]

Berryman's response shifts the ground from theology to anthropology. Faith is no longer validated by the conviction that it is objectively true but by the theologian's concrete experiences in community with the poor. This is, of course, a characteristically modern strategy, one which I have employed in my own theological writings.[19]

There are, however, difficulties with any attempt to verify liberation theology's fundamental assertion that God is preeminently the God of the poor. Liberation theology shifts the problem of verification from the present to an empirically unavailable but conveniently inexhaustible future. The cognitive element in verification is thereby downgraded in favor of future-oriented praxis. This, however, only postpones or evades the problem. Sooner or later, assurances of divine concern for the poor must be verified or they will be seen as pathetic illusions.

Moreover, the claim cannot be validated by any controvertible reading of traditional biblical theology. Admittedly, passages from Scripture can be cited as proof-texts of God's special concern for the poor. In this respect, the liberation theologians do not invent a new tradition.[20] On the other hand, the classical Jewish and Christian readings of Scripture tend to interpret large-scale misfortune as divine chastisement for sin. Lest I be misunderstood, I cite this tradition as an historian of religion; it is not a tradition to which I personally subscribe. For example, over the centuries both the church and the synagogue have regarded the negative vicissitudes of Israel's history as divine punishment for Israel's want of obedience to the divine covenant. Jewish and Christian thinkers have only disagreed concerning the nature of the sins for which Israel was alleged to have been punished.[21] If one is committed to the belief that God, as the unique, omnipotent Creator of the cosmos, is actively involved in human history, then the identification of misfortune as divine punishment is altogether plausible. In fact, as H. Richard Niebuhr has pointed out, certain branches of Christianity took poverty to be a sign of divine rejection and the ability to prosper in one's vocation as a sign of election and God's grace.[22] The hoary tradition that misfortune is a sign of divine rejection is entirely consistent with the tradition of an omnipotent God of history.

My purpose in recalling this very important element in biblical theology is not to enter into debate concerning the proper reading of a source as admittedly complex as the books of the Old and New Testament. It is rather to suggest that liberation theology's claims that God is the God of the poor cannot be verified either by the empirical events of history or by an incontestable reading of Scripture. Liberation theology's demand for liberation *praxis* can be understood as the attempt to realize in the empirical world a religiously derived ideal vision that awaits verification. In the meantime, there is always the danger that the promise of a felicitous future can be utilized by future-oriented religious and political ideologies to legitimate, if necessary, revolutionary action and even violence as a means of realizing the promised condition.

If the religious discourse of a faith that affirms the God-who-acts-in-history is to have a meaningful content, the objective veracity of Scripture's account of at least some crucial events will have to be convincingly affirmed and liberation theology's reading of Scripture will have to be convincingly demonstrated to be authoritative. This does not mean that every word in the Bible must literally be the word of God as fundamentalists, both Jewish and Christian, insist. Nevertheless, unless there is truth to Scripture's account of the covenant at Sinai as an objective event, the biblical understanding of Israel's history as a drama of disobedience, punishment, exile, and redemption will be seen as little more than an all-too-human attempt to ascribe cosmic significance to a series of power struggles in which the Israelites were ultimately defeated. Similarly, unless there is genuine credibility to the New Testament account that God actually took human form in the person of Jesus of Nazareth as the crucified and resurrected Savior of humanity, Christianity will be seen as a purely human attempt to give meaning, structure, and hope to human beings wholly enmeshed in the natural order.[23] Willy-nilly, liberation theology rests upon the credibility of the doctrine that God acts in history. Absent that fundamental conviction, liberation theologians are in the situation described by Paul of Tarsus two thousand years ago:

> Now if Christ be preached that he rose from the dead, how say some among you that there is no resurrection from the dead? But if there be no resurrection of the dead, then is Christ not risen: And if Christ be not risen, then is our preaching vain, and your faith is also vain. (I Cor. 15:12–14)

Paul understood the difference between the pagan religions of myth and the biblical religions of history. The latter cannot avoid the problem of credibility in either the first Christian century or the twentieth.

Earlier in this century, the problem of theological credibility was examined by the German Protestant scholar Ernst Troeltsch (1865–1923). Troeltsch observed that the methods and presuppositions of modern historical scholarship, in which he, like many of the liberation theologians, was superbly trained, are incompatible with traditional Christian faith. This writer would add that they are equally incompatible with normative Judaism. Both traditions claim to be exclusively and objectively true. These claims rest ultimately on belief in the supernatural inspiration of Scripture. By contrast, critical historians start with the methodological assumption that the Bible can only be understood in terms of its historical context. Moreover, the methods and the principles of interpretation by which one studies the Bible can be no different than those used to investigate any other ancient historical document. Scripture must be treated methodologically by the scholar as he or she would treat any profane document. Troeltsch insisted that every expression of truth and value was historically conditioned and that the critical historian was obliged to reject supernatural intervention as a principle of explanation. "History," Troeltsch argued, "is no place for absolute religion and absolute personalities."[24]

While Troeltsch was insisting that modern historical research into religion was of necessity value-neutral, his friend and colleague Max Weber (1864–1920) was spelling out the meaning of value-neutrality in the spheres of the economy and society. Although Weber identified himself as a Protestant, he described himself as "religiously unmusical." His definition of culture reveals the unremittingly secular character of his understanding of the human condition. It stands in radical contrast to the views of the liberation theologians. According to Weber, " 'Culture' is a finite segment of the meaningless infinity of the world process, a segment on which *human beings* confer meaning and significance."[25] Weber held that science, including the social sciences, is a morally neutral instrument available to its possessors for whatever purposes they have the power to implement. He distinguished between "knowledge of what 'is,' " what we would call factual knowledge, and "knowledge of what 'should be'" or "normative knowledge."[26] According to Weber, "It can never be the task of an empirical science to provide binding norms and ideals from which directives for immediate practical activity can be derived."[27] Value judgments, Weber argued, are "subjective" in origin. Whence then do we derive our value judgments? According to German historian Wolfgang Mommsen, Weber maintained that the "spontaneous decision of personality" is alone the foundation of all values in post-traditional society.[28] In this opinion, as in much else, Weber appears to be a disciple of Nietzsche.

Weber has also given us one of the most succinct descriptions of the moral limitations of the bourgeois capitalist market economy:

The market community as such is the most impersonal relationship of practical life into which human beings can enter with one another.... Where the market is allowed to follow its own autonomous tendencies, its participants do not look toward the persons of each other but only toward the commodity; there are no obligations of brotherliness or reverence, and none of the spontaneous human relations that are sustained by personal unions. They all would just obstruct the free development of the bare market relationship....[29]

No liberation theologian could take issue with Weber's description of the market community. On the contrary, it is precisely because the market community is as Weber described it that human misery and marginality have come upon Latin America's poor. Throughout his career, Weber sought to comprehend the character of the modern era. Impressed by its achievements, he was nevertheless pessimistic about its long-range consequences. Perhaps nowhere did Weber express his pessimism as bleakly as in his concluding reflections in *The Protestant Ethic and the Spirit of Capitalism:*

The Puritan wanted to work in a calling; we are forced to do so. For when asceticism was carried out of monastic cells into everyday life, and began to dominate worldly morality, it did its part in building the tremendous cosmos of the modern economic order. This order is now bound to the technical and economic conditions of machine production which to-day determine the lives of all the individuals who are born into this mechanism, not only those directly concerned with economic acquisition, with irresistible force. Perhaps it will so determine them until the last ton of fossilized coal is burnt. In Baxter's view the care for external goods should only lie on the shoulders of the "saint like a light cloak, which can be thrown aside at any moment." But fate decreed that the cloak should become an iron cage....

No one knows who will live in this cage in the future, or whether at the end of this tremendous development entirely new prophets will arise, or there will be a great rebirth of old ideas and ideals, or, if neither, mechanical petrification, embellished with a sort of convulsive self-importance. For of the last stage of this cultural development, it might well be truly said: "Specialists without spirit, sensualists without heart; this nullity imagines that it has attained a level of civilization never before achieved."[30]

As is well known, it was Weber's celebrated thesis that there was an "elective affinity" between Calvinism and the spirit of rational bourgeois capitalism. Hence, there was more than a little irony in bourgeois capitalism's combination of Protestant origins and contemporary functional godlessness. Admittedly, most Protestants of Weber's period continued to profess religious beliefs. Nevertheless, whenever the demands of the marketplace conflicted with those of religion, especially in large-scale transactions, the marketplace prevailed. It is in that sense that bourgeois civilization can be characterized as functionally godless.[31]

Although Weber speculated that a way out of the "iron cage" might be found through the emergence of "entirely new prophets," his basic posture was one of pessimism. He was under no illusion that socialism offered an improvement over capitalism. By contrast, Karl Barth (1886–1966), perhaps the most important Protestant theologian of the twentieth century, did see a way out for the believer, if not for the bourgeois civilization Weber had described so bleakly. Like Weber, Barth rejected Enlightenment optimism which held that autonomous, self-sufficient humanity, guided by reason, could create a felicitous human community, a Kantian kingdom of ends if not a Christian kingdom of God. Barth saw as clearly as did Weber that without an objective, transcendent frame of reference in terms of which human projects could be judged, reason and science would almost inevitably become the servants of power. Weber saw no currently available cultural value to prevent such an outcome. For Barth, Christ as the Word of God was the objective standard.

As a young pastor in this first community in Safenwil, Switzerland, Barth was convinced by the suffering of his "congregation of farmers and workers" of the importance of "the social question." This led him to take the side of the workers in the bitter class conflict he beheld.[32] Barth became so committed to socialism at this stage of his career that he declared, "Jesus Christ *is* the social movement, and the social movement *is* Jesus in the present."[33] In a similar spirit Barth declared that the social movement was the "direct result" of the continuing "spiritual power which Jesus brought into life and history."[34] When allowance is made for the differences of place and circumstance, there are obvious parallels between the young Barth's identification of the cause of the workers with the cause of Jesus Christ and liberation theology's identification of the cause of the poor as the cause of God. As Barth's theology developed, that identification was not to last. Barth's reasons for abandoning the identification may be instructive for understanding the dilemmas that await liberation theology as it continues to develop.

In addition to Barth's motives, it will be helpful to recall the intellectual and theological upheaval which attended the triumph of the scientific historical school of biblical scholarship to which I have already alluded. The most important response to the rise of the historical school, with its methodological denial of Scripture's privileged status, was the rise of Protestant liberalism, which relativized the dogmatic claims of biblical religion. Supernatural elements in Christianity were deemphasized in favor of a natural religion in harmony with reason.[35] The father of Protestant liberalism was Friedrich Schleiermacher (1768–1834). Albrecht Ritschl (1822–89) was one of its great representatives. Ritschl sought to introduce a form of Christianity that was free of the traditional, prescientific forms in which it had been encased. A fundamental aim of Ritschl and his school was the reconciliation of religion and culture. Ritschl's thought was rich, complicated, and sophisticated. For our purposes it will suffice to take note of one of his leading ideas: Only by involvement in work in the larger community for the sake of the common good, that is, by faithfulness in one's social calling, can one truly become an example of Christ: God and humanity together have a common task of realizing his kingdom, identified by Ritschl as "the association of mankind—an association both extensively and intensively the most comprehensive possible—through the reciprocal moral action of its members, action which transcends all merely natural and particular considerations."[36]

Concerning Ritschl's conception of the kingdom of God, H. Richard Niebuhr has commented: "All the references are to man and to man's work; the word 'God' seems to be an intrusion.... The conception...is practically the same as Kant's idea of the kingdom of ends."[37]

Niebuhr adds that Ritschl attempted to reconcile Christianity with those elements in the culture of his era which were most compatible with it. Unfortunately, those who came after Ritschl tended to identify Christianity with considerably less elevated aspects of German culture. For example, one of Ritschl's disciples, Wilhelm Herrmann (1846–1922), identified the traditional Protestant notion that the Christian is called upon by God to serve him in the workaday world with the idea of a citizen's "calling" (*Beruf*) in the Bismarckian *Kaiserreich*. In a period in which the first German Reich was undertaking its spectacular path toward becoming Europe's preeminent industrial power, Ritschl's disciple largely identified the Christian's vocation with worldly activity in the nascent Reich. As was later to be the case with liberation theology, Herrmann was less interested in *theoria* than *praxis*. Metaphysical and eschatological speculation was to be eschewed. For Herrmann, Christian religious life had a practical, worldly, and potentially nationalistic bent.[38]

The younger generation of Ritschlians tended to complete the historicization and, hence, the relativization of Christianity. In place of having a supernatural legitimation, Christianity came to be characterized as the "highest stage" in the evolution of humanity's religious consciousness and, as such, was largely identified with the values of German bourgeois culture. The latter was solipsistically seen as the highest stage in civilization's evolution. Where liberation theology sees God as taking sides with the poor, the later Ritschlians tended to see God as on the side of the German bourgeoisie.

Had it not been for the outbreak of World War I, it is quite likely that liberalism's bourgeois reconciliation of religion and culture would have remained unchallenged for many decades. World War I revealed the night side of bourgeois "progress." The rapid transformation of the great European powers from agrarian to advanced industrial societies had extraordinarily destabilizing social consequences. Industrialization brought in its train competition for raw materials, markets, and the capital necessary for further industrialization. The leaders of the Reich, a late-comer to European imperialism, became convinced that their nation's survival as an advanced industrial power required both territorial and economic expansion.[39] Once the war began, it became obvious that slaughter could be mechanized as easily as any process of production.

At the outbreak of World War I, Barth was twenty-eight years old. Initially, he had accepted the dominant liberal Protestantism of the period. The crucial event leading to his rejection of "nineteenth-century theology" was the unqualified support expressed in a proclamation issued by a group of German intellectuals in August 1914 for the war policies of Kaiser

Wilhelm II. The signatories included most of his former theology teachers. The proclamation was consistent with Protestant liberalism's identification of Christianity with German bourgeois culture. In reality, it was more of a surrender than an identification.[40] Liberalism had identified itself with a culture that had been responsible for the most pointlessly destructive war in all of human history. The historical experience of the war discredited both bourgeois culture and the Protestant liberalism which identified itself with it. An analogous surrender could await liberation theology to the extent that it becomes firmly allied to Marxist politics.

Barth understood clearly that a new beginning had to be made in theology. His impact as a theological leader dates from the publication of the second edition of his great commentary, *The Epistle to the Romans,* in 1921.[41] This is the period in which Barth ceased to identify socialism with the cause of Christ. Barth attacked the "subjectivism" of the liberal Protestant theology of this time, which he saw as an attempt to fit Christian revelation into the mold of conceptions of human origin. Concerning socialism Barth now warned, "The cause of divine renewal must not be confused with the cause of human progress."[42] From 1921 on, his fundamental concern was to prevent theology from becoming an ideology, that is, to prevent that which Barth regarded as the Word of God from being regarded as a product of human culture.

Barth argued that Protestant liberalism had mistakenly identified fallible, human values with the Word of God, thus destroying revelation as the spiritual Archimedean point of Christianity. According to Barth, both human will and reason have been vitiated by the Fall so that it is absolutely impossible for humanity to discover the truth about God by its own efforts. Only if and when God manifests himself can there be revelation. In this period of his career, Barth completely rejected natural theology and insisted upon the radical transcendence of God. Barth was not interested in attempting to "prove" the existence of God. He held that the Bible witnesses to God's acts; it does not prove his existence. Thus, true theology is wholly dependent upon revelation. As such, theology is rational inquiry into God's self-revelation insofar as human beings are capable of such an inquiry. And, for Barth, God reveals himself only in and through Christ. Hence, Barth held that theology has one and only one task, namely, to declare that God has become human in the person of Jesus Christ.

For Barth, Christian teaching is God's teaching about himself; Christianity is not, as are the world's religions, a human religious teaching. Barth's view of Christianity constitutes a thoroughgoing rejection of liberal Protestantism's historicizing attempts to achieve a synthesis of Christianity and modern bourgeois culture. In contrast to Ritschl's reconciliation of bourgeois culture and liberal Protestantism, Barth's theology announces the demise of bourgeois culture.

Nor is it accidental that it was the experience of World War I that led to Barth's rejection of the liberal synthesis of religion and culture. *The experience of that war, with its mass production of human slaughter and its origins in the dilemmas of bourgeois civilization, shook twentieth-century religion to its foundations.* Let us also recall that in a religion of history, an omnipotent God cannot easily be divorced from involvement in the empirical events of history. Having beheld the night side of culture, Barth refused to identify Christianity as the highest expression of human culture. For Barth there was an infinite qualitative distance between the Word of God and the highest in human culture. By the beginning of World War I, it was obvious to Barth that in the German cultural sphere such an identification was tantamount to identifying Christ with the imperialism of the wartime *Kaiserreich*.

Between 1933 and 1945, German clergy and theologians were faced with the problem of the extent to which they were prepared to accept an historicizing synthesis of religion and the dominant National Socialist culture, a far more malignant and demonic force than that of the *Kaiserreich*. The majority of German religious leaders, both Protestant and Catholic, had little difficulty in embracing National Socialism, many with great enthusiasm. Barth rejected any compromise with National Socialism. Refusing on religious grounds to pledge unconditional allegiance to Adolf Hitler, as was required of all German professors, Barth left Germany in 1935 and returned to his native Switzerland. Because of his Christian faith, Barth was never deceived about the demonic aspects of the secular culture of his era.[43]

Barth understood that without the Archimedean point of transcendent, divinely legitimated religious values, such as can be found in both non-liberal Judaism and Christianity, one is left with values that are wholly immanent in the secular world. In the political sphere, power becomes the dominant value; in the economic sphere, wealth divorced from moral values comes to dominate. Value-free instrumental rationality becomes the dominant mode of conducting the business of life. Barth believed that he had a spiritual Archimedean point, faith in the sovereignty of the self-revealing God. It was this faith that enabled him to take his stand against the Third Reich. Had he identified his faith with German culture, he would in all likelihood have supported National Socialism as did the majority of his theological peers.

It is generally recognized today that Barth's understanding of God changed considerably over the years. In his *Epistle to the Romans,* Barth stressed the radical incommensurability of the Word of God and the human word. In order to escape a relativism that reduced faith to culture, Barth stressed the radical transcendence of God, rejecting any hint of divine immanence. God, he asserted, was *ganz anders,* wholly other. In his *Church Dogmatics,* the magisterial, multi-volume work of his mature years, Barth continued to affirm Christianity as God's self-revelation; but he now came to stress the *humanity* of God rather than God's absolute transcendence. Barth now stressed that, far from being wholly other, "God reveals himself to man in the Person of Jesus Christ: Whoever says, 'revelation,' says 'The Word become Flesh.' "[44]

Thomas Altizer has suggested that Barth's change of his earlier position may have been due to the realization that insistence on the dichotomy between the Word of God and the human word must in the final analysis result in the negation of all human expressions of the meaning of faith, "including the creedal and dogmatic statements of the historic church...."[45] By insisting on the radical incommensurability of the divine and the human, Barth unintentionally invited the rejection of God as functionally irrelevant. And *functional irrelevance can easily lead to radical unbelief.* Some link had to be affirmed between God and humanity. For Barth, the Incarnate Christ was that link. Nevertheless, affirmation of the humanity of God in Christ did not solve the problem of functional irrelevance, nor did it really restore the credibility of the creedal and dogmatic assertions of the church. As Kenneth Hamilton has observed, in Barth, both early and late, it is always God who condescends to commune with humanity; that is, our knowledge of God always comes from God's side and is always an act of self-revelation.[46] Barth's faith in God as revealing himself in Christ is thus the *presupposition* of his entire theological system. While Barth's theology may help Christians to deepen their understanding of what is involved intellectually and spiritually in their inherited faith and the culture it has engendered, Barth's christological presuppositions take as axiomatic that which non-Christians find most difficult to accept in Christian belief.

Non-Christians, both Eastern and Western, can legitimately inquire of Barth, "What evidence can you offer for your assertion that the Christian understanding of God is in reality God's self-revelation?" As noted, a comparable question can be posed to liberation theologians. Traditionally, both Judaism and Christianity have answered questions of that sort by offering as evidence the biblical traditions that testify to God's revelation to Moses and Jesus' role as the crucified and resurrected Christ, respectively, as *real and indubitable events in history*. As noted above, such evidence retained its credibility as long as the biblical accounts were regarded as *accurate historical accounts of what actually took place*. That is why, as we have noted, fundamentalists, both Jewish and Christian, continue to insist upon the literal, historical truth of the accounts in Scripture. Fundamentalists respect the elementary requirement that assertions about reality be based upon credible evidence. Those trained in the scientific, historical study of religion question the evidence set forth by the fundamentalists, but there is no gainsaying the fact that the fundamentalists attempt to offer what they regard as credible evidence.

The same cannot be said of Barth, the liberation theologians, or those Christian thinkers who accept the scientific study of their basic text, the Bible. In Barth's case, history is treated with an ambiguity which, to an outsider, appears to obscure more than it clarifies. For example, the most decisive event in Christ's history is his resurrection. Absent the resurrection, Jesus is but a mortal Jewish teacher whose life is tragically cut off before his time; it is the resurrection that makes manifest his role as Christ the Redeemer. Yet Barth rejects the literal, historical character of the resurrection. He insists that the resurrection "is not a 'historical' event which may be placed side by side with other events. Rather it is the 'non-historical' happening, by which all other events are bounded."[47] Undoubtedly, such statements make sense within the circle of faith. Nonbelievers, however, are likely to observe that their requests for evidence have not been met and that they have been asked to accept at face value assertions about reality which have yet to be verified. Thus, Barth does not really escape the problems arising from his original assertion of the radical otherness of God. Barth's magisterial work is rightly entitled *Church Dogmatics*. Barth gives nonbelievers no credible evidence for his assertions about God and Christ even while faulting them for their lack of faith. Barth's whole effort can be likened to an Anselmian *fides quaerens intellectum*, faith seeking understanding. In defense of Barth one might object that Christianity never claimed that its truths could be validated by empirical evidence. It always insisted that faith was a divine gift through which God instilled in the believer the capacity to receive the Truth. Undoubtedly, many Christians will rest content with a view of faith as God's self-revelation made credible to the believer by an act of divine grace. Quite obviously, such a view will not offer the non-Christian a credible intellectual or spiritual basis for becoming a Christian.

Protestant liberalism was born when Friedrich Schleiermacher attempted to render Christianity credible to religion's "cultured despisers."[48] As noted, liberation theologians have expressed little interest in the "cultured despisers" of Christianity, and Karl Barth insisted that Schleiermacher had conceded far too much to culture in his defense of religion. Nevertheless, there was good reason for the concern of Schleiermacher, and of those who came after him, for the "cultured despisers." The latter were the forerunners of the kind of secularized consciousness which, according to Weber, was in the process of making of the future an "iron cage." As we have seen, Barth attempted to escape the worst dilemmas of the "iron cage" of modern Western civilization by asserting the reality of a Christian spiritual Archimedian point, namely, God's self-revelation in Christ. Believing in that Archimedian point, Barth was able to refuse to go along with some of the most destructive aspects of the culture of modernity. Unfortunately, the closer one looks at Barth's Archimedian point, the less certain one becomes that it constitutes a reliable defense against the ills of modernity. While Barth's thought may strengthen the resolve of those who possess a faith similar to his, it has little, if anything, to say to the kind of urban, educated, secularized professionals responsible for maintaining the "iron cage." They are hardly likely to rest content with Barth's assurances of the truth of the Christian view of God when their interests are at stake. One is forced sadly to conclude that religion's grandest attempt to escape the "iron cage" in the twentieth century cannot be thought of as having succeeded. Absent a more convincing teacher than Barth, we are left in the spiritually precarious situation of seeing religion as wholly blended into the texture of human culture, the very predicament Barth labored so valiantly to overcome.

Unverifiable claims about the radical transcendence of God constituted Barth's attempt to escape from the iron cage. As noted, unverifiable claims about God's role in history and humanity's role as God's partner in realizing God's kingdom constitute liberation theology's way out. Yet, liberation theology is as unlikely to overcome the crisis in modern theology as Barth was. It is the supreme irony of the biblical religions that they have a tendency to negate themselves. We cannot enter into this issue in detail save to note that the biblical idea of an omnipotent Creator God had the long-range cultural effect of desacralizing both the natural world and all human institutions. Its most important practical consequence has not been a significant diminution of religious affiliation but the functional irrelevance of religious constraints when personal, economic, or political interests are at stake. *Functional irrelevance is the most significant practical expression of the crisis of modern theology.* An important example of this development was manifest in the tension between the pope and large numbers of his American flock on his 1987 American tour.[49] In spite of the church's claims concerning the authority of the pope in matters of religion and morals, many American Catholics insist on their freedom to decide for themselves in matters of personal morality, a freedom wealthy Catholics had long ago taken for themselves in economic matters.

To the extent that the liberation theologians succeed in raising the consciousness of the poor and in ameliorating their economic, social, and political condition, they will foster their adaptation to modern secular society. Willy-nilly, this will include adoption of middle class values such as a commitment to functional rationality, prudential calculation, delayed gratification, and scientific problem solving, values that make for competence in a technological society in which mind counts for far more than matter. The consequence of such a development for new entrants into the middle class will be the same as it has been for their predecessors: Functional rationality is totalizing in its consequences. Under the impact of liberation theology, today's poor could become tomorrow's new secularized bourgeoisie. Then the iron cage will have moved from the North Atlantic to the Southern Hemisphere.

NOTES

1. Gustavo Gutiérrez, "Liberation Praxis and Christian Faith," in *The Power of the Poor in History,* trans. Robert Barr (Maryknoll, N.Y.: Orbis Books, 1984), p. 57.

2. On the relationship between Catholic social teaching and liberation theology, see Phillip Berryman, "Liberation Theology and the U.S. Bishops' Letters on Nuclear Weapons and on the Economy," chap. 11 of this volume.

3. Gutiérrez, "Liberation Praxis," p. 57.

4. Thomas Hobbes, *Leviathan,* ed. C. B. Macpherson (Harmondsworth, Middlesex: Penguin Books, 1968), Pt. I, chap. 10, pp. 151–52.

5. Richard L. Rubenstein, *The Age of Triage* (Boston: Beacon Press, 1983), p. 132. See also Michael A. Cavanaugh, "Liberalism and Rationalism in Modern Theology: The Sociological Hypothesis," *Review of Religious Research* 29 (September 1987): 25–43. The views expressed here rely heavily on the theory of cognitive dissonance. See Leon A. Festinger, "Cognitive Dissonance," *Scientific American* 207 (October 1962): 93–102.

6. On modernization, see Marion J. Levy, Jr., *Modernization: Latecomers and Survivors* (New York: Basic Books, 1972).

7. I follow Max Weber in understanding rationalization as "the methodical attainment of a definitely given and practical end by an increasingly precise calculation of adequate means." Weber, "The Sociology of the World's Religions," in *From Max Weber: Essays in Sociology,* ed. H. H. Gerth and C. Wright Mills (New York: Oxford University Press, 1946), p. 293.

8. Rubenstein, *The Age of Triage.*

9. See Max Weber, *Economy and Society,* 2 vols., ed. Guenther Roth and Claus Witich (New York: Bedminster Press, 1968), 2: 636–37.

10. Gutiérrez, "Liberation Praxis," p. 50.

11. See, for example, Gustavo Gutiérrez, *A Theology of Liberation,* trans. and ed. Sister Caridad Inda and John Eagleson (Maryknoll, N.Y.: Orbis Books, 1973), pp. 110–11.

12. Gutiérrez, *The Power of the Poor in History,* pp. 37–38.

13. See, for example, Juan Luis Segundo, S. J., *The Liberation of Theology,* trans. John Drury (Maryknoll, N.Y.: Orbis Books, 1985), pp. 13–18, 57–61; Phillip Berryman, *Liberation Theology* (New York: Pantheon Books, 1987), pp. 138–50.

14. Gutiérrez, *The Power of the Poor in History,* p. 63.

15. See, for example, Gustavo Gutiérrez, "God's Revelation and Proclamation in History," in *The Power of the Poor in History,* pp. 3–22; Leonardo Boff, O.F.M., *Jesus Christ Liberator: A Critical Christology for Our Time,* trans. Patrick Hughes (Maryknoll, N.Y.: Orbis Books, 1978); Segundo, *The Liberation of Theology.*

16. Gustavo Gutiérrez, "God's Revelation and Proclamation in History," in *The Power of the Poor in History,* p. 14.

17. Ibid., p. 21.

18. Phillip Berryman, *Liberation Theology,* pp. 61–62.

19. Two decades ago I argued that in a time of diminished credibility religion would not disappear: "It (religion) is the way we share and celebrate, both consciously and unconsciously, through the inherited myths, rituals, and traditions of our communities, the dilemmas and the crises of life and death, good and evil. Religion is the way in which we share our predicament; it is never the way in which we overcome our condition." (See Richard L. Rubenstein, *After Auschwitz* (Indianapolis: Bobbs-Merrill, 1966), p. 263.) The indispensability of an objective historical basis for Christianity's assertions about Jesus as the Christ is discussed by Van A. Harvey, *The Historian and the Believer* (New York: Macmillan, 1969) pp. 102–63. In addition to the question of the unity of the five Books of Moses, the historical veracity of Gospel narratives concerning the life and activities of Jesus has been a problem for Christian thought since the publication in 1834 of David Friedrich Strauss's *Life of Jesus,* trans. George Eliot (London: Swan Sonnenschein, 1906). Strauss applied critical historical scholarship to the study of the New Testament. He rejected the historicity, among others of the Gospel traditions, concerning Jesus' infancy, his baptism by John the Baptist, temptation, transfiguration, resurrection, and ascension. Strauss argued that these traditions arose as messianic legends and myths and had become attached to Jesus *after* his followers had come to believe that

he was Israel's Messiah. Later critics argued that Mark was the earliest Gospel, upon which both Matthew and Luke were largely dependent. However, the critics held that, far from being an historical account of the life or message of Jesus, Mark had taken isolated stories and sayings and had edited them in accordance with his own theological perspectives. (See Werner Georg Kümmel, *The Theology of the New Testament,* trans. John E. Steely (Nashville: Abingdon Press, 1973).) From the point of view of historical scholarship, the Gospels are a far more reliable source for what the early church believed about the life of Jesus than for the life of Jesus itself.

20. See, for example, Gutiérrez, "God's Revelation and Proclamation in History," in *The Power of the Poor in History,* pp. 3–24, and Berryman, *Liberation Theology,* pp. 45–62.

21. I have discussed this issue in detail in *After Auschwitz* and *The Religious Imagination,* 2nd ed. (Lanham, Md.: University Press of America, 1986).

22. H. Richard Niebuhr, *The Social Sources of Denominationalism.*

23. The indispensability of an objective historical basis for Christianity's assertions about Jesus as the Christ is discussed by Harvey, *The Historian and the Believer,* pp. 102–63.

24. Ernst Troeltsch, *Die Absolutheit des Christentums* (Tubingen: J.C.B. Mohr, 1902), p. 41. I am indebted to Harvey, *The Historian and the Believer,* p. 30, for this citation.

25. Max Weber, " 'Objectivity' in Social Science and Social Policy," in *The Methodology of the Social Sciences* (1904), trans. and ed. Edward A. Shils and Henry A. Finch (New York: Free Press, 1949), p. 81.

26. Ibid., p. 51.

27. Ibid., p. 52.

28. Wolfgang Mommsen, *The Age of Bureaucracy: Perspectives on the Political Sociology of Max Weber* (Oxford: Basil Blackwell, 1974), p. 7.

29. Max Weber, *Economy and Society,* II, 636.

30. Max Weber, *The Protestant Ethic and the Spirit of Capitalism,* trans. Talcott Parsons (New York: Charles Scribners' Sons, 1958), pp. 181–82.

31. On the functional godlessness of modern civilization, see Rubenstein, *The Age of Triage,* pp. 1–33.

32. Karl Barth, "Autobiographische Skizze," in *Fakultätsalbum der Evangelischen-Theologischen Fakultät in Münster* (1927), p. 309, cited by Eberhard Jungel, *Karl Barth: A Theological Legacy,* trans. Garrett E. Paul (Philadelphia: The Westminster Press, 1986), p. 84.

33. "Jesus Christus und die Soziale Bewegung," in *Der Freie Aargauer: Offizelles Organ der Arbeiterpartei des Kantons Aargau* (December 23, 1911), second section, p. 1; cited by Jüngel, *Karl Barth.*

34. Barth, cited by Jüngel, *Karl Barth,* p. 84.

35. For an overview of the rise of Protestant liberalism, see Karl Barth, *Protestant Thought: From Rousseau to Ritschl,* trans. Brian Cozens (London: SCM Press, 1959). For a succinct discussion of the development, see Peter Berger, *The Sacred Canopy: Elements of a Sociology of Religion* (Garden City, N.Y.: Doubleday Anchor Books, 1969), pp. 158–60.

36. Albrecht Ritschl, *The Christian Doctrine of Justification and Reconciliation,* trans. and ed. H. R. Mackintosh and A. B. Macauley (Edinburgh: T. and T. Clark, 1900), p. 284.

37. H. Richard Niebuhr, *Christ and Culture* (New York: Harper and Row, 1951), p. 99.

38. Gustav Kruger, "The 'Theology of Crisis' " in *European Intellectual History Since Darwin and Marx,* ed. W. Warren Wagar (New York: Harper and Row, 1967), pp. 135–39. Kruger, a German church historian, originally delivered this paper as a lecture at New York's Union Theological Seminary in 1927.

39. See Fritz Fischer, *War of Illusions: German Policies from 1911 to 1914* (New York: W. W. Norton, 1975), pp. 1–43.

40. Karl Barth, *The Humanity of God,* trans. Thomas Weiser and John Newton Thomas (Richmond: John Knox Press, 1960), p. 14.

41. Karl Barth, *The Epistle to the Romans,* trans. Edwyn C. Hoskyns (Oxford: Oxford University Press, 1933).

42. Jüngel, *Karl Barth,* p. 101.

43. See Robert E. Willis, *The Ethics of Karl Barth* (Leiden: E. J. Brill, 1971), pp. 406–14.

44. Karl Barth, *Die Kirchliche Dogmatik,* Vol. I/1 (Zurich: Evangelischer Verlag A. G. Zollikon, 1940), p. 122 (author's translation).

45. Thomas J. J. Altizer, "Theology and the Death of God" in Thomas J. J. Altizer and William Hamilton, *Radical Theology and the Death of God* (Indianapolis: Bobbs-Merrill, 1966), p. 105.

46. Kenneth Hamilton, *God is Dead: The Anatomy of a Slogan* (Grand Rapids: William B. Eerdmans, 1966), p. 46.

47. Barth, *The Epistle to the Romans,* p. 203.

48. Friedrich Schleiermacher, *On Religion: Speeches to Its Cultured Despisers* (New York: Harper Torch Books, 1958).

49. The rift between the teachings of traditional religious institutions and the claims of autonomous reason were apparent recently when Pope John Paul II spoke to the Roman Catholic bishops of the United States assembled in Los Angeles on September 16, 1987, on such issues as sexual morality, abortion, divorce, and remarriage. He noted that a "large number of Catholics" do not adhere to the church's position on these issues. He then declared: "It is sometimes claimed that dissent from the Magisterium is totally compatible with being a 'good Catholic' and poses no obstacle to the reception of the sacraments. This is a grave error that challenges the teaching office of the bishops of the United States and elsewhere…. Dissent from Church doctrine remains what it is, dissent; as such it may not be proposed or received on an equal level with the Church's authentic teaching." ("Pope Counsels Bishops to Hold to Christ's Teachings in the Face of Dissent," *New York Times,* September 17, 1987.)

    The pope's address was in response to the prepared remarks of four members of the American heirarchy, one of whom was Joseph Cardinal Bernardin. Cardinal Bernardin spoke from a perspective with which the majority of educated Americans, Catholic and non-Catholic, could identify. The cardinal said: "We live in an open society where everyone prizes the freedom to speak his or her mind. Many tend to question things which are important to them, as religion is." Cardinal Bernardin went on to tell the pope that Americans "almost instinctively react negatively when they are told that they must do something, even though in their hearts they know they should do it." (Quoted by Joseph Berger, "Dissent and Good Catholics Are Incompatible, Pope Says," *New York Times,* September 17, 1987.)

To this observer it would seem that Cardinal Bernardin sought to convey to the pope the irreversible commitment of educated American Catholics to autonomous reason as the ultimate arbiter of how they govern their personal lives. As is well known, a very large number of American Catholics refuse to concede that their fidelity to their church is flawed because of, for example, their use of unsanctioned methods of birth control or their resort to divorce and remarriage. The pope as leader of a church claiming both divine legitimation and universality could hardly have been expected to compromise on the issue of the authority of the magisterium.

4

Liberation Theology and the Interpretation of Political Violence

Frederick Sontag

It is impossible to remain loyal to Marxism, to the Revolution, without treating insurrection as an art.

—V. I. Lenin

THE ISSUES

Where liberation theology and its contributions to theological discussion are concerned, perhaps no issue has been more controversial than its association with violence. When it comes to Marxism-Leninism, there is no question of its dependence on the use of violence. The issue of violence, however, plagues all liberation theories, since on the one hand the ties that hold humans in bondage may be so strong that only violent means can be effective to release us. But on the other hand, it is well known that violence may not accomplish what it promises and that terror, more often than peace, results.

Probably there has never been a theory seeking to release human beings to their full potential which has not had to consider the issue of the use of violence to achieve its ends. Yet this issue takes on a new urgency in our time due to two significant changes in our situation: (1) Most communist proposals which have resulted in worldwide change have militantly asserted the necessity to use force if we are to be set free. (2) Although in recent times liberation theology has been espoused by some Christian theologians, the adoption of pacifism or the abhorrence of violence by many Christian groups is well known. The question of religion's intrusion into the political realm is problem enough, but to add to this the use of violence raises the issue to a high intensity.

Although various traditions have well-developed positions regarding violence and nonviolence, where Christianity is concerned it is always instructive to begin by looking at the life and work of Jesus. Christianity will be our frame of reference in discussing these issues, since liberation theology, as it has become known, developed in a Christian context. First of all we have to ask whether the use of violence to achieve political ends is always ruled out or whether circumstances might justify it as an acceptable tool for Christian use. Traditionally, Jesus is seen as rejecting the use of violence and as having suffered violence himself. Can anything change this image so that it would make violence acceptable on Christian grounds?

In considering this, we first have to note that Jesus lived under political oppression himself. In fact, when we consider the Jewish expectations for the Messiah, as this role came to be projected onto him, it is precisely the Jews' hope for release from Roman oppressors that centered such high expectations on Jesus. Although later Christians came to understand Jesus as a Messiah, nothing could be more clear than that he did not live to fulfill the role of political liberator. After his death and for centuries later, Jewish political fortunes went from bad to worse. Thus, the people's expectations of gaining release by the hand of Jesus did not result in a change in political fortunes. This does not mean that Christians have not entered into politics and governments in later years or that some welcome changes cannot be attributed to "Christian influence." But it does mean that such improvements cannot be directly attributed to Jesus' efforts in his own lifetime.

This leads us to one of the many points of conflict Christians have had with communist programs. Following the optimism of the modern scientific age, Marxism-Leninism claims that the age of science offers us the possibility for "utopia now." Christianity, on the other hand, is represented as offering release only later, delayed until some eventual heaven. Thus, the Christian must face the taunt that communism offers an achievable ideal state now, one within our reach due to scientific advances, whereas Christianity holds out little hope for us in this world. Certainly liberation theology arises at least partly as a Christian "answer" to the Marxist challenge. As is well known, of course, it does borrow some doctrines from Marxism-Leninism. One issue at the base of the question of the use of violence is the issue of Christianity's compatibility with Marxist-Leninist doctrine and philosophical assumptions. Can Christian liberation theologians accept parts of communist doctrine without compromising the core of their own belief?

If Christians cannot promise us immediate release, as Marxists can, then certainly they are at a disadvantage competing in a world dominated by revolutionary fever. Marxists have achieved the overthrow of oppressive political regimes. What can Christians offer to compete with this, other than a distant heaven? Christians do claim that we human beings can be born anew, achieving an internal renewal, but how can this mild and largely unseen change compete with revolutionary overthrow and the establishment of a new political order? Of course, if you are not a fan of Marxist regimes as they have emerged historically, you might begin by questioning whether violent revolutions have in fact achieved their promised full release for the citizens affected. Even so, it cannot be denied that revolutionary violence has yielded political change, and without the use of force some oppressive situations might well have simply remained stagnant and unchanging. What can Christians claim to achieve in the way of overt change, and what means can they legitimately and consistently employ?

Before exploring some of these basic issues further, or exploring what Christian beginnings and history would seem to allow as possible, let me state the thesis I will offer. This might seem to be reaching the conclusion before the analysis of the issue, but stating a thesis at this point may in fact clarify the issues. Anyone who deals with Christian texts and traditions has no choice except to pick some focal point as a reference. Once one makes this selection, other notions fall in around it. I believe there is no neutral focal point, except of course that some selections can be shown to be trivial or unusual. What I propose has often been selected as crucial for Christian interpretation, even if it has been a bit enigmatic in its interpretation, as many central sayings in Christianity often are.

You recall that, when Jesus was asked if it was proper to pay taxes to Caesar, he asked for a coin. Showing the image of Caesar on it, he is quoted as saying: "Render therefore unto Caesar the things which are Caesar's; and unto God the things that are God's."[1] Others have pointed out that, although this seems an astute reply, it is not so easy to interpret in its detail as it might at first seem. I would not dispute that conclusion, since I think all abstract principles are difficult to apply concretely and in detail. Their supposed clarity often becomes murky when practical decisions are required. However, I do not take this as a special fault of Jesus' utterances but as a fact of our moral life, that is, that no principle applies easily and universally without requiring difficult decisions on our part. This does not render general rules and principles useless, but it does mean that the enunciation of general principles is only the beginning of the human decision process.

In this case in particular, how does Jesus' neat division of the affairs of Caesar and the affairs of God help us to decide whether there is a legitimate Christian resort to violence to achieve change or whether violence is ruled out? Quite often this saying of Jesus is appealed to in order to argue for a rigid separation, which makes Christianity purely a thing of the spirit, to be conducted in isolation from mundane matters with which Christians are sometimes advised to have nothing to do. Religion becomes an interior, spiritual matter, leaving the affairs of state overtly unaffected. In contrast, I want to argue the reverse, that in fact this important saying can be interpreted otherwise and leaves Christians free in the practical world. This can be done with one crucial provision: Christians cannot appeal to Jesus or to religious principles to justify their political/public activity. Each person must accept responsibility and justify his or her actions on their own.

Although to say this may seem to compartmentalize religion, if seen in another way it actually authorizes any activity the individual may wish to undertake. It is just that he or she must take the responsibility for what is done. Nor does this outlook claim that religion, particularly Christianity, is purely an internal, spiritual affair with no external applications. It simply tells us that, if you feel some principle, such as compassion for those who are poor or suffering, requires action on your part, you must undertake what you deem necessary without putting responsibility off on other shoulders, particularly on Jesus'. Jesus clearly did not use violence and seems to have preached against its use. If you think now that violence is needed to release human beings from their suffering bonds, fine. But the means you adopt are your choice and the consequences are on your shoulders. Of course, most liberation theologians want to analyze Christian texts and traditions so that they justify their actions, even violence. But instead, I believe, God places all justification on our shoulders.

We know that any argument which seems to imply that *all* Christians must or should support some one program of action cannot be justified in the long run. No argument within Christianity has received (or I believe can receive) unanimous approval as expressing what all Christians must believe or do. This does not mean that all arguments claiming Christian support are equally valid. But it does mean that it is dangerous to try to fix one "Christian position" as binding on all. Our differences have not ceased to exist, and the only sense in which we might reach universal agreement would be if we agreed to stop trying to force all of Christianity into some single form or program. Diversity may be part of Christianity's essence. If we could accept this as fact, it might keep us out of internally destructive arguments, ones which make us appear headed toward unity but in fact promote division.

One can live in South Africa and claim justification for one's racial views, although never without dispute, since on this thesis neither God nor Jesus enjoins any one program. However, the stress on love and the love of enemies is so central that one does need to reconcile any particular outlook with that theme of Christianity. The medieval person who asserted the divine right of kings is as much at fault as the revolutionary who argues that Jesus offers liberation in a way that authorizes violence, if its use proves necessary to break "the ties that bind" us in debilitating life-styles. Surely Jesus not only did not resort to violence himself but in fact seems to have opposed it. Yet I believe even that fact does not prevent the dedicated Christian from arguing for the necessity of violence as a means, if he or she is convinced that it is the only way the oppressive structure will release us.

One central problem with this interpretation will be spotted quickly both by dedicated revolutionaries and by Christians who want liberation theology to result in social change. That is, effective liberation and revolutionary movements need unified support. To have the effective dedication required, they cannot simply sink into a "do as you please" attitude. We know that effective revolutionary action is of necessity intolerant where any opposition to the new program is concerned. The classical liberal tolerance for diversity in viewpoints is not a virtue that breeds success for revolutionary or liberation movements. We all know that such actions have not only often been intolerant of opposing views but have in fact felt that the destruction of the opposition is a prime requirement for success.

We are aware of the Marxist-Leninist insistence on toeing the line on dogma and its demand for conformity to doctrine. But can the Christian accept the singularity of interpretation which effective action seems to require? If the Christian liberation theologian argues that all Christians cannot be required to accept some program of action, he or she is limited by the division of plurality. But then neither, on the other hand, can the Christian revolutionary activist be told that his program is "unchristian" as judged by some singular, authoritative standard. Of course, the chief complication in saying this lies with a hierarchical church which establishes authorities to formulate doctrine. The Christian who wants to act differently from what the structure of such a church allows will either (1) have to find a way to act independently and still stay within that community; or (2) convince the hierarchy of the rightness of the position, in which case the church's official position becomes his own; or (3) rebel against the church and perhaps leave it for another less doctrinally rigid Christian community.

DOES LIBERATION NECESSITATE USE OF VIOLENCE?

Contrary to some of the claims we have examined above, it should be a question whether liberation necessitates use of violence. To deal with this question, we must first distinguish the inner and the outer human nature. As is known, Christianity tends to do this and has often itself claimed to offer a new inner freedom. It talks of being "born again" but tends to mean the inner nature, not the physical human being. Of course, external change is sometimes offered too, but usually it is to be at a later time, not now.

It is clear from Jesus' statements that, no matter what later church interpretations may conclude, Jesus' followers were enjoined to help the poor, heal the sick, and relieve suffering. No specific instructions are given as to how this is to be done (which is the basis for a Marxist complaint about the lack of an action program), but still the Christian intent is clear. I have argued that any implementation program is the responsibility of the individual and that no one is in its specifics as such enjoined by Christian doctrine. It is only said that some action should be undertaken. This provokes the individual Christian's crisis: I must do something for human relief, but the burden is mine as to how I choose to do this, no group plan being laid out.

Furthermore, where Marxism-Leninism is concerned, two problems plague Christianity: (1) the Marxist doctrine of "materialism," and (2) the stress on the use of revolutionary violence. The Christian appraisal does not deny that there are material causes of unhappiness and enslavement, but still it tends to stress (as Hegel does in opposition to Marx) the spiritual or internal causes, which must be addressed first and which were not necessarily materially determined but were perhaps independent in origin. How, then, one attacks the material/economic/political situation is not specified. It may be as Mother Teresa works, simply caring for the suffering individually. A political/material program may be proposed, too, although not as required of all by reason of their Christian belief.

The universalism and uniformity of doctrine generally so demanded by Marxism-Leninism as a condition for success are simply not there in Christian terms. Some church groups have attempted to impose uniformity of doctrine, but there is no evidence that any one interpretation can be required of all Christians but only insofar as they are members of a particular group. Uniformity of action on a "Christian" basis is excluded from the beginning, all of which does not bode well for a "Christian" revolution, and certainly it makes the use of violence to achieve "liberation" a matter of great debate.

With some of these issues and proposals in mind, let us look at some recent proponents of liberation theology in a Christian setting and use these as a test ground. Let us begin with a recent (and mild) statement, Cornel West's *Prophesy Deliverance: An Afro-American Revolutionary Christianity*. West professes to "an abiding allegiance to progressive Marxist social analysis and political praxis."[2] But that statement is hard for many Christians to understand, since it involves an allegiance to material/economic determinism, plus a commitment to political revolution, using violence as necessary. Marx's key theme stresses inevitable class strife and the necessity to use force to break these bonds.

West describes "the Christian people" as "the self-realization of individuality within community."[3] This involves a "this-worldly" liberation as well as otherworldly salvation, which is hard to argue with in general. But the issue is what "this-worldly" liberation means and what force is to be used to achieve it. Are the forces that bind us such that only violence and political revolution can break them? West notes that Marxism and Christianity "share a similar moral impulse,"[4] which is quite true and which often pits them against each other as rivals. But the issue is the analysis of "the binding structures" which must be attacked and the means which must be used. Otherwise only platitudes unite us all.

West then goes on to describe the two basic challenges confronting Afro-Americans as "self-image and self-determination."[5] Again, it is hard to argue with this, but what if violence and revolution are necessary to achieve self-determination? He urges a "dialogical encounter" between Afro-American Christian thought and progressive Marxist social analysis.[6] Again, dialogue is harmless enough, but what if the good Marxist argues for the necessity of violence, revolution, and the extermination of opponents who block the revolution? West then proceeds to an historical account of the Afro-American experience, which again skirts the issue of "what is to be done" and how.

Even if, as West says, "the alliance of prophetic Christianity and progressive Marxism provides a last humane hope for humankind,"[7] the issue at stake still concerns the role of violence in its realization, a question he does not address. Furthermore, there surely is no one agreed-upon definition of "prophetic Christianity" which all Christians can support. It is hard to see how a "last human hope" can rest on such a divided and splintered basis, something a Marxist knows to be a formula for a lack of political/social action. We begin to argue about what program a Christian ought to follow rather than uniting to achieve transformation. What is the evidence that "all Christians" have been or ever can be united on one platform?

One of West's theological statements is perhaps the most crucial: "God sides with the oppressed and acts on their behalf."[8] Christian literature certainly is full of concern for "the oppressed," but we must be careful to see what "oppressed" means and what the causes of the oppression are said to be. It cannot be argued that all Christians do or ought to fill in this definition as a Marxist might. True, God has been said by both Jew and Christian to "act." But do God's endorsed actions embrace revolution and violence? That is not easy to argue, particularly since God's incarnation in Jesus did not obviously undermine the Roman empire. Jesus was crucified, and the Jews were left politically subjugated.

West acknowledges that "one is hard put to find a sketch of what liberation would actually mean in the everyday lives of black people."[9] But if this is true, the shared concerns with Marxism fade into insignificance, unless a political/social action program can be agreed upon, particularly with regard to the use of or the rejection of violence. West suggests that "human liberation occurs only when people participate substantively in the decision-making processes in the major institutions that regulate their lives."[10] But this still leaves untouched the major and decisive issue of how this is to be achieved and whether any Christian program can become identical with a Marxist formula.

West sees that Marxism recognizes "the positive, liberating aspects of popular culture and religion,"[11] but there is a difference here that is crucial. The Marxist has a radically different view of the subjugating effect of religion and a stronger notion of what is needed to overcome human alienation. If so, little can be held in common when it comes to practical implementation. West is strong in supporting what one might call a cultural and intellectual revolution, but that outlook skirts the complex question of whether such "altered perspectives" are sufficient to achieve liberation.

The "revolutionary activity," which West seems to endorse, is going to have to be something quite different from Marxist revolution and violence, so that one must ask West what such a "revolution" can hope to achieve by way of radical reform.[12] West seems to feel he has found a "middle pathway," but it is hard to get a very clear picture of how this deals with revolution and violence.[13] The book ends on an extremely vague note. In fact, after its historical description of the changes in black theology, this can only leave the reader puzzled as to (1) what specifically is proposed, (2) whether revolution and violence are authorized, and (3) whether West really believes that *all* black theologians are likely to agree with what he has proposed.

Now working further back in time, let us examine a more clear-cut proposal concerning the use of violence, James Cone's *A Black Theology of Liberation*. This examination is not proposed as an assessment of all the writings and changes in positions Cone or other American liberation theologians may have gone through since 1970, but in this book by Cone we have an early example that raised the issue of authorizing the use of violent means. Cone states that Christianity "is essentially a religion of liberation," which is difficult to argue with.[14] But the issue still concerns liberation from what and by what means. Similarly, when Cone says that the Christian message is addressed to "the poor," the issue concerns the meaning of "poor" (that is, economically or spiritually poor?).

Cone argues that the gospel bestows on the poor "the necessary power to break the chains of oppression."[15] But again, what limits are set, if any, on the use of power? Like West, Cone asserts that black liberation "is the work of God himself."[16] But is this "work" by God such that it is physically evident now; and particularly, does it extend to violent revolution? If it does not, it may not succeed, in which case it would be a strange "work" of God indeed. Cone claims that all acts which destroy white racism are "Christian."[17] But again, does that put God on the side of violence? Cone also has God "taking sides in the struggle," which is a bit hard to visualize.[18] How does God do this? Why is this not evident to us, to all?

Cone advocates "a radical revolutionary confrontation" with white power.[19] But once again: Should this confrontation include the use of violence and human destruction, even if the power structures that block us can be overcome in no other way? Racism probably is incompatible with the gospel of Christ, but to say that means nothing until the issue of violence is faced. Cone does argue that we cannot take Jesus' actions as a guide and that we must be free "to make decisions without an ethical guide from Jesus."[20] But that simply raises the issue of what criteria Christians can use to justify any action as being within the limits of Christianity. Anyone, of course, may call any action, violent or otherwise, "Christian." Names are free, but how many who call themselves "Christian" would agree?

The meaning of "revolution" is involved with this question, since Cone asserts that the black revolution in America is the revolution of God, and he identifies this with black power. However, we know in advance that revolutions are difficult to establish as factual even though claims about them may be plentiful. And more importantly, what would "revolution" mean in the context of what has transpired in America in recent years? To say that "every blow for liberation is the work of God" leaves God open to responsibility for mass murder, and Cone clearly states that "they should have killed him [the oppressor] instead of 'loving' him," which is certainly a radical reversal of traditional Christian teachings.[21]

We know that the history of Christianity, as well as other religions, is full of killings in "holy" wars. Do we want to retreat to such destruction? Also we must realize that "holy wars" can be waged by social and political conservatives as well as by radicals. One cannot argue that "Christianity" is or has been on one political side only.

Cone claims that "love" means that "God meets our needs," but the history of Christianity offers countless examples of religious testing that are far from "God's meeting one's needs."[22] That God has consistently "met our needs" would be hard to make out in history. Cone will not allow human suffering to have "divine approval," but that is difficult if not impossible to claim if one accepts God as the world's creator as well as its liberator.[23] If God created our world, then in that sense divinity is responsible for much of the suffering our world contains. Of course, Cone's early writing left much vague and brought forth many objections. The issue for us is not the ensuing debate but the strange way in which Christianity is used to support violence and how "love" comes to be compatible with killing.

THE ORIGINS OF LIBERATION THEOLOGY

Gustavo Gutiérrez first brought liberation theology to wide attention in his *A Theology of Liberation*. Just as the situation of black people in America may be special, so it is clear that the Roman Catholic church is different in Latin America than in most parts of the world. Still, our concern is not the church's sociohistorical context, but how the origins of liberation theology relate to the use of violence. Gutiérrez begins by equating "liberation" with "salvation."[24] This notion is crucial, since most Christians are familiar with the idea of "salvation" but perhaps not with its link to the notion of "liberation."

Gutiérrez argues that theology changes and that theology as "critical reflection on praxis" (action) has recently become more accepted.[25] From a Protestant perspective, one could argue that others have long argued for Christianity's commitment to change, but of course Gutiérrez is speaking from a Roman Catholic and Latin perspective, as he says. Even more so, Marxism wants to transform the world, but the issue is: by what means?[26] From the beginning we need to recognize that Gutiérrez speaks almost entirely in terms of "the church," as no Protestant really can, although it is interesting to see Cone and West argue for a unified "black" perspective in the same way.

"Liberation," Gutiérrez recognizes, involves radical change. Although "salvation" as a more traditional term does too, it is not immediately socially and politically oriented. Gutiérrez does see the historical process as "the gradual liberation of man," but this involves a progressive, evolutionary perspective which may be hard to justify in fact.[27] If, as he says, "Christ is presented as the one who brings us liberation," much will depend on accepting the shift from "salvation" to the slightly broader notion of "liberation" and the question of what this involves.[28] Gutiérrez recognizes this, but he argues on an evolutionary basis that now "human reason has become political reason."[29] This may be difficult to accept without also accepting the arguable assumption that there is "social evolution."

Gutiérrez asks the question: Should the church actually lend support to "a dictatorial and oppressive government" by remaining friendly or silent?[30] This again assumes a Roman Catholic meaning of "the church," and it still leaves unsettled what action the church, or any religious person, should engage in. But as for Latin America, Gutiérrez feels that "the revolutionary process ought to embrace the whole continent," although he does not provide specifics about how this is to be done or how far it is authorized to go.[31] He also seems to assume some kind of purity of intent on the part of those who oppose current dictatorial government. But Reinhold Niebuhr could be right: there may be no one right side but only a choice of lesser evils.

As Gutiérrez says, "The coming of the Kingdom implies the building of a just society."[32] Clearly that is involved, but still the issue is: how, when, and by what means? No Christian needs to refrain from social action, but there is a question of whether our own actions can claim to accomplish this fully, as the Marxist's anticipated classless society does, or whether its full achievement is reserved for God's final action and the end of time. Gutiérrez urges the church to a "prophetic denunciation" of social injustice. That is an ancient tradition for both Judaism and Christianity. The question is whether one can move beyond this to violent revolution on a religious basis.

Speaking for Latin America, Gutiérrez wants the church to "place itself squarely within the process of revolution, amid the violence which is present in different ways."[33] Of course, Christians do not flee in the face of violence; those involved in any struggle must still be ministered to, and their human needs may be vast. But can the church, or any person claiming the support of Christianity, actively promote the revolutionary process and engage in violence, too? The church might put its weight behind social changes, as he argues, but does that endorse any particular program or plan of action? Gutiérrez treats "salvation" as something "otherworldly," but there is no reason to do so.[34] He wants a new chosen people and obviously a messiah who will be more of a political liberator than Jesus was in fact.

Gutiérrez paints a moving picture of Christian commitment to alleviate suffering and of the new world it works for, but on the whole he avoids the issue of the necessity of violence, as Cone did not. Perhaps he comes closest to the issue when he states: "To love one's enemies presupposes recognizing and accepting that one has class enemies and that it is necessary to combat them."[35] Yes, but by what means, and does this include the elimination of opposing parties by violence if necessary, as orthodox Marxism often assumes must be done? Gutiérrez wants us to participate in the class struggle, but does that mean to seek the elimination of certain existing classes?

He argues for a "solidarity *with the poor* and...a protest *against poverty*."[36] But is this protest to remain mainly verbal? Marxism would scoff at such ineffective "action." In all his analysis, Gutiérrez has not faced the Marxist challenge that the bonds that suppress us are material and therefore require radical action, revolutionary violence, that can break, eliminate, and eradicate the oppressive sociopolitical structures of our present world. Is this Marxist challenge true? If so, violence is necessary and our present order cannot remain. That is a possible theory, and it could be true, as Marxists have argued. But Gutiérrez has only argued for action without specifying the limits of action allowed, which is the issue at the heart of the matter and the origin of the surrounding controversy.

By way of assessment, review, and summary, let us consider briefly a book by Oscar Cullmann, *Jesus and the Revolutionaries*. Cullmann argues that Jesus could have joined the revolutionary movements of his time but that he did not. In fact, argues Cullmann, Jesus "cannot be simply viewed as belonging to any of the principal movements prevailing...at his time."[37] If this is true, it is a hard fact for all the advocates of revolution considered here—West, Cone, and Gutiérrez—to accept. They want to enlist Christian backing for specific causes, whereas it may be that Jesus joined none in his time and remained an enigma to his disciples because of this. Of course, Cone argued that Jesus should not be the role model for Christian action, but if we accept that statement, we will be hard pressed to identify any action as "Christian."

In Jesus' time the Zealots were the group advocating a political program, just as Cone, West, and Gutiérrez do. Yet Jesus did not join them. The Romans convicted Jesus of the crime of trying to establish a political kingdom. Yet we know the irony of his crucifixion is that he preached the coming of the kingdom from within. Jesus and the Zealots both proclaimed that the kingdom of God was at hand, and Jesus was condemned as a Zealot agitator. Yet we know he advocated nonviolence and viewed the Zealots as a diabolic temptation to be shunned. Still, Jesus' expectation of a coming kingdom is undeniable, although it is to be from God more than from us.

Most importantly, Jesus did not hate his enemies, a tendency we see in Marxism and in some liberation theologies. In fact, his attitude toward the Samaritans and Gentiles probably shocked the Zealots, "whose hate for the Gentiles was the most extreme."[38] So we need to ask: Can violent revolution be advocated without a basis in hatred, which, if not, is a block for most Christians? The forgiving of our enemies is difficult for a revolutionary program, and certainly it eliminates violence as an acceptable path. Jesus turns to the poor *and* to the rich; he shows no class distinctions, which presents a roadblock for all Marxism.

Even his disciples could not understand the conception of the kingdom of God which Jesus preached, so different was it from the current political options. He was a strange "Messiah." Jesus dismissed as a Satanic temptation the Zealot political concept of the Messiah (which is actually close to what Cone, West, and Gutiérrez advocate). It is not easy to understand the kind of "kingdom" Jesus wanted to inaugurate, but certainly it was not simply a political/economic one. Jesus compromised on the issue of political/religious allegiance, as we noted earlier, since not to pay one's taxes was considered by the Zealots as a test of faithfulness. Ironically, Jesus was condemned as a Zealot and yet he was no Zealot, which is a problem for West, Cone, and Gutiérrez. Jesus did not join the Zealots when the Jewish War broke out but fled to the other side of the Jordan.

In conclusion, let us glance at a later book by James Cone, *God of the Oppressed*. Since this book attempts to build liberation theology out of the black church experience, it is more mild in its tone. Yet Cone states: "God came and is present now, in order to destroy the oppressor's power to hold people in captivity."[39] But if so, this surely cannot be "power" in a political sense, since oppressors still wield political power. That outcome would seem to make God ineffective, if that was indeed the "power" he sought to break. God's intervention cannot be as immediate as Cone indicates, but if it is not, why not? Cone claims that "Jesus has not left us alone but is with us in the struggle for freedom."[40] That may very well be true, but it says nothing about Jesus and the question of using violent means in the struggle.

Jesus is the Expected One, "coming to liberate the oppressed from slavery."[41] Yes, but when, and what is his present action? To quote the phrase does not tell us. Cone calls black worship "a liberating experience,"[42] and it may be, but surely such "liberation" is far from political or violent and may have little economic effect. But then Cone returns to have "liberation" mean "revolutionary action against injustice, slavery, and oppression."[43] He speaks of "joining God in the fight against injustice," but Cone remains vague and ambivalent as to what means are permissible for us to use to accomplish this.[44]

Finally, then, I have argued that any individual, Christian or otherwise, can resort to violence and destruction if he or she wishes to take the responsibility for using such means. Marxist-Leninists can undoubtedly find clear doctrine to support using violence to break the prevailing social/political/economic/class structures which they assert prevent liberation. A Christian, on the other hand, may offer an individual reading of "Christianity" which authorizes the use of violence, but neither in the life and work of Jesus, nor in the New Testament, nor in most major theological interpretations, can one find justification for the use of violent means and for advocating destruction.

Certainly it is clear that no unanimity of all Christians will ever be centered on the acceptance of the use of violence, so antithetical is it to most Christian traditions. Yet we must face the Marxist-Leninist challenge that the structures which bind us cannot be broken other than by the use of violent means. Furthermore, whatever any Christian may feel authorized to do, the transformation of the world's basic structure depends at least in part on God's intervening power, even if it can be said that divinity interferes partially and subtly now. Still, the day of full and final release is not yet here, and surely we cannot be sure that the use of violence and terror will hasten its coming.

THE SPECIAL PROBLEMS IN SOUTH AND CENTRAL AMERICA

If one lives in the United States, it may be easy enough to pursue a nonviolent revolution. Martin Luther King, Jr., could be a Christian pacifist, follow Jesus and Gandhi, and still achieve a revolution in race relations. Gandhi inspired King because he achieved the independence of India while preaching nonviolence, even if violence did follow as a result of his work. Gandhi was dealing with a cultivated British democracy, even if as part of an empire, and King had United States constitutional appeals open to him. Although situations vary, it is hard to point to a single situation in South or Central America where military force is not the rule and where civil liberties are sacred.

When you face openly ruthless military power and autocratic political rule, where any protest might cause you to disappear from society, it can easily seem that nothing but force can accomplish change. Those who do not hold power under constitutions or through open democratic elections must know that only repression can keep them in power. Such rulers have everything to fear from protest and revolution and little to lose from ruthless oppression, particularly if astutely and cleverly applied. In such situations, to talk of "liberation" without a willingness to resort to force and violence may be to doom all such talk to either frustration or insignificance. "The church" often has both wealth and political influence. Why should this not be used to achieve a change otherwise doomed to failure?

Given such a context, all I have been saying about the questionable nature of any appeal to violence on a Christian basis would seem to doom religion to ineffectiveness. The problem is not so much finding a way to change or revise Christianity's traditional posture as to wonder how political interests, no matter how just their cause, could have thought of turning to Christianity, or to any of its churches, in support of a change that almost demands violence if the project is not to fail. Why not argue for change and for any means necessary to achieve it on a secular basis, just as Marx does? Of course, a monolithic church in Latin America can be a powerful instrument, whereas churches in the United States split their power among a vast variety.

In North America one can appeal to organized religion for spiritual or moral support and often raise powerful forces. But any hint of violence would at best divide support and perhaps even doom the movement to failure. In Latin America, violence may be necessary for success, and the Roman Catholic church stands out as one of the few institutions explicitly committed to the good of the people, whatever its actual past record of accommodation to political repression may be. One may be forced to consider the church as its ally or find little organized support. Odd, then, that violence appears on the horizon of Christianity (as it has in the past, although often as a means to repress dissent from within) as an alternative to potential revolutionary failure. However, what we must ask is whether any association with violence will tear apart Christian effectiveness rather than secure an otherwise unobtainable political change.

Listening to the rhetoric of recent liberation theologians, one detects two trends that have been dangerous in Christianity's past and may be potentially divisive again, especially when unity of action is desperately needed. These are: (1) a tendency to pit one group against another rather than to bring peace among factions, and (2) a stress on preaching the realization of the kingdom of God now.

Insofar as Latin American liberation theology incites hate against North American economic "oppressors," or even against local political oppressions, it draws strength from the stormy emotions of hate and retaliation, whereas Christianity has preached the love of enemies. Can any movement be accredited as "Christian" which in any way capitalizes on hate for an enemy rather than love? Furthermore, as often happens whenever hatred of a group or class is preached, any such appeal will divide Christians rather than unite them, even if some rally to the call.

Where Christian tradition is concerned, the issue of the Kingdom of God may pose the most difficult problem. Jesus' followers expected success in their time, and Jesus was crucified amidst disappointed hopes. The traditional expectation of Jesus' second coming seems to say that no realization of the Christian hope can come in any full or exact sense until that time. In this case, whatever Christians do in the interim to redress wrongs (which they are enjoined to do), the final resolution awaits God's action. If so, violence to achieve goals now appears to become less justifiable. Violence, if it is to be appealed to, can hardly be done as enjoined by Christian doctrine but must be an individual action.

NOTES

1. Matt. 22:21 (King James Version).

2. Cornel West, *Prophesy Deliverance: An Afro-American Revolutionary Christianity,* (Philadelphia: Westminster Press, 1982), p. 10.

3. Ibid., p. 16.

4. Ibid.

5. Ibid., p. 80.

6. Ibid., p. 83.

7. Ibid., p. 95.

8. Ibid., p. 106.

9. Ibid., p. 111.

10. Ibid., p. 112.

11. Ibid., p. 117.

12. Ibid., p. 131.

13. Ibid., p. 143.

14. James Cone, *A Black Theology of Liberation* (Philadelphia: J. B. Lippincott, 1970), p. 11.

15. Ibid., p. 23.

16. Ibid., p. 26.

17. Ibid., p. 33.

18. Ibid., p. 36.

19. Ibid., p. 41.

20. Ibid., p. 68.

21. Ibid., p. 101.

22. Ibid., p. 138.

23. Ibid., p. 149.

24. Gustavo Gutiérrez, *A Theology of Liberation: History, Politics and Salvation* (Maryknoll, N.Y.: Orbis Books, 1973), p. 2.

25. Ibid., p. 6.

26. Ibid., p. 9.

27. Ibid., p. 29.

28. Ibid., p. 37.

29. Ibid., p. 47.

30. Ibid., p. 65.

31. Ibid., p. 89.

32. Ibid., p. 110.

33. Ibid., p. 138.

34. Ibid., p. 151.

35. Ibid., p. 276.

36. Ibid., p. 301.

37. Oscar Cullmann, *Jesus and the Revolutionaries* (New York: Harper and Row, 1976), p. vii. S. G. F. Brandon, for instance, in his books, *The Trial of Jesus of Nazareth* and *Jesus and the Zealots,* argued for another side of this position, as we are well aware. But Cullmann, I believe, has effectively argued against the notion of Jesus as a Zealot.

38. Ibid., p. 23.

39. James Cone, *God of the Oppressed* (New York: Seabury Press, 1975), p. 99.

40. Ibid., p. 122.

41. Ibid., p. 129.

42. Ibid., p. 144.

43. Ibid., p. 152.

44. Ibid., p. 233.

Part II

Liberation Theology and Socioeconomic Problems

5

Liberation Theology, Latin America, and Third World Underdevelopment

Roland Robertson

The religious institution—under whatever spirit one envisages it—is the principal political institution.
—Saint-Simon, *Science de l'homme* (1813)

BASIC CONSIDERATIONS

From my perspective as a sociologist, the theme of this paper falls almost automatically into two parts —namely, liberation theology as a form of analysis of Third World underdevelopment on the one hand, and the analysis of the relationship between liberation theology and Third World underdevelopment on the other. The first requires discussion of the analytical and interpretive thrust of liberation theology with particular reference to the problem of "underdevelopment," while the second necessitates analysis and interpretation of the emergence and impact of liberation theology in Third World settings. Emphasizing that it is not possible—nor even, perhaps, desirable—to keep these two dimensions of discussion completely separate, it is nonetheless important at the outset to provide a rationale for my distinction between *liberation theology as analysis* and *the analysis of liberation theology* with respect to particular kinds of sociocultural setting.

Much of what has been written in explicitly liberation-theological contexts has involved the weaving together of classical Christian theology and secular-ideological, social scientific, and philosophical themes. Thus in considering liberation theology as a whole—when, in other words, one confronts and attempts to assess the cogency of liberation theology in the largest sense—one quickly faces debates on many different fronts. Unfortunately, very few people have been willing and able to come to terms with liberation theology on such a grand scale. For the most part, external discussion of liberation theology—as opposed to internal exposition, revision, or advocacy—has been highly compartmentalized, with some thrusts of liberationism receiving a lot of attention, others very little. Thus there has been much analysis of liberation theology from theological, philosophical, and ideological points of view, but relatively little from social scientific standpoints. In other words, while a number of theologians, philosophers, and ideologues have considered liberation theology (mainly of the Latin American kind) from "the outside" (with varying degrees of sympathy), few social scientists have dealt explicitly with the social scientific components of liberation theology, in the sense of engaging directly with the liberationists' generalizations about social structure, culture, sociocultural change, and so on.

There is, I believe, one major reason for the latter circumstance, namely, that many of the most relevant social scientists—that is, those who specialize in the study of one or more Latin American societies—have adopted large chunks of the social science aspect of liberation theology as premises of their own work. In particular, they have accepted—at least in broad outline—the dependency-theory components (or, if you will, the antimodernizationist or antidevelopmentalist aspects) of liberation theology. In so doing they have tended to see the latter as "a natural response" to Third World circumstances. In that perspective liberation theology expresses in ostensibly politicotheological terms what those same social scientists seek to say in "scientific" terms.

For one who does not regard the social scientific dimension of liberation theology uncritically and who is interested in the question as to why some social scientific perspectives are embraced and others eschewed by liberation theologians, it is clearly necessary to confront liberation theology to a much greater degree than is the case with those who, by and large, find the social science of liberation theology quite acceptable. However, I do not intend to engage in such a critique in the present context.[1] Rather, I will concentrate on the second aspect of the theme—that is, I will discuss the emergence, diffusion, and significance of liberation theology in Latin America, Africa, and Asia. That itself is a vast agenda and I can only in a relatively short discussion deal with those issues in a very general way. My approach will be to consider, first, relevant differences in historical experiences among the three Third World continents and, second, the nature and global circumstance of liberation theology's metatheological emphasis on the historical and, in the broadest sense, sociocultural settings of theology and religion. In the latter regard I consider liberation theology as a particular manifestation of the contemporary politicization of religion.[2]

Other contributors to this volume deal in varying detail with the ideational content of liberation theology, at least in its Latin American forms. I will simply invoke at this juncture an earlier attempt of mine to characterize the general thrust of Latin American liberation theology.[3] In that previous discussion I summarized the major claims of liberation theology along the following lines:

> 1. The traditional doctrinal focus upon inner spirituality and personal sin has prevented realization of the ideas that sin can be, and indeed should be, regarded as a structural property of society and that salvation can and should be considered primarily in collective and historical terms. This perspective is closely related to the claim that, whereas the dominant theological method has been ahistorical and apolitical, the Bible should be read with emphasis precisely on historicity and the inevitable conjunction of politics and religion. Thus Moses and the Promised Land and Jesus and the Kingdom of God are the exemplary biblical themes. In sum, theology should be existentialist rather than essentialist, homocentric rather than theocentric, inductive rather than deductive, biblical and circumstantial rather than scholastic and eternalistic.
>
> 2. Latin America's circumstances of widespread poverty and inequality, as well as its religious condition, result from a long history of imperialist or neocolonial subjection, by

Spain and Portugal in the sixteenth century, by other European countries (notably Britain) in the nineteenth century, and by the United States in the twentieth century. More specifically, the present Latin American condition is a consequence of the operation of a world system of economic and political exploitation. (For some liberation theologians Latin America has a privileged role to play in releasing the Third World from bondage.)

3. Vatican II in effect validated the idea of a church of and for the people, one having a greater concern with the material condition of humanity (more specifically, the poor, marginal, and excluded). According to Gutiérrez, traditional theology begins with the problem of the nonbeliever whereas liberationism begins with "the man who is not a man." Theology should be geared to the establishment of a terrestrial kingdom of God.

CONTINENTAL AND CIVILIZATIONAL VARIATION

Liberation theology is indeed most closely associated with Latin America, where it was first powerfully thematized and where it has had the most impact. However, in spite of liberation theology's now being regarded more inclusively as a Third World phenomenon with Latin America as its main source, it is worth noting that when the idea of the third world was beginning to take hold in the 1960s there was some uncertainty as to whether Latin American societies should be included within that category. Originally, the "Third World" mainly applied to the newly or about-to-become independent countries of Africa and Asia. (Some French intellectuals also included all Communist countries.) At the time when, mainly on the basis of a series of international conferences following the Bandung conference of nonaligned nations in 1955, the Third World began to be seen as a global institution, it was mainly along Afro-Asian lines. Precisely during that same period, the conception of societal *modernization* was developed by Western social scientists. It was an approach to the problem of economic and political underdevelopment applied to Latin American societies and to the new (and some old) nations of Africa and Asia. In Latin America during the late 1960s, groups of social scientists mounted serious attacks on modernization theories, mainly on the grounds that Latin

America was being held back economically and politically by indigenous cultural and social-structural deficiencies which could, nevertheless, be overcome on a society-by-society basis along trajectories traveled previously by the rich liberal democracies of North America, western and northern Europe, and Australasia.

A major reason for the early ambivalence concerning the Third World status of Latin America was centered upon the fact that most of the old Spanish and Portuguese colonies in the Western Hemisphere had achieved formal independence by the middle of the nineteenth century and thus their membership—if not their active participation—in "international society" predated the membership of even such significant twentieth-century societies as Germany, Italy, and Japan, not to speak of the non-European nations which gained independence after World War II. But it is precisely the disjunction between formal international equality and actual inequality with respect to socioeconomic standing—its relative deprivation—which has constituted the root of Latin America's revolt against North American and West European ideas concerning the economic structure of the world, even though Latin Americans are on average significantly better off than those in most Asian and African countries. The relative deprivation of Latin America has contributed to the idea that the Third World originated in the Iberian penetration of the Americas. Indeed, in the writings of some liberation theologians one can see the fusion of Pan Latin Americanism—the idea that Iberian America consists of a single "cosmic race" composed of Indians, blacks, and white Europeans and capable of a unique, globally relevant universalism—with the notion that Latin America is eschatologically destined to be the leader of a global proletariat.[4]

It should be added that during the nineteenth century, political elites in a number of the newly independent Latin American societies largely accepted and tried to import strategies concerning what in the mid-twentieth century came to be called societal modernization. Indeed, it may be worth noting in that regard that, while it is conventional to think of Japan as the first society in the modern period to copy self-consciously and systematically from the West (mainly because it has been so successful), it was in fact the new nations of Latin America which tried to do so first. (If, as Lipset cogently argued some years ago, the United States was the *first* new nation, then a number of Latin American societies are candidates for being regarded as the second.[5]) However, no Latin American society was successful in combining a sense of its own identity with self-generated capacity to internalize aspects of European or North American societies in such a way as to promote substantial "progress." During the post-Iberian phase Britain, the United States, and other (European) societies greatly intruded upon Mexico and South and Central America. Contrary to the view of many liberation theologians, however, that does not account for the failure of Latin American societies to "learn how to learn," which is an essential ingredient of the modernization process. In other words, the relative failure of Latin American societies to adapt to the global culture of modernity and modernization cannot be accounted for solely in terms of its encounters with powerful intrusive nations. Nevertheless, Latin America has in relatively recent years "borrowed successfully" from the West in the case of liberation theology, in the sense of importing radical philosophy, theology, and social science from Europe.[6] It has, in turn, made a significant—but at the same time controversial—contribution to the world as a whole; for liberation theology has, of course, become influential in various parts of Asia and Africa, notably via the Ecumenical Association of Third World Theologians (EATWOT), which held its first meeting in 1976. Well before that time Latin America had come to be widely thought of as a part of the Third World, and by the end of the 1970s the leading ideas of Latin American liberation theologians had deeply penetrated EATWOT, making it appropriate for that organization to meet in Latin America in 1980. It should also be emphasized that the World Council of Churches has played quite an important role in the diffusion of ideas close to those of liberation theology.

Liberation theology is a perspective which has developed almost exclusively among Christians (and more extensively among Catholics than Protestants), and it is important in that connection to note a major set of differences between the Christian churches in Latin America and those in Africa and Asia. Latin American Christianity (overwhelmingly Catholic historically, but decreasingly so in the modern period) is largely the result of the first wave of extensive European imperial expansion, which was occasioned in significant part by the Protestant Reformation and reaction to it in western and northern Europe in the first half of the sixteenth century, along with the fact that Islam had only recently been expelled from Iberia itself. For hundreds of years Catholic Christianity has enjoyed a hegemonic cultural position in Latin America, in spite of the attempts of nineteenth-

and twentieth-century political elites to secularize certain institutions along what were often perceived to be progressive European and North American lines and the fact that Catholicism has, in various places, been interwoven with indigenous religions and religions of African origin.

In considerable contrast, the Christian churches in both Africa and Asia derive mainly from a later stage of European expansion during the nineteenth and early twentieth centuries involving a greater degree of differentiation between imperialistic penetration and missionary endeavor than was the case with the sixteenth-century Spanish and Portuguese moves into Latin America. Moreover, some of the initial missionary effort in Africa and Asia in the nineteenth century was directed from within the United States, which at the time was not extensively engaged in expansionist activity outside the Western Hemisphere. Probably the most important contrast between the African and Asian circumstances is that in Asia, with the important exception of the Philippines, Christianity did not clearly triumph numerically or socioculturally over indigenous religions. On the other hand, the missionary effort in Africa has resulted in Christianity's being "either the majority religion, or about to become it, in almost all parts of the African continent south of the equator as well as in important parts north of the equator...."[7] That the vast majority of the population of the Philippines can be classified as Christian (with a quite militant Islamic minority) is due not to the nineteenth- and early twentieth-century European expansion but almost entirely to the earlier Iberian phase of imperialism. (Thus in a special sense the Philippines is as much a Latin American as an Asian society.) The only other case of an Asian country where Christianity is strong both numerically and institutionally is Korea (originally in the north but now in the noncommunist south). This is largely the result of its encounters with more powerful nations (Russia, Japan, China, and, to a lesser extent, Britain and France) and American missionaries before the United States was acting as an imperial power in Asia. The Philippines and South Korea are, of course, of great contemporary interest since they have recently taken steps in democratic directions, with religious leaders and groups playing a significant part in those developments. However, the role of religion differs in the two sets of circumstances, with liberation theology being much more significant in the Philippines than in South Korea.[8]

Christian penetration of Africa confronted, except in certain northern Islamic areas, very localized, magico-animistic religions which had virtually no experience of relating one religious world view to another and which were theologically unsystematized. The Christian arrival in Asia, by contrast, involved encounters with sophisticated civilizations containing systematic religions and long-standing experience of other cultures, religions, and philosophical traditions.[9] This is particularly true of East Asia. For many centuries China had been a site of complex and changing relationships among Confucianism, Mahayana Buddhism, Taoism, and yin yang thought (although by quite early in the twentieth century Chinese intellectuals had begun, somewhat ironically under Western influence, to reject both Eastern and Western religion). Under Chinese influence, Korea had undergone a similar experience, particularly with respect to the relationships between Buddhism, Confucianism, and its own relatively elaborate form of shamanism. In turn Korea had been a kind of transmission belt between China and Japan. For something like fourteen hundred years Japan had a "multireligious policy" involving all of the above-named religious orientations (but particularly Buddhism and Confucianism) in relation to its indigenous folk religion (Shinto).

The differences among the major continental carriers of contemporary liberation theology (Asia, Africa, and Latin America) are of considerable significance in appreciating its dimensions and significance. Their differences have been reflected in variations in how the notion of liberation has been interpreted, centering upon the degree to which liberation *per se,* as opposed to the process of *inculturation,* has been emphasized as a primary task for the Christian. In its starkest form the difference between the Latin American conception of liberation and the Afro-Asian conception of inculturation revolves around the issue of whether individuals and groups are to be released from a "pre-human" condition—which has, as the argument goes, been inflicted upon them—or whether, on the other hand, individuals and collectivities are to be enabled to realize their humanity by bringing their Christianity into alignment with traditional beliefs, customs, and practices.

The emphasis on liberation in the Latin American context has thus been centered upon the claim that it is first necessary to be "humanized"—released from degrading exploitation and poverty—before becoming a religious Christian; but since the humanization process involves the comprehension of *the conditions* which have historically created the phenomenon of "the man who is not a man" (to use the well-known phrase of Gutiérrez) that process is inevitably not simply one of spiritualization. It also must involve, according to the liberationists, a process of consciousness-raising along "secular lines" *(concientización)*. This concern with humanization may well derive indirectly from the debate in Spain in the sixteenth century as to the degree to which the natives of the New World should be regarded as fully human, or at least able to achieve adulthood. While there were subsequent versions of that debate in some of the countries and churches which led the Western penetration of Africa and Asia much later, they were nowhere near so explicit. This was true in large part because—with the possible exception of Portuguese "ultracolonialism"—the second wave of European expansion did not involve such far-reaching attempts to dominate and reconstruct the indigenous culture.

In any case, in Asia, if not nearly so much as in Africa, the problem of comprehending the indigenous cultural system was much more salient to missionaries (and other functionaries in the imperialist societies). Given that historical circumstance, which partly caused the relatively slow rate of conversion and the modern situation of the minority status of Christianity in Asia, it is not surprising that there should be much more emphasis upon *adapting to* local sociocultural conditions in the non-Latin parts of the Third World. In Latin America, much more than in other parts of the Third World—with the exception, again, of the Philippines —liberation theology has had *two* fairly distinctive but intersecting thrusts: one against the perceived local and global centers of politicoeconomic exploitation, the other against the dominant groups within the Catholic church. The major reason for this difference is that in Latin America the Catholic church hierarchy traditionally had been associated with conservative ideological forces, and, at least until the Second Vatican Council, the leadership of the Latin American church was clearly subordinate to the Vatican.

The contrast between liberation and inculturation can, however, be given too much weight. Indeed, in recent years what was once a source of divergence between Afro-Asian and Latin American theological "radicals" has become greatly attenuated. On the Latin American front liberation-theological and other sympathetic intellectuals have apparently become increasingly interested in inculturation with respect to the perceived protorevolutionary ingredients of Amerindian religion.[10] Thus there has been an incorporation of inculturation into the theme of liberation; and on the African and Asian fronts a meeting point between the themes of liberation and inculturation has been reached via the notion of *contextualization*,[11] which all along has been a theme of liberation theology. Nearly all of the leading Latin American theologians have insisted that the theological enterprise does not begin hermeneutically with theology per se— that is, with discussion of transcendental or spiritual matters— but rather with analysis of the concrete sociocultural and historical situation in which theologizing "proper" occurs.

In spite of this convergence among the transnational elites in the Third World liberationist movement, there remain important differences in emphasis and circumstance. Particular attention should be drawn to the remarkable proliferation of independent churches and religious movements of a syncretic nature, involving mixtures of Christianity and indigenous religion, in central and southern Africa during the twentieth century. Many of these have been thaumaturgical, reformist, or nativist in inclination rather than millennial or revolutionary, although Africa has seen many millennial movements, often protorevolutionary in nature, during the twentieth century. In any case, there are many internal alternatives to the attractions of explicit liberation theology—which has, nonetheless, made its mark in both Catholic and Protestant mission-founded churches of a more "mainline" orientation. In spite of the large number of African independent churches, the mainline churches still attract the vast majority of African adherents to formally institutionalized religion in Africa south of the Sahara.

LIBERATION THEOLOGY AND THE IDEA OF CONTEXTUALIZATION

In maintaining that theology must reflect explicitly on its own context as well as stimulate the "everyday theology" of the poor and underprivileged, liberationists insist that theology has always been, if only implicitly, political and ideological as well as reliant upon extra-theological resources. Thus liberation theology sees both a level of *meaning* which stands over theology as such—a sense of history and contemporary circumstance which is necessary for interpretation of the Bible and of extant theological texts—and a political *power* dimension in all theology. It is this

connecting of meaning and power which is one of the most salient ingredients of liberation theology as one considers it from a sociological
perspective. This characteristic enables us to place liberation theology in a
larger context; for there has been a virtually worldwide politicization of
religion in recent years. The idea that "church" and "state" can and should
be clearly *separated* is, of course, of recent historical origin; it received its
first, full-fledged expression in America at the end of the eighteenth century. Ironically, however, it was precisely in reference to the newly independent United States that Tocqueville applied the dictum that religion is
the major political institution.[12] Subsequently, under considerable influence from the American model, the idea became widely, if unevenly,
diffused across the world that the state should be basically secular and that,
on the other hand, religion is a basically private matter (with some public-
ethical consequences). At the same time the category of "religion" has become highly manipulable. If it is the case that one of the major problems
with the contemporary state is that it has problems of legitimacy (traditionally given to it by dominant religions), it is not surprising that the category
of religion should have become politicized. The protection which
"religion" has been given on a more-or-less global basis in the last few
decades—even if only by lip-service in many societies—provides the possibility to use religion as a lever for either legitimation or delegitimation.
Regardless of whether societies across the world are undergoing processes of desecularization, we must consider carefully the extent to which
religion as a category has become manipulable. More specifically, I would
argue that the "use" of religion must be addressed before we can tackle the
direct question of secularization. In any case, insofar as "religion" is
regarded as a category of transcendent discourse which can be employed
as protection against dominant political powerholders, theological reflection and, more particularly, religious activity will be susceptible to
politicization.

   Such considerations have an important bearing on two major aspects of
the notion of contextualization—namely, the fusion of theology and social
theory and the alignment of Christianity with Marxism. These two aspects
overlap considerably since Marxism is often taken to be a form of social
science. Liberation theology came to the fore in Latin America in the 1960s
when societal modernization theories (involving the central idea that the
move away from underdevelopment should consist of basically internal

changes along the same tracks as those taken by Western liberal democracies) were at their peak and Marxist thought of a primarily non-Soviet type was rapidly entering the Western academy. As has often been noted, the increased influence of Marxism in Western Europe had a big impact in Latin America because a considerable number of young European Catholics went as priests or religious to Latin America during that period.

The kind of intellectual Marxism which was diffused in the West and other noncommunist parts of the world at that time had two main strands. On the one hand, there was a kind of *cultural* Marxism, which drew upon Hegelian aspects of Marxist thought, articulated some of the ideas of the neo-Marxist Frankfurt school of social theory, and involved interest in the work of Gramsci with respect to the idea of cultural hegemony and the claim that religion is a form of politics. Needless to say, such orientations have fitted rather neatly into contexts where religious culture appears to be a stumbling block with respect to progressive societal change. On the other hand, some of the Marxism which began to develop outside of Soviet-type communist contexts has been, at the other extreme, *economistic* in its tendency. I speak of dependence and dependency theories, which were to a considerable extent Latin American in origin, but which nonetheless stand within the Trotskyist stream of Marxist thought when taken to their logical conclusion, as they were in North American world-system theory. By this I mean that, in attributing the internal condition and global politicoeconomic position of a society to the operation of the worldwide economic system, such theories deny the possibility of "socialism in one country"; they reject the idea of relatively autonomous societal change or "modernization."

It is rather obvious why such perspectives have taken hold so strongly in various parts of the Third World, and most firmly in Latin America. Beyond the obvious it should be said that these analytical and ideological tendencies, when taken together with other mid-twentieth-century turns in Western social science—such as the heightening of interest in hermeneutics (itself largely a consequence of the relativization of traditions and cultures) and the idea that social reality is largely *constructed*—have had a great appeal among intellectual and ideological elites in much of the Third World. They appear to provide accounts of both the material impoverishment of most third world societies and the cultural circumstances which sustain them. Recent social science theories provide ways of making sense of the often bewildering variety of religious, political, and politicoreligious views in the contemporary world. More particularly, the kind of secular thought (most of it North American or West European in origin) upon which liberation theology has drawn provides simultaneously and paradoxically both deterministic accounts of Third World circumstances and voluntaristic programs for surmounting those circumstances.

The realization among Third World Christian elites (there are now more Christians in the Third World than in North America and Europe combined[13]) that their Christianity has been heavily conditioned by extraneous circumstances has much to do with their search for and acceptance of "explanatory" and praxiological ideas. At one and the same time this tendency manifests secularizing and desecularizing tendencies—in my view making much of the debate about secularization in the conventional Western sense almost redundant. Meaning and power—primordially united, but "officially" disconnected in much of the world during the present century—are, whether we like it or not, being reunited, particularly in the Third World. On the other hand, the Third World is a category of decreasing relevance insofar as the newly industrialized countries are growing in number in Asia and, to a lesser degree, in Latin America. That development has implications which cannot be explored here.

THE POLITICAL THEMATIZATION
OF LIBERATION THEOLOGY

Much of the external discussion of Latin American liberation theology involves, as I have said, critical engagement with the writings of prominent intellectual producers and advocates of that mode of thought. Very little, on the other hand, has been done to assess the strength of liberation theology as a movement and its actual consequences. In fact, discourse about liberation theology rests in large part on an ironic "agreement" between pro-liberationists and anti-liberationists that liberation theology is a strong and growing movement—at least in Latin America. From a sociological point of view the circumstances of that agreement—specifically, the manner in which Latin American liberation theology has been thematized in a highly political form —are crucial, not least because from the sociological observer's standpoint neither group has produced much evidence to substantiate its claims concerning the strength and importance of liberation theology. Sociological skepticism about pro- and anti-liberationist claims concerning the strength of liberationism in Latin America does not, however, require an adamant denial of them. All that it does is to draw attention to the lack or misleading use of evidence and require consideration of the interests producing *the claim* that liberation is a formidable phenomenon.

One of the ways in which both sides of the conflict over Latin American liberation theology—but particularly the pro-liberationists —have tried to exhibit the strength of liberationism is by pointing to the rapid growth of the Christian base communities as carriers of a radical message, engaged in what some liberationists themselves freely call "subversive activity." Typically, writers on the base communities (CEBs) "estimate" there are so many hundreds of thousands of base communities in Latin America, implying (correctly) that we have very little idea how many there are. (There does appear to be rather firm evidence that the majority of them are in Brazil.) More important, the claim made by many writers that the base communities are overwhelmingly vehicles of liberation theology is, at best, misleading given their apparent heterogeneity with respect to purpose, activity, size, and survival. In fact, the few clear-cut examples of CEBs' playing the kind of role which both protagonists and antagonists of liberation theology have attributed to them are mainly in Central America, the most frequently cited case being the Christian community at Solentiname in southern Nicaragua. That community was founded by Ernesto Cardenal in the mid-1960s and did play a significant supporting role in the Nicaraguan revolution of 1979—along with Cardenal himself, who, among other priests, subsequently joined the Sandinista government.[14] (Solentiname has by now acquired great symbolic status among both proponents and opponents of liberation theology.) However, we simply do not have much idea as to the overall extent of base-community liberationism in Latin America. Certainly it is not likely that the CEB phenomenon is of greater long-term significance than the remarkable surge of Protestant evangelicalism in Brazil and elsewhere.

What seems to have brought the question of the political significance of Latin American liberation theology to prominence, what has led to the insertion of liberation theology into ideological debate in the United States, is the controversy about the Sandinista regime in Nicaragua. Indeed, many on both sides of the debate about liberation theology have helped to establish the idea that Nicaragua since 1979 constitutes a test case for liberation theology. Contra supporters perceive the survival of the Sandinista regime as an example of the implications of liberation theology, while many American adherents to liberation theology consider that regime to be worthy of religious legitimation or, at least, defense against the Contras and their American supporters. Thus "the political problem" of Latin American liberation theology has been partly produced by an ideological conflict *within* the United States concerning Nicaragua.

To put the matter even more sharply in perspective, it should be said that the visibility which Latin American liberation theology has attained in the United States is, in large part, due to the extensive promotion of the writings of a small number of Latin American intellectuals by Orbis Books, the publishing arm of the Maryknoll order. While liberationism has undoubtedly had considerable impact on the Catholic church in Latin America (and thus also on the Roman Catholic church generally) and certainly cannot be dismissed as an insignificant phenomenon, there is much to be said for the view that its general political significance has been greatly exaggerated— a circumstance which itself deserves much more discussion.

NOTES

1. I have, on the other hand, done some of that in my essay, "Liberation Theology in Latin America: Sociological Problems of Interpretation and Explanation," in *Prophetic Religion and Politics* ed. Jeffrey K. Hadden and Anton Shupe (New York: Paragon House, 1986), pp. 73–102.

2. I discuss this phenomenon in "Global Aspects of the Contemporary Politicization of Religion," in *The Changing Face of Religion,* ed. James Beckford and Thomas Luckmann (London and Beverly Hills, Calif.: Sage Publications, 1988).

3. Roland Robertson, "Latin America and Liberation Theology," in *Church-State Relations: Tensions and Transitions,* ed. Thomas Robbins and Roland Robertson (New Brunswick, N.J.: Transaction Books, 1987), pp. 217–18. For a more comprehensive characterization see my "Liberation Theology in Latin America: Sociological Problems of Interpretation and Explanation."

4. See Enrique Dussel, *History and the Theology of Liberation,* trans. John Drury (Maryknoll, N.Y.: Orbis Books, 1976). See also Larry Rohter, "Southern Summit Rekindles Old Dreams of Latin Unity," *New York Times* (November 29, 1987): E, 3, for discussion of some of the roots of modern Pan Latin Americanism.

5. Seymour Martin Lipset, *The First New Nation: The United States in Historical and Comparative Perspective* (London: Heinemann, 1963).

6. I cannot enter here into detailed substantiation of this claim. See Alan Neely, "Liberation Theology in Latin America: Antecedents and Autochthony," *Missiology: An International Review* 6, 3 (1978): 343–69. See also Edward Norman, *Christianity in the Southern Hemisphere* (Oxford: Clarendon Press, 1981).

7. Adrian Hastings, "Christianity in Sub-Saharan Africa," in *The Encyclopedia of Religion,* vol. 3, ed. Mircea Eliade et al. (New York: Macmillan Publishing Company, 1987), p. 411.

8. Christianity has considerable continuity with Korean folk religion and its populist tendencies. Minjung theology is a kind of South Korean equivalent of liberation theology. For South Korean attitudes

towards liberation theology see Korean Theologians, "Reflections by Korean Theologians on the Final Statement," in *Asia's Struggle for Full Humanity,* ed. Virginia Fabella (Maryknoll, N.Y.: Orbis Books, 1980), pp. 167–70.

9. I am omitting from my discussion the Middle Eastern (as well as the Soviet) portions of Asia—which relieves me of the great problem of discussing whether Shi'ite and other militant branches of contemporary Islam are to be considered as distant "cousins" of liberation theology. (Certainly, the early part of the speech of the president of Iran to the United Nations General Assembly on September 22, 1987, was couched very much in the language of popular-religious liberationism.) In turn I avoid in the present context consideration of the degree to which Christian liberation theology is a form of fundamentalism.

10. See, for example, Gonzalo Castillo-Cardenas, *Liberation Theology from Below: The Life and Thought of Manuel Quintim Lame* (Maryknoll, N.Y.: Orbis Books, 1987).

11. Virginia Fabella, "Introduction," in *Asia's Struggle for Full Humanity,* p. 4.

12. Attributed to Saint-Simon and quoted in Emile Durkheim, *Socialism,* trans. Charlotte Sattler and ed. Alvin W. Gouldner (New York: Collier Books, 1962), p. 223.

13. See Harvey Cox's introduction to Fidel Castro, *Fidel and Religion,* trans. Cuban Center for Translation and Interpretation (New York: Simon and Schuster, 1987), pp. 11–27. I should also point out, as many others have, that Latin America may well soon become the dominant area in global Catholicism. Moreover, while there is a shortage of Catholic priests in the First World, there is a surfeit in the Third World. That should *not,* however, lead us into thinking that the arrival in Europe and North America—or, for that matter, in Latin America—of a growing number of African Catholic priests will amplify the liberation theological presence. There is much to suggest that the new generation of African priests and bishops is very *conservative.* This seems to be particularly true of Nigeria and Zaire, two of the major exporters of Catholic functionaries in recent years.

14. For discussion of the degree to which Cardenal's theology is representative of liberation theology in Nicaragua, see Donald C. Hodges, *Intellectual Foundations of the Nicaraguan Revolution* (Austin: University of Texas Press, 1986), pp. 256–91.

6

Myths and Realities of Liberation Theology: The Case of Basic Christian Communities in Brazil

W. E. Hewitt

INTRODUCTION

One of the most discussed—yet least understood—developments within Latin American Catholicism in recent years is the phenomenon of the basic Christian communities or CEBs (*comunidades eclesiales* or *eclesiais de base*).[1] Owing to their reported ability to transform unjust social structures, these small faith-inspired circles, which proliferate primarily among the urban and rural lower classes, have attracted an unprecedented amount of attention from within the ranks of social scientists and religious personnel alike. What the CEBs have to offer to these and other interested observers, it would appear, is a unique and irresistible opportunity to witness firsthand the societally transforming potential of religion in a concrete setting.

For Roman Catholic liberation theologians, in particular, whose work on the groups has long dominated the literature, the CEBs possess a special relevance within church and secular realms. Most often, the groups are cited as "proof" of the liberationist perspective itself; that is, as evidence that the long-gestating radicalism of the masses, operating within a religious context, has finally reached the surface of Latin American society. As the prinicipal carriers of this revolutionary fervor, the CEBs, liberation theologians claim, will ultimately bring about the people's total emancipation from centuries-old social, economic, political, and even religious oppression.

Much of liberationist analysis, however, is without solid empirical grounding. In place of standard investigative techniques, most studies of the genre rely heavily upon the highly subjective, personal accounts of individual priests, nuns, or laypersons working intimately with the CEBs. Overall, moreover, the work appears to be as much oriented toward promoting the groups as toward objectively describing them.

Such methodological imprecision and open bias have, not surprisingly, prompted many over the years to voice certain concerns about the validity of liberationist findings where the CEBs are concerned. Yet it is only quite recently, with the publication of social scientific research on the phenomenon, that the very real limitations of the liberationist approach have been fully exposed. Briefly stated, these more recent studies—while concurring with the notion that the groups do indeed have an important role to play in Latin American society—reveal the CEBs' societal impact to be far more subtle, indirect, and multifaceted than liberationism has envisioned.

In this paper we undertake to summarize the results of one such social scientific study dealing with CEBs in one specific country, Brazil—a nation of some 135 million which is home to the largest concentration of base communities in Latin America. The empirical findings presented offer a challenge to liberationist assumptions about the CEBs in a number of key respects related to their origins, activities, internal organization, sociopolitical implications, and future prospects. In addition, the data shed new light on the role of leadership within the groups. While liberationists have tended to downplay this factor, the more recent research we cite shows the quality of leadership to be of prime importance to a complete understanding of the CEBs' essential character and orientation.

The study to which we refer was conducted by the author in 1981 in the Archdiocese of São Paulo, an ecclesiastical unit of some eleven million inhabitants located in southeastern Brazil. Over a period of six months, detailed information on CEB activities and organization was obtained from a sample of twenty-two groups chosen from a wide range of social and geographic settings. These data were collected from a variety of sources at the institutional church and CEB level using informal interviews, self-administered questionnaires, and participant observation.

Prior to discussing the findings of this research and their significance for the liberationist perspective, however, it will be useful to provide some background on the CEB phenomenon as it exists today in Brazil.

THE CEB PHENOMENON IN BRAZIL

Information about the physical extent of CEB penetration in Brazil is extremely difficult to obtain and inherently unreliable. Most informal estimates, however, would put the number of CEBs operating in the country at somewhere between seventy and eighty thousand[2]—a figure which, in all probability, would account for at least half to three-quarters of all base communities now in existence in Latin America.[3] Membership figures, where these are offered, tend to be mere projections based on the total number of groups. Using a base of forty to fifty, some have suggested, for example, that there are anywhere from two to four million Brazilians presently involved in CEB activities.[4] Most of these, it is further held, are drawn from the rural and semi-urban lower classes in the central-west, northeast, and southeast regions of the country.[5]

Such lack of precision surrounding the CEBs' demographic profile extends as well to the ways in which they are defined. Certainly as yet there has emerged no one generic description of the groups which has found widespread acceptance among CEB analysts. In official church documents, the groups are routinely defined by breaking the term CEB (*comunidade eclesial de base*) into its constituent parts. Thus, for example, according to the National Conference of Brazilian Bishops (CNBB), the CEBs are *communities,* because they are composed of people who live in the same neighborhood; they are *ecclesial,* because their members belong to the universal Catholic church; and finally, they are *basic,* since their participants are ordinary lay people.[6] In still another account, provided by CEB analyst Mariano Baraglia, the groups are described in somewhat less formal terms.[7] According to this author, the CEBs should be conceptualized as small, freely forming associations of ordinary Catholics who meet on a regular basis to deepen their knowledge of the gospel, to reflect upon community needs and seek adequate solutions to those needs, to celebrate victories and share defeats together in the Eucharist, and to spread the word of God.

It is only, perhaps, with respect to the general historical conditions which have helped facilitate CEB emergence and growth that there has existed any measure of consensus (albeit fragile) among students of the groups.[8] According to most reliable accounts, the CEBs appeared about twenty to thirty years ago, coinciding with a unique conjuncture of both religious and political circumstances. On the one hand, most CEB analysts point to the universal church's postwar move to greater emphasis on lay group formation—often through the promotion of Catholic Action cells—as offering the incipient thrust to CEB activation. This initial push, it is further held, was reinforced by pronouncements emanating from two important sources: the Second Vatican Council (1962–1965) and the 1968 Latin American bishops' meetings in Medellín, Colombia. On the other hand, CEB watchers also point to the sense of urgency lent CEB formation by increased social, political, and economic repression occurring in the wake of Brazil's 1964 military coup. Under the watchful eye of an increasingly activist church, they argue, the CEBs effectively offered the poor and oppressed a protected political space from which they could actively challenge the arbitrary policies of the newly implanted military regime.

THEORETICAL INTERPRETATIONS OF THE CEBs' CURRENT SOCIETAL ROLE

To date, the CEB literature originating in Brazil and elsewhere has been dominated by Catholic priests, theologians, and active laypersons with strong liberationist sympathies. For the most part, these individuals have tended to interpret the CEBs' current role in Brazilian society as part and parcel of a popular reaction to historic social injustice. According to Gutiérrez[9] and Dussel,[10] for example, the CEBs must be seen as a class-rooted and class-oriented phenomenon through which the poor are shaping their struggle for liberation from the tyranny of centuries-old social, economic, and political oppression. Similarly, for others such as Barreiro[11] and Boff,[12] the CEBs are the leading edge of a newly renovated church, and through their evangelizing practices are stimulating the *conscientização* (political awakening) of the lower classes. This in turn, they claim, will result in the birth of a new social order in Brazil.

In practical terms, the societal transformation envisioned by these and other authors begins as the CEBs assume "responsibility for matters ranging from 'aid to the needy, to...greater problems, such as labor unions and land.' "[13] "The quest for a new world," states Betto, for example, is only really initiated as the people of the CEBs undertake "concrete actions, arising from their immediate interests."[14] Such actions, he adds, may range from fighting city hall for running water, to lobbying politicians to control the rising cost of living.

From these beginnings, and as a direct consequence of "the form in which they organize themselves, divide tasks, and internally democratize power," the groups ultimately, Boff affirms, "establish the miniature model of a new society."[15] This new social order, he further maintains, will be opposed to bourgeois principles, and will instead incorporate the values of the kingdom of heaven. Concurring with this forecast, Betto as well sees the CEB-inspired society to come as one which will be "popular, democratic, [and] socialist."[16]

A major assumption which presents itself again and again in these accounts is that the CEBs represent a rather homogeneously structured collectivity, uniformly oriented towards radical social change. This homogeneity of form and action envisioned by liberationists is ostensibly related to the experience of poverty endured by ordinary CEB members who, over time, learn to use their faith to deal with the reality of oppression.

Recent research reveals, however, a much more heterogeneous CEB phenomenon, in terms of form and aim, than that portrayed in the literature to date. Moreover, it would appear that the class-related factors cited by liberationists as essential for CEB activation play only a secondary role in determining what the groups are and do. The common denominator linking the CEBs which empirical analysis shows to be of major consequence in this regard is related to the quality of church-based leadership exercised within specific groups.

Before we consider the precise impact of this variable, though, let us first examine in detail the exact extent of CEB heterogeneity revealed by the data with respect to the groups' basic features, activities, and organization.

HETEROGENEITY OF CEB FORM

One of the most elementary ways in which CEB heterogeneity manifests itself is in the great variety of background characteristics displayed by the groups. To begin with, the CEBs are not, as the liberationist literature has so often suggested, exclusively lower class. While surveys done by both the National Conference of Brazilian Bishops[17] and Afonso Gregory[18] affirm that the bulk of Brazilian CEBs are formed among the rural and semi-urban poor, both also indicate that a sizable minority can be found in strictly urban areas, the preserve of the middle classes. In the bishops' study, 17 percent of CEBs polled were situated in urban residential areas, while the figure for the Gregory report is about 9 percent. Bruneau as well, in his 1982 study of Catholic lay groups in Brazil, concludes that the CEBs were not exclusively communities of the poor and oppressed. As a strategy, claims Bruneau, the CEBs relate to all social classes.[19]

These early findings with respect to social class are confirmed by our own study of CEBs in the Archdiocese of São Paulo. As table 1 shows, the social location of the basic communities chosen for analysis is extremely diverse, with groups located in every possible type of setting, from well-manicured middle-class neighborhoods to *favelas* (slums) on the outskirts of the city.[20]

Area	Number of CEBs (n=22)
Upper Middle Class	3
Middle Class	8
Working Class	8
Favela or Cortico	3

Table 1. Social Location of Sample CEBs

The sample demonstrates a high degree of CEB heterogeneity in other respects as well, such as group maturity, size, and age of members. Group ages, for instance, as summarized in table 2, range anywhere from one to seventeen years, while the number of participants in each group varies from five to fifty. In addition, though females and older people are dominant within many groups, different CEBs do, nevertheless, tend to attract different proportions of the two constituencies. And, finally, the sample data reveal a relatively high level of fluidity within CEBs. This is evidenced by a high degree of turnover especially within more mature groups. Though table 2 shows at least eight groups aged nine to seventeen years, only one or two CEB members indicated on questionnaires that they had been affiliated with their group for more than seven years.

Characteristic	Number of CEBs (n=22)
Group Age	
0–3 years	8
4–8	6
9–17	8
Group size	
5–15 members	9
16–30	8
31–50	5
Sex Ratio	
Predominantly female (over 60%)	14
Even	6
Predominantly male (over 60%)	2
Members' mean age	
Under 40	6
Over 40	16

Table 2. Basic Features of Sample CEBs

DIVERSITY IN CEB ACTIVITIES AND ORGANIZATION

Such diversity of background features is reflected as well in the kinds of activities which the CEBs undertake and the organizational systems they have developed in support of these. Rather than pursuing a limited range of societally transforming activities, as the liberationist literature seems to suggest, in actuality the CEBs engage in an almost limitless array of religious and political functions operationalized through a variety of means. Contrary to the view implicit within liberationism, moreover, this constellation of activities and organizational structures adopted by individual CEBs appears to bear little relationship to the class origins of group members or the length of time which they have had to confront the social or political "realities" of their situation.

The principal activities in which our sample CEBs are engaged can be grouped into two broad categories. The first group consists of the more traditional functions of a kind which have been historically practiced in Catholic lay groups. These would include: (1) Bible study (in the strict interpretive sense), (2) charity work, and (3) the planning of festive occasions to mark holy days. Secondly, there are the more innovative activities which have largely appeared in the wake of Vatican II and have come to be synonymous with the CEB phenomenon in Brazil. Such functions, which possess significant political implications for both the church and Brazilian society generally, include: (1) the preparation and offering (often by lay ministers) of local religious services known as *celebrações*, (2) preparation for, and offering of, certain other sacraments (baptism in particular), (3) reflection and discussion where CEB members critically discuss biblical teaching in light of the existing social reality, (4) political consciousness-raising (designed to awaken the local citizenry to the reality of social, economic, and political oppression), and finally (5) community action projects. This last innovative activity is perhaps the most politically explicit function which the CEBs have adopted. In lower-class, semi-urban or rural areas, the community projects are normally designed to secure basic services, infrastructural improvements, or legal land title for residents. In more affluent urban neighborhoods, where local needs are obviously somewhat different, community action usually takes a less dramatic form, involving perhaps *mutirões* (joint-labor initiatives), neighborhood crime watches, food cooperatives, or CEB promotion in adjacent slum areas.

The organizational structures which the CEBs have adopted are almost as varied as the activities they are intended to support. With respect to the structure of group leadership, first of all, a number of options exist. Some CEBs are simply directed by individual lay leaders or *pastoral agents* dispatched by the church. Others maintain lay-run *conselhos* (councils) which are either elected or volunteer-based. Furthermore, depending upon the complexity, type, and the number of activities undertaken, groups may or may not maintain auxiliary subgroups or teams which are given responsibility for coordinating specific functions or facilitating these functions in a more intimate setting. CEBs which emphasize religious functions also often possess their own locally trained lay ministers. Even the range of CEB meeting times and places is quite varied. Some CEBs meet once a week, others less frequently; some meet in members' homes, some in church basements, and still others in their own locally constructed community centers.

Based upon the various combinations of activities and organizational forms present within the sample groups, one may, for purposes of analysis, construct a number of CEB types or categories. Elsewhere,[21] we have delineated and described in detail some six types, ranging from simple devotional groups (type I) which, operating out of members' own homes, practice basic religious functions such as Bible reading and charity work with a minimum of fanfare, to classical or ideal typical CEBs (type VI) which possess their own community centers, are run by elected *conselhos,* and are regularly involved in an intricately organized web of complex religious and advanced political activities. A summary of these types and their basic attributes is presented below in chart 1.

The very existence of such a typology is sufficient to negate the portrait of CEB homogeneity painted by the liberationists. Further, however, it serves as a useful tool for dispelling corollary assumptions of this religious current which link social class and CEB maturity to a supposed tendency within the CEBs for political progressiveness. There is simply no evidence provided by the data to suggest, for example, that the ranks of the most advanced CEBs are open only to groups of lower-class origin. Nor is it evident that the CEBs move through a kind of staging process, where, seasoned by the hardships of confronting their social and political reality, they eventually reach advanced levels of political engagement.

These assertions can be effectively substantiated by breaking down each of the CEB types by social location and age, as has been done in table 3. With respect to social location, first of all, the table reveals that both lower- and middle-class groups are capable of adopting a variety of forms. Certainly, it *is* true that some CEB types tend to occur more frequently in certain settings. For example, CEBs of types III, IV, and V tend to be more popular within middle-class areas, while the most advanced CEBs of type VI are exclusively lower class. Nevertheless, before drawing conclusions from this finding, two observations must be made.

Feature	CEB Category					
	I (n=5)	II (n=1)	III (n=4)	IV (n=5)	V (n=1)	VI (n=6)
Traditional activities						
Charity work	❖	❖	❖	❖		❖
Bible study	❖	❖	❖	❖		❖
Festive days	❖	❖	❖	❖		❖
Innovative activities						
Preparation and offering						
of *celebrações*		❖		❖		❖
of other sacraments		❖		❖		❖
Reflection and discussion		❖		❖		❖
Political consiousness-raising			❖	❖	❖	❖
Basic community action				❖		
Advanced community action					❖	❖
Organizational features						
Functional subgroups		❖		❖	❖	❖
Conselho		❖		❖	❖	❖
Lay ministers		❖		❖	❖	❖
Meet in community center		❖		❖	❖	❖

Notes:
❖ Indicates presence of feature in question
Designated names of CEB types are as follows:
I—Simple Devotional   II—Devotional Mini-Parish
III—Elementary Devotional/Political   IV—Politically Oriented Mini-Parish
V—Politically Oriented Missionary   V—Classical or Ideal-Typical

Chart 1. Typology of CEBs

Feature	CEB Category					
	I (n=5)	II (n=1)	III (n=4)	IV (n=5)	V (n=1)	VI (n=6)
Social location						
Lower class	3	1	1	–	–	6
Middle class	2	–	3	5	1	–
Group age						
Under 5 years	3	–	1	1	–	4
Over 5 years	2	1	3	4	1	2

Designated names of CEB types are as follows:
I—Simple Devotional   II—Devotional Mini-Parish
III—Elementary Devotional/Political   IV—Politically Oriented Mini-Parish
V—Politically Oriented Missionary   V—Classical or Ideal-Typical

Table 3. Social Location and Age of CEB Types

First, the table shows that within the more politically advanced types generally (IV to VI), lower- and middle-class groups are almost equally represented. It might be pointed out here, as well, that the predominantly middle-class CEBs of type IV differ from type VI CEBs only with respect to the quality of the political activity which is undertaken. Where type IV CEBs engage in community service activities, type VI groups are active in projects designed to improve the local infrastructure. These two types of activities, though not of equal intensity, are not entirely dissimilar either. Rather, they should be seen as simply appropriate to the social setting in which they are undertaken.

Second, it should be noted that there exists a clear tendency for the lower-class groups to adopt more *primitive* forms (types I and II) than their middle-class counterparts. Just as the less affluent CEBs have no monopoly on organizational complexity and political involvement, so too, consequently, are they not excluded from the ranks of the simpler CEBs.

As in the case of social class, group age, which reflects the length of time which a CEB has had to interact with the environment, also has no apparent effect on politicization and organizational development. Newer

CEBs, table 3 shows, are just as likely as older ones to adopt more advanced, or conversely, more elementary forms.

THE IMPORTANCE OF LEADERSHIP FOR CEB ACTIVATION

The apparent absence of any profound impact of variables such as social class or group age on the emergence of various CEB types does not mean that there are no constants which delimit or explain what activities or organizational forms which individual CEBs will adopt. In fact, the sample data reveal at least one variable which does consistently emerge as a reasonably reliable predictor of what the CEBs are and do. That factor is related to the quality of leadership present within the CEBs. Often, this leadership originates at the level of the institutional church, which sets policy for CEB formation and action, but also tends to exhibit itself rather succinctly through the actions of institutionally dispatched pastoral agents who operate at the local level.

As we suggested earlier, the liberationist perspective, for the most part, tends to stress the spontaneity and inherent democratic character of the CEBs. The groups, according to this view, are born of a popular desire for liberation, and in them the people work in unison for total emancipation. External activists, be they the bishops or their designated agents (who most often are recruited from within the ranks of the middle classes), act as mere advisers, helping only to guide the people's own emergent political consciousness. Borrowing a term from Italian neo-Marxist Antonio Gramsci, Clodovis Boff has described such individuals as "organic intellectuals" who aid—but do not directly excite—the revolutionary potential of the popular will in specific sociohistorical contexts.[22]

The Gramscian approach to CEB activation has been lent further credence in recent works by North American students of the Brazilian church such as Adriance,[23] and to a lesser extent, Mainwaring.[24] While recognizing the currently powerful role played by the institutional church or its agents in encouraging the CEB phenomenon, they nevertheless tend to emphasize the importance of the people's own desire for change in oppressive situations as the indispensable factor both for CEB activation directly and for the establishment of official policy supporting it.

Other analysts, such as Bruneau, have dealt with the leadership issue in a somewhat different fashion. He sees CEB promotion generally as part of a strategy of influence orchestrated by the elite of the institutional church.

In response to the Brazilian reality of political repression, blatant social inequality, and competition from other value movements—all of which has contributed to a diminution of its religious authority—the Brazilian church, claims Bruneau, has sought to encourage the CEBs (along with other innovations) to create a new and more just society, in which Christianity will become more inherently meaningful.[25] According to this view, then, the bishops who set official policy are the authors of a blueprint for societal transformation designed to restore institutional relevance or influence. The pastoral agents for their part (and indeed many of the liberationists) are the "foot soldiers" of this movement; their attempts to stimulate and enhance the CEB phenomenon are part of overall church strategy.

The portrait of church personnel involved with CEB promotion which Bruneau establishes thus negates the Gramscian "organic intellectual" conception promoted by Clodovis Boff and others. Rather, these individuals are highly reminiscent of Weber's "civic strata" who, because of their urban locus and orientation to production and trade, have served throughout history as the principal carriers of new religious ideas stressing action in this world.[26]

Bruneau has backed up his claims with respect to the elite-orchestrated operationalization of church strategy, by providing survey data which show that the CEBs tend to arise mainly where the local bishop is favorable to their presence. Conversely, where the local hierarchy is not disposed to the phenomenon, Bruneau claims, the groups remain dormant.[27] Similar findings were reported in a 1981 CNBB-sponsored research report. In this study, the authors noted a direct link between the emergence of CEBs and institutional planning. "In those regions," stated the report, "where there exists a Joint Pastoral Plan in which the [base] community line is defined as a priority task, the CEBs encounter a very favorable climate for their emergence and growth."[28]

Certainly São Paulo, where the CEBs are currently flourishing, falls squarely into the "favorable climate" category. Since the early 1970s, when CEB formation was first designated as one of four top-priority areas in official archdiocesan pastoral plans, the number of groups has grown from a mere handful to over eight hundred.[29] Much of this success is attributable to the church's practice of dispatching younger, ostensibly more politically progressive pastoral agents to promote CEB development in predominantly lower-class target areas located for the most part on São Paulo's urban periphery.

At the local level, the effectiveness of this strategy is clearly demonstrated in a parish-by-parish analysis conducted by the author as part of the 1984 CEB study, which shows a respectable correlation (r=.377) between presence of youthful pastors and group density.[30] The study also revealed that most priests and nuns involved with the groups clearly perceived their role as that of "agents" for the implementation of church policy, as opposed to "organic intellectuals" in the Gramscian sense. For example, of twenty pastoral agents surveyed, all but two expressed total agreement with the church's current policy of elite-directed CEB formation, while fourteen affirmed the necessity of close and continuing ecclesiastical supervision of the CEBs.[31] Some of these same individuals, it might be noted as well, tended to undertake their role a little too zealously—to the point of inciting a good deal of hostility among a somewhat overwhelmed CEB membership.[32]

Strong linkages between the institutional church and base community activation are similarly revealed by certain features and activities of the sample CEBs discussed earlier. As table 4 shows, there can in fact be little question that the CEBs are firmly a part of ecclesiastical structure and fall squarely under the authority of religious personnel. For example, while admittedly only a slim majority regularly sends representatives to institutionally sponsored CEB conferences or use church-prepared liturgical or discussion aids, fully seventeen of twenty-two groups maintain normal and frequent contact with various other parish groups. Also noteworthy is the fact that some sixteen of the CEBs owe their very existence to the active involvement of church-dispatched priests or nuns.

Type of Linkage	Number of CEBs (n=22)
Send representatives to CEB-related conferences	12
Use official liturgical or discussion aids	13
Maintain regular contact with other parish groups	17
Priests or nuns involved in group formation process	16

Table 4. CEB Linkages to Institutional Church

Perhaps most importantly of all, the sample data reveal a definite association between the continued presence of pastoral agents and various aspects of group life. The precise nature of this relationship is represented in table 5. Here we have broken down the CEB types delimited previously by the quality of pastoral agents' presence. The political orientation of religious personnel and the degree to which they spent time in individual CEBs were determined through interviews and participant observation. Priests and nuns designated as progressive were those who generally upheld the church's "option for the poor" and the political role of the CEBs, while those deemed traditional tended to avoid political or class-related themes. To be designated directly present, religious personnel had actively to serve their CEB in a leadership capacity.

	CEB Category					
	I	**II**	**III**	**IV**	**V**	**VI**
Quality of Leadership	(n=5)	(n=1)	(n=4)	(n=5)	(n=1)	(n=6)
Pastoral agent directly present and politically oriented	1	–	–	–	1	4
Pastoral agent not present and/or not politically oriented	4	1	4	5	–	2

Designated names of CEB types are as follows:
I—Simple Devotional   II—Devotional Mini-Parish
III—Elementary Devotional/Political   IV—Politically Oriented Mini-Parish
V—Politically Oriented Missionary   V—Classical or Ideal-Typical

Table 5. Effect of Leadership on CEB Type

What table 5 indicates is that group type complexity is directly and positively linked to the presence of church representatives active in a leadership capacity. Among the more basic group types (I to III), first of all, politically active pastoral agents are all but nonexistent. At the other end of the scale, where the more advanced group types (IV to VI) are concerned, the situation is slightly more complex, yet consistent with the general pattern. Pastoral agents, while not present in type IV groups— which in any case tend to undertake more basic forms of political activity—are rarely absent in types V and VI, which engage in the most explicit forms of community action.

Not only, then, does the institutional church exert considerable influence over when, where, and how the groups will emerge, it has a good deal of input—through the manner in which pastoral agents are selected, trained, and dispatched—in the determination of the organizational structure and activity profile of individual CEBs.

SOCIOPOLITICAL IMPLICATIONS OF THE CEBs

In pointing to the strength of such ties between the institutional church and the CEBs, it is not our intention to imply that the groups are mere puppet organizations. Certainly, lay members are able to exercise a certain amount of control (within ecclesiastically approved guidelines) in matters affecting the direction and organization of their group and in fact are strongly encouraged to do so. At times, differing visions held by pastoral agents and the membership with respect to what the CEBs should be and do has even created a good deal of hostility between the two constituencies.[33]

Nor do we wish to suggest that ecclesiastical control left the CEBs devoid of any authentic or lasting sociopolitical significance. The truth is that the CEBs do have very important implications both for the lives of their members and for Brazilian society generally. However, we would argue that such consequences are much less immediate or obvious than those envisioned by liberation theologians.

The primary benefit of the CEBs, in our view, is the contribution which they make to the establishment of a sense of citizenship, especially among lower-class participants. Long enveloped in the patron-client mentality which has traditionally defined class relations in Brazilian society, the poor through the CEBs are for the first time cooperating to create a world of their own making. In working together with pastoral agents to press local officials for sewers, streetlights, or land reform, they are learning that sometimes the best way to achieve their goals is not by appealing as individuals to omnipotent authorities, but by working together for the common good. They are developing, in other words, that spirit of "enlightened self-interest" which Tocqueville attributed to those proud and simple folk who laid the groundwork for America's political culture in the early nineteenth century.[34] And just as in the United States of Tocqueville's era, there is every chance that in Brazil the "enlightened self-interest" inspired in the CEBs will ultimately contribute, in some measure, to the emergence of a responsible, involved citizenry. This, in turn, may eventually help to create a stable democratic polity in which the majority of the Brazilian population (that is, the poor) truly participate for the first time.

Tentative evidence for this assessment of the CEBs' political impact lies in an anomaly of CEB growth and activation which is well known to church workers—the fact that the CEBs tend to multiply primarily among the more "affluent" poor, such as the urban working classes on the outskirts of São Paulo—among people, in other words, who in some ways closely resemble Tocqueville's early Americans.[35] These individuals may live in what many would call slum areas, yet they do own their land and homes and have thus achieved at least some measure of success in life. They see, moreover, the potential for achieving more, a potential which may be satisfied quite nicely through mutual cooperation in the CEBs. As many of the CEB members interviewed during the course of our research were quick to point out (and often to the dismay of more radical pastoral agents), working together for running water and garbage pick-up not only improves the look and the quality of the neighborhood, it serves as well to increase the value of one's own property![36]

By contrast with their better-off counterparts, the poorest of the poor (the residents of *favelas* or inner-city *pensões*) are rarely the successful targets of church-directed CEB promotion efforts. This, we would argue, can be attributed to the fact that such individuals often have little or no stake in their community, either because they plan to move on to a better life, or because they have lost all hope of ever resolving their predicament. Among individuals such as these, consequently, collective action as a form of "enlightened self-interest" makes little sense and offers few obvious or immediate benefits.

FUTURE PROSPECTS FOR THE BRAZILIAN CEBs

The changes which the CEBs are forging among at least some sectors of the population will likely not occur overnight. Rather, transformations in the popular psychology (which may come to be reflected in the sociopolitical structure of the nation) will occur only gradually. This will require, moreover, given what we now know of CEB growth patterns, a substantial and sustained commitment on the part of the church to preserve what gains have been made, and to bring the benefits of the groups to as many additional individuals as possible.

Whether, however, such church support for the CEBs will indeed be forthcoming as in the past is now open to question. To begin with, the Brazilian church appears of late to be moving away from promoting the CEBs per se as the principal instruments of social change. Instead, it now seems to be encouraging greater participation of CEB members in popular movements active within the secular sphere, such as trade unions and political parties.[37] This development may signal a change in church strategy, or may simply be a rationalization put forth by the hierarchy to account for a growing defection of CEB members to other popular movements within the secular sphere. Either way, the CEBs' this-worldly impact may be in process of diminution.

Second, in the course of Brazil's ongoing transition to democratic rule, the episcopate seems to be demonstrating an increasing lack of decisiveness with respect to the continued operationalization of the "preferential option for the poor," the major ideological force behind CEB formation. In the absence of any clear-cut antagonistic enemies of the people, the bishops appear to have lost their direction, pronouncing as much on newly liberalized sexual mores and family planning initiatives as criticizing the pace of social and political reform.[38]

And finally, there is evidence of a growing wave of conservatism within the Vatican, which may ultimately have a dramatic effect on all forms of social activism within the Brazilian church, including the CEBs. This development is signaled by recent warnings reportedly given liberationists such as Leonardo and Clodovis Boff to tone down the more radical aspects of their theology, by stepped-up vigilance over course content in the seminaries of more progressive archdioceses such as São Paulo, and by the recent appointment of more moderate clerics to diocesan posts.[39]

Whether recent events such as these are indicative of a long-term trend of dire consequence for the CEBs in Brazil remains to be seen. For now, certainly, the phenomenon continues to prosper, and reports of CEB involvement in various issues and causes continue to appear. Any assessment of permanent damage to the CEBs' mandate will require, consequently, longer-term study and evaluation.

NOTES

1. Spanish and Portuguese spellings, respectively.

2. See Thomas C. Bruneau, "Church and Politics in Brazil: The Genesis of Change," *Journal of Latin American Studies* 17 (1985): 271–93.

3. Author's estimate only. The precise number of basic communities operating in Latin America is not known, as few, if any, national churches have ever conducted an inventory of groups within their jurisdiction. See also, Thomas C. Bruneau, "Basic Christian Communities in Latin America" in *Churches and Politics in Latin America,* ed. Daniel H. Levine (Beverly Hills, Calif.: Sage Publishing Co., 1980), p. 225.

4. Irmão Michel, "Comunidades católicas de base são o fruto de colaboração entre duas classes sociais, a pobre e a média," *Revista Eclesiástica Brasileira* (hereafter *REB*) 42 (1982): 120.

5. Conferência Nacional dos Bispos do Brasil (hereafter CNBB), *Comunidades: Igreja na base* (São Paulo: Paulinas, 1977), pp. 20–21.

6. CNBB, *Comunidades eclesiais de base na igreja no Brasil* (São Paulo: Paulinas, 1983), pp. 13–14.

7. Mariano Baraglia, *Evolução das comunidades eclesiais de base* (Petrópolis: Vozes, 1974), p. 42.

8. Even here, however, disagreement frequently appears where the timing and impact of precipitating events are concerned.

9. Gustavo Gutiérrez, "The Irruption of the Poor in Latin America and the Christian Communities of the Common People," in *The Challenge of Basic Christian Communities,* ed. Sergio Torres and John Eagleson, trans. John Drury (Maryknoll, N.Y.: Orbis Books, 1981).

10. Enrique Dussel, "Current Events in Latin America," in *Basic Christian Communities*.

11. Alvaro Barreiro, *Basic Ecclesial Communities,* trans. Barbara Campbell (Maryknoll, N.Y.: Orbis Books, 1982).

12. Leonardo Boff, "Theological Characteristics of a Grassroots Church," in *Basic Christian Communities*.

13. Barreiro, *Basic Ecclesial Communities,* p. 58.

14. Frei Betto, *O que é comunidade eclesial de base?* (São Paulo: Brasiliense, 1981), p. 46 (author's translation).

15. Leonardo Boff, "CEBs: A igreja inteira na base," *REB* 43 (1983): 469 (author's translation).

16. Betto, "As comunidades eclesiais de base como potencial de transformação da sociedade brasileira," *REB* 43 (1983): 503 (author's translation).

17. CNBB, *Comunidades: Igreja na base,* pp. 20–21.

18. Afonso Gregory, "Dados préliminares sobre experiências de comunidades eclesiais de base no Brasil," in *Comunidades eclesiais de base: Utopia ou realidade?* ed. Afonso Gregory (Petrópolis: Vozes, 1973).

19. Thomas C. Bruneau, *The Church in Brazil* (Austin: University of Texas Press, 1982), p. 140.

20. Social location was determined with the aid of a homogeneous-area mapping scheme devised by the São Paulo state government. See W. E. Hewitt, "The Structure and Orientation of Comunidades Eclesiais de Base (CEBs) in the Archdiocese of São Paulo" (Ph.D. dissertation, McMaster University, 1985), chap. 3.

21. See W. E. Hewitt, "Basic Christian Communities (CEBs): Structure, Orientation and Sociopolitical Thrust," *Thought* (Special Edition, forthcoming); in a similar manner, Welsh has developed a number of CEB types based upon his experience with basic communities in São Paulo state. See John R. Welsh, "Comunidades Eclesiais de Base: A New Way to Be Church," *America* 8 (1986): 85–88.

22. Clodovis Boff, "Agente de pastoral e povo," *REB* 40 (1980): 216–41.

23. Madeleine Adriance, *Opting for the Poor: Brazilian Catholicism in Transition* (Kansas City: Sheed and Ward, 1986), pp. 106–25.

24. Scott Mainwaring, *The Catholic Church and Politics in Brazil, 1916–1985* (Stanford: Stanford University Press, 1986), pp. 14–17, chap. 9.

25. Thomas C. Bruneau, *The Political Transformation of the Brazilian Catholic Church* (London: Cambridge University Press, 1974).

26. H. H. Gerth and C. W. Mills, eds., *From Max Weber: Essays in Sociology* (New York: Oxford University Press, 1946), pp. 283–85.

27. Bruneau, *The Church in Brazil*, p. 109.

28. CNBB, *Comunidades eclesiais de base no Brasil* (São Paulo: Paulinas, 1981), p. 45 (author's translation).

29. See *3o Plano Bienal de Pastoral, 1981–1983* (São Paulo: Archdiocese of São Paulo, 1981); and *Guia geral da Arquidiocese de São Paulo* (São Paulo: Archdiocese of São Paulo, 1983).

30. Hewitt, "Structure and Orientation," pp. 117–18.

31. Ibid., pp. 104–6.

32. W. E. Hewitt, "Strategies for Social Change Employed by Comunidades Eclesiais de Base (CEBs) in the Archdiocese of São Paulo," *Journal for the Scientific Study of Religion* 25 (1986): 25.

33. Ibid., p. 25.

34. Alexis de Tocqueville, *Democracy in America,* Vol. 2 (New York: Vintage Books, 1945), chap. 8.

35. Hewitt, "Structure and Orientation," pp. 101, 241–43.

36. Hewitt, "Strategies for Social Change," p. 27.

37. This trend was, in fact, noted in the literature as early as 1980. See Thomas G. Sanders, "The Catholic Church in Brazil's Political Transition," *American Universities Field Staff Reports* 48 (1980).

38. W. E. Hewitt, "Whither Goeth the Option for the Poor in Brazilian Catholicism," paper presented at the Annual Meeting of the Society for the Scientific Study of Religion, Louisville, Kentucky, 31 October 1987.

39. See "Duplo castigo," *Veja,* 15 (May 1985): 67; "Vaticano observa seminários de SP," *Folha de São Paulo,* 30 May 1984, p. 6; "O pastor do planalto," *Isto É,* 2 May 1984, p. 44; and "Acerto em Roma," *Veja,* 19 March 1986, pp. 100–101; for a thorough overview of the entire process, see Mainwaring, *Catholic Church,* chap. 11.

7

Catholics
and the Marxist Left
in Latin America

Michael Fleet

During the last fifteen years large numbers of Latin American Christians have undergone political radicalization. This phenomenon has been closely associated with the propagation of liberation theologies and with active Christian involvement in "popular" social and political struggles.

Liberation theologies represent a new way of doing theology, one rooted in a prior commitment to the struggles of poor people and drawing on social science to approach the context in which they take place. These theologies vary in content. They are also embraced with varying degrees of consciousness and coherence by particular communities of Christians. Their relationship to the church, to the Christian community movement, and to Christian radicalization generally is conditioned by social forces and processes that vary according to country and sociopolitical contexts.

Diverse institutional interests, antagonisms, and responsibilities of church authorities, party officials, and labor and popular-sector leaders, for example, condition their reaction to theological currents. Grassroots leaders, activists, and followers, on the other hand, while less adept at theoretical or analytical matters, are likely to have fewer partisan or institutional encumbrances. Their experience with poverty, exploitation, and repression leads them almost reflexively to work together with others in similar circumstances. Liberation theologies do not determine social and political commitments, but they do help to reconcile such commitments with Christian faith.

At the core of Christian radicalization in virtually all instances have been improved relations between Christian and Marxist groups. In the past, strong anti-Marxist fears and sentiments had kept Christians from moving left despite the pull of other factors and forces. Of late, however, shared struggles under repressive authoritarian regimes have converted many Christian and Marxist antagonists into allies, although others continue to resist all suggestions of association, and even advocates of collaboration often disagree as to the form and direction it should take.

Recent scholarship has concentrated on liberation theology, on the politicizing of religiously based groups in authoritarian settings, and, somewhat tangentially, on Christian Democratic parties. Little work has been done on Christian-Marxist relations in individual countries or in comparative terms.

This essay looks at relations between Christians and Marxists in Brazil, Peru, and Chile over the past twenty-five years. It describes changes in orientations and relations during this period, attempts to characterize current positions and relations, and speculates as to what factors and forces might account for the several patterns that emerge.

THE HISTORICAL EXPERIENCES
Brazil

Progressive Brazilian Christians have pursued closer ties with the Marxist world for more than thirty years. During the 1960s Catholic university students and young Catholic workers rebelled against a still highly conservative Catholic hierarchy and aligned themselves with the historically weak Brazilian Left, adopting elements of Marxist analysis and strategy. In effect, they became "Christian Marxists." During the early years of military rule many were active in urban and rural guerrilla efforts.

Several things appear to have given rise to this radicalization. One was the string of economic failures experienced under the previous four administrations. Another was the generalized agitation and polarization during the Goulart period (1961–64). But of even greater importance were the absence of a solidly reformist Christian Democratic party and the hostility of most church authorities. The existence of a progressive Christian reform movement might have channelled student aspirations and impulses along more moderate lines. And a hierarchy less identified with the country's dominant economic and political elites might not have provoked them into challenging established structures and guidelines. In the absence of middle-of-the-road alternatives, however, radicalization may well have been inevitable.

With the 1964 coup, progressive Catholic activists became active in various resistance and guerrilla efforts. These were crushed with relative ease; most of the young radicals were arrested and either exiled or forced to abandon their political work. Between 1974 and 1982, however, they joined with Marxist and other "popular-sector" (that is, working class and slum dweller) forces in a movement that ultimately forced the military to relinquish power.

These ties between Christians and Marxists were never consolidated. With transition to civilian rule contacts between the two groups have diminished appreciably. Many progressive Christian activists and some Marxists have joined the *Partido dos Trabalhistas* (Workers' party, or PT), but so far have failed to develop a solid political base, even in the Christian communities with which they once worked. In fact, it seems that most "popular sector" Christians have supported candidates of the less progressive but more influential traditional parties.

Several factors account for the failure of radical Christians and Marxists to extend their political association. First, the would-be partners were robbed of their common enemy. Second, the clientelistic parties and party coalitions of the post-military period effectively monopolize political space and make it difficult for other political forces to gain a foothold. As a result, Christian, Christian-Marxist, and secular Marxist leaders who do not belong to one of the smaller, less important parties are either not active in party politics or form a minority left wing within one of the larger parties, where they must compete with very differently minded factions.

It is also clear, however, that Brazilian Christians and Marxists continue to harbor doubts regarding each other. On the Christian side, the typical member of a *comunidade eclesial de base* (CEB) is suspicious of party politics generally and of elite domination of social and political movements, particularly those of the Left. A few appear to recognize the need for strong political organization at the national level. But most "committed"

Christians distrust politics. They prefer to work in their own localities, with people and organizations they know, and in the language of their own tradition.

As for the Marxists, a majority of their intellectuals and activists continue to view religion in fairly orthodox terms. For most, religious sentiment is simply false consciousness, incompatible with the purposes of a revolutionary movement and a proper "object of struggle." More conciliatory spirits contend that attacking Christians for their "false consciousness" will simply strengthen reactionary elements and thereby dilute Christian support that is essential for the achievement of important social objectives. But even they concede that problems of compatibility exist over the long run.[1]

Instrumentalism of this sort does not sit well with rank-and-file Christians. Indeed, it heightens their fears of "being used" by others. Party and intellectual elites might value collaboration independently of the intentions for which it is entered into, but ordinary followers are less likely to do so.

Unless there are substantial changes in political context and attitudes, therefore, it seems unlikely that Christians and Marxists will be working together as such, although both may be found in movements and parties (such as the PT) that neither side controls but in which each can pursue its various objectives free of manipulation and contamination by the other.

Peru

In Peru relations between Christians and Marxists have developed furthest. There, an *Izquierda Unida* (IU) has brought together practicing Catholics, Marxists who no longer "believe" but who bear the imprint of an earlier Christian formation, and secular Marxists of varied orientations and backgrounds. It is presently the country's second political force behind the ruling American Revolutionary Popular Alliance (APRA), with an electoral following that has averaged over 30 percent of the national vote since 1978.

This success has been a function of social, demographic, and political factors unique to Peru. These include: (a) the crisis of Peru's political system during the 1960s and the consequent alienation and rapid radicalization of a new generation of political elites, (b) the inundation of Lima and other cities by poverty-stricken rural migrants available for social and political mobilization, (c) the reforms undertaken but subsequently scuttled or diluted under the Velasco government (1968–75), (d) church activities directed at the popular sector and capable of filling the social and political spaces created or permitted during this period, (e) the adoption by Catholic intellectuals and activists of elements of Marxist analysis (even as their faith and their ties to the church grew stronger), and (f) the absence of a Christian Democratic movement capable of attracting young Catholic elites and popular-sector Christians generally.

Historically the Peruvian Left has been small and the Catholic church conservative. During the 1960s and 1970s, however, oligarchic political institutions collapsed, the Cuban revolution emerged as a symbol and model for progressives, and "popular" elements grew more active and assertive within the church. As a result, a majority of the Peruvians coming of age politically during this period turned their backs on established institutions and organizations, and embraced ideologies and strategies calling for total transformation of society.

A few of these young radicals came from non-Christian families and backgrounds, that is, from public grammar schools, secondary schools, and universities like San Marcos. But most were graduates of Catholic high schools or the Pontifical Catholic University who had abandoned their faith during adolescence or later came to regard it as incompatible with revolutionary political commitment. These groups were highly critical of established parties and of the "excessively cautious" *Partido Comunista del Perú* in particular. Attracted to notions of revolutionary politics, armed struggle, and popular war, they were active in the *Vanguardia Revolucionaria* and other small Maoist groupings formed during the late 1960s.

A third group consisted of practicing Catholics who sought to reconcile their Christian and Marxist convictions. They were encouraged and sustained by Father Gustavo Gutiérrez, an advisor to the *Unión Nacional de Estudiantes Católicos* (UNEC), for whom faith and sociopolitical analysis formed complementary rather than competing dimensions ("planes") of human existence.[2] A few of these *unecos* joined the Peruvian Christian Democratic party (PDC), where they formed a vocal but ineffective left wing before leaving in 1971. Most, however, refused to have anything to do with the "timidly reformist" PDC, and either joined one of the new revolutionary organizations or chose not to become identified with any political party.

The radicalization of these activists was tempered by the crushing of the rural guerrilla insurgency in 1965 and by the coming to power in 1968 of a reformist military regime. The first of these events closed the door on armed struggle; the second cast reformism in a more promising light. Following Velasco's nationalization of the International Petroleum Company and implementation of agrarian reform, some radicals accepted posts in his government while others looked on with growing sympathy and expectation. Most, however, kept their distance, arguing that Velasco was no reformer or that reformism itself would be disastrous for the Peruvian people.

Progressive Catholics were among those accepting posts in Velasco's government. Most did not, however, preferring to collaborate in church-sponsored projects in the burgeoning Lima slums or in one of the recently established "alternative" research and promotional centers.[3] In either case they worked closely with priests, nuns, and laypersons in popular-sector programs, and soon became visible and admired fixtures in these communities.

Their activities frequently led to confrontations with government authorities, who found it difficult to accept criticism. The government's reformist initiatives and rhetoric had stimulated demands it was unable (or unwilling) to satisfy and spaces within which popular organizations were able to develop.

With the onset of economic difficulties in 1971, Velasco's government began to lose its reformist zeal. Along with other erstwhile supporters, Catholic intellectuals and activists gradually moved into opposition. Conflict increased steadily through 1975, when Velasco was overthrown by army General Morales Bermudez, whose more conservative and repressive policies led to a heightening of tensions. Priests, nuns, and grassroots activists led or joined with others (including Marxist groups) in protest marches, demonstrations, and strikes. Conditions rapidly assumed crisis proportions, and by the middle of 1977 the country had become ungovernable. At that point the military decided to return to its barracks, setting in motion a process of transition to democracy that would culminate in presidential and parliamentary elections in 1980.

Some on the Left were skeptical of these moves. They boycotted the constituent assembly elections of 1978 on grounds that they were simply an alternative means of detaining the popular movement. Most applauded the return of electoral politics, however. Many saw electoral work as useful, if not essential, in the building of a broader political base. Radical Catholics, most of whom considered themselves democratic socialists, defended elections in principle but were also clearly anxious to capitalize on their work in the popular sector.

The *Izquierda Unida* was launched in 1980 as an electoral coalition of Christian and Marxist groups. In the seven elections held since 1978, it has polled an average of 30 percent of the national vote. Its various internal factions remain divided on both strategic and programmatic questions, however; and at this point it is more a vehicle for registering protest than a viable political option in its own right.

It is difficult to estimate the relative strength of the IU's component elements. Several of its leading figures (former Lima mayor Alfonso Barrantes and the so-called independents, for example) are not affiliated with any particular party. Others, although identified with one of the two main component groups, the *Union de Izquierda Revolucionaria* (UNIR) and the *Partido Unificado Mariateguista* (PUM), belong to factions or tendencies (the *Movimiento de la Izquierda Revolucionaria* (MIR), the *Vanguardia Revolucionaria,* the *Bandera Roja-Trinchera Roja*, for example) that have their own, and in some cases highly sectarian, constituencies.

Independent Catholics such as Rolando Ames, Manuel Piqueras, Javier Iguíñiz, and Michel Ascueta have been closely identified with the church and its popular-sector work over the last fifteen years, and at some point might be able to put this to politically advantageous use.[4] But the Christians active in the new popular organizations are difficult to organize and mobilize politically. On the one hand, their desperate socioeconomic circumstances frequently oblige them to (re)turn to parties like APRA, for example, or to agencies which they have criticized in the past. At the same time, their moralistic style and orientation have bred in them a fundamentalist aversion to the kind of bargaining (with allies and adversaries) that the building of an effective political movement often requires.

Chile

In Chile, Christian-Marxist relations have been more conflictive than collaborative. Progressive Christians have been seeking closer ties with the Marxist Left for more than forty years but have been resisted by a powerful Christian Democratic party (of which some had been or still were members) and by communists and socialists primarily interested in absorbing Christians into their own partisan ranks.

The idea of a Christian-Marxist alliance has found echo since 1973 among Christian and Marxist workers, slum dwellers (*pobladores*), and students who, with parties at less than full strength, have found it easier to work together. It has also been endorsed by "renovated" Marxist intellectuals, and by some Marxist-Leninists who have overcome their former disdain for believers. But most party and organizational leaders, Christian and Marxist alike, cling to perspectives and strategies that exclude one another over the longer run.

Their failure to come to even minimal terms during the last twenty-five years has carried a high price: it helped to undermine both the Frei (1964–70) and Allende (1970–73) governments and today facilitates the persistence in power of a dictatorial regime with virtually no popular support.

Chilean Christian radicalism initially grew out of the university student movement. When young Chilean Catholics entered politics (some in the 1940s and 1950s, others in the early 1960s), Christian reformism had yet to be tested and seemed full of promise. It attracted these younger elements (first in the *Falange* and subsequently in the *Partido Democrata Cristiano, PDC*), and for two decades managed to contain if not deflate their radicalism. Within the party they formed a minority left wing whose occasional pronouncements helped the party to appear more progressive than it really was.

Following Frei's election in 1964, these radicals sought to close the breach with the Left. They adopted Marxist perspectives on capitalism and the inadequacy of gradual reform and sought to accelerate the pace of Frei's "Revolution in Liberty." For five years they struggled in vain to bring Marxists and Christians together. When the PDC decided to enter its own candidate in the 1970 presidential election against candidates from both the Right and the Left, they left to form the *Movimiento para la Acción Popular Unitária* (MAPU).

The radicals failed to take many followers with them. Most Christian Democratic workers and peasants looked to Frei, not to the party's left wing, for solutions to national problems. Indeed, they had always seen the PDC as an alternative to Marxism, and for years had struggled against Communist and Socialist rivals in their workplaces and union organizations. Over the years an intense and abiding antagonism arose between the two sides, and for most Christian Democrats even minimal collaboration with Marxists was simply unthinkable.

In leaving the party many of these radicals also broke with the church. Some had ceased believing or practicing their religion during adolescence for reasons unrelated to politics. Others, captivated by the structural Marxism of Althusser, renounced their religious convictions for philosophical reasons. For most, however, their break with the church was more an angry reaction to what they saw as its identification with the political fortunes and anti-Marxist sentiments of the PDC. In fact, it is probably safe to say that they were moved more by the desire to end the division of popular forces than by Marxist doctrine as such.

With Allende's election in 1970, Christian radicals came to occupy important positions in his government and for the next several years worked closely with the Chilean Communists. Additionally, some eighty priests, many of whom lived in poorer neighborhoods and had worked closely with these former Christian Democrats during the Frei years, launched the Christians for Socialism movement in an effort to generate greater Catholic support for Allende. In August 1971 another group of progressive Christian Democrats abandoned the PDC to form the *Movimiento de Izquierda Cristiana* (IC). They proposed forming a single "radical" Christian party. But the *mapucistas* declined. They were less interested in projecting their Christian identity and even thought that Christian principles might be an obstacle to truly revolutionary politics. The groups accordingly remained apart, although several of MAPU's leading figures did cross over to the IC.

With the serious economic and political problems of 1971 and 1972, both groups experienced radicalization. At the end of 1972 the MAPU divided into two factions, the *MAPU-Obrero Campesino* headed by Jaime Gazmuri and the MAPU led by Oscar Guillermo Garretón. The latter was the more intransigent, although both adopted Leninist outlooks and forms of organization. For their part, IC militants moved closer to the ultra-radical MIR, though without ever embracing Marxism as such or calling their Christian convictions or identity into question.

Following the coup, Christian and non-Christian supporters of the Allende government were detained, jailed, or forced into exile. The coup and subsequent experiences caused many to reconsider their ideological views. Some were able to study in Europe and the United States, where they were supported by solidarity committees and exposed to liberal, social democratic, democratic socialist, and Eurocommunist influences. Those remaining in Chile were forced to confront evidence of UP mistakes and of widespread dissatisfaction with Allende's government. Amidst repression and disillusionment, however, both Catholics and non-Christians found refuge, support, and sympathy in the church, under whose protection they became involved in social assistance projects and were able to work in defense of human rights, in popular educational programs, and in social research and promotional institutions.

As a result of these experiences many radical intellectuals revised their views of democratic institutions and practices, religion and culture, and education and political organization. Without abandoning Marxism, they began to worry about more than objective class interests or relationships. A majority embraced the notion of a democratic socialist society to be constructed politically over time, and toward which the formation of a broad antidictatorial front would be a first step.

Another important aspect of the post-1973 period was the appearance of labor and popular organizations in which Catholic Left activists, Christian Democrats, and secular Marxists have worked together. Organizations that had been suppressed and dismantled following the coup were resurrected and have become more independent from the political parties on which they had previously depended.[5]

The local-level leaders of these organizations are affiliated with parties ranging from the centrist PDC through the two MAPUs, the IC, and the various socialist factions, to the MIR and Communist party on the "nondemocratic" Left. Typically, however, the Christians (and non-Christians) within each work better with each other than with Christians (or Marxists) of differing strategic positions. And, as in Peru, many local-level Christian activists tend to be critical of traditional parties, of incrementalist or evolutionary strategies, and of the idea of negotiating with political adversaries.

The leadership of the Communist party and many within the Almeyda faction of the Socialist party continue to defend notions of militant class struggle, "popular" (as opposed to liberal) democracy, and armed (as well as political) opposition to the Pinochet regime. Some appear to do so with enthusiasm, while others are more interested in distancing themselves from more radical groups and from their own increasingly belligerent bases. Other secular Marxist intellectuals and party leaders, those of the Nuñez Socialist faction, for example, have embraced "renovated" Marxist conceptions, but like the radical Christians they have had difficulty selling this perspective to some of their base-level activists.

As for the Christian Democrats, they retain a substantial following among popular-sector Catholics. Although some of their labor and student leaders work closely with Communists and other Marxists, the party's leadership, its professional sector, and most labor and popular sector leaders and activists continue to view Marxists (particularly Communists and Almeyda Socialists) as permanent adversaries, thereby helping to perpetuate the division of anti-Pinochet forces.

CURRENT POSITIONS AND RELATIONS

In defining the range of positions and state of relations among Christians and Marxists in these countries, I have conducted interviews and carried out attitudinal surveys. I have interviewed some seventy Chilean and thirty-five Peruvian intellectuals, national party and organizational leaders, and local-level leaders representing the various party, ideological, and functional groupings within the Christian and Marxist communities. I have also surveyed 518 local-level activists in Chile and 485 in Peru. I have only begun to sift through these data. I have thirty more interviews to do in Peru and have yet to begin the interviews and the survey in Brazil.

What follows, therefore, are initial though informed impressions of the Chilean and Peruvian cases, plus references to Brazil based on a reading of the secondary literature. After characterizing the positions of various political elements and their relationships in each country, I will attempt to account for some of the patterns and then identify questions for further inquiry.

Perhaps most noteworthy is the diversity of views within each of the communities. Among Christians, for example, one can identify five subgroupings. They are:

> a. *Revolutionaries*—those who accept conventional class categories and the notion of contradictory class interests, embrace revolutionary methods of struggle, and favor joining forces with the nondemocratic Left
> b. *Progressives*—those who have adopted a class perspective but value democratic methods and processes, and are therefore not interested in alliance with the nondemocratic Left

c. *Skeptics*—progressives willing to work with people from the other side but skeptical of parties, of politics generally, and of the possibility and propriety of understandings with antipopular forces

d. *Moderates*—those who reject a class perspective but are willing to cooperate with democratic leftists (even if Marxist) over the short run

e. *Antis*—those who reject class perspectives and want nothing to do with Marxists of any sort

Among non-Christian Marxists, on the other hand, one can distinguish the following:

x. *The orthodox*—those who regard democracy as a possibly useful "tool," but insist that the popular movement be led by representatives of the working class, refuse to confine themselves to the rules and spaces of existing economic and political structures, and are interested only in short-term collaboration with Christian institutions and forces

y. *The renovated*—those who value democracy and political activity for their own sake, are willing to join a coalition of "democratic" forces without claiming a vanguard role, and agree to pursue socialist goals within existing national and international structures

z. *Skeptics*—progressives willing to work with people from the other side but skeptical of parties, of politics generally, and of both the possibility and propriety of reaching understandings with antipopular forces

These ideological groups vary in relative strength across country and level lines. The following table identifies four levels of activity (that is, intellectuals, national-level leaders, local-level leaders, and base-level elements or activists) within each community. The dominant orientations at each level are given, with those in parentheses being of lesser but still significant incidence.

Brazil	Catholics	Cultural Christians	Non-Christians
Intellectuals	a,b	b	x
National Leaders	b,d,e	b,d,e	x,y
Local Leaders	a,b,d	a,b,d	x
Base Elements	c,(b,d)	c,d	x
Peru			
Intellectuals	b	a,b	x,y
National Leaders	b,(d,e)	a,(b)	x,(y)
Local Leaders	a,b	a,b	x,y
Base Elements	a,b,c,(d)	a,c	x,z
Chile			
Intellectuals	b,d	b,d,(a)	y,(x)
National Leaders	d,(b,e)	b,d	x,y
Local Leaders	a,d,e,(b)	b	y,(x)
Base Elements	c,(a,b,d)	a,c,d	x,y,z

Ideological and strategic divergence within both Christian and Marxist communities is thus considerable. Among Peruvian Christians, revolutionary and progressive orientations predominate, with organic Catholics tending to be progressive (that is, moderate) rather than revolutionary. In both Brazil and Chile, on the other hand, both Catholics and cultural Christians are more evenly distributed across categories. Among non-Christian Marxists, the Brazilians tend to be orthodox, the Chileans renovated (that is, revisionist), and the Peruvians generally mixed. In all three countries, finally, a substantial number of base elements in all three groups are skeptics.

In terms of Christian-Marxist relations, two observations are in order: First, they are warmest and of the greatest political import in Peru. They are weakest in Brazil and occupy a middle ground in the case of Chile. Second, collaboration has been greater at the grassroots level and (to a lesser extent) among intellectuals than among institutional authorities.

These characterizations must be qualified, however, given intracommunity heterogeneity. In effect, some Christians (and Marxists) get along better with those on the other side who share their ideological and strategic views than with fellow Christians (or Marxists). Christian-Marxist relations can thus be good—that is, substantial numbers of Christians and Marxists can favor working closely with the other side (as in the Chilean case)—without Christians and Marxists constituting a united or dominant political force.

A number of questions arise from these findings: For one, why the greater radicalization among Peruvian Christians? For another, why the greater incidence of revolutionary perspectives among cultural Christians in Peru than in Chile? Third, why the greater incidence of renovated perspectives among Chilean Marxists? Fourth, why the greater attraction to "renovated" perspectives among intellectuals and national leaders (as opposed to local-level leaders and activists) in all three countries? Finally, why the greater interest in permanent association at the local-leader and base-element levels?

In terms of the differences among countries (the first three questions), demographic and class patterns, socioeconomic conditions, the party system, the nature of the country's Communist and Christian Democratic parties in particular, and the pastoral orientation of its Catholic hierarchy are all important factors. At this point, however, I would stress the unifying impact of shared experiences under repressive military regimes, the more extensive political space available in Peru from 1968 to 1975, the seven years of economic and political frustration since the return to formal democratic rule in 1980, and finally the presence (also since 1980) of a broad-based and increasingly effective insurrectionist movement (*Sendero Luminoso*). The more radical orientation of Brazilian Marxists, on the other hand, is probably related to their limited following and political influence since the late 1960s.

Differences among strata (the fourth and fifth questions) reflect the breaches existing between political *aparati* and their "bases" in each of the countries. These breaches have to do with (1) the limitations imposed on party activities during particularly repressive phases of military rule (in Chile, from 1973 to 1983), (2) the difficulties of coordinating political work even when more open conditions have prevailed, and (3) the need (in the late- and post-dictatorial periods) to confront more vexing issues (how, for example, to oppose the dictatorial regime and what to do with power once it is obtained) than the human rights and basic needs questions around which base-level activity and collaboration initially developed.

In fact, many Christians and Marxists at the local level are skeptical of politics generally and of the leaders, parties, and practices of earlier periods (on which they blame the country's difficulties and the ensuing period of military rule). Some of this can be accounted for in generational terms, that is, as the predictable means by which a new generation would hope to accede to positions of power and influence. But it also reflects a certain fundamentalist spirit that has arisen in recent years, the result perhaps of the morally charged formations and struggles to which many (young and old, Christian and Marxist alike) have been exposed.

CONCLUSIONS AND HYPOTHESES

These impressions are drawn from an initial review of some of the relevant data. More definitive pronouncements must await the completion of additional interviews and analysis. At this point, however, several observations and hypotheses can be suggested. In general, relations *within* and *between* Christian and Marxist communities appear to be the consequence of both objective and subjective factors: (a) demographic, socioeconomic, and political conditions; (b) the ideological orientations of those involved; and (c) perceptions regarding political strengths, strategic options, and their likely outcomes.

Collaborative relations appear to require a certain level of Christian radicalization. Such radicalization, although legitimated theologically, is the product of a complex web of demographic and class structures, the evolution of economic conditions over time, the policies of the existing government, available political alternatives, and the response of church leaders. The absence of a strong or progressive Christian Democratic party and the hostility of the Catholic hierarchy are particularly important factors in this regard, although these relationships need to be studied more fully.

Beyond Christian radicalization, however, each side must want to work with the other. Christians appear more likely to do so when (a) they have experienced repression or been involved in social projects with Marxists, (b) they sense they have little influence or credibility within so-called "popular" sectors, and (c) no powerful orthodox Communist party exists. As for Marxists, their interest in collaboration is likely to be greater when (a) they lack influence or support within the "popular" sector, (b) they have experienced theoretical or strategic "renovation," and (c) the church has afforded them refuge and the opportunity to engage in social and political activity.

With both Christians and Marxists, however, one might ask whether collaboration will continue once military rule is ended. In Brazil, for example, relations have cooled since the advent of "distention" in 1982. In Chile, although relations have improved since 1973, they continue to falter around the question of how to oppose Pinochet and what to do once power reverts to civilian hands. In Peru, on the other hand, relations grew stronger between 1978 and 1986 and have begun to experience strain only recently. Evidently contradictory pressures are at work in these cases.

With a reduction in repression and the return to constitutional politics, it is likely that (a) human compassion will recede, (b) Marxists will have less need for institutional refuge, (c) matters on which agreement is more difficult to reach (socioeconomic as opposed to human rights policy, for example) will come to the fore, and (d) each community will be seeking to expand its own institutional political base. But it is also possible that (e) the impetus of previous collaboration will carry over and intensify, (f) elections will confirm the strength of one or both groups, thereby increasing the incentive for collaboration, and (g) the two sides will face a common political rival, such as APRA in Peru.

The character and consequences of the return to civilian rule will be greatly affected by the incidence of "fundamentalism" among grassroots Christians and Marxists. This phenomenon needs to be examined more closely, although at this point its impact appears to be threefold: (a) it strengthens the more radical tendencies within each community, (b) it increases apoliticism among followers on both sides, and (c) it helps to perpetuate internal division and organizational ineffectiveness.

Grassroots fundamentalism also raises questions regarding the assumption that the Christian base community movement will be a foundational element in future democratic societies in Latin America.[6] It is true that base communities are seedbeds of anti-dictatorial sentiment and activity, and that most either practice or aspire to participatory democracy in the conduct of their own affairs. However, the formation and practice of democratic politics at the national level also require that citizens make concessions to adversaries, that they align for political advantage with people who want different things, and that they accept the institutions and practices of representative (as opposed to direct) democracy. And these, unfortunately, are skills and tolerances that many CEB members do not appear to possess and to which some feel positively adverse.

NOTES

1. The second of these positions was voiced by ex-*jucista*, one-time Christian-Marxist, and now (simply) Marxist editor Duarte Pacheco Pereira in the roundtable discussion appearing in Helen Salem (coord.), *A igreja dos oprimidos* (São Paulo: Brasil Debates, 1981).

2. This position is developed by Gutiérrez in his *Lineas pastorales de la iglesia en América Latina* (Lima: CEP, 1970).

3. They devoted themselves primarily to the *pueblos jóvenes* (literally "young towns") that were erected on the sand dunes and flats of Lima's northern, eastern, and southern cones, on which hundreds of thousands of economic refugees from other parts of the country began to settle during the early 1970s. In some cases, that of *Villa el Salvador*, for example, Catholic radicals organized the initial invasion and settlement, and went from there; in others, they moved in to organize among squatters settled by the Velasco government or by other political groups. Among the more prominent of the centers, on the other hand, were DESCO (established, ironically, by people associated with the strongly anti-Marxist Belgian Jesuit, Roger Vekemans), CELADEC (an ecumenical center set up by the Methodist church), and Gustavo Gutiérrez's Bartolomé de las Casas Center.

4. Ames is a political science professor at the Catholic University who was elected to the Senate in 1985. Piqueras is a sociologist and a member of the Chamber of Deputies who has spent several years working factory jobs and organizing workers and slum dwellers. Iguiñiz and Ascueta are native Spaniards. Iguiñiz is an economist and the principal drafter of the IU's 1985 presidential platform. Ascueta is a former seminarian and lay missioner who is serving his third term as mayor of *Villa el Salvador*.

5. Among the factors contributing to this phenomenon were the fact that the parties themselves (both Marxist parties and the PDC) no longer dominated political space and logic as in preceding years, the emergence of a new generation of Christian Democratic activists (in both the labor and popular sectors) less imbued with anti-leftism than their forebears, and the shift by many Catholic Left intellectuals and activists to educational and promotional work in the popular sectors.

6. See, for example, Charles A. Reilly, "Latin America's Religious Populists," in *Religion and Political Conflict in Latin America*, ed. Daniel H. Levine (Chapel Hill: University of North Carolina Press, 1986).

8

Liberation Theology and Dependency Theory

William R. Garrett

INTRODUCTION

Liberation theologians in Latin America have relied heavily on the rubrics of neocolonial dependency theory as a framework of analysis for understanding that region's poverty and political plight. The overriding purpose of this essay is to assess the significance of dependency theory, with its neo-Marxist orientation, in shaping the central concepts of liberation theology. We begin by introducing the modernization-developmental paradigm which emerged from structural-functional theory in the 1950s and 1960s. Next, we trace the evolution of dependency theory—along with other neo-Marxist variants—as they took shape in the 1960s as an alternative to developmentalism.

Against this backdrop, liberation theology is interpreted as a fusion of Christian precepts with a neocolonial understanding of the Latin American situation. By this approach, not only is capitalism rejected but revolutionary tactics are also entertained as a viable means for redressing the continent's inundating problems. We conclude by contending that dependency theory exerts a determinative influence that mutes liberation theologians' capacity to engage in independent, critical reflection with respect to their movement.

THE BACKGROUND TO THE EMERGENCE
OF DEPENDENCY THEORY

The Great Transformation—as modernization in the West has been described—can be regarded, in its most generalized sense, as *the* substantive preoccupation of academic sociology's founding fathers.[1] Comte, Spencer, Marx, Weber, Durkheim, Simmel, Toennies, as well as a whole host of lesser lights among the classical theorists of the discipline from the late nineteenth to the early twentieth centuries, sought above all else to provide cogent accounts of how economic, cultural, technological, and political forces conspired to produce the modern social order. By the mid-twentieth century, social scientists manifested a renewed interest in modernization theory, but this time the problem definition was markedly different: the overriding concern was not so much the historical question of how modernity originated; rather, it was the developmental issue of how traditional societies could alter their structures and institutional patterns so as to enter into the processes of modernization.[2]

Given the prominence of Parsonian theory in sociology as well as in the related disciplines of economics, anthropology, and political science during the post-World War II period, structural-functional constructs overwhelmingly informed the salient theoretical models of modernization. The orthodox paradigm most commonly employed by social analysts in North America was typically described as "developmental theory," even though the discrete variables cited as essential for economic take-off and political maturation were far from uniformly identified in the sundry perspectives included under the broad "developmental" rubric.[3] Despite these variations on a common theme, however, consensus was apparent within this body of literature in the reluctance to utilize Marxist or neo-Marxist categories of interpretation. Members of the New Left (such as C. Wright Mills[4]) and, later, adherents of radical sociological perspectives (such as Alvin Gouldner[5]) viewed the absence of Marxist concepts as a clear indication of the essentially conservative, business-oriented character of academic sociology generally and Parsonian theory in particular.

Such criticisms from the Left possessed only limited validity at best.[6] To be sure, structural-functional theory came to maturity during the Cold War era, but there were ancillary reasons for the limited interest in Marxist interpretations, reasons which derived from theoretical—rather than political—considerations. Not least was the fact that many of the writings of the young Marx were not widely known and available in translation until the 1950s and developmental theory was well on its way toward being framed at this time.[7] Furthermore, Marx could be more readily ignored prior to the revival of neo-Marxist studies that followed from the discovery of his early manuscripts. Perhaps most important, however, was the then conventional view that Marx proffered a monocausal system of analysis which attributed deterministic significance to economic factors while giving short shrift to cultural, ideological, and voluntaristic aspects of social reality.[8]

By contrast, structural-functional theorists manifested a concerted effort to develop multicausal models. Although Talcott Parsons' early work stressed ideational and voluntaristic factors,[9] he had moved to a position that resolutely opposed all types of determinism—behavioristic, cultural, material, and idealistic—by the time the working papers in action theory were published.[10] A cursory survey of the major contributions to modernization theory likewise indicates that, while cultural factors were often accentuated by those researchers following up clues from Weber's Protestant ethic thesis, the more common course was to strive for some modicum of balance among interpretative variables. Accordingly, structural-functionalists typically approached modernization by insisting that development would almost certainly require a program which addressed simultaneously the economic, political, and valuational questions on the agenda of any society striving to attain an economically advanced status.

DEPENDENCY THEORY AS A COUNTERPOINT TO DEVELOPMENTALISM

Dependency theory, which derived from Marxist reflection relative to colonial imperialism, was developed in diametric opposition to developmentalism. Marx himself devoted remarkably little space to a discussion of colonialism—apart from his brief, final chapter in *Capital*[11] and only a meager theory of imperialism can be discerned from his copious literary output. Perhaps, as Schumpeter has suggested, Marx was too competent an economist to trust very far that line of argument which laid great stress on the "monopolistic restriction of output" and the subsequent rise of "protectionism" against the intrusion of other capitalist societies.[12] At any rate, it was left to Lenin[13] and a whole cortege of neo-Marxist theorists—including Rosa Luxemburg and Fritz Steinberg—to conflate Marx's cryptic notion of colonialism with the infrastructure tendency toward capitalist concentration, a trend which they portrayed as the overriding characteristic of capitalist development at the turn of the twentieth century.

The result was an argument advancing the claim that imperialism represented the final stage of capitalism, a stage wherein monopolies and finance capital have established themselves in the metropolitan center, exhausted their exploitable labor force, and hence are compelled to turn outward toward the economic/political domination of overseas territories as the last frontier for favorable investment where capital could yield a markedly increased level of return.[14] Imperialism, Lenin contended, merely signaled the entrance of capitalism into a final, parasitic, and decaying form whose very success in exploitation only hastened its necessary destruction.[15]

The conspicuous failure of industrial nations to conform blithely to the scenario Lenin laid down set the stage for the enunciation of a recrudescent Marxist theory of neo-imperial colonialism. Paul Baran, Paul Sweezy, and Andre Gunder Frank emerged as three of the chief architects of this new paradigm. Although their empirical focus was primarily on Latin America,[16] they jointly concluded that capitalism worldwide was at once the producer and sustainer of underdevelopment among the "have-not" nations.[17] The features which differentiated neocolonial dependency theory, as it subsequently became popularly known, from earlier critiques of imperialism include the following: Dependency theory asserts that advanced capitalism exhibits a capital-intensive, rather than a labor-intensive, character.[18] That is to say, the metropolitan center (a term denoting a first economic power) resists direct military intervention in the political affairs of satellite nations and opts, instead, to penetrate their social structures through the exportation of capital itself. Metropolitan interests accomplish this goal by creating alliances with indigenous elites in Third World nations through the extension of loans and direct capital investment. Local elites oversee foreign investment on behalf of metropolitan capitalists and reduce de facto free societies to a position of dependency by encouraging the accumulation of excessive debts and financial obligations to First World banks and corporations. Peripheral nations, for their part, afford capitalist enterprises a new source of cheap labor as well as economies easily manipulated by virtue of capital dependency. The manufactured commodities resulting from Third World factory production are, for the most part, not for local consumption but for foreign markets. Accordingly, metropolitan centers enjoy high rates of return on their investments from both loans and manufacturing operations, while satellite societies realize little internal development—apart, of course, from the benefits to indigenous elites coopted by the metropolitan centers. For the peripheral economy, therefore, the expropriation of economic surplus along with the loss of local economic control not only retards development but actually results—to use Frank's popular phrase—in the "development of underdevelopment." [19]

RECENT REFINEMENTS IN DEPENDENCY THEORY

Advocates of neocolonial dependency theory have generated considerable empirical research over the last two decades.[20] Chief among the objectives pursued in these investigations has been the effort to demonstrate the lines of penetration from core to peripheral nations and the sorts of consequences generated by the introduction of foreign capital. Another central feature of these studies turned on the utilization of more sophisticated mathematical and econometric procedures,[21] and less reliance on theoretical/ideological constructs. With the availability of more precise data, a succession of subtle criticisms and refinements began to emerge with respect to the original neocolonial paradigm.[22]

Meanwhile, other schools of neo-Marxist theory came into prominence as the Left experienced something of an intellectual fragmentation in recent decades. World systems theory arose during the early 1970s, for example, partly as an historically more sophisticated competitor to and complement of dependency theory. Inspired in part by the work of Fernand Braudel[23] and pioneered by Immanuel Wallerstein, the central claim of world systems theory held that the whole planet was united willy-nilly in one global capitalist, economic system. As a Marxist variant, world systems theory employed much of the same language, logic, and ideological assumptions as dependency theory, but the linkage between the two schools has been tenuous at best.

A more independent course of theoretical innovation derived from the Frankfurt school whose propositions came to be known collectively as "critical theory."[24] While members of this critical school engaged in somewhat more abstract analyses than other Marxist variants, nonetheless they did provide a supplementary critique of capitalist culture and its organizational dynamics. Likewise, Louis Althusser[25] and Antonio Gramsci[26] have proffered markedly different stances related to the Marxist tradition, stances which have been quite independently appropriated by contributors to the burgeoning literature of liberation theology.

The full range of these neo-Marxist analyses with their nuanced differences cannot, of course, be critically examined in this brief essay. One salient trend in this research tradition is worth noting, however, especially in view of its relevance to the sorts of claims advanced by liberation theologians which are to be considered below. The line of interpretive analysis to which we shall call attention pertains to the "development of underdevelopment" thesis of Andre Gunder Frank and the ancillary claim that this process results in the creation of inequality among peoples in satellite nations. The initial contention of dependency and world system theorists was that developed core nations both exacerbated the underdevelopment of peripheral societies and widened the gap between the "haves" and the "have-nots" in dependent economic orders. This pattern of unequal development was hypothesized to be a function of the reliance of liaison elites in dependent countries on the external power of core nations to oversee the distribution of scarce resources in a manner favorable to coopted functionaries in the periphery.[27] In other words, it is decision-making power exercised by actors in the core which results in uneven development in the periphery, according to this perspective.[28]

Research undertaken to demonstrate the accuracy of this stance began to produce discordant results by the early 1980s. Evans and Timberlake demonstrated, for example, that the penetration of foreign capital generated economic inequality *when* the investments of multinational corporations distorted the structure of the labor force in the direction of augmenting the tertiary, rather than the secondary, sector of the economy. Why this should be the case, the authors admitted they were unable to explain—in part, we may assume, because the obvious explanation would have challenged the cogency of their theoretical perspective. Meanwhile, a whole series of subsequent studies confirmed the empirical accuracy of the basic finding reported by Evans and Timberlake that service sector expansion retarded development and promoted dependency, while the growth of manufacturing heightened independence and narrowed class divisions.[29] A collateral study by Delacroix and Ragin[30] confirmed that the detrimental effects of dependent development could be ameliorated substantially by the structural blockage provided by state activism among satellite nations. That is to say, where governmental officials in semiperipheral and peripheral societies actively directed the reinvestment of economic surplus generated by core penetration into areas that stimulated further growth in satellite nations, then the drift toward dependency and indigenous class inequality was positively curtailed.

The significance of these studies, taken collectively, can be interpreted in the following fashion: Whereas dependency theorists assert that the economic power of the core determines the outcome of dependency and class inequality, the mounting evidence now seems to suggest that reinvestment decisions made by local elites exercise a much more significant influence over the movement toward dependency or development among Third World nations than do multinational corporations of the core. Indeed, the Chilean economist Joseph Ramos, while recognizing that dependent economic relations exist between core and periphery, that is, between the United States and Latin America, nonetheless claims that the fundamental problem of Latin America now is no longer development or dependence but the problem of economic distribution.[31] Two pieces of data are worth considering in this connection: First, the United States puts only one percent of its total investments (domestic and foreign) into Latin America.[32] It strains credulity to imagine that the whole continent is thrust into a dependent status by virtue of this small capital transfer, or even that such United States investments constitute a significant exploitive venture. Second, Latin America has sustained rather impressive growth rates of between 5 and 7 percent annually from 1967 to 1980.[33] Unfortunately, however, substantial growth rates do not automatically "trickle down," and the poor in most Third World nations in Latin America are now worse off than they were, say, twenty-five years ago, before sustained growth was achieved.

Thus the conclusion would appear intractable that, when elites in dependent nations who are aligned with multinational corporations reinvest their substantial earnings outside the country by depositing these funds in First World banks or buying stocks in First World corporations or, again, when governmental officials in Third World nations illegally siphon off internal investment profits to enhance their personal wealth, then dependency along with income inequality will be the necessary outcome of the penetration of core capital. Conversely, however, when the surplus from core investments is returned to the indigenous economy to build up the manufacturing infrastructure and when governmental policies, regulations, and licensing procedures encourage, rather than frustrate, entrepreneurial ventures, then independent growth as well as income redistribution can be effectively accomplished. As a spokesman for dependent societies, then, Ramos would appear to be directly on target when he observes that "economic development and the elimination of poverty do not depend so much on what others do for us, but on what we do for ourselves. Despite our dependency, we have a sufficient degree of freedom to eliminate these problems with policies within our reach...."[34]

Anyone who draws this conclusion, of course, runs the risk of being charged with "blaming the victims" for their plight. Certainly, it is not our intent to argue that Latin American peasants have by miscalculation, ignorance, or naivete thrust themselves into a position of dependency with its attendant misery and deprivation. Nor do we mean to absolve transnational corporations of the capacity to engage in rapacious behavior with respect to the economic lives of Third World peoples. The more modest point, rather, is to suggest that investment decisions by Third World leaders—economic and political—constitute an intervening variable of crucial significance for determining the outcome of peripheral development and income distribution.[35] Dependency theorists typically manifest the tendency to succumb to the much-too-simplistic portrayal of core corporations and their supporting governments—especially the United States—as the sole perpetrators of Third World poverty and economic crisis. The pernicious consequences flowing out of this interpretive stance can be assessed somewhat more concretely in the following section, where we examine the incorporation of dependency theories of greater or lesser degrees of elegance into the foundational presuppositions informing the leading varieties of liberation theology.

LIBERATION THEOLOGY AND DEPENDENCY THEORY

Liberation theology had its inspiration in Latin America, although it has subsequently spread to other troubled areas around the globe such as Ireland, Africa, Asia, and even North America. Theologically, it represents a melange of Christian religious precepts fused with social scientific categories of analysis, especially as these constructs appropriated from the social sciences have been understood within the Latin American context.[36] The qualification just appended is of utmost importance because, as John Coleman has astutely observed, Latin Americans have demonstrated a tendency to identify "scientific Marxism" with social scientific analysis *tout court*.[37] Accordingly, liberation theology derives much of its distinctiveness from the bold attempt to predicate a reinterpretation of the Christian symbol system on an infrastructure extracted from Marxist social theory. Wherever it has appeared, liberation theology has exhibited a pronounced affinity for political orientations that range well left of center, as well as a willingness to legitimate revolutionary action as a means toward fulfilling those political ambitions.[38]

The concerted effort to forge a new posture for Latin American theologizing by integrating Marxist categories of analysis into theological discourse has embroiled liberation theologians in a heated controversy almost from the outset of their new venture in religious reflection. Indeed, liberation theologians have expended a great deal of energy attempting to convince Vatican officials and North American critics that they are not mere doctrinaire Marxists.[39] Although Joseph Cardinal Ratzinger may not yet be fully convinced on the score,[40] most contemporary observers are less concerned with the *fact* of Marxist influences than they are with discerning the extent to which such constructs have facilitated or confounded the creation of a viable theological posture.

Although that larger issue remains a matter of considerable interest, our more circumscribed purpose in this analysis pertains to the sort of influence exerted by the incorporation of dependency theory as a presuppositional foundation for liberation theology. Specifically, the argument will be advanced below that, although several varieties of dependency theory have been employed by liberation theologians, the most generalized consequence of utilizing dependency theory concepts has been to necessitate locating the solution to Latin American problems in some form of Marxist revolutionary strategy, precisely because the definition of the situation has been couched in Marxist categories of analysis. Thus, while liberation theologians have attempted of late to establish a degree of social distance between their own perspectives and Marxist social theory,[41] they have been hampered in that effort by constraints imposed on their theological reflection by the potent ramifications originating from the dependency frame of reference.

The most appropriate point of departure for assessing the role which dependency theory plays in liberation theologies is the work of Gutiérrez and Segundo. There is more than a germ of truth in Michael Novak's observation that Gutiérrez and Segundo have done "the lion's share" of innovation with respect to liberation theology and that all the rest remains largely commentary—although there are some supporters of the Latin American initiative who have swiftly taken issue with this judgment.[42]

However, if one takes the linguistic identification of this theological school seriously—as indeed I think one should—then the first question which springs to mind is, Liberation from what? The answer uniformly given, by its major proponents is quite simply "dependence," by which they mean, in the shorthand of contemporary religiopolitical parlance, the economic, political, and cultural repression and exploitation of Latin America by First World countries and primarily the United States. Segundo put the issue in unequivocal terms when he asserted:

> As is well known by now, liberation theology arose as a reaction against the developmentalist theories and models formulated by the United States for Latin America in the decade of the sixties. The developmentalist model was characterized by the fact that it covered over and tried to hide the critical and decisive relationship of dependence versus liberation.[43]

This bold assertion on the part of Segundo merely echoed the already distinctive stance taken by Gutiérrez in what is perhaps still the most formative statement of liberation theology penned to date.[44] In almost pure dialectical progression, Gutiérrez charted a course of historical reconstruction for Latin America which cast the decade of the 1950s as an era of developmentalism, the 1960s as the decade of the discovery of dependency, and the 1970s as the period of the advent of liberation themes.[45] There can be no doubt that for Gutiérrez (as for other liberation theologians) it was precisely the sociopolitical "reality" of dependency which made necessary the development of liberation theology. In Gutiérrez's own words, in fact, the assertion is advanced that "*dependence* and *liberation* are correlative terms."[46]

The source from which Gutiérrez[47] derived a goodly portion of his original dependency theory was the work of such moderates as Fernando Henrique Cardosa, Raul Prebisch, and their colleagues who explicitly rejected a neocolonial Marxist reading of the Latin American situation.[48] In the same connection, however, Gutiérrez also integrated Frank's notion of the development of underdevelopment. The lack of conceptual symmetry between the moderate presuppositions of Cardosa and the neo-Marxist assumptions of Frank unfortunately passed by the board without ever being addressed in Gutiérrez's diligent effort to conflate these two perspectives. Thus, the extent to which Gutiérrez actually embraced the Marxist implications deriving from Frank's dependency theory has remained shrouded in a troublesome cloud of ambiguity.

Other liberation theologians have similarly paid high tribute to the analyses of Cardosa, et al., for providing the analytical underpinnings for the development of Latin American theological precepts,[49] and again without pausing to resolve the ideational discordance between moderate and neocolonial presuppositions. The customary procedure of liberation theologians had entailed simply sketching out a dependency theory in highly generalized terms as a focal point for justifying a theology of liberation, but without specifying whether a given conception of this model of inequitable economic relations derived from non-Marxist or Marxist sources.[50] Over the course of the movement's brief history, however, references to Cardosa and the moderates have declined significantly in liberationist literature, while the conceptual center of gravity has shifted more and more in the direction of the Frank neocolonial interpretation. Indeed, liberation theologians have followed an international pattern wherein Marxist versions of dependency theory have grown in popularity at the expense of more moderate interpretations.[51]

Unanimity has prevailed from the outset, meanwhile, in condemning the international capitalist system for the poverty and oppression experienced by the peasants of Latin America,[52] in accord with the line of interpretation laid down by the neocolonial variant of dependency theory. Consequently, liberation theologians—almost without fail—have endorsed some variety of socialism as the only viable alternative to capitalist exploitation. And in the process, they have reiterated time and again that their embracing socialism does not necessarily mean that they have appropriated an orthodox Marxist vision of the structures and processes of post-liberation society. To establish the prima facie validity to such a claim, we need only to recall that Daniel Bell—who is often described nowadays as a neoconservative, an epithet which he regards as essentially meaningless—has recently depicted his point of view as that of a socialist in economics, a liberal in politics, and a conservative in culture.[53] To his credit, however, Bell subsequently spelled out the ramifications attending each of these discrete aspects of his general theoretical perspective.

Unfortunately, little effort has been directed thus far toward identifying precisely what meaning should be attached to the term "socialism" in the writings of liberation theologians. Segundo undoubtedly speaks for most of his fellow liberationists when he declares, "We give the name of socialism to a regime in which the ownership of the means of production is removed from individuals and handed over to higher institutions whose concern is the common good."[54] The relatively facile intermixture of normative with empirical components, along with the absence of conceptual precision in this formulation, fosters the suspicion, not that liberation theologians are striving to camouflage ulterior motives under the guise of disingenuous rhetoric, but rather that they simply have not yet settled on a cogent conception of the sort of regime which ought to achieve institutionalism after the revolution. For the present, then, liberationists have managed to do little more than express a vague hope for ultimately instituting a new social order which occupies a middle ground between North American capitalism and Soviet Marxism.[55]

Liberation theologians, therefore, have adopted a series of propositions, each building upon its predecessor in syllogistic fashion, and finally culminating in a predictable set of political judgments. First, in subscribing to the tenets of dependency theory, advocates of liberation theology have been drawn ineluctably toward the conclusion that Nicaraguan deprivation is a direct function of First World economic practices.[56] An inference of this sort follows logically from the decision to employ Marxist analytical categories for delineating the plight of the oppressed. Second, the appropriate response to a definition of reality couched in dependency terms is liberation from oppression—through revolution if necessary and especially if other more efficacious alternatives are unavailable. The celebrated postulate of W. I. Thomas is worth recalling in this connection, namely, that "situations which are defined as real, are real in their consequences." In other words, the theological development of the liberation movement is constrained by the manner in which dependency theory informs the definition of the situation out of which its reflection arises. And finally, the option for a socialist political strategy follows immediately from the designation of capitalism as the exploitive system responsible for the marginalization and oppression that made liberation theology necessary in the first place.

The crucial point to be made on the basis of this analysis can be summarized as follows: While liberationists have sought to argue—and no doubt genuinely believe—that Marxist analyses have been important to their reflection *only* at the point of providing a social scientific infrastructure to their interpretation of reality, the very dynamics of their thought precludes attributing such a limited and benign role to Marxist influences. For example, Míguez Bonino claims that, while Marxism has supplied the "method of analysis" as well as a "framework for study," this sociological foundation simply serves as a point of departure for that faith dimension out of which the articulation of authentic theological propositions arises.[57] Although the enterprise outlined by Míguez Bonino merits high praise for its noble intentions, it fails to reckon seriously enough with the extent to which such a posture is held captive to the ideological assumptions embedded in its analytical theory. For once dependency theory has been enjoined to provide a definition of the empirical situation, then this has a crucial and determinative effect on shaping the content of liberation theology and in consolidating a preferential option for socialism. The dismissal of Marxist influences by claiming that they merely represent a set of analytical categories for understanding the Latin American condition grossly underestimates the final significance of these interpretive rubrics. Ideas do, indeed, have consequences—vulgar Marxist conceptions of the epiphenomenal role of ideology in relation to material substructures to the contrary notwithstanding. And ideas which control the definition of the situation have extraordinary power in shaping all subsequent responses to reality so conceived.

Thus, liberation theologians present their interpreters with a curious conundrum. On the one hand, they castigate as unscientific or reactionary anyone who would challenge the validity of interpretive assessments founded on dependency theory. On the other hand, they seek to absolve their theological contribution from too intimate an affiliation with Marxist ideological conceptions. The obscurantism running rife in liberationists' writings is due, in generous part, to a fundamental lack of intellectual rigor and conceptual clarity. (See the criticism of Neuhaus on this score.[58]) Yet, the issue runs much deeper than this. The fate of liberation theology is inextricably tied to the enduring cogency of dependency theory. Should subsequent research on Third World economic-political dynamics or a paradigm shift among sociological theorists discredit dependency theory, then liberation theology would almost certainly be impossible to sustain, or at the very least it would require such drastic alterations that little of its former substance would remain in evidence. Indeed, among contemporary social analysts, few schools of thought have a larger investment in the enduring cogency of dependency theory than the liberation theologians of Latin America.

CONCLUSION: DEPENDENCY AND LIBERATION

The literature of liberation theology is riddled with Marxist concepts— such as praxis (and orthopraxis), class struggle, capitalist exploitation, ruling class hegemony, material forces, alienating labor, economic oppression, revolutionary process, dominant class repression, and the like. Our concern in this analysis has not been to examine either the full range of Marxist schools of thought or the various instances of Marxist influence on liberation theology as evidenced by the adoption of these sundry concepts. Rather, our concern has been to follow up one type of influence, namely, that which has derived from the appropriation of neocolonial dependency theory.[59]

Whereas much of the Marxist rhetoric employed by liberation theologians can be dismissed as peripheral to the central thrust of this school, dependency theory enjoys a status that is far from marginal for the movement as a whole. Indeed, the programmatic orientation of liberation theology is directly founded on the distinctive tenets of dependency theory, both with respect to the basic problem definition and with respect to the appropriate solution for ameliorating the plight of Latin Americans caught in the throes of abject poverty. Moreover, as a discrete set of religious ideas, liberation theology lies sandwiched between the specification of the problem and the identification of corrective measures. Although Segundo contends that the function of theology in this situation should be understood as *fides quaerens intellectum* (faith seeking understanding),[60] in point of fact the theological contribution remains narrowly delimited to providing a religious warrant for that "understanding" of the historical context already derived from neo-Marxist constructs. One searches in vain through the extensive writings of this school for clear indications of where its theological rubrics have fostered independent criticism, clarification, or qualification of neocolonial interpretations.

Defenders of liberationists have, on occasion, challenged such a con- clusion by means of a counterargument which asserts that theologians of this school are engaged in day-to-day ministry in the barrios and peasant villages of Latin America, and therefore they should not be expected to master the subtler nuances of academic social theory. Apart from the fact that such a defense implicitly acknowledges a lack of critical discernment with respect to the theoretical infrastructure utilized by this theological school, the more curious, and perhaps original, feature of this defense is that it justifies a toleration of theological naivete on the grounds of personal involvement. In an earlier era, certainly, no one suggested that Karl Barth's *Letter to the Romans* should be indulged any theological misconstructions because the author was a young country pastor in Switzerland at the time or, again, that Reinhold Niebuhr's early forays into political-theological analysis should be absolved of the need for realistic rigor because he was serving a parish in Detroit. Why the normal criteria of evaluation should be suspended in the case of liberation theologians has never been adequate- ly explained. Surely a preferential option for the poor need not entail a preferential option for poor theologizing.

Moreover, a number of occasions immediately spring to mind wherein liberation theologians might make a more substantive contribution to the resolution of those inundating economic-political problems now plaguing Latin America. In this first instance, liberationists would better serve their cause of ameliorating the misery of Latin American peasants if they at- tended more readily to the burgeoning literature critical of dependency theory as well as the qualifications and refinements developed by advo- cates of the dependency paradigm. No interest in undertaking such a criti- cal review of this sort has yet been manifested among the leading figures of the liberation movement. Assmann provides, albeit somewhat inadver- tently, a ready account for this reluctance, when he observes that "one thing virtually all the documents so far published agree on is that the starting- point of the theology of liberation is the present historical situation of domination and dependence in which the countries of the Third World find themselves."[61] Liberation theologians have such a formidable stake in the "dependency-liberation formula" that any questioning of the validity of the dependency paradigm would inevitably shake the movement to its very foundations. Naive acceptance of dependency theory as established scientific fact, therefore, readily serves the vested ideal interests of the movement's constituents. Furthermore, when one moves beyond the literate leadership of the liberation movement to peasants in the countryside and the urban poor mobilized in the barrios, then appreciation for the subtleties of dependency theories is promptly reduced. Cardenal's transcripts of conversations with peasants in Solentiname, for example, reveal a drastic simplification of basic liberation themes, so that the "dependency-liberation formula" assumes a starkly reductionistic end even belligerent form.[62] This formula functions at the level of popular consumption less as a method of analysis than as a depiction of reality which calls for a specific type of responsive action.

A second instance wherein liberationists might exercise a positive influence relative to redressing the political problems currently facing Latin Americans relates to the clarification of those "ends and means," goals and practices, embodied in the revolutionary cause. Yet liberationist writings to date have concentrated more attention on the ways in which the Eucharist, biblical interpretation, prayer, meditation, ethics, ecclesiastical structures, and so forth can be made relevant to the revolutionary process than they have on how these ecclesiastical elements can help contain the demonic forces arising out of class struggles and revolutionary violence. The rhetoric of liberation theologians in legitimizing revolutionary action can only be deemed conscionable insofar as they are willing or able to adduce criteria for adjudicating whether a given foray into violence advances meritorious ends and holds forth a reasonable probability of ushering in a more humane social order. The generalized condemnation of contemporary repressive regimes and the sanguine faith in the ability of post-revolutionary masses to devise an equitable political structure simply do not inspire much faith in the critical seriousness of liberation advocates. The lack of clarity—both with respect to current failings of regnant regimes and subsequent remedies of a political-economic nature—suggests that liberation theologians have allocated the hard decisions to others relative to the sort of future social order which ought to be institutionalized.

Such a posture might well be understandable for political ideologues who have no independent point of reference on which to predicate judgments of this sort, but theologians have access to a whole range of ethical standards for evaluating precisely these kinds of valuational issues. The fact that liberationists have engaged in a wide ranging ethical critique of First World nations and repressive Latin American regimes, while stalwartly refusing to bring ethical criteria to bear on the means employed in revolutionary action by their own partisans or to define what justice in the new social order would have to entail, merely serves to underscore the essential marginality of theological discourse to the liberationist movement as a whole. Taking recourse to abstruse formulations which announce that participants in the liberation process are committed to the "creation of a just society" and "a new man"[63] without delineating the project in more concrete terms is at once theologically suspect and politically dangerous, especially when revolution with its attendant potential for violence is endorsed as one's mechanism for attaining social change.

On balance, therefore, the central failing of liberation theology can be reduced to the following terms: on the one hand, it assigns too narrow a role to theology and the church while, on the other hand, it invests too much faith in the cogency of dependency theory and the likelihood that its prescribed solution of revolutionary struggle will produce a benign outcome. This criticism is not founded on a bias against political theologies generally. Rather, it relates to the particular style of theologizing embraced by this school of thought, namely, its relegation of religious ideas to a position wherein they essentially provide a warrant for the economic interpretation of dependency theory and legitimation for a political strategy of revolutionary action. Other political theologians have made a concerted effort to retain a critical stance, even toward those movements facilitating social change which they generally favor. That such a critical posture has failed to develop among liberation theologians has left them vulnerable to the charge that, by dint of their project, "...Marxists are transformed into Christians by transforming Christians into Marxists."[64]

NOTES

1. Peter L. Berger and Hansfried Kellner, *Sociology Reinterpreted* (Garden City, N.Y.: Doubleday and Co., 1981), pp. 3–8; Daniel Chirot, "The Rise of the West," *American Sociological Review* 50 (April 1985): 181–95.

2. S. N. Eisenstadt, "Reflections On A Theory Of Modernization," in *Nations By Design,* ed. Arnold Rivkin (Garden City, N.Y.: Doubleday and Co., 1968), pp. 35–37.

3. Several of the more prominent contributions to this extensive body of literature include: David E. Apter, *The Politics of Modernization* (Chicago: University of Chicago Press, 1965); Robert N. Bellah, *Tokugawa Religion* (Boston: Beacon Press, [1957] 1970); Reinhard Bendix, *Nation-Building And Citizenship* (Garden City, N.Y.: Doubleday and Co., 1964); Leonard Binder et al., *Crises and Sequences in Political Development* (Princeton: Princeton University Press, 1971); Szymon Chodak, *Societal Development* (New York: Oxford University Press, 1973); S. N. Eisenstadt, ed., *The Protestant Ethic and Modernization* (New York: Basic Books, 1968); Guy Hunter, *Modernizing Peasant Societies* (New York: Oxford University Press, 1969); Daniel Lerner, *The Passing of Traditional Society* (New York: Free Press, 1958); Marion J. Levy, Jr., *Modernization and the Structure of Societies* (Princeton: Princeton University Press, 1966); Seymour Martin Lipset, *Revolution and Counter-Revolution* (Garden City, N.Y.: Doubleday and Co., [1963] 1970); David McClelland, *The Achieving Society* (New York: Free Press, 1961); Fred R. von der Mehden, *Politics of the Developing Nations* (Englewood Cliffs, N.J.: Prentice-Hall, 1964); Robert A. Nisbet, *Social Change and History* (New York: Oxford University Press, 1969); J. Roland Pennock, ed., *Self-Government in Modernizing Nations* (Englewood Cliffs, N.J.: Prentice-Hall, 1964); Lucian W. Pye, *Politics, Personality, and Nation Building* (New Haven: Yale University Press, 1962); W. W. Rostow, *The Stages of Economic Growth* (New York: Oxford University Press, 1960); and I. Robert Sinai, *The Challenge of Modernization* (New York: W. W. Norton, 1964). One common feature of these studies was their conspicuous avoidance of Marxist

and neo-Marxist interpretive schemes, and, indeed, several embraced an explicitly anti-Marxist stance.

4. C. Wright Mills, *The Sociological Imagination* (New York: Oxford University Press, 1959).

5. Alvin W. Gouldner, *The Coming Crisis in Western Sociology* (New York: Avon Books, 1970).

6. See Jeffrey C. Alexander, *The Modern Reconstruction of Classical Thought: Talcott Parsons,* Vol. 2 of *Theoretical Logic in Sociology* (Berkeley: University of California Press, 1983).

7. See Robert Tucker, *Philosophy and Myth in Karl Marx* (New York: Cambridge University Press, 1961).

8. Such a facile view of Marxist materialism has recently and ably been critiqued by Dupré and McLellan. See, Louis Dupré, *Marx's Social Critique of Culture* (New Haven: Yale University Press, 1983); and David McClellan, *Karl Marx: His Life and Thought* (New York: Harper and Row, 1973).

9. Talcott Parsons, *The Structure of Social Action* (New York: Bantam Books, [1937] 1949); *The Social System* (New York: Bantam Books, 1951).

10. See Talcott Parsons et al., *Working Papers in a Theory of Action* (New York: Free Press, 1953); and Francois Bourricaud, *The Sociology of Talcott Parsons* (Chicago: University of Chicago Press, 1981), pp. 190–91.

11. Karl Marx, *Capital* (New York: Random House, 1906), pp. 838–48.

12. Joseph A. Schumpeter, *Capitalism, Socialism, and Democracy* (New York: Harper and Row, [1942], 1962), pp. 50–51.

13. V. I. Lenin, *The Essential Works of Lenin* (New York: Bantam Books, 1966).

14. Ibid., pp. 236–45; James O'Connor, "The Meaning of Economic Imperialism," in *Readings in U.S. Imperialism,* ed. K. T. Fann and D. C. Hodges (Boston: Porter Sargent, 1971).

15. Lenin, *Essential Works,* pp. 266–68.

16. David McClellan, *Marxism after Marx* (New York: Harper and Row, 1979), pp. 250–53.

17. Andre Gunder Frank, *Capitalism and Underdevelopment in Latin America* (New York: Monthly Review Press, 1969), p. xi.

18. Peter L. Berger, *Pyramids of Sacrifice* (Garden City, N.Y.: Doubleday and Co., 1976), pp. 49–51.

19. Andre Gunder Frank, *Latin America: Underdevelopment or Revolution?* (New York: Monthly Review Press, 1969), pp. 3–120, 145–218.

20. Although this lengthy literature cannot be fully cited here, some of the more important contributions, especially those generated by sociologists, include the following: Christopher Chase-Dunn, "The Effects of International Economic Dependence on Development and Inequality: A Cross-National Analysis," *American Sociological Review* 40 (December 1975): 720–38; Richard Rubinson, "The World-Economy and the Distribution of Income within States," *American Sociological Review* 41 (August 1976): 638–59; Immanuel Wallerstein, *The Modern World-System* (New York: Academic Press, 1974); *The Capitalist World-Economy* (Cambridge: Cambridge University Press, 1979); *The Modern World-System II* (New York: Academic Press, 1980); Peter B. Evans and Michael Timberlane, "Dependence, Inequality, and the Growth of the Tertiary: A Comparative Analysis of Less Developed Countries," *American Sociological Review* 45 (October 1980): 531–52; Kenneth Bollen, "World System Position, Dependency, and Democracy: The Cross-National Evidence," *American Sociological Review* 48 (August 1983): 468–79; Albert Bergesen, ed., *Crisis in the World-System* (Beverly Hills, Calif.: Sage Publications, 1983); Robert Fiala, "Inequality and the Service Sector in Less Developed Countries: A Reanalysis and Respecification," *American Sociological Review* 48 (June 1983): 421–28; York W. Bradshaw, "Dependent Development In Black Africa: A Cross National Study," *American Sociological Review* 50 (April 1985): 195–207; and William Rau and D. W. Roncek, "Industrialization and World Inequality: The Transformation of the Division of Labor in 59 Nations, 1960–1981," *American Sociological Review* 52 (June 1987): 359–69. One of the significant features with respect to much of this literature is the gradual shift from strict dependency theory to some variant form of world systems analysis.

21. Paul A. Baran and Paul M. Sweezy, "Economics of Two Worlds," in *Marx and Modern Economics,* ed. David Horowitz (New York: Monthly Review Press, 1968), p. 291.

22. See Ernest Mandel, *Late Capitalism* (London: NLB, 1975), pp. 535–40.

23. See Fernand Braudel, *Civilization and Capitalism, 15th–18th Century* (New York: Harper and Row, 1981, 1982, 1984).

24. Among the leaders of the Frankfurt school are: Max Horkheimer, *Critical Theory* (New York: Herder and Herder, 1972); *Critique of Instrumental Reason* (New York: Seabury Press, 1974); Theodor Adorno, *Negative Dialectics* (New York: Seabury Press, 1973), and with Max Horkheimer, *Dialectic of Enlightenment* (New York: Herder and Herder, 1972); Herbert Marcuse, *One-Dimensional Man* (Boston: Beacon Press, 1964); and more contemporaneously, Jürgen Habermas, *Knowledge and Human Interests* (Boston: Beacon Press, 1971), *Theory and Practice* (Boston: Beacon Press, 1974), and *The Theory of Communicative Action,* Vol. 1 (Boston: Beacon Press, 1981). Critical theorists have devoted relatively little attention to the issue of dependency, but they have provided an alternative Marxian approach to economic-political relations. Liberation theologians have typically not been terribly conversant with critical theory, except perhaps for the work of Marcuse.

25. Louis Althusser, *For Marx* (New York: Random House, 1970); and Louis Althusser and Etienne Balibar, *Reading Capital* (New York: Pantheon Books, 1970).

26. See Antonio Gramsci, *The Modern Prince and Other Writings* (New York: International Publishers, 1957).

27. See Chase-Dunn, "Economic Dependence," pp. 732–33.

28. See Rubinson, "The World Economy."

29. See in this connection: Fiala, "Inequality and the Service Sector," and Rau and Roncek, "Industrialization and World Inequality."

30. Jacques Delacroix and Charles C. Ragin, "Structural Blockage: A Cross-National Study of Economic Dependency, State Efficacy, and Underdevelopment," *American Journal of Sociology* 86 (May 1981): 1311–47.

31. Joseph Ramos, "Dependency and Development: An Attempt to Clarify the Issues," in *Liberation South, Liberation North,* ed. Michael Novak (Washington, D.C.: American Enterprise Institute, 1981), pp. 61–64.

32. Ramos, ibid., p. 61.

33. Michael J. Francis, "Dependency: Ideology, Fad, and Fact," in *Latin America: Dependency or Interdependence,* ed. Michael Novak and Michael P. Jackson (Washington, D.C.: American Enterprise Institute, 1985), p. 96.

34. Ramos, "Dependency and Development," p. 67.

35. See Peter L. Berger and Michael Novak, *Speaking to the Third World* (Washington, D.C.: American Enterprise Institute, 1985), p. 12.

36. The exponential growth of writings by liberation theologians—as well as the critical commentary on this school—precludes any exhaustive summary in this brief essay. We can, however, identify several of the more important contributions that have served to define the boundaries of this variegated tradition, including: Gustavo Gutiérrez, *A Theology of Liberation* (Maryknoll, N.Y.: Orbis Books, 1973); Juan Luis Segundo, *The Liberation of Theology* (Maryknoll, N.Y.: Orbis Books, 1976); Hugo Assmann, *A Theology for a Nomad Church* (Maryknoll, N.Y.: Orbis Books, 1976); José Míguez Bonino, *Doing Theology in a Revolutionary Situation* (Philadelphia: The Westminster Press, 1975); Leonardo Boff, *Liberating Grace* (Maryknoll, New York: Orbis Books, 1979), *Ecclesiogenesis: The Base Communities Reinvent the Church* (Maryknoll, N.Y.: Orbis Books, 1986); Leonardo Boff and Clodovis Boff, *Liberation Theology: From Confrontation to Dialogue* (Maryknoll, N.Y.: Orbis Books, 1986); Ernesto Cardinal, *The Gospel in Solentiname* (Maryknoll, N.Y.: Orbis Books, 1976–82); José Comblin, *The Church and the National Security State* (Maryknoll, N.Y.: Orbis Books, 1979); Enrique Dussel, *History and the Theology of Liberation* (Maryknoll, N.Y.: Orbis Books, 1976); Matthew L. Lamb, *Solidarity with Victims* (Maryknoll, N.Y.: Orbis Books, 1982); and José Miranda, *Marx against the Marxists* (Maryknoll, N.Y.: Orbis Books, 1980), *Communism in the Bible* (Maryknoll, N.Y.: Orbis Books, 1982).

37. John A. Coleman, S. J., "Civil Religion and Liberation Theology in North America," in *Theology in the Americas,* ed. Sergio Torres and John Eagleson (Maryknoll, N.Y.: Orbis Books, 1976), p. 133.

38. See William R. Garrett, "Religion and the Legitimation of Violence," in *Prophetic Religions and Politics,* ed. Jeffrey K. Hadden and Anson Shupe (New York: Paragon House, 1986).

39. See Deane William Ferm, *Third World Liberation Theologies* (Maryknoll, N.Y.: Orbis Books, 1986), pp. 107–15.

40. See Joseph Cardinal Ratzinger and Vittorio Messori, *The Ratzinger Report* (San Francisco: Ignatius Press, 1985), pp. 186–88.

41. See in this connection, Boff and Boff, *Liberation Theology,* and Segundo Galilea, "Liberation Theology And The New Tasks Facing Christians," in *Frontiers of Theology in Latin America,* ed. Rosino Gibellini (Maryknoll, N.Y.: Orbis Books, 1979), p. 170.

42. See Ferm *Third World Liberation Theology,* p. 111.

43. Segundo, *Liberation of Theology,* p. 37.

44. See Gutiérrez, *Theology of Liberation.*

45. Ibid., pp. 81–99.

46. Gutiérrez, *Theology of Liberation,* p. 81.

47. See Ibid., pp. 82–83, 92–93.

48. Michael Novak, *Will It Liberate? Questions about Liberation Theology* (New York: Paulist Press, 1986), p. 131; Peter L. Berger, *The Capitalist Revolution* (New York: Basic Books, 1986), p. 124.

49. See Boff, *Liberating Grace,* pp. 218–19; Míguez Bonino, *Doing Theology,* pp. 36–37.

50. See, for example, Assmann, *Nomad Church,* pp. 45–56; Segundo, *Liberation of Theology,* and Comblin, *National Security State,* pp. 31–38.

51. See, Berger, *Capitalist Revolution,* pp. 124–25.

52. See, Christine E. Gudorf, *Catholic Social Teaching on Liberation Themes* (Washington, D.C.: University Press of America, 1981), pp. 170–71.

53. See Daniel Bell, *The Cultural Contradictions of Capitalism* (New York: Harper and Row, 1978), p. xi.

54. Juan Luis Segundo, "Capitalism-Socialism: A Theological Crux" in *Liberation South, Liberation North,* ed. Michael Novak (Washington, D.C.: American Enterprise Institute, 1981), p. 15.

55. See, in this connection, Comblin, *National Security State,* pp. 127–32; Míguez Bonino, *Doing Theology,* pp. 33–36; Assmann, *Nomad Church,* p. 97; Dussel, "Historical and Philosophical Presuppositions for Latin American Theology" in *Frontiers of Theology in Latin America,* ed. Rosino Gibellini (Maryknoll, N.Y.: Orbis Books, 1979), p. 205; and Boff, *Liberating Grace,* p. 42.

56. One of the most glaring oversights by liberation theologians in pondering the causes of Latin American poverty is the role which former colonial powers—especially Spain and Portugal—exerted on shaping the basic institutions of the continent. Indeed, the legacy of colonial practices may well, on balance, be more significant than the role of multinationals from the United States. See, for example, Ivan Vallier, *Catholicism, Social Control, and Modernization in Latin America* (Englewood Cliffs, N.J.: Prentice-Hall, 1970); Sheldon B. Liss, *Marxist Thought in Latin America* (Berkeley: University of California Press, 1984); and Roland Robertson, "Liberation Theology in Latin America: Sociological Problems of Interpretation and Explanation," in *Prophetic Religions and Politics.*

57. Míguez Bonino, *Doing Theology,* pp. 34–35.

58. Richard John Neuhaus, "Liberation Theology and the Cultural Captivity of the Gospel," in *Liberation Theology,* ed. Ronald Nash (Milford, Mich.: Mott Media, Inc., 1984), pp. 219–36.

59. One of the more conventional defenses raised in support of liberation theologians is that, since Marxism itself has become such a diverse phenomenon, it is no longer very meaningful to label this school Marxist. One cannot gainsay the general validity of this observation, yet the liberationists themselves often describe their analyses as Marxist, and with little apparent recognition of the nuanced strands of Marxist theory. Indeed, the central theme of this research endeavor is to establish the thesis that liberationists

generally have in mind some form of dependency theory when they describe their position as Marxist or informed by Marxist precepts.

60. Segundo, "Capitalism-Socialism," p. 16.

61. Assmann, *Nomad Church*, p. 53.

62. See Cardenal, *Solentiname*.

63. These phrases are from Gutiérrez, *Theology of Liberation*, p. 213.

64. Dale Vree, "A Critique of Christian Marxism," in *Liberation Theology*, ed. Nash, p. 214.

┌─────┐
│ 9 │
└─────┘

Liberation Theology and the Latin American Revolutions

Humberto Belli

Revolutions in Latin America are taking place in a largely Christian environment. That the fate of these revolutions is entwined with dynamics of that environment is a safe assumption. At any rate, that became the explicit assumption of one of the most influential revolutionary leaders of Latin America, the legendary Che Guevara. He once said: "When the revolutionary Christians dare to give an integral testimony, that day the Latin American revolution will be irreversible." [1]

To find out how Marxist revolutionaries came to this awareness and how this affects the political dynamics of Latin America, we must go back to the early days of the Cuban revolution.

REVOLUTIONARY STRATEGY IN LATIN AMERICA

As the first Marxist victory in the region, the Cuban Revolution sparked an unprecedented wave of revolutionary fervor among Latin American radicals. It also forced a rethinking of the strategies best suited to the overthrow of ruling regimes. Traditionally, communists in this part of the world had faithfully abided by Moscow's reservations about the wisdom of armed struggle as a means of attaining power. In the Latin Americans' view,

199

objective conditions in their region were not ripe for that type of confrontation. What Marxist revolutionaries had done was patiently to build working class organizations and to wait for the growth of a more sizable urban proletariat. Until organization of the proletariat was complete, they believed, violent tactics were doomed to failure.

The epic of the young Castroist guerrillas' descending in triumph from the mountains suddenly challenged these views. Among many younger Marxists, less inclined by temperament to the gradual buildup of proletarian forces, the experience of Cuba seemed to show that the objective conditions for the unleashing of successful wars against oppressive regimes could be precipitated. All it took was a handful of courageous armed militants who were able to create a revolutionary "focus" in remote areas of the countryside, protected by the terrain and by the support of the local peasants. Acting from their hideouts, the guerrillas would gradually engage the armies of the bourgeois government by using hit-and-run tactics. The revolutionary focus would then galvanize the discontented segments of the population and gradually demoralize the enemy.

The best exponent of this strategy came to be not a Latin American but the Frenchman Régis Debray, whose book, *Revolution in the Revolution?* published in 1966, became a primer for the new cohort of strategists. But not for too long. Wherever the advocates of the "foco" theory put it to the test, they were met with disaster. In 1967 alone, Che Guevara met a lonely death at the hands of the Bolivian army, Debray ended up in prison, and the Sandinista guerrillas in Nicaragua were almost annihilated. Scores of Latin American revolutionaries suffered similar fates.

The setbacks forced a reappraisal of the strategies used. Some Marxist leaders concluded that they had tried to replicate too closely or too mechanically the Cuban experience. In an effort to salvage the basic strategy of armed struggle, some abandoned the foco theory and went into designing more eclectic approaches. At times they followed the teachings of Mao, who relied on mobile peasant armies. At times they favored urban-based guerrilla networks and warfare. Quite often militants quarreled among themselves on these issues and caused splits in many of their organizations.

No matter what variations were tried, however, the new strategies were of no avail. Despite their strategic imagination, in country after country revolutionary movements suffered defeat after defeat.

In Brazil, Carlos Marighella, who tried to shift the struggle to urban areas, was killed by the police in 1968. In Venezuela, most of the guerrillas gave up their struggle and reintegrated themselves into civic life, except for a band led by Douglas Bravo who soon fell into oblivion. In Peru and Bolivia, armed groups were unable to regain the footholds they had lost in disastrous confrontations with the armies in 1966 and 1968. In Uruguay, the famous Tupamaros urban guerrillas, who for a few years made headlines in the international media with their bold and imaginative strikes, were completely disbanded by 1971. The Marxist armies in Colombia stagnated, and those in Guatemala and Argentina were unable to hold their ground before the onslaught of military and right-wing groups. The Allende experiment in Chile was finally aborted by a coup in 1973.

By the beginning of the seventies, and after more than a decade of attempted revolutions, the radical Left found itself in a dismal situation. Not only had they been beaten on the battlefield, but they had failed to transcend the limits of being small elite groups of university-based conspirators. On the domestic front they had been unable to spark the enthusiasm of the masses. On the international front they had been unable to arouse the sympathy and media attention that had proven so instrumental to Fidel Castro's victory.

SUCCESSFUL REVOLUTION

The new stalemate brought another round of soul-searching, splits within groups, and strategic proposals. Then, while the dust of past defeats was still settling, an extraordinary event occurred, with a suddenness reminiscent of the Cuban revolution. Armed guerrillas were victorious in Nicaragua while hosts of other Marxist combatants made the government of El Salvador shake and stumble. There was a new upsurge of guerrilla movements in Central America, and they were scoring unprecedented successes.

Still more significantly, in the case of Nicaragua the guerrillas were able to ignite a nationwide fire, while at the international level both Nicaraguan and Salvadoran revolutionaries found an unprecedented reception among journalists and church people.

Why this turnaround? What strategic novelty had at last succeeded in Central America?

Alan Riding of the *New York Times* confronted these questions in 1981 and provided valuable insight into the nature of the change in Central America. The success of the Marxist revolutionaries, he contended, was not due to the intensity of Central American poverty, which had not markedly increased at the end of the seventies, but was the result of a wholly novel factor—the successful blend of Marxism and Christianity in the region.[2] Riding chose for his article a significant title: "The Sword and the Cross." Possibly it was this kind of symbolism Guevara had in mind when he made his prophetic statement about the great revolutionary potential in a confluence of Marxists and Christians.

In retrospect, events indeed suggest that the initial failure of the Latin American revolutionaries to emulate the Cuban experience rested not in trying to copy the revolution, but in failing to pay enough attention to Guevara's comment. The irony is that Guevara himself seems to have neglected his observation. In spite of his earlier statements about the political potential of having Christians embrace the cause of revolution, his writings about strategy and tactics shared the same views and emphases as the host of revolutionary analyses that prevailed throughout the sixties. Their focus was military and centered on how different guerrilla strategies could produce or promote different political outcomes. They neglected ideological aspects and, hence, overlooked one of the decisively important aspects of the Cuban revolution. In the phase before their triumph, Cuban revolutionary leaders had called for and obtained the collaboration of Cubans of all social strata and beliefs—including militant Christians such as Frank Pais and some Catholic bishops.

How were the Cubans able to achieve such support? Although several specific factors in Cuban society at that time contributed to the outcome, a key element was the conscious effort among top leaders of the revolution not to present themselves as Marxist-Leninists, in order to avoid alienating their broader domestic and international audiences. In other words, the Marxist leaders of the revolution weighed the strong anticommunist sentiment of the Cuban people, characteristic of the Catholic heritage prior to Vatican II, and presented themselves as liberal, bourgeois reformers. They did not produce a theology of revolution, but they were careful to articulate their calls to action in ways that took into account "the religious factor." This was not a sufficient condition for the revolutionary victory, but it was without question one of the necessary conditions.

The revolutionaries who took their rifles into the jungles and slums of Latin America during the sixties failed to apply this important lesson of the victorious Cubans. A reason for their neglect may be that they were misled by their own ideology. To explain the Cuban success in Marxist terms, they had to refer to abstract processes such as "the worsening of contradictions in neocolonial societies" or to strategic considerations. It would have been inappropriate, and embarrassing, to single out deception as an important tactical instrument.

Another reason for their failure during the 1960s was the obvious difficulty of replicating a strategy that had already alerted most non-Marxist leaders in Latin America. That Castro himself publicly confessed his Marxist-Leninism after coming to power, and that the Left in other countries rushed to support him, precluded other revolutionaries' denial of their ideological allegiances. What is more, the euphoria engendered by the triumph in Cuba prevented many revolutionaries from defining this situation as problematic. When they took to the hills, they saw their action as heralding a most profound strategic break with old-guard communists. Yet, in a very important respect, the new revolutionaries shared with the older communists their advocacy of sectarian, Marxist-Leninist ideas. And in many ways they harvested the same result: They caused the disaffection of scores of peasants, students, middle-class professionals, and, very significantly, those educators and value transmitters who are so important in Latin America—priests, nuns, pastors, and members of religious orders.

Insightful leaders such as Guevara had the intuition that in order to win or at least to neutralize the non-Marxist forces in the region, Latin American Marxists had to devise new strategies. By the end of the sixties, however, few were able to envision them.

RELIGIOUS ANTICOMMUNISM

Fear of communism among large segments of the traditionally Roman Catholic and agrarian societies of Latin America posed a formidable obstacle. The Roman Catholic church, influential as it was in the education establishment, among the upper and middle classes, and among the peasantry, militantly and almost unanimously preached against communism. Several papal encyclicals and church documents explicitly and unambiguously condemned it. As early as in 1846, Pope Pius IX had called communism an "infamous doctrine."[3]

Leo XIII had defined communism as "the fatal plague which insinuates itself into the very marrow of human society only to bring about its ruin."[4]

Even more stern were the expressions of Pius XI. In his famous encyclical, *On Atheistic Communism,* he referred to "the most persistent enemy of the church," "a satanic scourge," which used a "propaganda so truly diabolical that the world has perhaps never witnessed its like before."[5] Pius XI concluded that "Communism is intrinsically wrong, and no one who would save Christian civilization may collaborate with it in any undertaking whatsoever."[6]

The ban on any collaboration between Christians and Communists became official church policy in 1949, under Pius XII, when a decree of the Holy Office forbade Catholics to join the Communist party or encourage it in any way.[7] Before theological relativism and pluralism were acceptable in Latin America, Vatican views were taught and understood as possessing near-absolute authority.

Among Protestants, anticommunism was a strong feature as well. Nurtured in many instances by the tradition of North American evangelical fundamentalists, many of the Protestant denominations working in the region shared a deeply ingrained distaste for political activism and easily saw in communism the work of the devil, though some Protestant theologians, such as Tillich and Niebuhr in the 1920s and 1930s, felt freer than Catholics to explore different alternatives and considered socialism and Marxism with some openness. No matter how strong the longing for an earthly utopia, however, neither Protestants nor Catholics were able to come up with theological and theoretical means to bring about reconciliation between Christianity and communism.

The anti-Christian, antireligious tradition of nearly all communist movements and regimes also conspired to deepen the division between Marxists and Christians. Castro himself expelled the bulk of the Cuban Catholic clergy, squarely placing his regime in the anti-church tradition of Marxist governments all over the world. At the ideological level, a good many postrevolutionary radical documents in Cuba still rejected religion as the opiate of the masses; and it was the customary policy among revolutionary Marxist movements to prevent Christian conversion. There were, however, Marxist voices that pointed out the disadvantages of such antireligious policies. The Peruvian intellectual, José Carlos Mariátegui, advised the Left to consider Christianity an integral part of the people's consciousness in

Latin America. It could be used for one purpose or another—if not for revolution, then for reaction. Not to seek control of this powerful lever would be to abandon it to the enemy.[8] Yet, such admonitions went unheeded, and the schism between Marxists and Christians remained a deep divide.

VATICAN II AND CHRISTIAN-MARXIST DIALOGUE

How could this stalemate be broken? The opportunity came at the end of the sixties, when patterns had dramatically changed inside the Catholic and Protestant world, and when the bitter taste of repeated defeats had humbled the Left. Landmarks of the change in the Christian world were Vatican II and the Latin American Bishops' Conference at Medellín, Colombia (1968). Although neither of these events explicitly questioned the traditional teachings of the church about communism, they brought significant changes in emphasis and style, together with some new openings that set in motion long-dormant forces and launched proposals with unforeseen consequences. A discussion of whether these and similar results were a faithful reflection of the spirit and intent of those who framed Vatican II falls outside the scope of this analysis. Suffice it to say that in the wake of the council, changed circumstances made it easier for new theological interpretations to gain a foothold within the church.

With Vatican II there came from many quarters militant calls for theological pluralism and experimentation. At the same time the dropping of former defenses and the search for reconciliation with non-Christians, including Marxists, came to be ruling concerns of many Catholic intellectuals. The new attitude was epitomized by the title that Roger Garaudy, chief theoretician of the French Communist party gave to his book, *From Anathema to Dialogue*. In many places in Western Europe and North America new interest in Christian-Marxist dialogue produced countless encounters and writings. The process, however, was not symmetrical. As many scholars have documented, many Christians went to great lengths to build bridges, even at the expense of doctrinal integrity, while the Marxists barely moved an inch. It has even been suggested that part of what stimulated the eagerness to find common ground with Marxists was, in many cases an unconscious desire to buy into someone else's belief system,[9] thus betraying the existence of a deep, and possibly widespread, identity crisis among Christians.

In regard to Marxism and communism, positions of Christians in Central America at that point ranged from the earlier distrust and unambiguous rejection, through advocacy of understanding and dialogue (while warning about potential dangers and incompatibilities) to implicit or explicit defense of the Marxist analysis.

A fact of the utmost importance when viewing the range of standpoints is that the unity of vision about communism that had characterized the church before Vatican II was now considerably weakened, if not defunct. An end result was that the Catholic laity, as well as the armies of relatively perplexed priests, nuns, and seminarians, saw many of the old and perhaps too-rigid certainties replaced by a vast array of contradictory theological visions, each struggling for recognition and each claiming to represent the true Catholic spirit. Now there were theologians and church representatives who saw communism as enemy, competitor, or friend. Although Catholics of different views criticized and even harshly attacked each other, none of them was reprimanded by the highest church authorities. On the other hand, as author Dale Vree has indicated, "in 1970 the French Communist party expelled its chief theoretician, Roger Garaudy, from the Politburo (on which he had served for fourteen years) and the party itself (of which he was a member for more than thirty years). His offense was revisionism—including, in the background, his pioneering role in the dialogue."[10] No Catholic theologian suffered excommunication on similar grounds. There were no more heresy trials at all after the council.

At a time when tolerance and openness toward new ideas was the prevailing attitude, it took considerable courage to take stands that might appear authoritarian or, even worse, "preconciliar," a highly derogatory adjective that came to be feared almost as much as "heretical" had been feared in the Middle Ages. A "preconciliar" Catholic or theologian did not risk excommunication but something deemed worse by contemporary man—irrelevance.

LIBERATION THEOLOGY

For a variety of reasons, interpretations of those who tended to view Marxism as a friendly set of ideas found very fertile soil among Latin American theologians and religious who had studied or were studying in Europe, and who had been influenced by different European liberal theologians, especially Germans like Moltmann, Bultmann, and Metz. Many of these Latin American theologians became co-authors and advocates of what is known as liberation theology, particularly after the Peruvian priest, Gustavo Gutiérrez, published a book in 1971 in which he expounded systematically the key tenets of such a theology.

The originality of Gutiérrez and his followers' views was not their call for social justice or their call for political involvement on behalf of the poor—as it is often assumed in less-informed church and journalistic circles in the developed world. Such concerns had been present among Christian Democrats and among socially minded Christians in the tradition of Jacques Maritain and Pierre Teilhard de Chardin. The magisterium of the church, as expressed in several encyclicals such as Leo XIII's *Rerum Novarum* (1891), had also upheld the rights of workers to demand just wages and had issued calls on behalf of social justice.

New in Gutiérrez's thought, however, was his adoption of the idea of class struggle as framed by Marx: that society is divided into two irreconcilable social classes, the oppressed and the oppressors; that conflict—not reconciliation—between the two must lead to a classless, harmonious society once the private ownership of the means of production is abolished; and that all views and institutions (theology and the church included) respond to either the class interests of the oppressed or to the interests of the oppressors.[11]

Gutiérrez provides an explicit summary of the movement's adoption of Marx's perspectives:

> Only a class-based analysis will enable us to see what is really involved in the opposition between oppressed countries on the one hand and dominant peoples on the other....
>
> [The] people must come to power if society is to be truly free and egalitarian. In such a society private ownership of the means of production will be eliminated because it enables a few to expropriate the fruits of labor,...generates class division in society, and permits one class to be exploited by another....
>
> Only by eliminating private ownership of the wealth created by human labor will we be able to lay the foundations for a more just society. That is why efforts to project a new

society in Latin America are moving more and more toward socialism.[12]

Even a superficial acquaintance with Marxist doctrine readily suggests that these views are indistinguishable from those espoused by Communist and Marxist organizations around the world. But in fact, the liberationists' originality was their attempt to express the idea of class struggle in Christian terms, or, that is to say, their effort to provide theological legitimacy for many of Marx's key ideas. Sin was identified, for practical purposes, with unjust social structures, namely, capitalism and Western imperialism. Deliverance from sin, salvation—oftentimes made synonymous with liberation—was to be achieved by revolution. The revolutionary cadre, the party, was to be the Moses or the Messiah, leading the people away from oppression into the promised land, or into the kingdom of God—oftentimes identified with socialism. That society was divided into the oppressed and the oppressor meant that Christians had to take sides with the former as against the latter.[13] No neutrality in this regard was possible, either for the individual Christian or for the church. Both had to take an "option for the poor"—usually identified as the oppressed or the proletariat— which necessarily meant entering the conflict-ridden arena of politics and embracing the projects of the poor.[14] The catch here is that by "the poor" liberationists meant, practically and theoretically, the revolutionary poor, those aware of their class interests and actively seeking the overthrow of capitalism.[15]

For Christians to side with the revolutionary poor in their struggle was no longer truly an option but a duty. Liberationists saw commitment to the revolution as an essential part of what it meant to be a Christian. Since it was in the poor that Jesus dwelt in a hidden but real way, for Christians not to commit themselves to the revolution would be for them to turn their backs on Christ. In other words, one could not be a Christian without being a revolutionary, a conclusion that immediately raised a question: Can one be a Christian just by being a revolutionary? Reknowned liberation theologians answered in the affirmative, expanding Karl Rahner's idea of "the anonymous Christian" and claiming that orthopraxis—the right kind of action—was more important than orthodoxy—the right beliefs.[16] Atheists, Marxist militants, those struggling to liberate the oppressed—and therefore to serve Christ—could be considered unconscious Christians or "incognito Christians."

Although allowance should be made for a certain diversity of positions among the liberationists, the centrality of revolution (the belief that revolutionary political action against the ruling socioeconomic order is the way to make Christian love for the poor truly effective) became the distinguishing mark of the theologians who are either identified or who identify themselves with this perspective.

Deprived of two characteristics, however, the primacy of political action and of revolutionary goals, liberation theology would be difficult to distinguish from other Christian stands. Keep the option for the poor and take away political militancy and one gets Mother Theresa of Calcutta. Keep political militancy and take away revolution and you get Christian democracy or reformism.

Liberationists also shared among themselves and with the Latin American Marxists the belief that the basic—although to some of them not the exclusive—source of the misfortune and oppression of the poor in Latin America was to be found in the dependency of the economies of the subcontinent or their subjugation under the yoke of Western imperialism.

In view of the basic premises of liberation theology and of their justification in religious terms, it is easy to see how it provided for the first time a means to build a bridge between Marxists and Christians, and how it could help to achieve the type of integration of Christians into the revolutionary process of which Che Guevara had once dreamt—a feat of portentous consequences.

ALLIANCES WITH THE CHRISTIAN LEFT

Whether the bridge created is theologically sound does not concern us here. The empirical fact is that, for some Christians in Latin America and elsewhere, liberation theology seemed sound and began making inroads in the church. It attracted Catholic and Protestant theologians, priests, seminarians, nuns, and a few lay leaders. Amid the pluralism and openness after Vatican II, the views of the liberationists seemed, perhaps, a legitimate trend. Liberation theology's advocates were accredited theologians of the church, teaching at Catholic (or Protestant) seminaries, working as parish priests or pastors, as members and even leaders of religious orders. Some of their views could be contested by other theologians and a few bishops, but the full weight of the church's authority—already questioned with the rise of relativism and other trends—did not make itself felt in the theological disputes.

Advocates of liberation theology at this time argued that their views were faithful to both the council and to Medellín. There were in fact some expressions in the bishops' statement from the Medellín conference that liberationists found very helpful. In particular, the statement's near endorsement of dependency theory in claiming that "the principal guilt for economic dependence of our countries rests with powers *inspired* by uncontrolled desire for gain, which leads to economic dictatorship and the 'international imperialism of money.' "[17] Once again, the intent of the framers of the Medellín documents may have been oceans apart from some of the radical interpretations given to them, but the ambiguity of the text helped establish the liberationists as part of a legitimate and, indeed, mainstream force inside the church.

By the end of the sixties and beginning of the seventies, the spread and influence of the new interpretations was remarkable, particularly in religious societies such as the Jesuits and the Maryknoll order, as well as in several Protestant denominations of the World Council of Churches. All over Latin America, with bases of support in the United States and Europe, centers for the dissemination of liberation theology sprang up: Priests for the Third World, in Argentina, in 1965; ONIS (Oficina Nacional de Investigación Social) in Peru, in 1968; CIDOC (Centro Iberoamericano de Documentación) in Cuernavaca, Mexico, in 1969; Christians for Socialism, in Chile, in 1972.

What was happening, in the meantime, among the members of the Marxist Left? Although they were not experiencing the identity crisis of their Christian counterparts, many of them, perhaps subdued by the several defeats of the sixties, were questioning the wisdom of their old assumptions. Gradually, some of them began to grasp the potential of the number of Christians being radicalized while still claiming to adhere to the church and its teachings. During the Allende regime in Chile, Castro pioneered a series of contacts with "revolutionary Christians" in order to explore what he called "strategic alliances with the Christian Left." One of the participants explained such a meeting:

> Fidel invited us to Cuba. We spent three weeks getting to know the Cuban process and, at the end, we spent about ten hours discussing, also with Commander Fidel, these issues on

the Alliance.... Fidel was deeply convinced that there would be no revolution in Latin America without the Christians.[18]

REVOLUTIONARY CHRISTIAN EDUCATION

The first country to use the Marxist-Christian alliance on a significant scale was Nicaragua. The results were awesome. Two liberationist priests, Fathers Ernesto Cardenal and Uriel Molina, who were enchanted by the Cuban revolution and founded the first two Christian base communities (CEBs) in Nicaragua, were approached by Sandinista leaders in 1969 and 1971. The priests felt honored by these overtures and began working in coordination with the Sandinistas. Their key role was to teach the basics of liberation theology to mostly middle-class Catholic young people. Part of the instruction was a conscientious effort to wash away the students' possible misgivings about communism and to teach them the virtues of "Marxist analysis." The next step was preaching the Christian duty of siding with the poor in a concrete, historically effective way. Invariably they concluded that in Nicaragua Christian duty meant joining the Sandinista Front. In the words of Father Cardenal:

> What is interesting is that from this commitment with the people the youngsters found that the way was the FSLN [Sandinista Front of National Liberation]. This was always successful— perhaps in as many as 97 percent of the cases.[19]

For the Sandinistas the revolutionary Christian recruits that Father Molina was educating in his base community in Managua proved to be an attractive discovery. As mostly upper-class youngsters, the revolutionary Christians were able to provide the Sandinistas with some key logistical support (cars, farms, homes, and so on). But they offered far wider opportunities also. Its association with the revolutionary Christians gave the FSLN an air of greater legitimacy and increased its appeal domestically and abroad.[20]

In these circumstances the Nicaraguan Marxists decided to allow liberationist Christians into their ranks without extracting the customary show of loyalty to Marxist-Leninist doctrine. The latter prerequisite would be kept for the members of the inner circle only. Commander Mónica Baltodano described this procedure in the following terms:

All this was decisive for the incorporation of the people.... It was hitting the mark for the Frente Sandinista. For the Frente saw the reality of our people—a very Christian people, a very Catholic people. It did not position itself as if it were Marxist and had to convert people to Marxism. It was seen that the key thing was not whether the people were Marxists but whether the people were ready to fight against the dictatorship. Within this framework, there was no need of anything else.[21]

DEALING WITH THE RELIGIOUS FACTOR

Young converts to liberationism flocked to the Sandinista Front, while internationally a handful of Catholic priests involved with the Sandinista revolutionaries championed the Sandinista cause and even made appeals in the United States Congress to cut off aid to Nicaragua's dictator, Anastasio Somoza. Simultaneously, committees of solidarity with the people of Nicaragua appeared around the world, oftentimes under the auspices of church-related groups. Finally, a Marxist revolutionary movement in Latin America was following one of the lessons of the Cuban revolution—to deal with the religious factor—and non-Marxists were being drawn to their cause while the Marxist-Leninist top leadership remained firmly in command. Over subsequent years the Sandinistas suppressed their criticism of religious beliefs and distinguished between the "true" Christians, the ones who supported them, and the false ones, the ones who did not.

In contrast with the Cuban case, the Nicaraguan revolutionaries did not face the potential problem of democratic allies who could become disillusioned on discovering their true politics, or who would attempt to wrest control for themselves. Significantly, the Nicaraguan Marxists soon found that they had nothing to fear from the Christian liberationists. The dynamics of their theology was such that with the passing of time many adherents totally embraced the cause of Marxist Leninism, including its atheistic aspect. In a set of interviews with the North American Marxist Margaret Randall, Father Fernando Cardenal confessed how many of the converts to liberation theology ended up abandoning their Christian faith, an experience also undergone by the twelve student founders of Father Molina's first base community.[22] And even if some converts did not follow the entire process, the way they defined key religious concepts was such that they all fit, without representing a challenge, into the Marxist ideological framework. This was evident with some of the priests who admitted that one could not be a Christian without being a Marxist.[23]

Liberation theology had another feature that made its adherents ideal collaborators for the Marxists: its reluctance to suggest its own agenda, or program, for the transformations that ought to follow the victory of the oppressed. Such an omission, considered by some scholars as the greatest weakness of this theology,[24] is traceable to the way liberation theology sees the "option for the poor." In this regard the liberationists see themselves as people who have decided to join the poor, to share their yearnings and "historical projects." Such a commitment has an unavoidably passive ring; the liberationist does not approach the poor in order to lead them but to support them in their struggles. Claims to possess a uniquely Christian agenda and attempts to offer leadership are humbly surrendered to the revolutionary vanguard. In some writings theologians explicitly argue against Christians' telling the proletariat what to do.[25]

A very interesting note during the Nicaraguan revolution was the Sandinistas' decision for many liberationists who had become Marxist-Leninists to remain inside their original Christian organizations. One of these, Commander Mónica Baltodano, refers to one of the advantages of this tactic: "We were definitely less subject to repression. We would arrive in a barrio and say some things, but we were there 'with an umbrella' because we were Christians."[26]

The penetration of Christian organizations through the activism of liberationists allowed the Sandinistas to involve some basic Christian communities in their struggle. One Sandinista said they were like "quarries" for organizing by the FSLN. CEPA (Center for Agricultural Education and Training), a church program for rural leaders, eventually provided a network linked to the Sandinistas and was the embryo of the ATC (Association of Rural Workers), today the official Sandinista farmworkers union.[27]

On July 19, 1979, the Sandinista revolution triumphed. Its leaders knew that a key ingredient of their success had been the participation of Christians. In the words of a communique of the Sandinista Front, Christians had taken part in the revolution "to a degree unprecedented in any other revolutionary movement in Latin America and perhaps in the world. This fact opens new and interesting possibilities for the participation of Christians in revolutions elsewhere...."[28]

Father Ernesto Cardenal came to a similar conclusion:

> The revolution in Nicaragua was the first of its kind to be ac-
> complished with the mass support of Christians, a fact that
> cannot fail to influence the further development of revolution-
> ary movements in the whole of Latin America, whose in-
> habitants are predominantly Christian. Radical revolutionary
> changes can't, therefore, be brought about without the active
> presence of Christians, or against their will.[29]

THE NICARAGUAN EXAMPLE

Post-revolutionary developments in Nicaragua came to show how liberation theology could be instrumental not only in the quest for power but also
in its preservation. In fact, the support that the local and international advocates of this theology gave to the Sandinista regime has proved to be a very
important element in the survival of the Nicaraguan revolution. As I summarized it in my book, *Breaking Faith; The Sandinista Revolution and Its
Impact on Freedom and Christian Faith in Nicaragua,* the role that the
liberationists have played in Nicaragua is fourfold:

> 1. They have provided a theological rationale for the mes-
> sianism of the Sandinistas by making revolution a near
> synonym of salvation, with the party as its only agent.
> 2. They have lent credibility to the Sandinistas' contention
> that their regime is not so much Marxist-Leninist as it is one
> in which Christianity and revolution can walk together.
> 3. They have served as a visible front to attack the Chris-
> tian churches and to undermine their authority and teachings,
> thus reducing for the Sandinistas the political cost of a more
> direct confrontation.
> 4. They have been instruments of a subtle ideological cam-
> paign to substitute the Marxist creed for the Christian gospel,
> and loyalty to a totally secular political organization for loyal-
> ty to Christ or the church.[30]

There are many indications that the Nicaraguan revolution furthered in
the international Left an awareness of the importance of the religious factor and the promise offered by liberation theology. Spokesmen of the Mar-

xist Left from the United States to Cuba to Moscow were amazed. The editors of the North American radical magazine *Monthly Review* went to Nicaragua in 1982 and reported being "impressed—by the attitude, the evident commitment, and the familiarity with Marxism on the Christian side. The more we looked into the matter, the more convinced we became that something new was happening in the Christian churches, both Catholic and Protestant." The visitors reported that the attitudes of the Nicaraguan liberationists were "remarkably close to our own."[31] They were also pleased by the way in which liberation theology shared the outlook and goals of Marxists. Confirming that the theologies of liberation more and more explicitly equate liberation with revolution, the editors commented:

> But what is true is that these new currents in religious thinking lead straight into realms of theory and practice where Marxists have long been active. Those who accept the identification of liberation with revolution can hardly avoid a confrontation with the Marxist world view and its associated analysis of the transformation of social structures through class struggle. Theologies of liberation and Marxism—with their respective supporters and adherents—increasingly occupy the same terrain and share the same or similar goals.[32]

THE "BAPTIZING" OF MARXISM

By the early eighties the multifold political advantages that liberation theology was offering to the radical Left were becoming apparent. A most important advantage was its contribution to weakening the old barrier that religion had represented for the advancement of communism. In this regard, liberation theology not only has tried to make Marxism acceptable to Christians but has in a way "baptized" most basic Marxist concepts. Another related contribution has been to provide a medium through which Marxist ideas can be presented to the public, using a terminology that, because of its reliance on biblical and theological terms, does not alienate the faithful. This new, "edited" version of Marxism, has also helped to revitalize it among some segments of the Western intelligentsia, at a time when its prestige was fading. Liberationism provides new ground for political utopianism, although one which is now less sociologically based than it is theologically inspired—thus making it more immune to scientific refutation.

The effectiveness of this approach is complemented by the fact that it is often promoted by religious personnel, who are more likely to be trusted than are traditional political activists. In this regard, the bulk of the Marxist political message—revolutionary class struggle against Western capitalism to impose collectivistic socialism—has gained access to a vast pool of human resources strategically located in the societies of Latin America. Priests and religious activists are heavily involved in the education establishment at all levels. They are also prominently represented in the written and spoken media and connected in a vast, sometimes resourceful, international network. Moreover, they are, for the most part—as Max Weber put it—"dispensable," people who can allocate their time with greater freedom than most and who can therefore devote a greater amount of energy to political endeavors.[33] In some instances the religious become a paid bureaucracy at the service of revolution. As church people, they can easily move into poor barrios and middle-class neighborhoods, and they can take the lead in secular organizations.

What was done in Nicaragua involving some basic Christian communities and agricultural organizations like CEPA has been done in several other countries. In El Salvador FECCAS (Federation of Christian Peasants of El Salvador) was transformed into a militant organization that later joined the BPR (Revolutionary People's Bloc), which was linked to the guerrillas. According to Phillip Berryman, "there is a direct line from basic Christian communities' pastoral work to the popular organizations to a Marxist guerrilla organization."[34]

A similar process has been followed in Guatemala, with the CUC (Committee for Peasant Unity), an outgrowth of the pastoral agents of the Justice and Peace Committee; in Brazil, where some of the basic Christian communities work with the Marxist PT (Workers' party); and in several other countries.

A side effect of these developments has been distrust and hostility toward church people in general among some Latin American regimes. Religious who are actively involved in social and political issues are frequently labeled as "subversives" or "communists," either as a result of genuine confusion or as a premeditated effort to discredit them. In either case, those who benefit the most from this indiscriminate labeling are the liberationists. This is precisely what happened in Nicaragua when the Somoza regime accused democratic-minded Archbishop Obando y Brava of Managua of being a communist sympathizer. The charge was obviously unfair in regard to the archbishop, though it was not when applied to some other priests, such as Father Uriel Molina. Yet Father Molina could point to the falsehood or inaccuracy of the charges against the archbishop in order to suggest the unfairness of those against himself. In some other cases, the labeling of church activists as leftist revolutionaries has led to the retaliatory victimization of Christians committed to orthodoxy and democracy, an outcome that does as much damage to the regimes where those deeds occur as it promotes the radicalization of moderate Christians. The participation of church people in leftist movements has helped to obscure, especially in the developed world, the true nature of the revolutionary movements' power struggles and of the conflicts in the region.

Liberationists in the developed world also articulate the revolutionaries' struggles and goals in a vocabulary which no longer elicits distrust. To the stock of Christian terms with Marxist content provided by liberation theologies, liberationists in the developed nations add a vocabulary of human rights and democratic-liberal concepts. Another end result of these approaches is that many church people who get a good deal of their information from activists or sympathizers of liberationism tend to see local conflicts as confrontations between poor and rich, oppressed and oppressors, democracy and dictatorship. The fact that this may be, at times, partially valid tends to leave out other aspects and complexities of considerable importance. The Marxist-Leninist element and the real participation of Cuba and Soviet bloc interests are usually discounted as reactionary propaganda or as a secondary by-product of the struggle. No wonder, thus, that in the last decade, the center of gravity for the advocacy of Third World revolutionary causes has passed from secular leftist organizations to church groups. Liberationist Phillip Berryman celebrates the shift in the following terms:

> Liberation theology is having a rebound impact on the United States. At almost any public action in protest of U. S. policy in Central America, half or more of the participants have become involved through church organizations. Some of the major initiatives have come from religious groups.[35]

UNDISGUISED JOY

In view of these and many other considerations, it is hardly surprising that Fidel Castro praised liberation theology in his book-interview *Fidel and Religion*.

> There is no need to be very perspicacious to understand that we fully sympathize, in absolute coherence with everything that we have talked and stated, with the church making an option on the side of the oppressed....And of course, the liberation theologians have been the ones who have carried the banner for this encounter with the poor. In this sense it is almost necessary to say that I see with deep sympathy the effort that these men, whom we could call "enlightened ones," have made in this direction.[36]

That communist leaders such as Castro are fully aware of the revolutionary potential of liberation theology is something that he also expresses in unambiguous terms:

> Liberation theology is a re-encounter of Christianity with its roots, with its most attractive history, with its most beautiful, most attractive, most heroic and most glorious history—this I can tell—of such a magnitude, that it forces the whole Left in Latin America to take it into account as one of the most fundamental events taking place in our times.[37]

The undisguised joy of communists at the phenomenon of liberation theology could be a cause of potential embarrassment for some liberationists, which may have been one of the reasons behind recent attempts of some of these theologians to deny the Marxist character of their theology and the movements they support. Father Ernesto Cardenal candidly admitted in an interview that "some liberation theologians maintain that they are not influenced by Marxist philosophy at all. In this case it is necessary to discern whether they say this for tactical reasons, so as not to be compromised politically."[38] Yet, it is also plausible that some liberationists may feel uncomfortable with the real possibility of becoming agents of totalitarian political ideologies, and that they are now trying to work for a distinguishable Christian liberation. To what extent this effort should be recognized as a genuine one will depend largely on the theologians' willingness to renounce the Marxist myth that class struggle is the road to a classless society—as was the Vatican's instruction on liberation theology in 1984; on their capacity to develop a more specific— and democratic— agenda of social change; and on their readiness to denounce oppression from either the Left or the Right, implying their willingness to sever ties with, or distance themselves from, Marxist dictatorships. As long as these criteria are not met, it will be legitimate to consider liberation theology as an ideology that, independently from the original motivations of its framers, wonderfully serves the interests of very concrete political forces— the Marxist Left, and most particularly the interests of the Soviet Union and Cuba.

As the cases of Cuba and Nicaragua indicate, the tactical blurring of the revolutionaries' true goals has been a decisive element in their victories. Liberation theology has come to enrich their arsenal of tactics, providing not only a means to cancel out the potential obstacles of the religious factor, but a way to harness it in behalf of the revolutionaries' agenda. In some respects, it may not be out of proportion to refer to the prevailing type of liberation theology as a true Trojan horse, whereby the aged and relatively decadent Marxist-Leninist ideology has found a new capacity to penetrate the Christian churches and the West—this time in religious garments.

What it takes to confront such a challenge is something to be answered by serious study and effort. The first step, however, is to realize that the challenge is very serious.

NOTES

1. Quoted in Pablo Richard, "The Experience of Christians in Chile during the Popular Unity Period," *Cristianos Revolucionarios II*, No. 4, (Managua: Instituto Histórico Centro Americano, 1980), p. 31 (author's translation).

2. Alan Riding, "The Sword and the Cross," *New York Times*, May 28, 1981, p. 6.

3. Pius IX, *Qui Pluribus*, Encyclical November 9, 1846 (Acta Pii IX, vol. I, p. 13). Cf. Syllabus, IV, (A.S.S., vol. III, p. 170).

4. Leo XIII, *Quod Apostolici Muneris*, Encyclical December 28, 1878 (Acta Leonis XIII, vol. I, p. 46).

5. Pius XI, "On Atheistic Communism," in *Seven Great Encyclicals*, ed. William J. Gibbons, S.J. (Glen Rock, N.J.: Paulist Press, 1963), St. Paul Editions, p. 209.

6. Ibid., p. 199.

7. In Henri Chambre, S.J., *Christianity and Communism*, trans. R. F. Trevett (New York: Hawthorn, 1960), p. 27.

8. José Carlos Mariátegui, "Siete ensayos de interpretación de la realidad peruana," quoted in Donald C. Hodges, *Intellectual Foundations of the Nicaraguan Revolution* (Austin: University of Texas Press, 1986), p. 279.

9. Dale Vree, *On Synthesizing Marxism and Christianity* (New York: John Wiley and Sons, 1976), p. 4.

10. Ibid., p. 6.

11. This statement appears in Friedrich Engels, Preface to the German Edition of 1883, of the *Communist Manifesto*, in *The Marx-Engels Reader*, 2d ed., ed. Robert C. Tucker (New York: W. W. Norton, 1978), p. 472.

12. Gustavo Gutiérrez, "Liberation Praxis and Christian Faith," in *Frontiers of Theology in Latin America*, ed. Rosino Gibellini (Maryknoll, N.Y.: Orbis Books, 1979), pp. 17, 1–2. This essay contains several other expressions resembling those of Marx and Engels.

13. Ibid., p. 9.

14. Ibid.

15. Ibid., p. 8.

16. Raul Vidales, "Methodological Issues in Liberation Theology," in *Frontiers of Theology in Latin America*, p. 50.

17. From the official English translation of the Medellín documents, "The Church in the Present-Day Transformation of Latin America in the Light of the Council," cited in Michael Novak, *The Spirit of Democratic Capitalism* (New York: Simon and Schuster, 1982), p. 272.

18. Uriel Molina, "El sendero de una experiencia," in *Nicarahuac*, No. 5 (Managua: Ministerio de Educación, 1981), p. 23 (author's translation).

19. Fernando Cardenal quoted in Margaret Randall, *Cristianos en la revolución nicaraguense* (Caracas: Poseidon, 1983), p. 193 (author's translation).

20. Humberto Belli, *Breaking Faith; The Sandinista Revolution and its Impact on Freedom and Christian Faith in Nicaragua* (Westchester, Ill.: Crossways, 1985), p. 22.

21. Baltodano, in Randall, *Cristianos en la revolución*, p. 187 (author's translation).

22. This information is gathered from Randall, pp. 212–14, 220, and is summarized in Belli, *Breaking Faith*, p. 23.

23. Ernesto Cardenal, "El evangelio me hizo marxista," cited in Belli, *Nicaragua: Christians under Fire* (Garden City, Mich.: Puebla Institute, 1984), appendix A.

24. See Michael Novak, *Democratic Capitalism*, pp. 293–95.

25. Richard, "Christians in Chile," p. 31.

26. Baltodano cited in Randall, *Cristianos en la revolución*, p. 187 (author's translation).

27. Phillip Berryman, "Basic Christian Communities and the Future of Latin America," in *Monthly Review* 36 (July–August 1984): 36.

28. "Communicado oficial de la dirección nacional del FSLN sobre la religión," in *Barricada*, Managua, October 7, 1980 (author's translation).

29. Ernesto Cardenal, "Is Liberation Theology Marxist? An Interview with Ernesto Cardenal," *Crisis* (June 1987), p. 39.

30. Belli, *Breaking Faith,* p. 242.

31. Preface from the editors, *Monthly Review* 36 (July–August, 1984): 7.

32. Ibid., p. 5.

33. Max Weber, as cited in Lewis Coser et al., *Introduction to Sociology,* 2d ed. (San Diego: Harcourt, Brace, Jovanovich, 1987), p. 504.

34. Berryman, "Basic Christian Communities," p. 35.

35. Berryman, *Liberation Theology* (New York: Pantheon, 1987), p. 20.

36. This statement appears in *Fidel Castro y la religión* (La Habana, Cuba: Oficina de Publicaciones del Consejo de Estado, 1985), p. 305 (author's translation).

37. Ibid., p. 291 (author's translation).

38. Cardenal, "Is Liberation Theology Marxist?" p. 39.

PART III

Liberation Theology and Public Policy in the United States

The Great Enemy? How Latin American Liberation Theology Sees the United States and the USSR

John K. Roth

Our every action is a battle cry against imperialism and a call for the peoples' unity against the great enemy of mankind: the United States of America.
>   — Ernesto "Che" Guevara

Provoked by hunger, poverty, exploitation, and premature death, Latin American liberation theology, in the words of Brazilian priests and brothers Leonardo and Clodovis Boff, is a "chant of the Third World transformed into a reflection of messianic hope for a society of freedom, a society that will become a communion of brothers and sisters."[1] This religious-political movement—rooted in the Bible, the social theory of Karl Marx, and above all in the plight of impoverished people—intends to change the world radically. Its aims put Latin American liberation theology on a collision course with the United States. American policymaking must reckon with that fact.

FROM TOCQUEVILLE TO GUEVARA AND BEYOND

To get the analysis under way, consider that Latin American liberation theology did not exist when Alexis de Tocqueville (1805–1859) studied early nineteenth-century democracy in the United States. Even then, however, that French observer's keen insights targeted factors throughout the Americas that would eventually conspire to produce this theological-political development, which may yet rival Islamic fundamentalism as the most politically volatile religious upsurge of the twentieth century's second half.

Egalitarianism, individualism, an influential role for religion, a propensity to let majority rule form public opinion—these were among the qualities Tocqueville found most pronounced among United States citizens. He regarded something else, however, as "the characteristic trait which now distinguishes the Americans most particularly from all other nations."[2] According to Tocqueville, the origins of life in the United States, coupled with the nation's politics, social environment, and geography, resulted in Americans' becoming "an almost exclusively industrial and trading community."[3] Although Tocqueville took "their principal interest" to be "exploitation" of the "huge new country," he also saw American appetites reaching well beyond those borders.[4] In the United States, international trade "would become a national interest of the first importance."[5]

This commercial republic, believed Tocqueville, was destined to be the dominant economic power in the New World. The implications for Latin America seemed clear to him. Long under Spanish and Portuguese hegemony, those regions were industrially backward. That fact, however, had little to do with their natural condition. "Where in the world," mused Tocqueville, "can one find more fertile wildernesses, greater rivers, and more untouched and inexhaustible riches than in South America?"[6] Tocqueville held that no part of the earth was more naturally blessed. Yet he put his claim in question form because he wondered why the economic disparity between the Americas was already so extreme. Differences in colonizing philosophies—essentially English on the one hand, Spanish and Portuguese on the other—stood at the heart of that matter. For our purposes, though, the key point is his conclusion. "Every nation that comes to birth or grows up in the New World," said Tocqueville, "does so, in a sense, for the benefit of the Anglo-Americans."[7]

Tocqueville's appraisal of American democracy was approving, ambivalent, and anxious all at once. Convinced that the United States was a power to deal with, he worked to identify and understand the most dynamic forces at work in its people. Domestically, democracy and "trade and industry" nourished each other, and Americans knew it. Although that symbiotic relationship might inform United States foreign policy, Tocqueville sensed that economics alone would largely determine U.S. foreign relations. If correct, his judgment further suggested that there could be no foregone conclusions about the sorts of regimes the United States would support or resist in Latin America. It was clearer, Tocqueville implied, that United States support of or resistance against a particular foreign government would be a function of a regime's economic benefit to the United States, that "national interest of the first importance."

Few interpreters have done as much as Tocqueville to enhance self- understanding in the United States. As far as this essay's subject is concerned, his contributions reach well beyond the pages of his justly celebrated *Democracy in America*. Having discerned early on the centrality of the nation's commercial spirit, Tocqueville aids comprehension of the vision of the United States that exists, one way or another, among the various outlooks that comprise Latin American liberation theology. Those outlooks pivot around the conviction that economic self-interest does indeed govern United States policies toward the nation's southern neighbors.

One difference between Tocqueville and the liberation theologians of Latin America is that the latter see this relationship as far more deleterious than Tocqueville anticipated. This is not to say that Tocqueville would have been surprised by the resentment toward the United States that festers in Latin America today. Current American understanding must be equally perspicacious. Grasping the contents of and the reasons for the vision of the United States that characterizes Latin American liberation theology, how that vision compares and contrasts with liberation theology's stance toward the Soviet Union, and how the United States might best respond to all of these factors—such topics are not only matters for serious religious reflection. They are of vital political significance for public policy as well.

By the year 2000, Latin America's population may exceed 600 million. It will include half of the world's Roman Catholics. Presently a majority of Latin Americans are impoverished. At the same time, large numbers of the region's Christians, inspired by leaders as politically astute as they are theologically sophisticated, are organized locally and committed to the work of liberation theology. That reality deserves close attention when one recalls that a seminal influence on the movement continues to be that of Ernesto "Che" Guevara, the Argentine medical student who became radicalized during the Cuban Revolution, worked to overthrow Bolivia's government, and then was captured, tortured, and executed by Bolivian soldiers in 1967. His commitment made him a martyr in the eyes of many who support liberation theology's agenda for Latin America.

Che Guevara's charge that the United States is "the great enemy of mankind" opened this essay.[8] Perhaps nothing summarizes his symbolic importance as well as a vignette recounted by José Míguez Bonino, a leading Protestant liberation theologian from Argentina and former president of the World Council of Churches. Young people from an Uruguayan shanty town, he reports, once performed a play in a well-to-do Protestant church. In the ensuing discussion, one member of the troupe was asked, "Who, then, is Jesus Christ?" The actor answered: "For us, ...Jesus Christ is Che Guevara." What the answer meant, according to Míguez Bonino, is that "liberation and revolution are a legitimate transcription of the gospel."[9]

Whatever the differences of theme and emphasis among the Latin American liberation theologians—and those differences are considerable—their opinion of the United States is remarkably uniform. Guevara's indictment, the young Uruguayan's answer, Míguez Bonino's theological interpretation of the latter— elements like these have thus far been foundational for this movement. As theological voices, to say nothing of chants, resound variations on these themes almost everywhere in Latin American liberation theology, United States policies will be ill-made unless serious attention is paid to the liberationists' indictment, implicit if not explicit, that the United States is, indeed, the great enemy.

This chapter is primarily descriptive. By providing a catalog of representative views drawn from leading liberationists in a variety of places, it details how Latin American liberation theology portrays the United States and, to a lesser extent, the Soviet Union. Generous quotations permit these writers to speak for themselves. If the words "United States" and "Soviet

Union" do not often appear explicitly in these passages, it is not difficult to translate their indirect discourse so that its words convey, non-euphemistically and accurately, what they really mean. The crucial point to understand is that liberation theologians fault capitalism for most of what is wrong in Latin America. Wherever capitalism operates, according to their analysis, the deadly presence of the United States is working, too. What results, then, is a condemnation of the United States far harsher than any criticism that the Latin American liberation theologians level at the USSR.

LIBERATION FROM DOMINATION

Latin American liberation theologians do not necessarily disagree with President Ronald Reagan's pre-*glasnost/perestroika* claim that the Soviet Union is an evil empire. Mainly, however, they reserve such judgments for the United States. As we document that point, note that Latin American liberation theologies criticize what they call the abstractness of European and North American theology. By contrast, they regard theirs as concrete and particular. It is ironic, therefore, that on most occasions they do not speak directly about the United States or the USSR. Even indirectly, they have relatively little to say about the USSR, but that is hardly true where the United States is concerned. In the vocabulary of Latin American liberation theology, "capitalism" is at least a four-letter word. One never misses the bullseye by much in thinking that the liberationists mean "capitalism" to be code for the United States.

"Among more alert groups today, what we have called a new awareness of Latin American reality is making headway. They believe that there can be authentic development for Latin America only if there is liberation from the domination exercised by the great capitalist countries, and especially by the most powerful, the United States of America."[10] So writes the Peruvian Gustavo Gutiérrez, who is generally acknowledged to be the preeminent Latin American liberation theologian. His colleagues join Gutiérrez in viewing life from its bottomside— that is, from the perspective of the poor. They read Scripture and hear the Christian gospel specifically as a promise of release from oppression. This release has political and economic dimensions of the most practical kind. It clearly means freedom from the exploitation that Latin American liberation theology finds inextricably bound up with capitalism. According to this outlook, which relies heavily on Karl Marx's nineteenth-century critique of capitalism, the

United States in particular oppresses Latin America. This domination not only subjects millions to poverty as the rich take the profits, but it leaves the poor doubly impoverished because they become dependent on the rich for the crumbs that are left to them. "Reforms," predicated on the claim that the lot of the poor and powerless will be relieved if capitalist development advances, are not trustworthy. Hence, the call must be for liberation from American domination.

"We must come right out and say it, loud and clear: *liberation is the social emancipation of the oppressed*. Our concrete task is to replace the capitalist system and move toward a new society—a society of a socialistic type."[11] Clodovis Boff thus expands Gutiérrez's rejection of capitalistic control by the United States. This particular statement comes at the end of one of Boff's discussions, and he does not elaborate what his socialistic society would be like. In that regard he is similar to many of his fellow liberationists: quite definite about what he is against, quite imprecise about what he wants instead. On the latter score, Latin American liberation theology, its criticisms of theological abstraction notwithstanding, remains vaguely visionary with its countless references to "brother- and sisterhood," "a more just society," and "the creation of a new human person." Unambiguous, however, is the imperative to move beyond the existing state of affairs. Insofar as the United States has national interests in those affairs, the pronouncements of Latin American liberation theology against capitalism and for socialism cannot be comforting. Latin American liberation theology serves notice that the United States is essentially foe, not friend.

"The choice we have to make is not between society as it exists in the USA or society as it exists in the Soviet Union."[12] The words are those of the Uruguayan Juan Luis Segundo, S. J., author of the five-volume *Theology for Artisans of a New Humanity* and one of the most prolific writers among the Latin American liberation theologians. Segundo argues for Latin American self-determination, a key ingredient in liberation. If the option between socialism and capitalism requires a breaking of United States domination, it likewise demands that Latin America not be subservient to the USSR. The latter emphasis does little, however, to soften the blow that Segundo's analysis strikes at the United States. Shared by all Latin American theologies of liberation, says Segundo, is "the view that men, on a political as well as individual basis, construct the Kingdom of God from within history now."[13] At the heart of that project must be a decision "whether we are going to leave to individuals and private groups, or take away from them, the right to possess the means of production which exist in our countries. This is what we call the option for capitalism or socialism."[14] Segundo leaves no doubt about the correct decision. The immediate needs of impoverished people require the setting aside of economic competition and profit—capitalism, in a word—and their replacement by socialism, "a political regime in which the ownership of the means of production is removed from individuals and handed over to higher institutions whose concern is the common good."[15]

In "Capitalism-Socialism: A Theological Crux," the essay in question here, Segundo does not say much more to define the socialism he advocates. Critics probe his ambiguous silence: How shall the common good be defined? What higher institutions will and/or should have authority? What ensures that they will act rightly? Does Segundo's call to "take away" certain rights incite, if not endorse, revolutionary violence?

The latter issue is especially problematic, not only in Segundo's case but for every other Latin American liberationist as well. Different essays in this volume deal explicitly with the relations between liberation theology and violence. Here it must suffice to say that Deane William Ferm's conclusions—"I find very little advocacy of violence on the part of Third World liberation theologians" and "I do not know of any...living Latin American liberation theologians who make explicit and unconditional statements advocating that social change must be achieved by force..."— hardly settle the matter.[16] For Ferm, a knowledgeable as well as sympathetic interpreter of the movement, is also quick to recognize that Latin American theologians such as Míguez Bonino, Richard, Leonardo Boff, and others have argued that physical violence may well be necessary. This is true, the liberation argument contends, because violence—personal and institutional—has clearly been done first and continuously by the capitalistic power of oppressors such as the United States. If the liberation movements of Latin America do resort to violence, this line of thought continues, presently they can do so in good conscience because their struggle is a just war. Again the code-like quality of liberation theology's rhetoric bears remembering. Overt advocacy of violence may not occur often, but as Scripture puts the point, "He who has an ear, let him hear" (Rev. 2:7). The spirit of Latin American liberation theology does little to close the door on violent revolutionary responses. No one should be caught by surprise if revolutionary violence erupts in Latin American situations where liberation theology has exerted influence.

Returning specifically to Segundo, in a way he anticipates some of the questions posed by his critics. His strategy points out the urgency of immediate need, acknowledges that no one can foresee or control the future, recognizes that not every socialistic step may be completely right, and contends that his critics' objections are more likely rooted in ideological interests that defend the status quo than in an honest search for knowledge and justice. Although the point dwells largely between his lines, the United States, insofar as its capitalism functions in Latin America, is still a great enemy for Segundo. Some of the liberationists' best friends, of course, may still be American. But Uncle Sam is not among them.

THE REIGN OF JUSTICE IS AT HAND

Scripture announces that the kingdom of God is at hand. Time's passage, however, leaves the meaning of that claim open to conflicting interpretations. Karl Marx's alternative regarded human history as a struggle between socioeconomic classes that was inevitably moving toward the justice of a classless society here on earth. To the extent that Latin American liberation theologians are Marxists, it is not owing to atheism or materialism on their parts. On the contrary, it is just because they take God's reality, as well as the power of the human will, so seriously that they have hope for the future. At the same time their interpretation of that hope gives their Christianity a distinctly Marxist cast.

The liberationists' interpretation of Latin American history rests on the belief that theirs is an epistemologically privileged perspective. That perspective grasps the truth because it discerns reality from the vantage point of the oppressed and exploited. That perspective finds history to be primarily a struggle between social classes. An essential key to the just resolution of that struggle, which enjoins the faithful commitment of the oppressed, is the abolition of private ownership of the means of production. Finally, no matter what costs must be borne, there is the conviction that victory for the cause of liberation will not ultimately be denied.

This latter point, of course, is not a theme peculiar to Marxism alone. The notion that God or history is "on our side" belongs to many ideologies, and the reason is not hard to find. The idea is powerful; men, women, and children will die for it. Even less is there anything necessarily Marxist about the liberationists' claim that Christianity enjoins preferential treatment for the poor and downtrodden. It takes considerable myopia, to say nothing of blindness, to read Scripture without admitting that the God portrayed in its pages is especially concerned about the poor and the powerless. But Latin American liberation theology adds to those points the nearly canonical Marxist framework noted above. Whether Latin American liberation theology will be saddled forever with its questionable Marxist leanings remains to be seen. In the foreseeable future, however, one can scarcely imagine a non-Marxist liberation theology in Latin America. That fact has an important consequence, namely, that those who are inspired by the liberation movement will carry out their plans with a determined sense of confidence about the rightness of their ways. Such confidence entails that the dominant ways of the United States must go.

"The good news takes a very concrete form. The central message is this: the situation cannot continue as it is; impoverishment and exploitation are not God's will; but now there is hope, resurrection, life, change. The reign of God, which is the reign of justice, is at hand."[17] Elsa Tamez, author of the preceding words, is a Costa Rican professor of biblical studies who flatly asserts that "the accumulation of wealth is incompatible with Christianity, since any accumulation of possessions is at the cost of the very poor."[18] The entire biblical drama, her reading of Scripture emphasizes, vindicates the poor in their perennial struggle against the rich, the mighty, and the comfortable.

According to Tamez, Jesus acted decisively in the class struggle of his day. At that time, she contends, the ordinary people of Palestine were exploited not only by the Roman Empire but also by those among the Jewish people who collaborated with their Roman overlords. In the midst of this oppression, Jesus brought good news: the reign of justice is at hand.

Contemporary Latin America, says Tamez, parallels Jesus' time. So the good news now is the same as it was then. Women, children, and men are to be liberated "from everything and everyone that keeps them enslaved."[19] This message is directed especially to the poor, a biblical identification that includes "the helpless, the indigent, the hungry, the oppressed, the needy, the humiliated." The people who fit that description, Tamez continues, exist in this situation neither naturally, nor by some historical inevitability, nor by chance. Instead "they have been unjustly impoverished and despoiled by the powerful."[20]

It follows that the news brought by Jesus is not so good for the oppressors, except insofar as God's judgment produces a spirit of repentance that liberates by chastening the sinful and hastening the reign of justice that humanizes everyone. Poverty not only "reflects the socioeconomic conditions of inequality in which people live," writes Tamez, it challenges God, who "takes sides and...favors the poor.... The Bible makes perfectly clear this divine predilection and option for the poor."[21]

Explicitly, Tamez says little about the United States. But her code language is not too indirect. When attacking oppression, her primary target is less the Soviet Union than the United States. In fact, like those of other liberationists, Tamez's biblical interpretations come close, at least by implication, to demonizing the United States as the anti-Christ. Paradoxically, that demonization clinches the case against the United States. For however powerful the anti-Christ may be, its powers will not ultimately prevail against God's predilection for the poor. "The eschatological promise of justice," concludes Tamez, "is drawing ever nearer to fulfillment and, with it, the end of poverty."[22] If correct, her vision of that promise portends nothing less than the demise of America-as-anti-Christ.

"For a Christian to claim to be anticommunist...without doubt constitutes the greatest scandal of our century."[23] That claim is José Miranda's. He has taught at the Universidad Metropolitana Tztapalapa in Mexico City and significantly influenced the thought of Elsa Tamez. Miranda asserts that communism is essentially a Christian imperative. Denial of that proposition only testifies to the failure of church and Western society alike to be true to their Christian origins. Miranda's New Testament scholarship stresses that the early Christians held goods in common and distributed them according to need. Centuries later when Karl Marx urged people to produce according to their ability and to receive according to their need, he was building on the largely-forgotten communist ethic of the New Testament.

Miranda contends that the genuine Karl Marx, as opposed to the misconstrued Marx of various "Marxisms," was a humanist who actually identified closely with the radical social teachings of Jesus. Miranda has to criticize many of Marx's interpreters, to say nothing of reading Marx selectively himself, so that his view of the authentic Marx will stand. The avowed purpose of this enterprise, however, is less to defend Marx than to make clear that Jesus *"was in fact a communist."*[24] Presumably Jesus' true followers will be, too.

According to Miranda, not Marx but Jesus is the original inspiration for a classless society. He explicitly intended that such a society should be realized on earth and within human history. Christians have been lax, if not apostate, in failing to preach and practice that gospel. Whatever their errors may be concerning the proper reading of Marx's texts, the Marxists have at least heard the right good news and tried to make the world fit it. Miranda credits them with "doing us [Christians] a favor by propagating the idea of communism in our absence—our culpable absence."[25] Miranda does not imply that such credit extends to the Soviet Union. In fact, he speaks of "the failure of Russian communism." This failure is no failure of communism rightly understood, however. For according to Miranda, the USSR is not truly communistic. Instead he conveniently calls its system "state capitalism."[26] But even that posture implies that the real enemy is where the most formidable capitalistic enterprises are to be found, namely, in the United States.

The choice is either capitalism or communism; "there is no third way," asserts Miranda, for people who love freedom.[27] A choice between the two must be made. That choice, moreover, goes far toward determining who is a Christian. Being a Christian is optional. But if one chooses to be a Christian, argues Miranda, that decision is incompatible with capitalism. If nothing else, Miranda's views are radical, and not every Latin American liberation theologian makes the polarities so extreme. The salient element here is the extent to which most United States Christians must be special foes for Miranda. Most of them are of a much more capitalistic persuasion than Miranda finds tolerable. In his interpretation "ugly Americans" are legion. They inhabit the offices of Wall Street and Pennsylvania Avenue, and plenty of them attend church as well.

> Those of us from the West, and particularly Christians, should be careful before indulging in self-righteous denunciation of "Stalinist terror" and "communist oppression" without realising that at least as much terror and oppression—often even without hope—is abroad in the Western world under the pretence of defending "Christian values" and "the Christian way of life." Nothing that a "horrified" European bourgeois

can read about Soviet terror in Solzhenitsyn's *Gulag Ar-chipelago* is new to the subjects of the "most Christian" governments of Brazil, Uruguay or Chile![28]

José Míguez Bonino, whose voice we have heard before, held that view in 1976, and it still seems to be in effect. No thinking person will contest that injustice is less than rife in Latin America. Míguez Bonino correctly suggests, moreover, that hypocrisy is also rife when critics target terror and oppression in the Soviet bloc to the exclusion of injustice that stems from corruption and repression within the regimes of the West. A significant factor to note, however, is that, in contrast to his evaluation of the United States, Míguez Bonino's critique gives the Soviet Union a comparatively clean bill of health.

The USSR has been the major seedbed for the political practice of what Míguez Bonino calls Marxist socialism. He believes that movement has proved to be "a powerful and efficient motor of social change, economic development and scientific progress.... Whatever our misgivings, it is difficult not to feel a sense of admiration and gratitude for a movement that, in less than a century, through its direct action in some areas and through indirect influence in labour movements and other social forces in others, has raised to a human condition the life of at least half of the human race!"[29]

Míguez Bonino admits that neither the Soviet Union nor the Marxist socialism inspired by that state has lived up to its revolutionary potential. Yet the accolades he pays to both, however qualified, are absent when he focuses on the Western democracies. In a context that uses Stalin as an example, moreover, Míguez Bonino speaks about communist dedication and avers that "however repulsive the manifestations of this total devotion may be, we have to respect them and to recognise that they have also appeared—both in their sublime and in their repugnant forms—at the crucial and most decisive points in the history of Christian spirituality."[30] Furthermore, insofar as the Western democracies exhibit social justice, Míguez Bonino gives much of the credit to the inspiration of Marxist socialism at work in those places.

The message of Míguez Bonino is hard to miss. While the choice may be the lesser of evils, Soviet ways have more to commend them than do those of the United States. Although Latin American liberation theology tries to distance its Marxist socialism from the Soviet orbit, these two movements still have more reason to be friendly toward each other than is the case where the interests of the United States and Latin American liberation theology are concerned. Neither United States Christians nor the foreign policy of the United States can overlook that fact with impunity.

GOD HAS ENEMIES

Latin American liberation theologies recognize that the United States possesses immense power. While arguing that the oppressed must win their own liberation, liberation theology understands, too, that its cause depends considerably on United States responses. About that point there will be more to say, but first consider one place where the liberation theologians think they and their people have an edge. It involves the intensity of their politically motivated religious faith.

"God's love is not neutrality; it is a demand for justice. And therefore God has enemies."[31] Another Costa Rican theologian, Victorio G. Araya, makes that claim. He does so in an article that contrasts the low intensity of most American religious life with the vitality of a Latin American spirituality that is motivated by liberation themes. Symptomatic of the former is a preoccupation with the issue of whether God is dead. For those moved by liberation theology, that concern is a non-issue; its God is alive and well. For example, governing the religious life of liberation theology is the conviction that "God is the ever open horizon leading to creativity and historical initiative, he is the demand for justice and love, the one who beckons to us to go forward, reminding us of our vocation to transform nature and create a more just world."[32]

United States history documents how revolutionary such ideas can be. As Tocqueville understood, similar religious motives explain much of the power that the United States possesses. The political significance of Latin American liberation theology resides in the recognition that faith, as the old saying has it, can move mountains. Americans love to sing "God Bless America." Latin American liberation theology inclines toward a revision that exclaims "God Damn America." According to the liberationists, that change can be made with the courage of a justified religious conviction.

As previously noted, liberation theologians from Latin America are not precluded from saying, "Some of my best friends are U.S. citizens, and Christians are among them." But those are the exceptions who prove a rule that directs Latin American liberation theology. It holds that most Americans aid and abet what Victorio Araya calls "the violent, antilife structures that are crushing [the exploited peoples of our continent] and turning their world into a graveyard of capitalism."[33] Precisely because such rhetoric is religiously inspired, its political significance is intensified.

"The modern capitalist system is growing more religious and pious by the day."[34] An initial reading of this proposition by Pablo Richard, a Chilean biblical scholar and sociologist, seems to contradict Araya, but in fact his statement amplifies the latter's contentions. For Richard, idolatry is the central issue. If faith in God is lukewarm in the United States, devotion to idols is hot and heavy. He believes that the accumulation of wealth and the maintenance of political domination have been idolatrously sacralized in capitalist regimes and in the United States particularly.

As Richard sees it, the struggle between the oppressed and their capitalistic oppressors is different from the battle that would exist if capitalists were truly atheistic. The "death of God" may be experienced in the capitalistic way of life but not the death of the gods. On the contrary, the struggle under way is religious, a latter-day repetition of Yahweh's encounter with the false gods of ancient Canaan and their supporters. Religious battles are often the most impassioned and bitter. The one in question here may prove to be no exception. Once more, however, the liberationist analysis provides an edge for that side. The biblical message, Richard explains, is pure and simple: ultimately, God prevails against the gods.

Granted, Scripture does not indicate that a full triumph against idolatrous exploitation occurred during biblical times. Richard contends, however, that the current situation is newly hopeful. There is now reason to think that such a victory lies within reach. "In biblical times," he writes, "the possibility of a radical and conscious transformation of the economic and political structure of an idolatrous system did not yet exist. Today this possibility exists."[35] Thanks to the liberation movement and its Marxist analysis of the socioeconomic structural changes that are necessary, the liberating God and his followers can accomplish what the Bible promised long ago.

The cause of Latin American liberation theology becomes a kind of holy war twice over. It is not simply a struggle against injustice but a battle against the false divinities of wealth and power—the man-made "sacred" rulers that use all they can for their own advantage. It bears remembering that, impoverished though they may be, people who organize themselves around such religious inspiration are rich with potency to change the world dramatically.

"There is always a political aspect to the way in which theology is made."[36] So writes Hugo Assmann, a Brazilian theologian and sociologist who, like so many of his liberationist colleagues, received his intellectual training in Europe before returning to South America, where his identification with the plight of the poor has caused him to suffer political exile. His point echoes and sums up a view that characterizes the entire liberation movement. As Assmann sizes up the situation, the dependence of Latin America on capitalist nations such as the United States is where the liberationists' political theology needs to focus.

According to Assmann, "if the state of domination and dependence in which two-thirds of humanity live, with an annual toll of thirty million dead from starvation and malnutrition, does not become the starting-point for *any* Christian theology today, even in the affluent and powerful countries, then theology cannot begin to relate meaningfully to the real situation. Its questions will lack reality and not relate to real men and women."[37] His dependency theory holds that, as developed capitalist countries moved into Latin America, their objectives permitted development of those regions only to a point of continuing underdevelopment that leaves them exploited and dependent at once. Liberation means social change that breaks these neo-imperialistic shackles. Christianity's distinctive contribution toward that end will be to keep the liberation movement concentrated on "what is specifically and fully human, in the line of fidelity to all that is involved materially in loving one's neighbour. But theoretical insistence is not enough: we have an overall vision of the purpose of man to urge us to action."[38]

Hugo Assmann's was one of the two or three founding voices of Latin American liberation theology in the late sixties and early seventies. It is therefore important to note that his thought—the same can be said for others—is not frozen but remains on the move. During the past twenty years, as the overall Latin American political scene has advanced somewhat away from dictatorships and tyrannies toward more democratic regimes, Assmann has apparently become much more concerned to consider how democracy can work on behalf of the poor.[39] Nevertheless, insofar as the United States strives to keep Latin America dependent, and insofar as the work of North American Christian theologians fails to respond in solidarity with Assmann's cause, they remain not only his opponents but presumably God's as well. Trusting that the answer to the New Testament's question—"If God is for us, who is against us?" (Rom. 8:31)— will vindicate the cause of liberation theology, the odds rise in favor of Latin American social upheaval that will be unfriendly to the United States.

RESPONDING TO THE INDICTMENTS

Summing up one line of thought in her *Cry of the People*, Penny Lernoux targets a dilemma focused in this chapter. "It isn't pleasant to be called an oppressor," she writes, "yet that is how many people in Latin America see the United States."[40] More recently, William M. Ramsay expands Lernoux's understatement. Commenting on liberation theology's tendency to blame Latin America's woes on the United States, he remarks that "it is difficult for us, who have prospered in this system and who love our country, to hear this criticism with much sympathy."[41]

Some North American theologians not only think the United States ought to listen sympathetically but also believe that the nation should hear how ominous the liberationist outlook can be. For example, Robert McAfee Brown, one of the movement's most sympathetic American interpreters, makes the following point: Insofar as Latin American liberation theology asserts that the present United States capitalist system must go, the nation is under "a genuine threat, because with the disappearance of the system would go our securities, our status, our luxuries, possibly our necessities, perhaps even our lives."[42]

Brown's approach is to turn this threat into a challenge. Met especially by a revitalized Christian community, that challenge could mitigate liberation theology's indictment of the United States. Emphasizing that much of liberation theology depends on a dualism between oppressor and oppressed, he admits this distinction can be "overwhelming because it puts so many of us on the wrong side of the division, where we are overwhelmed either with guilt at being found there or with frustration at not being sure how to change things."[43] Nevertheless, Brown hopes that Americans can move beyond being overwhelmed and bring about some reconciling changes.

Chances in favor of that outcome, Brown adds, will be increased if it is understood that oppressors are themselves oppressed because oppression dehumanizes everyone. He indicates that this insight should help United States citizens in particular to see that as the oppressed of Latin America seek to liberate themselves, they are also working to liberate the United States from its own dehumanization. Nurtured by openness to what liberation theology offers the United States as well as Latin America, American citizens could in turn be moved toward greater solidarity with their brothers and sisters to the south. "None are free," Brown contends, "until all are free."[44] If Americans select the right key, he believes, everyone can move toward the liberation that people need together.

In addition to a constituency among essentially white, liberal American Protestants and Catholics, Brown has allies in the black and feminist communities. The Argentine Enrique Dussel suggests that additional sympathizers should be found in the Spanish-speaking population that burgeons in the United States. Estimating that by the year 2000 fifty percent of United States Catholics will be of Latin American origin, he urges "Christian Latin American-Chicanos" to recognize that they are "a dependent and oppressed people within an 'imperial nation' who must become aware in order to liberate themselves and 'to liberate the poor nations of the world.' "[45]

Indictments of the United States brought by Latin American liberation theology live within as well as outside of United States borders. This can be healthy if it leads the United States to respond sensibly. The boundaries of this paper's topic permit no more than a concluding comment in that direction, but the crux of the matter involves a continued United States revisioning of the future for its capitalist economy.

That economy does not serve everyone well at home or abroad. Unless the people of the United States are hypocrites, however, the vast majority of them understand that their well-being depends upon the sound functioning of this system. In addition, Americans do not want to be oppressors. "In democracies," as Tocqueville said, "a self-sacrificing man is rare," but his judgment that "Americans...are hardly ever insensitive" has merit, too.[46] Precisely at that point the issue is joined, for Latin American liberation theology finds capitalism at the center of its target.

Unless that movement substantially recasts its identity, little that the United States can do, short of scrapping our capitalist ways altogether, is likely to win full favor from those quarters. Granted, United States capitalism can and should be altered so it serves society better at home and overseas. But to the extent that United States capitalism remains—and it must unless Americans, including American Christians, are willing to deny their identity—the United States will likely remain a major scapegoat in the perspective of Latin American liberation theology.

Modifications and reformations both within American capitalism and within the liberationists' outlook may avert the collision course that presently exists between them. Yet in conclusion it must also be said that insofar as the liberationist perspective retains its unmistakably Marxist flavor, the potential for Soviet encouragement of that movement and its spinoffs remains. Disavowals by the liberation theologians notwithstanding, conditions could evolve so that such encouragement would even be welcomed. So the signs all point in a similar direction. The United States and its people, Christian or not, should begin their response to Latin American liberation theology by asking honestly and self-critically: Is the United States the great enemy?

NOTES

1. Leonardo Boff and Clodovis Boff, *Liberation Theology: From Dialogue to Confrontation*, trans. Robert R. Barr (San Francisco: Harper and Row, 1986), p. 1.

2. Alexis de Tocqueville, *Democracy in America*, ed. J. P. Mayer and trans. George Lawrence (Garden City, N.Y.: Doubleday Anchor Books, 1969), p. 621.

3. Ibid.

4. Ibid.

5. Ibid., p. 407.

6. Ibid., p. 306.

7. Ibid., p. 406.

8. The statement quoted from Guevara appears in Irving Louis Horowitz et al., eds., *Latin American Radicalism: A Documentary Report on Left and Nationalist Movements* (New York: Random House, 1969), p. 620. It is also cited in Deane William Ferm, *Third World Liberation Theologies: An Introductory Survey* (Maryknoll, N.Y.: Orbis Books, 1986), p. 13. Hereafter the latter is abbreviated *TWLT, Survey*.

9. See José Míguez Bonino, *Doing Theology in a Revolutionary Situation* (Philadelphia: Fortress Press, 1975), pp. 2–3.

10. Gustavo Gutiérrez, *A Theology of Liberation: History, Politics and Salvation*, trans. and ed. Sister Caridad Inda and John Eagleson (Maryknoll, N.Y.: Orbis Books, 1973), p. 88. Significantly, in his footnote to this statement, Gutiérrez observes that nearly a century and a half earlier—not much before Tocqueville's *Democracy in America*—Hegel wrote that "America is...the land of the future where in years to come world history will be forged *perhaps by the antagonism between North and South America.*" See Gutiérrez, *Theology of Liberation*, p. 96, n. 32. The italics are his. While the topic reaches beyond the scope of this essay, it is worth wondering whether Japan will begin to feel heat from Latin American liberation theology. Not only has Japan's economy eroded United States hegemony in numerous sectors, its capitalistic power in Latin

America is expanding rapidly. Richard L. Rubenstein's introductory essay also takes note of such developments. See p. 10 above.

11. Clodovis Boff, "Society and the Kingdom: A Dialogue between a Theologian, a Christian Activist, and a Parish Priest," in Leonardo and Clodovis Boff, *Salvation and Liberation*, trans. Robert R. Barr (Maryknoll, N.Y.: Orbis Books, 1984), p. 116. The italics are Boff's.

12. Juan Luis Segundo, "Capitalism-Socialism: A Theological Crux," trans. J. P. Donnelly, in *Liberation South, Liberation North*, ed. Michael Novak (Washington, D.C.: American Enterprise Institute, 1981), p. 8.

13. Ibid., p. 13.

14. Ibid., p. 15.

15. Ibid.

16. See Ferm, *TWLT, Survey*, p. 116 and also "Rubenstein on Liberation Theology," *International Journal on World Peace* 4 (April–June 1987): 7–8. The latter is Ferm's letter to the editor concerning Richard L. Rubenstein's "The Political Significance of Latin American Liberation Theology," *International Journal on World Peace* 3 (January–March 1986): 41–55. In this article, which has also been published in monograph form by the Washington Institute for Values in Public Policy, the author explores themes related to those under discussion in this essay.

17. Elsa Tamez, "Good News for the Poor," in *Third World Liberation Theologies: A Reader*, ed. Deane William Ferm (Maryknoll, N.Y.: 1986), p. 190. Hereafter this volume is abbreviated *TWLT, Reader*. The selection reprinted in Ferm's edition is from Tamez's *Bible of the Oppressed* (Maryknoll, N.Y.: Orbis Books, 1982), pp. 66–74.

18. Ibid., p. 193.

19. Ibid., pp. 190–91.

20. Ibid., p. 192.

21. Ibid., pp. 194–95.

22. Ibid., p. 195.

23. José Miranda, "Christianity Is Communism," in *TWLT, Reader*, ed. Ferm, p. 160. The selection reprinted in Ferm's edition is from

Miranda's *Communism in the Bible* (Maryknoll, N.Y.: Orbis Books, 1982), pp. 1–20.

24. Ibid., p. 172. The italics are Miranda's.

25. Ibid., p. 161.

26. Ibid., p. 162.

27. Ibid., p. 168.

28. José Míguez Bonino, *Christians and Marxists: The Mutual Challenge to Revolution* (London: Hodder and Stoughton, 1976), p. 87.

29. Ibid., p. 88–89.

30. Ibid., p. 135.

31. Victorio G. Araya, "The God of the Strategic Covenant," in Pablo Richard et al., *The Idols of Death and the God of Life: A Theology*, trans. Barbara E. Campbell and Bonnie Shepard (Maryknoll, N.Y.: Orbis Books, 1983), p. 110.

32. Ibid., p. 111.

33. Ibid., p. 105.

34. Pablo Richard, "Biblical Theology of Confrontation with Idols," in Richard et al., *The Idols of Death and the God of Life*, p. 3.

35. Ibid., p. 24.

36. Hugo Assmann, *Theology for a Nomad Church*, trans. Paul Burns (Maryknoll, N.Y.: Orbis Books, 1976), pp. 57–58.

37. Ibid., p. 54.

38. Ibid., p. 144.

39. On this point and others concerning Assmann, see Michael Novak, *Will It Liberate? Questions about Liberation Theology* (New York: Paulist Press, 1986), pp. 246–48. Also relevant are Novak's "Notes on Dinner with Assmann," pp. 236–42.

40. Penny Lernoux, *Cry of the People: United States Involvement in the Rise of Fascism, Torture, and Murder and the Persecution of the Catholic Church in Latin America* (Garden City, N.Y.: Doubleday and Co., 1980), p. 456. Lernoux's sequel to this book provides further insights into her reasons for believing that the dim view of the

United States held by many Latin Americans is justified. See *In Banks We Trust* (Garden City, N.Y.: Anchor Press/Doubleday, 1984).

41. William M. Ramsay, *Four Modern Prophets: Walter Rauschenbusch, Martin Luther King, Jr., Gustavo Gutiérrez, Rosemary Radford Ruether* (Atlanta: John Knox Press, 1986), p. 69.

42. Robert McAfee Brown, *Theology in a New Key: Responding to Liberation Themes* (Philadelphia: Westminster Press, 1978), p. 134.

43. Ibid., p. 146.

44. Ibid., p. 154.

45. Enrique Dussel, *History and the Theology of Liberation: A Latin American Perspective*, trans. John Drury (Maryknoll, N.Y.: Orbis Books, 1976), pp. 171, 176.

46. Tocqueville, *Democracy in America*, pp. 571–72.

11

Liberation Theology and the U.S. Bishops' Letters on Nuclear Weapons and on the Economy

Phillip Berryman

More than one observer has noted a connection between liberation theology and the recent pastoral letters of the U.S. Catholic bishops, *The Challenge of Peace* (1983) and *Economic Justice for All* (1986). For example, in developing his argument that the U.S. bishops have "abandoned" crucial aspects of Catholic teaching on peace, George Weigel devotes particular attention to liberation theology and the bishops' position on Central America. Alerting the church to the flaws and dangers in the pastoral letters and in liberation theology has also been a central concern of Michael Novak's, in recent years.[1]

One need not agree with (neo)conservative critics to note clear affinities between the letters and liberation theology. "Affinities" is a deliberately weak and vague term: I am not claiming that the U.S. bishops have been heavily influenced by Latin American liberation theology, but simply that both enterprises have something in common.

The aim of this chapter is to explore some of these affinities, while pointing to the divergences as well. Such a question is only indirectly relevant to policymakers insofar as highlighting the parallels and differences between the pastoral letters and liberation theology may contribute to a more nuanced understanding of Catholicism and its incidence in the public sphere.

BISHOPS AND THEOLOGIANS

At the outset, it should be noted that bishops and theologians play different roles in the church. A bishop occupies an office, or a ministry, that of oversight or leadership in a diocese. A theologian as such has no authority or office. Thus the most direct Latin American analog to the pastoral letters would not be the writings of theologians but the documents of the Latin American bishops produced at major conferences in Medellín, Colombia (1968), and Puebla, Mexico (1979), as well as hundreds of documents produced by national episcopal bodies since the 1960s.[2]

By their nature episcopal documents represent a degree of consensus, at least among the bishops themselves. Part of the role of theologians, on the other hand, is to explore *quaestiones disputatae*. By no means, however, is their relationship inherently adversarial. In fact, Latin American theologians have devoted a great deal of attention to further elaborating the themes sketched out in episcopal and papal documents. In some instances, especially in Brazil, there has been a close working relationship between theologians and bishops. One can surmise that theologians have been involved in drafting statements of the Brazilian bishops. When Cardinals Lorscheider and Arns accompanied Leonardo Boff to Rome for his 1985 meeting with Vatican officials, they were signifying the Brazilian episcopacy's support for him as a theologian and his right to explore even questions that ruffle feathers in Rome.

For their part, the U.S. bishops in *The Challenge of Peace* urge the development of a "theology of peace" which would draw on "biblical studies, systematic and moral theology, ecclesiology, and the experience and insights of members of the church who have struggled in various ways to make and keep the peace in this often violent age." In other words the "praxis" of peace activists would seem to be a *locus* for such a theology. They go on to say that the theology they have in mind should ground the task of peacemaking solidly in the biblical vision of the Kingdom of God, then place it centrally in the ministry of the Church. It should specify the obstacles in the way of peace, as these are understood theologically and in the social and political sciences. It should both identify the specific contributions a community of faith can make to the work of peace and relate these to the wider work of peace pursued by other groups and institutions in society. Finally, a theology of peace must include a message of hope (25).[3]

If one were to substitute the word "liberation" for "peace" or "peacemaking" in the passage above, it would sound remarkably like a description of what liberation theologians are attempting. Although *Economic Justice for All* contains no similar passage, it seems clear that the U.S. bishops have issued an invitation to a collaborative work by theologians and others to develop something analogous to Latin American liberation theology.

POST-VATICAN II QUESTIONS

Both liberation theology and the pastoral letters are concerned with the relationship between Christian faith and economic and political issues—indeed, with the very shape of our institutions and our society. This "social question," as it has been called, is not new. One can find antecedents in the Protestant "social gospel" and Catholic papal encyclicals starting with *Rerum Novarum* (1891). The work of Father John A. Ryan, the major author of a 1919 pastoral letter "On Reconstructing the Social Order," influenced a generation of priests who fostered Catholic support for New Deal reforms. George Weigel correctly indicates that the bishops had dealt with peace-related issues before Vatican II.[4]

Nevertheless, I believe both liberation theology and the recent bishops' letters should be seen as qualitatively new phenomena which reflect a changed situation of the church since the council.

Even prior to the council, some Latin American Catholics were wondering whether they might not need to develop their own specific pastoral methods and their own theology. How could they reach the vast numbers of poor people, scattered in villages or massed in urban barrios or favelas? What should be done about the institutional church's ties to existing elites?

What was the significance of the growing awareness that the existing development model was not improving the lives of the impoverished majority? Out of such questioning emerged new pastoral approaches (base communities, for example) and a new theological approach (liberation theology). Instead of simply repeating a "Catholic" (that is, Roman) theology presumed valid for all, Latin Americans began to develop their own specific theology. In the post-Vatican II period, the Catholic church in Latin America has developed its own distinctive style.

While its manifestation is less dramatic, something similar has been happening in the United States. Although Catholics have been present since colonial times, they formed only a small minority until the massive immigrations of the later nineteenth century. Catholicism continued to bear an immigrant stamp until the post-World War II generation when significant numbers began to share in the American dream: they moved to the suburbs and their children went to college. In the 1950s Catholics were still striving for full recognition in white Protestant America.

No sooner had that recognition occurred—symbolically represented in the election of John F. Kennedy as president—than the church was plunged into the maelstrom of Vatican Council II. Initially, the council seemed to be about internal church matters: liturgy, biblical scholarship, church authority, and so on. The document on the church in the modern world (*Gaudium et Spes*) only took shape slowly during the council years and was promulgated at the end of the council (1965). Moreover, during the immediate post-council years, the sharpest controversies seemed to swirl about matters of personal morality or church authority, for example, the reactions to Paul VI's "birth control" encyclical, *Humanae Vitae* (1968).

During this same period there was an expansion of Catholic activism for peace and justice, both unofficial and official, like the antiwar protests of the Berrigans and others and the eventual formal opposition by the bishops (1971) to the United States involvement in the Vietnam War. Such efforts were spurred by developments in worldwide Catholicism, such as the 1971 synod on justice in the world held in Rome which declared that "action on behalf of justice" is a "constitutive dimension of the preaching of the Gospel," and hence central to the church's mission. An important institutional expression in the United States has been the Campaign for Human Development with its strong emphasis on empowering grassroots groups.

The analogy with Latin America is that in a slower and less dramatic way, United States Catholicism was further developing its own distinctive identity. One example is the development of a more democratic style and at least some tolerance for expression of dissent. The very process of the recent letters, involving public discussion of three major drafts, is an example of the "Americanizing" of Catholicism. Moreover, American Catholicism now feels self-confident enough to take a critical stance toward United States institutions to a degree that would have been unthinkable when Catholics were still striving for full acceptance. One might wonder how it was possible that Catholics could coexist peacefully with nuclear weapons for almost forty years before the appearance of *The Challenge of Peace,* but there is little mystery to those who grew up in the 1950s when Catholic anticommunism went hand in hand with a bipartisan Cold War consensus.

Novak, Weigel, and others see the bishops' letters as reflecting the "anti-Americanism" which they regard as the trendy masochism of the "Catholic Left." However, to raise critical questions about the United States need not be anti-American, and may indeed be a high form of patriotism. The bishops' letters, including the process behind them as well as the questions they raise, may represent a coming-of-age more significant than the 1960 election. Just as liberation theology and the Medellín and Puebla documents express the emergence of a specifically Latin American Catholic church, the letters on nuclear weapons and the economy may be important elements in the emergence of a specifically American kind of Catholicism.

REFORMIST OR RADICAL?

Insisting that Christians "must assess the extent to which the structures and practices of the economy support or undermine their moral vision" (127), the U.S. bishops note that different people come to different conclusions. After contrasting the views of those who "argue that an unfettered free-market economy…provides the greatest possible liberty, material welfare, and equity" with those who see capitalism as "inherently inequitable" and "fatally flawed," the bishops insist that "Catholic social teaching has traditionally rejected these ideological extremes because they are likely to produce results contrary to human dignity and economic justice" (128, 129). They describe their own approach as:

pragmatic and evolutionary in nature. We live in a "mixed" economic system which is the product of a long history of reform and adjustment. It is in the spirit of this American pragmatic tradition of reform that we seek to continue the search for a more just economy (131).

In keeping with this orientation the bishops' policy recommendations are generally compatible with the shape of the modern Western welfare state.

Their overall stance differs markedly from that of liberation theologians, who, like many Latin American social scientists, criticize capitalism itself and call for a new model of development. Nevertheless, they describe the kind of socialism they have in mind in only the most general terms and emphasize that it would not be a copy of any existing model.

That the bishops and Latin American theologians diverge is confirmed by a critique of the U.S. bishops' letter on the economy written by the Brazilian theologians Leonardo and Clodovis Boff. While finding much to admire, the Boffs believe the bishops remain at a "descriptive" level and fail to arrive at an adequate analysis of the source of the problems they treat. Their "functionalist" method of analysis prevents them from seeing the depth of conflict in our world. Although the bishops show some familiarity with "dependence" theory, it is overriden by their insistence on "interdependence."[5]

In passing, I would note that the Latin American bishops, both in national conferences and at their continent-level meetings in Medellín (1968) and Puebla (1979), are perhaps somewhere between the positions of the Boffs and the U.S. bishops. They are not nearly as specific about policy recommendations as are the documents of their United States counterparts and they are more prone to generalize about ideological, economic, and political systems. At Medellín the bishops called for basic changes in society and showed sympathy with notions of revolution, understood not as violence but as a process in which the people become active agents in social transformation. At Puebla they had strong words about the present order but alongside critiques of "liberal capitalism" and the "national security state" one finds equally strong critiques of "Marxist collectivism." Although they can be fairly described as reformist, these documents can be given more radical readings.

The reformist thrust of the U.S. bishops' letters is obvious from their general tenor as well as from the passages quoted above. While the reaction of the Boff brothers is understandable, it seems unrealistic and unhistorical of them to have expected the U.S. bishops to condemn capitalism. To begin with, it would not have represented any consensus within the church or United States society. More importantly, while it is perhaps possible for Brazilians and other Latin Americans to have some sense of what "socialism" might mean for them, it is far less clear what it might mean for an advanced Western economy and especially for the United States. As they end the letter on the economy the bishops state that it is "but the beginning of a long process of education, discussion and action" (359).

A closer look at the letter on the economy shows the bishops raising systemic questions. In the very passage in which they stress their "pragmatic and evolutionary" approach, the bishops go on to insist that Catholic social teaching

> bears directly on larger questions concerning the economic system itself and the values it expresses—questions that cannot be ignored in the Catholic vision of economic justice. For example, does our economic system place more emphasis on maximizing profits than on meeting human needs and fostering human dignity? Does our economy distribute its benefits equitably or does it concentrate power and resources in the hands of a few? Does it promote excessive materialism and individualism? Does it adequately protect the environment and the nation's natural resources? Does it direct too many scarce resources to military purposes? (132)

The bishops explicitly urge continued scrutiny and exploration of such "systemic questions."

Moreover, they make bold hints when they speak of completing "the unfinished business of the American experiment" (296).

> The nation's founders took daring steps to create structures of participation, mutual accountability and widely distributed power to ensure the political rights and freedoms of all. We believe that similar steps are needed today to expand economic participation, broaden the sharing of economic power, and make economic decisions more accountable to the common good (297).

This sounds like a call for what many on the Left call "economic democracy."

Although *Economic Justice for All* is reformist in the sense that it assumes the continuity of the present economic system, the letter can be read as raising questions so fundamental that they point toward a qualitatively different kind of society. In that sense, a radical reading is also legitimate.

There is a similar double track in *The Challenge of Peace*. While its policy thrust sounds similar to the approach of liberal arms control advocates such as George Kennan and Robert McNamara, one also finds another kind of discourse.

> We fear that our world and nation are headed in the wrong direction. More weapons with greater destructive potential are produced every day. More and more nations are seeking to become nuclear powers. In our quest for more and more security, we fear we are actually becoming less and less secure.
>
> In the words of our Holy Father, we need a "moral about-face." The whole world must summon the moral courage and technical means to say "no" to nuclear conflict; "no" to weapons of mass destruction; "no" to an arms race which robs the poor and the vulnerable; and "no" to the moral danger of a nuclear age which places before humankind indefensible choices of constant terror or surrender (332, 333).

In their treatment of "The Superpowers in a Disordered World" (245–58) one has the impression that the bishops want to suggest the possibility of a different kind of relationship between the United States and the Soviet Union. However, most of the section is devoted to making it clear that they are not equating the two superpowers. Thus, warnings about the "trap of anti-Sovietism" are more than counterbalanced by references to the "Soviet threat," the "Soviet imperial drive for hegemony," the "Soviet system of repression," and so forth. With many such qualifiers, the bishops nevertheless insist that

> the Soviet people and their leaders are human beings created in the image and likeness of God. To believe we are condemned in the future only to what has been in the past of U.S.-Soviet relations is to underestimate both our human potential

for creative diplomacy and God's action in our midst which
can open the way to changes we could barely imagine (258).

In another visionary passage, the bishops, referring to existing papal
teaching, point to the need for surpassing the present situation in which
there is no effective political authority above the nation-state. They call for
"a properly constituted political authority with the capacity to shape our
material interdependence in the direction of moral interdependence" (241).

Finally, we may note the bishops' explicit acknowledgement of nonviolence as part of the "Christian theological tradition" alongside just-war
theory. The names of Gandhi, Dorothy Day, and Martin Luther King, Jr.,
are explicitly invoked, and pacifism is accorded full citizenship within
Catholicism (111 ff.). The bishops even devote several paragraphs to ur-
ging that the possibility of nonviolent popular defense be seriously explored (221–30).

In short, while both *The Challenge of Peace* and *Economic Justice for
All* are in some sense mainstream documents—situated, however, toward
the left-liberal end of the spectrum of United States debate—they may
legitimately be given a more "radical" reading. To the extent that they raise
fundamental questions about central issues in our society from a faith
perspective, they have strong affinities with liberation theology.

PRACTICE

"Peacemaking," say the bishops, "is not an optional commitment. It is
a requirement of our faith. We are called to be peacemakers, not by some
movement of the moment, but by our Lord Jesus" (333). In a similar spirit
they say that the concerns of the economics pastoral "are not at all
peripheral to the central mystery at the heart of the Church" but "integral
to the proclamation of the Gospel and part of the vocation of every Christian today" (60).

Although both letters are written with policy elites in mind, they are
aimed primarily at the Catholic community. Not only do they urge that
Catholics become involved in issues of peacemaking and economic justice, but they are themselves products of committed activity by many
people. Years of engagement by Catholic peace activists unquestionably
were decisive in pricking the conscience of the Catholic community, including the bishops. In the 1950s, for example, Dorothy Day and other

Catholic Worker associates prompted reactions of both mystification and admiration when they refused to legitimate the arms race by participating in nuclear attack drills in Manhattan.

I would suggest here a similarity to liberation theology's relationship to praxis. Although the theologians' writings often seem highly abstract, they are a response to real questions asked by priests, sisters, and active lay people at the village and barrio level. What emerges in the form of theological essays and books is the product of innumerable local-level efforts by base communities and others to struggle for justice and dignity and is intended as a service to those involved in such struggles.

Similarly, the U.S. bishops' letters are far more than an attempt to influence public opinion or perhaps the voting patterns of Catholics. Rather, the letters are invitations for individual Catholics, organizations and groups, parishes, and dioceses to become engaged with the issues as the bishops did, to study those issues and become involved in action at the local level. In so doing they will run up against problems, possibly even opposition and conflict. Along the way they will reflect and pray. Although the setting is different, the overall process will be similar to the kind of "action-and-reflection" that liberation theologians call "praxis."

HEARING THE BIBLE IN THE SAME "KEY"

One finds strong affinities between the biblical sections of the pastoral letters and the use of the Bible in liberation theology. For example, in paragraphs 30–55 the economic pastoral letter surveys the themes of creation, exodus/covenant/people, prophets/justice in the Hebrew scriptures, when speaking of Jesus highlights the commandment to love (especially Matthew 25:31–46), and devotes special attention to biblical perspectives on wealth and poverty (48–52). These are the very themes Latin American theologians have emphasized. They are central to the Scriptures themselves, of course, but fundamentalists and others reading the same Bible would highlight very different themes.

Explicitly mentioning the "preferential option for the poor," the bishops spell out the challenge posed to the church by the example of Jesus, who "takes the side of those most in need, physically and spiritually."

> It imposes a prophetic mandate to speak for those who have
> no one to speak for them, to be a defender of the defenseless,

who in biblical terms are the poor. It also demands a compassionate vision that enables the Church to see things from the side of the poor and powerless, and to assess lifestyle, policies, and social institutions in terms of their impact on the poor. It summons the Church also to be an instrument in assisting people to experience the liberating power of God in their own lives so that they may respond to the Gospel in freedom and in dignity. Finally, and most radically, it calls for an emptying of self, both individually and corporately, that allows the Church to experience the power of God in the midst of poverty and powerlessness (52).

Both liberation theology and the pastoral letters understand the Bible "in a new key" (Robert McAfee Brown).

CATHOLIC SOCIAL TEACHING

The two pastoral letters are explicitly based on Catholic social teaching, which the bishops see as "rooted in the Bible and developed over the past century by the popes and the Second Vatican Council" and as "dynamic and growing." At some points they invoke previous teaching extensively, as in the delicate question of deterrence, where long quotes from Vatican II and John Paul II's talk to the UN Second Special Session on Disarmament are included.

At one time Catholic social "doctrine," as it was then called, was largely identified with papal encyclicals and tended to view the world from Europe. Shifting away from this Eurocentric view, Paul VI's *Populorum Progressio* (1967) focused on the Third World. His *Octogesima Adveniens* (1971) seemed to acknowledge that the diversity of situations in the world would not admit of univocal formulas, thus inviting local churches to develop Catholic social thought in response to their own particular situations.

Medellín and Puebla can be seen as expressing Latin American developments of Catholic social teaching. Those documents have been central to the work of liberation theologians. Moreover, it is interesting to note that Pope John Paul II's encyclical *On Human Labor* (1981), which made little immediate impact on United States Catholicism (although its influence is explicit in the economics pastoral), was received enthusiastically in Latin

America. For example the DEI (Departamento Ecuménico de Investigaciones) group in Costa Rica published a local edition of the text with its own commentary. The Peruvian theologian Ricardo Antoncich has written a work on the church's social teaching for the "Theology and Liberation" series, a projected fifty-volume "summa" currently being produced by liberation theologians.[6]

Are liberation theologians opportunistically twisting the meaning of Catholic social teaching or simply ignoring parts they find inconvenient, such as strong condemnations of Marxism? There is no single understanding of what "Catholic social teaching" means—different writers come up with very different intepretations (compare, for example, the numerous works cited in chapter 2, footnote 17, of *Economic Justice for All*). Moreover, liberation theologians generally agree with many critiques of "really existing socialism." Along with most of the Latin American Left, they would see it as bureaucratized and as embodying its own form of oppression. What they would emphasize, however, is that they must be concerned with the economic system under which Latin Americans *presently* suffer rather than criticize the USSR, Eastern Europe, or Cuba. They must serve the Latin American effort to find a valid new model of development and discover the path in that direction, taking advantage of historical experience, including the partial successes as well as the failures of existing Third World socialism, including Cuba.

In any case, both these theologians and the U.S. bishops see themselves as standing in the tradition of Catholic social teaching and contributing to its development.

VISIONS OF PERSON, COMMUNITY, SOCIETY

The letter on the economy opens with these words:

> Every perspective on economic life that is human, moral, and Christian must be shaped by three questions: What does the economy do *for* people? What does it do *to* people? And how do people *participate* in it? The economy is a human reality: men and women working together to develop and care for the whole of God's creation (1).

A few paragraphs later we find the lapidary statement, "People shape the economy and in turn are shaped by it" (5).

What the bishops are asserting is that the economy is not to be considered a given, something beyond critique, but that on the contrary Christians must examine existing economic institutions in the light of higher principles.

> We have outlined this moral vision as a guide to all who seek
> to be faithful to the Gospel in their daily economic decisions
> and as a challenge to transform the economic arrangements
> that shape our lives and our world (127).

These arrangements, say the bishops, "embody and communicate social values and therefore have moral significance." Christians

> must be concerned about how the concrete outcomes of their
> economic activity serve human dignity; they must assess the
> extent to which the structures and practices of the economy
> support or undermine their moral vision (127).

The general tenor of these and other statements, admittedly rather philosophical in nature, seems to run contrary to the widespread assumption that economic activity is that of individuals, each pursuing his or her own goals. It is interesting to note that Milton Friedman takes exception not only to the thrust of the bishops' policy proposals but to their "collectivist moral strain." He objects to the notion that a country or a society has a moral duty, and asserts the contrary view that a country or a society is "a collection of individuals; ...the basic entity is the individual, or more fundamentally, the family, and...only individuals can have moral obligations."[7] This is not the place to discuss Friedman's atomistic view of society and economics, but simply to note that he underscores the deep divergence between himself and the bishops.

On the other hand, one finds in the letters an affinity with the Latin American conviction expressed at Medellín that people are to be "subjects of their own development." This seemingly abstract terminology makes sense to church people doing pastoral work at the village or barrio level who have observed striking examples of a kind of conversion when people cease to accept the world fatalistically as it is, and become involved in efforts to change it. Although to our ears the notion of shaping destiny may have a Promethean ring, these efforts are embodied in modest ventures such as peasant leagues, unions, barrio organizations, or cooperatives, which are nevertheless regarded as steps toward a more just kind of society.

This process is at once practical, (learning how to organize, run meetings, articulate demands, and so forth), and yet philosophical, enabling poor people to become active agents pursuing their own destiny—and it is ultimately a theological process. In church documents the process is sometimes referred to in the phrase "integral development."

It may seem ironic that poor people who have so little wealth and power believe they can become "subjects of their own development" and that their efforts can lead to a different kind of world, whereas citizens of the world's most powerful country regard as utopian the notion that by their concerted activity they might "transform...economic arrangements."

In a little-noticed text the U.S. bishops observe that even before Christ "the Greeks and Romans spoke of the human person as a 'social animal' made for friendship, community, and *public life*" (emphasis added). It is a commonplace to note, as the bishops do, that "human beings achieve self-realization not in isolation, but in interaction with others" (65). What I find striking is that they explicitly see being involved in "public life" as part of the full definition of being human. Put another way, the bishops seem to be implying that a life spent in purely private pursuits or in the circle of family and intimate acquaintances is lacking in something essential to a full human life: active pursuit of the common good through involvement in public life. They immediately add, "The virtues of citizenship are an expression of Christian love more crucial in today's interdependent world than ever before" (66).

WEALTH, POVERTY, AND JUSTICE

The U.S. bishops adopt the Latin American expression "preferential option for the poor." Dealing with poverty is not only desirable—it is a matter of distributive and social justice.

> Minimum material resources are an absolute necessity for human life. If persons are to be recognized as members of the human community, then the community has an obligation to help fulfill these basic needs unless an absolute scarcity of resources makes this strictly impossible. *No such scarcity exists in the United States today* (70, emphasis added).

The bishops say that basic justice "calls into question extreme inequalities of income and consumption when so many lack basic necessities."

They do not advocate "a flat, arithmetical equality of income and wealth"(74), however, and they explicitly state that the option for the poor "is not an adversarial slogan that pits one group or class against another." Rather, they believe that "the deprivation and powerlessness of the poor wounds the whole community" (88). Justice demands not only adequate welfare provisions—what the bishops call "a floor of material well-being on which all can stand" (74)—but overcoming marginalization, whether political or economic and within the United States or internationally.

> Stated positively, justice demands that social institutions be ordered in a way that guarantees all persons the ability to participate actively in the economic, political, and cultural life of society (78).

Again, one finds strong affinities with the underlying aims of liberation theology, which has devoted a great deal of attention to the theme of poverty. The primary difference is the scope of poverty. Using United States government official estimates, the bishops state that over 33 million people—one American out of seven—are poor. In Latin America, by any definition the poor are an absolute majority, and their poverty is in material terms far greater than that of the poor in the United States. It is at least arguable that poverty can be eliminated in the United States through the kinds of reform measures mentioned by the bishops (job creation, job training, welfare reform, and so on). In Latin America, on the other hand, what is required is a fundamental shift in power and priorities

THE UNITED STATES AND THE THIRD WORLD

Paragraphs 251–92 of *Economic Justice for All* deal with "The U.S. Economy and the Developing Nations: Complexity, Challenge, and Choices." We have already noted that Leonardo and Clodovis Boff do not give the bishops very good grades for the letter itself, and especially on this section—perhaps an A-minus for their moral concern but only a C-plus for their analysis and recommendations. The bishops' "functionalist" framework makes them see "contrasts" rather than "conflict" and to see problems as "dysfunctionalities" within a system that is in overall harmony.

Since the need for fundamental systemic change seems so obvious to them, the Boffs are frustrated at what they see as the failure of vision and nerve in the pastoral letter on the economy. The bishops invoke the usual global statistics about 800 million people in "absolute poverty" and a half-billion chronically hungry, 15 percent of children in those situations dying before the age of five, and so forth. They also admit that "the gap between rich and poor countries and between rich and poor people within countries is widening" (290). Yet they seem more confident when discussing welfare reform, saving family farms, or avoiding plant closings than they do when discussing the international economy. What they propose about aid, trade, finance (including the national debt), and investment seems to presuppose that the world will continue on its present course and that the United States must adjust, do more, shift priorities, and so forth.

The Boffs are dismayed that the bishops take what seems to be "a strictly moral and not a political approach to the question."

> The subjects of the episcopal recommendations are individuals and existing social institutions, seen as functions and categories, and not seen as people and classes. From this point of view, it appears that the United States has no fault regarding the poverty of the Third World! What we see is a situation of backwardness, not one of domination.[8]

They are especially disturbed at the treatment of the transnationals.

> How is it possible not to see, alongside the indisputable economic and technical development, the immense social, political and cultural dislocation and manipulation that the transnationals have perpetrated in the poor countries? Why not speak of blatant exploitation and plunder in relation to our countries?[9]

The Boffs believe the bishops are "working out of an older mindset, that of 'manifest destiny'" and "attribute a messianic function to America."

> In this way, the United States appears as the savior of the Third World, not as one of the parties responsible for its present misery! Rather than culprit, it becomes the defender! This is a typical case of "ideological inversion."[10]

While the Boffs' frustrations are understandable from a Third World viewpoint, a closer examination will find some suggestive passages. For example, in the final passage of this section the bishops state that

To restructure the international order along lines of greater
equity and participation and apply the preferential option for
the poor to international economic activity will require
sacrifices of at least the scope of those we have made over the
years in building our own nation (291).

In order to pursue justice and peace on a global scale, *we
call for a U.S. international economic policy designed to empower people everywhere and enable them to continue to
develop a sense of their own worth, improve the quality of
their lives, and ensure that the benefits of economic growth
are shared equitably* (292, emphasis in original).

At first glance this seems like standard development jargon. However,
the bishops should be aware that *empowering* the poor majority in Latin
America runs contrary to the kind of development being pursued by the
military, agroexport, and business elites. A shift in "economic arrangements" that really empowers the poor and enables them to have real participation would be revolutionary and is indeed the essence of revolution.
That is why popular movements are met with violence and why, until
now, those in favor of basic change have tended to see armed struggle as
a necessary component of struggle for change. On the other hand, today
in some places church people are hopeful that widespread grassroots nonviolent popular movements can lead to genuinely revolutionary change.

Perhaps the greatest lack in this section of the letter is any explicit
reference to people's own efforts to organize and struggle for change. Consequently, by default, the bishops' recommendations end up assuming the
present institutional order, even though their moral principles call for a
deeper shift. Despite this weakness, they nevertheless make important observations. They severely criticize the fact that United States Third World
policy has "become increasingly one of selective assistance based on an
East-West assessment of North-South problems, at the expense of basic
human needs" (262). They also see the United States in international
forums as "resisting developing-country proposals without advancing
realistic ones of our own" (263). They note that "we lag proportionately
behind most other industrial nations in providing resources and seem to
care less than before about development in the Third World" (265). They
urge an examination to see whether United States overseas investment
takes advantage of exploited labor. With strong words they note that the

"global *system* of finance, development, and trade established by the Bretton Woods Conference in 1944...seems incapable, without basic changes, of helping the debtor countries—which had no part in its creation—manage their increasingly untenable debt situation effectively and equitably" (273, emphasis in original). While they offer no single suggestion for resolving the Third World debt crisis, they note that "it is the poorest people who suffer most" from IMF-imposed austerity measures, and suggest a number of approaches, most of which would be difficult for the banks to accept:

> moratorium on payments, conversion of some dollar-denominated debt into local-currency debt, creditors' accepting a share of the burden by partially writing-down selected loans, capitalizing interest, or perhaps outright cancellation (274).

While the bishops' document does not satisfy the Boffs, and presumably most other Latin American liberation theologians, nevertheless one can find many points of contact between the respective concerns on both sides.

CONCLUDING REMARKS

The modest purpose of this chapter has been to find affinities and points of contact between liberation theology and the recent U.S. Catholic bishops' letters on nuclear weapons and on the United States economy. The material cited is primarily intended by way of example; no doubt other examples could be cited.

The argument here is based not so much on textual similarities (for example, use of similar expressions such as "preferential option for the poor") as it is on a similar kind of underlying logic. The differences derive primarily from the different roles of bishops and theologians and from the different situations of the Catholic church in Latin America and in the United States. If there are such affinities, it is not—*pace* George Weigel—because the bishops have somehow been manipulated by doctrinaire leftists, but because both liberation theologians and the U.S. bishops have drawn on, and further developed, a late twentieth-century understanding of Catholicism to serve the mission of the church for Latin America and the United States.

NOTES

1. George Weigel, *Tranquillitas Ordinis: The Present Failure and Future Promise of American Catholic Thought on War and Peace* (New York: Oxford University Press, 1987); Michael Novak, "Moral Clarity in the Nuclear Age," *National Review,* April 1, 1983; Michael Novak and William Simon (Lay Commission on Catholic Social Teaching and the U.S. Economy), *Toward the Future: Catholic Social Thought and the U.S. Economy—A Lay Letter* (New York: Lay Commission, 1984); Novak and Simon, "Liberty and Justice for All" (statement issued November 4, 1986); Michael Novak, *Will It Liberate? Questions about Liberation Theology?* (New York: Paulist Press, 1986).

2. Over a thousand pages of such documents can be found in José Marins et al., eds., *Praxis de los padres de América latina: Los documentos de las conferencias episcopales de Medellín a Puebla (1968–1978),* (Bogotá: Ediciones Paulinas, 1978).

3. Subsequent references to the bishops' letters will be indicated parenthetically in the text by paragraph number.

4. Weigel, *Tranquillitas Ordinis,* pp. 55 ff.

5. Clodovis Boff and Leonardo Boff, "Good News of Bishops' Economics Pastoral and Bad News Left Unmentioned," *National Catholic Reporter,* August 28, 1987, pp. 14, 23.

6. Cf. Ricardo Antoncich, *Christians in the Face of Injustice: A Latin American Reading of Catholic Social Teaching* (Maryknoll, N.Y.: Orbis Books, 1987). The Spanish original dates from 1980 and hence does not incorporate *Laborem Exercens.* The new volume for the Theology and Liberation Series is largely a reworking of the earlier work, incorporating the encyclical.

7. Milton Friedman, "Good Ends, Bad Means," in *The Catholic Challenge to the American Economy: Reflections on the U.S. Bishops' Pastoral Letter on Catholic Social Teaching and the U.S. Economy,* ed. Thomas M. Gannon, S. J. (New York: Macmillan, 1987) pp. 99, 105.

8. Clodovis Boff and Leonardo Boff, "Good News," pp. 24–25.

9. Ibid., p. 25.

10. Ibid.

12

Liberating without Being Liberationist: The U.S. Catholic Bishops' Pastoral Letter on the Economy

Dennis P. McCann

It may seem out of place to discuss the American Catholic bishops' letter, *Economic Justice for All: Pastoral Letter on Catholic Social Teaching and the U.S. Economy,* in a book on the politics of Latin American liberation theology. The process of drafting the letter, however, did involve consultation with Latin American bishops, and the letter itself addresses in passing an issue of grave concern to Latin Americans today, namely, the debt crisis. While the letter cannot be said to have been inspired by Latin American liberation theology, the American bishops' call for a "preferential option for the poor" does echo Latin American liberation theology and the Catholic church's response to it worldwide.

These links raise an important issue for concerned United States citizens and policymakers: What is and what is not the political significance of liberation theology within the American Catholic community? My belief is that if the connections between the views in the bishops' letter and those of Latin American liberation theologians are interpreted as the bishops intended them—namely, as showing solidarity with their fellow Catholic bishops in Latin America, but not as expressing a point of view essentially in sympathy with the more radical perspectives among the liberation theologians—a needless and counterproductive distortion can be avoided in United States public policy discussion. The best way to minimize the risk of this distortion, I contend, is to focus on the bishops' recent thinking not about Latin America but about the political economy of the United States itself.

The burden of this chapter is to show that the American Catholic bishops' reflections in *Economic Justice for All* can provide a model for a practical or public theology that is liberating without being liberationist.[1] This model, I hope to show, is useful not simply for understanding the American church's religious and moral claims upon the political economy of this nation. It also promises to be a crucial contribution to the church's universal understanding of the relationship between Christianity and democracy, between a moral commitment to human rights and the political institutions of representative government. Seen in this light, the American bishops' call for a "new experiment in democracy" provides both a timely corrective to Catholic social teaching and an alternative to liberation theology. Once the alternative is fully appreciated, not only may the National Conference of Catholic Bishops' (NCCB) statements on Latin America make more sense, but certain fears about the influence of liberation theology should be minimized.

THE AMERICAN EXPERIMENT

Let us begin where the ideological link between Latin American liberation theology and the NCCB's pastoral letter may seem strongest, namely, the American Catholic bishops' advocacy of a "preferential option for the poor." Though the terminology may have been inspired by their desire to express solidarity with the work of the Latin American bishops assembled at Puebla, Mexico, in 1979, the pastoral letter's use of it intends not the overthrow of the institutions of political democracy but their expansion to meet the challenges of an advanced industrial economy, especially the new pressures resulting from a situation of global economic interdependence. By defining the "moral priorities for the nation" in terms of the option for the poor, the U.S. bishops merely insist that whatever is done to respond to the challenge of global interdependence be done in such a way that the poor "become active participants in the life of society."[2] The poor, in other words, are not to be written off as global competitive pressures force us to restructure the American economy. Indeed, it is precisely the scale of this economic challenge that provides a unique opportunity to empower the poor. A nation whose economic base will be defined increasingly in terms of the native intelligence, sturdy moral values, and educational achievements of its people simply cannot afford any longer, if it ever could, to allow a significant minority to be marginalized socially and economically. The bishops' answer to the problem of "marginalization," however, is a "new experiment in democracy."

Understanding the NCCB's "new experiment in democracy," of course, means asking first of all what the bishops think of the older experiment. That is, what is their basic attitude toward the experiment in self-government that issued from the American Revolution of 1776? Though that attitude is overwhelmingly positive, I must emphasize that it is not to be taken for granted. These American bishops, after all, are Roman Catholics; that is, they are men whose professional careers have been shaped by an institution that only very recently has begun to face up to the revolutionary traditions that constitute modernity. Being an American Catholic is not a given, but a project, one that requires a conscious effort to confront the traditions of Roman Catholicism with the church's experience in this country.[3] The separation of church and state that lies at the heart of the United States Constitution is not a Roman Catholic idea. The separation of powers and the theory of representative government articulated in *The Federalist* did not correspond to Catholic social teaching at the time they were devised. Though a century ago American Catholics struggled impressively and perhaps precociously to convince the Vatican of the merits of the American experiment in democracy, their efforts provoked from Pope Leo XIII, that totem-like patron of modern Catholic social teaching, condemnation as heresy. Only during and after Vatican Council II (1962–65), did American Catholics manage to secure the church's recognition of the unique fruits of their participation in the American experiment. (I refer, of course, to Vatican II's epoch making *Declaration on Religious Freedom,* whose principal author was the American Jesuit, John Courtney Murray.[4])

Seen in this context, the pastoral letter's appreciation for the genuine achievements of the original American experiment is itself revolutionary. "As *Americans*," the bishops insist, "we are grateful for the gift of freedom and committed to the dream of 'liberty and justice for all.'... We are proud of the strength, productivity, and creativity of our economy, but we also remember those who have been left behind in our progress. We believe that we honor our history best by working for the day when all our sisters and brothers share adequately in the American dream."[5] In spelling out the rationale for the "new experiment in democracy," the pastoral letter makes explicit its parallel with the original American experiment:

> In order to create a new form of political democracy they were compelled to develop ways of thinking and political institutions that had never existed before. Their efforts were arduous and their goals imperfectly realized, but they launched an experiment in the protection of civil and political rights that has prospered through the efforts of those who came after them. *We believe the time has come for a similar experiment in securing economic rights: the creation of an order that guarantees the minimum conditions of human dignity in the economic sphere for every person.*[6]

In contrast to Marxist-inspired ideologies, which tend to play off economic rights against civil and political rights, the U.S. bishops clearly envision the new experiment as an expansion of self-governing institutions, not their usurpation by the state.

Consistent with appreciation of our nation's historic experience, the bishop's experiment is less a scheme for the redistribution of existing economic assets than a strategy for the creation of new ones. As the fourth chapter of the pastoral letter, "A New American Experiment: Partnership for the Public Good," makes clear, what the bishops have in mind is a social experiment that necessarily begins in the private sector of the economy and involves public intervention only as the scale and complexity of efforts at cooperation warrant it.[7] The policy recommendations outlined at the various levels of economic organization—that is, partnerships (1) within firms and industries, (2) at the local and regional levels of community, (3) at the national level, and (4) at the international level—have been selected not just with the option for the poor in mind, but as a strategy for economic empowerment that cannot help but result in greater productivity if the experiment is successful. Of course, the argument in favor of these policies is weighted heavily toward the traditional themes of Catholic social teaching, in particular the surprisingly resilient "principle of subsidiarity" by which the bishops "out-federal" even *The Federalist*.[8] Nevertheless, the bishops clearly recognize that the criteria for success in this experiment are economic as well as moral. Indeed, the pastoral letter implies that further progress toward social justice, even in the United States of America, can be achieved only on the basis of genuine economic development. What the bishops have discovered—too many other observers have failed to grasp it—is that democratic institutions based on the principle of self-government are an important element in any strategy for sustaining economic development, not just politically but also and especially in the way in which business corporations, civic associations, and even schools and churches are internally organized.

To recapitulate the argument so far: The "preferential option for the poor" advocated by the U.S. Catholic bishops takes its concrete political meaning not from Latin American liberation theology but from the "new experiment in democracy" also proposed by the pastoral letter. To opt for the poor is to help the poor to empower themselves, to remove whatever obstacles there may be to their efforts to overcome "marginalization," a complex social phenomenon with political as well as economic consequences. To opt for the poor is to opt for an experiment seeking to implement the full spectrum of human rights, economic as well as civil and political. It does not mean engaging in a class struggle that would pit the economic rights of some against the civil and political rights of others; nor does it presuppose that social conflict must be analyzed in such terms.[9] On the contrary, the U.S. bishops' option for the poor, while recognizing the realities of social conflict, assumes that such conflicts can fairly and peaceably be resolved, however tentatively, through an experiment in democracy bent on creating new wealth through more equitable forms of social and economic participation. The new experiment in democracy, in short, refers to the process, while the comprehensive understanding of human rights provides the moral content of the U.S. bishops' option for the poor. It is primarily the democratic process espoused by the bishops that distinguishes their option from the one advanced by most advocates of Latin American liberation theology.[10]

PREFERRING THE POOR

When one moves beyond the concrete political meaning of the U.S. bishops' option for the poor to the theological vision underlying it, the parallels between the pastoral letter's formulation and those theological views current in Latin America become more apparent. In order to understand these parallels, it may be useful to review the Latin American discussion of this theme. The "preferential option for the poor" first emerges, as far as I can tell, in the *Final Document* produced by the meeting of the Latin American Bishops' Conference (CELAM) at Puebla, Mexico, in 1979.[11] The section devoted to it comes at the beginning of Part IV of the document, which outlines a pastoral strategy for Christian witness in the world. It is important to note that this part also includes a "preferential option for young people";[12] indeed, the *Final Document* is studded with any number of pastoral "options," the plurality of which at least suggests a reason why the otherwise redundant term "preferential" may have been accepted by the Latin American bishops. Within their *Final Document* the option for the poor is preferential in the sense that it is more central or enjoys a higher priority than the other pastoral options proposed.[13]

Yet when one tries to determine what the Latin American bishops mean by a pastoral "option," the *Final Document* is not very forthcoming. It speaks in passing of a "choosing process" which "enables us, after pondering and analyzing both positive and negative realities in the light of the Gospel, to find and adopt the pastoral response to the challenges posed by evangelization."[14] So the key to the options proposed at Puebla is still "evangelization." The language found in the *Final Document* seems to go no further than the program of "scrutinizing the signs of the times" outlined in Vatican II's *Pastoral Constitution on the Church in the Modern World (Gaudium et Spes).*[15] An "option" is thus a pastoral strategy proposed by the bishops, resulting from their attempt to interpret the gospel in the current situation confronting the churches in which they exercise their authority.

This thoroughly traditional understanding of "preferential option," however, was immediately taken up by Latin American liberation theologians as an endorsement of their own thinking about a spiritual and theological "privilege of the poor." In his commentary on Puebla, "Liberation and the Poor: The Puebla Perspective," Gustavo Gutiérrez, the architect of liberation theology, treats the preferential option as a kind of *imitatio Christi.*[16] Quoting from a briefing paper for the Puebla meeting that he had written for the Peruvian bishops, he contends:

> The privilege of the poor, then, has its theological basis in God. The poor are "blessed" not because of the mere fact that they are poor, but because the Kingdom of God is expressed in the manifestation of his justice and love in their favor.[17]

To underscore the point, Gutiérrez quotes Pope John Paul II's salute to the poor in his address to the Barrio of Santa Cecilia, "The pope loves you because you are God's favorites." The preferential option, in Gutiérrez's view, thus amounts to a divine imperative.

In the context of contemporary Roman Catholic theology, Gutiérrez's perspective is best understood in terms of the so-called "fundamental option," which Karl Rahner and his disciples introduced into Catholic moral theology at the time of Vatican II.[18] In his phenomenological investigations of the Christian moral life, Rahner, a student of Heidegger but not of Marx, was attempting to highlight the reality of Christian conversion, the overall intentionality of a person's self-realization either for or against God, as opposed to the morality of individual actions that had become the dominant focus of ethical reflection among Catholic theologians. Though his elaboration of this "fundamental option" was consistently formal, it did establish two important points conducive to the development of a "preferential option for the poor": (1) it lent authority, among professional Catholic theologians at least, to the jargon of "options"; and (2) it provided a basis for understanding the "option" as life's most crucial "choosing process," namely, the one in which the mystery of one's personal salvation unfolds. Given Rahner's formal understanding of a "fundamental option," all that is needed to accept Gutiérrez's "preferential option for the poor" is certain substantively biblical convictions about the revelatory authority of the poor as "God's favorites" in history.

Who, then, are the poor, and why are they God's favorites? As Gutiérrez affirms, they are real people who suffer conditions of material deprivation and destitution. They are the dispossessed and the destitute, those unwitting victims of modernizing industrialization who have fled the increasingly overcrowded rural areas of Latin America only to be thrown together with countless others trying to live from day to day in the barrios surrounding the major cities. Unlike the poor in the United States, they constitute the majority among Latin Americans; theologically, however, they are identified with a biblical minority, "the poor of Yahweh," the *Anawim*, who are the first to respond to God's offer of salvation.[19] I will assume that the biblical teaching is not unfamiliar, but what needs to be noted here is that by asserting this theological identification, Latin American liberation theologians have created an ambiguity that is ripe for ideological exploitation.

For to be counted among the *Anawim* means that today's poor bear a special role in the history of salvation, just as once the *Anawim* were the first to recognize the kingdom of God in Jesus of Nazareth and have it preached to them. Liberation theology, among other things, has been an attempt to interpret this special role. Its more rigorous advocates, on this basis, have asserted a "hermeneutical privilege of the oppressed": "To truly understand the Bible is to read it through the eyes of the oppressed, since the God who speaks in the Bible is the God of the oppressed."[20] Though Gutiérrez avoids the terminology, he does seem to hold out for such a privilege:

> Solidarity with the poor, with their struggles and their hopes,
> is the condition of an authentic solidarity with everyone—the
> condition of a universal love that makes no attempt to gloss
> over the social oppositions that obtain in the concrete history
> of peoples, but strides straight through the middle of them to
> a kingdom of justice and love.[21]

Clearly, the option for the poor is no ordinary option. It is neither optional nor is it simply a moral imperative. It involves conversion to a substantively theological vision of how God is acting in human history and a serious attempt to reconstruct one's way of life in response to it. The new vision authenticates itself through solidarity with the oppressed, whose spiritual and moral discernments now are accepted as normative for the church as a whole.

The ideological problem, of course, is what counts as "solidarity." Critics of liberation theology—most recently Humberto Belli in his impressive statement, *Breaking Faith: The Sandinista Revolution and its Impact on Freedom and Christian Faith in Nicaragua*—describe the process by which Christian base communities, in which such "solidarity" is to be lived, have too often become indoctrination centers for promoting the ideology of Marxist-Leninism and the praxis of socialist revolution.[22] What Belli describes is precisely what I had predicted elsewhere as one possible outcome of the methodological problems involved in liberation theology.[23] What I feared was that, in some cases, the "hermeneutic privilege" of the oppressed would become a methodological warrant for legitimating the Marxist-Leninist version of international "class struggle" as the key to authentic participation in God's action in history. Though there may be forms of liberation theology that do not assume a Marxist-Leninist reading of Latin American history, the classic texts of the movement do seem to open themselves to this ideological perspective.[24] Other essays in this volume provide sufficient documentation to make this problem apparent; precisely this Marxist ideological content renders an otherwise plausible theological concept morally dubious and spiritually dangerous.

A similar argument can be found in the Vatican's two recent discussions on liberation theology. Almost five years after Puebla and the warnings issued by Pope John Paul II on that occasion, the Vatican issued its *Instruction on Certain Aspects of the Theology of Liberation*. It points out specific "deviations, and risks of deviations, damaging to the faith and to Christian living, that are brought about by certain forms of liberation theology which use, in an insufficiently critical manner, concepts borrowed from various currents of Marxist thought."[25] Though the instruction did not repudiate the option for the poor, it proscribed the use of "Marxist analysis" to create a new hermeneutic that, in the Vatican's view, does lead to a "reductionist reading of the Bible." The biblical portrait of the *Anawim*, in short, is not to be used to legitimate Marxist-Leninist class struggle within either the church or society; it is not to become the pretext for a politicization of the gospel.

What the option for the poor might mean apart from such a "deviation" was not fully clarified until the Vatican issued a second document more than a year later, an *Instruction on Christian Freedom and Liberation*. In that statement, the option for the poor is interpreted as a "preferential love of the poor."[26] The biblical *Anawim* and their special significance in the ministry of Jesus are reaffirmed, and the human misery that normally accompanies material poverty is denounced as "the obvious sign of the natural condition of weakness in which man finds himself since original sin and the sign of his need for salvation." But the emphasis in this preferential love is clearly upon fidelity to the gospel and upon the traditional practices of "detachment from riches" and compassionate "solidarity" as among the hallmarks of Christian witness: "The disciples of Jesus bear witness through love for the poor and unfortunate to the love of the Father himself manifested in the Saviour." Yet even while thus endorsing an option for the poor, the Vatican reiterates its earlier condemnation of the Marxist-Leninist "deviation" from Catholic orthodoxy. The option for the poor must not be interpreted "by means of reductive sociological and ideological categories which would make this preference a partisan choice and a source of conflict."

LIBERATIONISTS' RESPONSE

Response to the Vatican's two instructions by Latin American liberation theologians has been perplexing. With the notable exception of Juan Luis Segundo, the general pattern has been to deny teaching the caricature of Christianized Marxism denounced in the first statement, and to welcome the second statement as a further endorsement of the ongoing development of liberation theology. This pattern is not an unfamiliar one; for the papal condemnations of Americanism and modernism at the turn of the century were similarly received by most of those targeted by the Vatican.[27] There are two possible readings of this situation: either the liberation theologians are responding in good faith, or they are not. If they are responding in good faith, then critics of liberation theology, including myself, either have attributed Marxist perspectives to theologians who do not espouse them or have fixated on an early stage in the development of liberation theology that has subsequently been overcome through further reflection on political and social conditions in Latin America, which now include a significant movement in the direction of genuine democracy. On the other hand, they may not be responding in good faith. In this case their response may simply be a cover-up designed to mislead both sympathizers and critics about the true nature of their hard-core ideological commitments.

Normally, it makes sense to assume that most people, including theologians, are acting in good faith. Certainly I would welcome any development in liberation theology that clearly indicates disenchantment with Marxism-Leninism, both in theory and in praxis, and a more mature understanding of the necessary connection between economic progress, representative government, and respect for human rights. The only factor that keeps me from taking the liberationists' response to the Vatican at face value is testimony, such as that provided by Humberto Belli, about the dynamics, moral as well as political, of Marxist-Leninist "popular front" strategies. It would be unwise to assume that all liberation theologians are feigning a new theological and ideological maturity, but it would be equally unwise to take their recent statements simply at face value. Thus, further inquiry into the political significance of Latin American liberation theology is faced with the painstaking task of examining the intellectual and political development of each theologian on a case-by-case basis.

Whatever the outcome of such an inquiry, certain points necessary for the present discussion already are clear. There are at least three different interpretations of the "preferential option for the poor" operative in Latin American Catholicism today: (1) the "preferential option" described in the *Final Document* at Puebla, which I can now describe as a *minimalist* interpretation, because it exists within a plurality of pastoral options for evangelization; (2) the "privilege of the poor" apparent in the writings of liberation theologians after Puebla, a *maximalist* interpretation insofar as it makes this option the fundamental criterion of Christian authenticity today and more or less consistently understands it politically and ideologically in terms of the agenda of revolutionary socialism; and (3) the "preferential love of the poor" outlined in the Vatican's instructions on liberation theology. The latter I will now call a *mediating* interpretation. It apparently accepts the liberationists' general point on the connection between justice for the poor and Christian authenticity but rejects the political and ideological cooptation of both the poor and Christian faith that it detects in the writings of some theologians. It is not yet clear which of these interpretations will capture the hearts and minds of educated Christians in Latin America.

These distinctions, however, are crucial for understanding what is and is not meant by the U.S. bishops in adopting the "option for the poor" as the central teaching of their pastoral letter on the economy. For the option for the poor advocated by the U.S. bishops does conform to the "mediating" interpretation outlined by the Vatican's instructions. This is apparent, not only because the pastoral letter refers approvingly to the *Final Document* from Puebla as well as the Vatican's *Instruction on Christian Freedom and Liberation,* but also because the American bishops' remarks are structured similarly to those of the mediating interpretation.[28] As presented in the pastoral letter, the option for the poor is clearly a hallmark of Christian authenticity. The whole of the bishops' review of basic themes in Catholic theology points toward this option. Their reading of biblical teaching regarding creation, covenant, and the community that discipleship makes converges toward a recognition of God's special concern for the poor and their unique role "throughout Israel's history and in early Christianity...[as] agents of God's transforming power."[29] The option for the poor, in short, stands at the heart of the gospel's vision of how human persons are to relate to one another in community. This vision has profound economic consequences:

> Though in the Gospels and in the New Testament as a whole the offer of salvation is extended to all peoples, Jesus takes the side of those most in need, physically and spiritually. The example of Jesus poses a number of challenges to the contemporary Church. It imposes a prophetic mandate to speak for those who have no one to speak for them, to be a defender of the defenseless, who in biblical terms are the poor. It also demands a compassionate vision that enables the Church to see things from the side of the poor and powerless, and to assess lifestyle, policies, and social institutions in terms of their impact on the poor. It summons the Church also to be an instrument in assisting people to experience the liberating power of God in their own lives so that they may respond to the Gospel in freedom and in dignity. Finally, and most radically, it calls for an emptying of self, both individually and corporately, that allows the Church to experience the power of God in the midst of poverty and powerlessness.[30]

As the U.S. bishops see it, then, the option for the poor is an essentially religious act, a fundamental response to God's offer of fellowship and salvation. But their view of it, I am arguing, is liberating without being liberationist.

As Michael Novak has observed, "The 'option for the poor' *is* the correct option. Everything depends, however, upon the next institutional step."[31] The first institutional step, for the U.S. bishops, is to recognize that the "option" makes a claim primarily upon the church and only secondarily upon society as a whole. The paragraph from the pastoral letter just quoted is an exhortation to Christians covenanted as a church. The complex structure of moral argument offered by the letter does translate the option for the poor into a set of "moral priorities for the nation." But these priorities are suggested in an argument that presupposes the reality of American pluralism, guaranteed by the constitutional separation of church and state, as the context for public policy discussion and implementation. The "next institutional step" for the U.S. bishops, then, is to implement the option for the poor in a "new American experiment in democracy," which, as we have already established, builds upon the American principle of self-government without seeking to dismantle it.

Yet in some subtle ways the U.S. bishops' option for the poor is closer to that of liberation theology than it is to the Vatican's. For the pastoral letter is ideologically agnostic without being innocent of ideology. In reading the Vatican's instructions, one still get the impression of what Latin American liberation theologians like to denounce as *tercerismo*.[32] Consistent with the historic strategy of modern papal social teaching, *tercerismo* is the pattern of even-handed condemnation of both capitalist and socialist political economies in behalf of a third, substantively Catholic alternative. *Tercerismo* is unabashedly anti-modernist and castigates these modern social systems for their Godless materialism, whether explicitly theoretical or merely practical. The distinctiveness of the Catholic alternative, however, is usually established by holding out for a posture of ideological innocence. The Catholic alternative is neither modern nor exclusively premodern, though it would hope to be postmodern; its innocence is that of visionary protest.

By advocating a "new American experiment in democracy," however, the U.S. bishops have moved beyond ideological innocence. Like Latin American liberation theologians, the bishops seem to understand that it is impossible to maintain a strict separation between religious faith and political ideology, that any attempt to understand the meaning of Christian faith in the historic situation that confronts us cannot help but be ideological. The trick is to adopt or create an appropriate ideology and to do so for the right reasons, that is, reasons that are morally and intellectually consistent with the religious vision that animates the effort in the first place. Where the pastoral letter differs from typical examples of liberation theology, however, is that the former remains ideologically agnostic, while the latter emphatically are not. During the drafting process for the pastoral letter, the U.S. bishops seriously examined a whole host of systemic "social analyses" but found none of them clearly compelling as an explanation of the concrete workings of the American political economy. It is not as though they were ignorant of systemic social analysis and therefore blindly muddling down the path of piecemeal reformism. On the contrary, their proposals for implementing the option for the poor became reformist precisely because there was no more radical alternative that did not involve some unwarranted leap of faith to overcome the inadequacies of the arguments offered in its behalf. Rather than make an unwarranted leap of faith in that direction, the U.S. bishops chose to renew their civic faith in the processes of democratic self-government, a faith they knew to be justified by the American Catholic community's collective experience as part of the United States.

By contrast, Latin American liberation theologians, at least in their earliest publications, tended to adopt an almost gnostic faith in the validity of Marxist social analysis. Typically, they argued not just that faith and ideology are inextricably interrelated, but that one particular ideology of revolutionary socialism is the uniquely appropriate expression of authentic Christian faith today.[33] If I understand them correctly, the U.S. bishops would not try to defend Catholic social teaching by reverting to some ideal state of ideological innocence, but they would advocate agnosticism in the face of ideological conflict so long as compelling arguments are not forthcoming. The U.S. bishops, in the words of the pastoral letter, recognize that Christians as well as ordinary citizens can disagree in good faith regarding the "prudential judgments" involved in one ideological perspective or another, one policy choice or another.[34] Their recognition of the role of prudential judgment, in short, implies an ideological agnosticism that I have yet to find in any liberation theology from Latin America.

This "ideological agnosticism," however, is also an ideology. Indeed, it is the typical legitimation of American-style politics.[35] As such it is a crucial presupposition of the U.S. bishops' call for a new American experiment in democracy. But the ideological commitment here is not to some utopian sketch plan for an ideal society. Rather, it involves a process by which the inevitable social conflicts in any real society can be adjudicated as justly as humanly possible. After all, what the bishops advocate is an *experiment* in democracy; that is, given their agnosticism at the moment, perhaps a new truth will emerge or an old truth be rediscovered as we make every effort to develop full social participation in the economy.

Furthermore, it is also an experiment in *democracy*; that is, the attempt is made to see whether institutionalized procedures of unrestricted dialogue and public consensus-formation, if developed throughout our economic system, can actually make for both greater social justice and increased economic development. This commitment to a process, that is, to a new experiment in democracy, as I have argued elsewhere, is one appropriate response to the religious vision operative in the tradition of Catholic social teaching.[36] But rather than preserve Catholic social teaching by retreating into some false ideological innocence, the U.S. bishops' pastoral letter tries to renew Catholic social teaching by becoming ideologically engaged even though for the moment it remains agnostic ideologically. This strategy, I am arguing, is not only a novelty in the history of Catholic social teaching, it is also a promising model for that tradition's further development.

VISIONS FOR CENTRAL AMERICA

Let me conclude this discussion by turning now from the pastoral letter to the U.S. bishops' more recent statements on Latin America. My purpose in doing so is, first, to point out a remarkable consistency between these statements and the perspective of the pastoral letter and, second, to illustrate the relative insignificance of Latin American liberation theology as an influence upon the bishops' foreign policy recommendations in that area. For purposes of this inquiry I have restricted my focus to the bishops' statements from 1983 to 1987 on Central America in general and Nicaragua in particular.[37] The most recent of these, a "Joint Communique" from a meeting of U.S. and Central American bishops, July 21–23, 1987, in San José, Costa Rica, provides a fitting summary of the NCCB's basic perspective on that region.[38]

Over the years various U.S. bishops, as well as representatives from the United States Catholic Conference (USCC), have testified before the United States Congress in opposition to military aid to the Contras. This much is generally known. Usually not understood are their reasons for doing so and the policies they might propose as alternatives. Their opposition to military aid is not based on sympathy with the Sandinista government; on the contrary, they have consistently protested its pattern of human rights violations and repressive policies toward the Catholic church in Nicaragua. The bishops are not ignorant about the Marxist-Leninist scenario apparently unfolding in that country. They object to military aid because of a humanitarian concern for the poor, who inevitably suffer the most during a civil war, and because they doubt whether a military solution to the Nicaraguan conflict is possible without direct and massive United States military intervention.

Alternatively, they recommend "diplomatic initiatives," ranging from the Contadora process to the recent Central American peace proposal developed by President Oscar Arias of Costa Rica. Within this context, they typically insist upon what amounts to a demilitarization of Central America. Their purpose is emphatically not to disarm the Contras so that the Sandinistas will have the field to themselves. They recommend new experiments in multilateral assistance for economic development, some of them involving nongovernmental organizations, such as the churches, in creative efforts to make sure that foreign assistance actually reaches those most in need of it. Above all, they insist that Nicaragua's problems cannot be solved apart from a new national "dialogue" within the country itself, one involving the local churches and the full range of political and other civic organizations. Presumably, they would acknowledge the right of representatives of the Contras to participate in any such dialogue. Finally, they urge the United States government to explore ways to use the possibilities of nonmilitary aid to modify the Sandinista government's human rights practices. In short, their approach emphasizes the procedural. Though they apparently share with Contra sympathizers their opposition to Marxist Leninism, they urge a package of nonviolent, nonmilitary strategies for transforming the situation in Nicaragua. Their remarks on social conditions in the other Central American nations follow a similar pattern: a generalized advocacy of human rights, economic development, and nonviolently democratic means for achieving them.

What are the strengths and weaknesses of this approach? At this point it should be impressive for its consistency with overall NCCB thinking on Catholic social teaching; for it is as if the answer to Central America's problems lies in having Central Americans conduct a "new experiment in democracy" of their own. Like the pastoral letter on the economy, this approach is to be commended for recognizing the realities of social conflict without losing faith in the prospects for a peaceful, political solution to such conflict. Like the pastoral letter, this approach envisions a role for the local churches, a kind of moral leadership in facilitating the public "dialogue" that will not be without political and economic consequences. Its strength is that of the Arias plan itself, an attempt to develop a regional political solution, but one in which the churches and other voluntary associations may be encouraged to play an important role in mediating local conflicts. Its weakness, if there is any, is implicit in its very strength; that is, the bishops' commitment to "diplomatic initiatives" may betray a naivete about the relationship between such initiatives and the threat of military force. The bishops must ask themselves whether the Sandinistas' apparent willingness to negotiate a settlement within the Arias plan would have developed apart from the growing strength and prestige of the Contras. If that is the case, then how morally responsible is it to oppose consistently any military aid to the Contras? I have no answer to this question, for I have been and remain sympathetic to the U.S. bishops' intentions. Still, it is a morally legitimate question.

Needless to say, the U.S. bishops' position on Central America differs significantly from that typical among supporters of liberation theology. Those differences should now be apparent. My point here, in conclusion, is that those differences are significant; they should not be minimized simply because the U.S. bishops oppose military aid to the Contras. In this chapter I have tried to show that the bishops' position rests upon a religious vision of the human person in community that differs in important respects from that offered by Latin American liberation theology. Although the two may have certain points in common as they both have emerged from the tradition of Catholic social teaching, the U.S. bishops' views have been decisively shaped by their positive and fruitful experience of democracy in the United States, an experience that leads them to conceive of further economic and social reform in terms of further experiments in democratic self-government. Yet, despite the decisively American cast to their approach to Catholic social teaching, what the U.S. bishops have learned may still be relevant to their fellow Catholics in Latin America, especially in light of the dramatic increase in popular support for democratic institutions over the past few years. For the U.S. bishops have not only engaged in fruitful dialogue with both the Latin American bishops and their critics among the liberationists, but they have also been a consistent voice for human rights, democracy, and peaceful progress toward social justice here and in Latin America. Their recent pastoral letter, *Economic Justice for All*, shows that it *is* possible to preach a liberating gospel without falling into the trap of liberationism.

What, then, from this perspective is the political significance of Latin American liberation theology? Almost a decade ago I criticized liberation theology as "a sincere but confused protest, a call to conscience that challenges us to rethink the theory and practice of Christian realism in light of the problems that await us in the 1980s."[39] Though my argument unfolded primarily in theological terms, today it is even more applicable to liberation theology on political grounds. The past decade has witnessed the eclipse of revolutionary socialism both as ideology and as praxis. Whether one is inclined to be dismayed or cheered by that turn of events, the fact is that the political options confronting Latin Americans today are broader than they were very recently. If liberation theology is to remain faithful to the methodology of "critical reflection on praxis," it will have to change as the context to which it is addressed has changed. My reading of the present moment suggests that liberation theology is not now, nor is it ever likely to become, the only politically significant religious ideology available for Roman Catholics. Though its influence is not insignificant, it should no longer provoke the apocalyptic hopes and fears that too often clouded our first impressions of it. Most of all, it should not be used as the prism through which to interpret the Catholic church's initiatives for social justice and peace, either in the United States or in Latin America.

284 The Politics of Latin American Liberation Theology

NOTES

1. See Max Stackhouse, *Public Theology and Political Economy* (Grand Rapids: William B. Eerdmans, 1987). For a methodological study of the elements common to both public theology and all other forms of practical theology, see Dennis P. McCann and Charles R. Strain, *Polity and Praxis: A Program for American Practical Theology* (Minneapolis: Winston Press/Seabury Press, 1985).

2. National Conference of Catholic Bishops, *Economic Justice for All: Pastoral Letter on Catholic Social Teaching and the U.S. Economy,* in *Origins: NC Documentary Service,* Vol. 16, No. 24 (November 27, 1986): 421.

3. See Dennis P. McCann, *New Experiment in Democracy: The Challenge for American Catholicism* (Kansas City: Sheed and Ward, 1987).

4. *Declaration on Religious Freedom (Dignitatis Humanae),* in *The Documents of Vatican II,* ed. Walter M. Abbott (New York: America Press, 1966), pp. 675–96.

5. National Conference of Catholic Bishops, *Economic Justice for All,* p. 410.

6. Ibid., p. 422.

7. Ibid., pp. 440–43.

8. Ibid., p. 442. As formulated by Pope Pius XI in 1931, the principle of subsidiarity states: "Just as it is gravely wrong to take from individuals what they can accomplish by their own initiative and industry and give it to the community, so also it is an injustice and at the same time a grave evil and a disturbance of right order to assign to a greater and higher association what lesser and subordinate organizations can do." The "federalist" notions detected in this principle have to do with its recognition of the need for limited government, and the separation of powers implicit in its approach to decentralized government. See McCann, *New Experiment in Democracy,* pp. 136–39.

9. National Conference of Catholic Bishops, *Economic Justice for All,* pp. 425–26.

10. I wish to subscribe to the more optimistic reading of recent trends in Latin American liberation theology expressed in this volume by Paul E. Sigmund's "The Development of Liberation Theology." In particular I am intrigued, as is Sigmund, by Hugo Assmann's apparent willingness to link the process of democratization with the agenda of liberation theology. See Hugo Assmann and Nicholas Eberstadt, "Democracy and the Debt Crisis," *This World* 16 (Spring/Summer, 1986): 83–103.

11. See *Puebla and Beyond: Documentation and Commentary*, trans. John Drury, ed. John Eagleson and Philip Scharper (Maryknoll, N.Y.: Orbis Books, 1979).

12. "Preferential Option for Young People," in *Puebla and Beyond*, pp. 267–72.

13. Marcos McGrath, "The Puebla Document: Introduction and Commentary," in ibid., pp. 108–9.

14. *The Final Document*, ibid., p. 283.

15. *Pastoral Constitution on the Church in the Modern World (Gaudium et Spes)* in *The Documents of Vatican II*, pp. 201–2.

16. Gustavo Gutiérrez, "Liberation and the Poor: The Puebla Perspective," in *The Power of the Poor in History,* trans. Robert R. Barr (Maryknoll, N.Y.: Orbis Books, 1983), pp. 125–65.

17. Ibid., p. 138.

18. Karl Rahner, "The Fundamental Option," in *A Rahner Reader,* ed. Gerald A. McCool (New York: Seabury Press, 1975), pp. 255–62.

19. See John L. McKenzie, "Poor, Poverty," in *Dictionary of the Bible* (Milwaukee: Bruce Publishing, 1965), pp. 681–84.

20. See Elisabeth Schüssler Fiorenza, "Toward a Feminist Biblical Hermeneutics: Biblical Interpretation and Liberation Theology," in *The Challenge of Liberation Theology: A First World Response,* eds. Brian Mahan and L. Dale Richesin (Maryknoll, N.Y.: Orbis Books, 1981), p. 100. See also Juan Luis Segundo, *The Liberation of Theology,* trans. John Drury (Maryknoll, N.Y.: Orbis Books, 1976).

21. Gustavo Gutiérrez, "Liberation and the Poor," p. 129.

22. Humberto Belli, *Breaking Faith: The Sandinista Revolution and its Impact on Freedom and Christian Faith in Nicaragua* (Garden City, Mich.: Puebla Institute, 1985).

23. See Dennis P. McCann, *Christian Realism and Liberation Theology* (Maryknoll, N.Y.: Orbis Books, 1981), pp. 208–31.

24. Ibid., pp. 156–81.

25. Vatican Congregation for the Doctrine of the Faith, *Instruction on Certain Aspects of the "Theology of Liberation,"* in *Origins: NC Documentary Service* 13 (September, 1984).

26. Vatican Congregation for the Doctrine of the Faith, *Instruction on Christian Freedom and Liberation* (Vatican City: Vatican Polyglot Press, 1986).

27. See McCann, *New Experiment in Democracy*, pp. 9–19.

28. National Conference of Catholic Bishops, *Economic Justice for All*, p. 449.

29. Ibid., p. 417.

30. Ibid., p. 418.

31. Michael Novak, *Freedom with Justice: Catholic Social Thought and Liberal Institutions* (San Francisco: Harper and Row, 1984), p. 192.

32. See McCann, *Christian Realism and Liberation Theology*, p. 141.

33. See Juan Luis Segundo, "Capitalism—Socialism: A Theological Crux," in *Liberation South, Liberation North,* ed. Michael Novak (Washington, D. C.: American Enterprise Institute, 1981).

34. National Conference of Catholic Bishops, *Economic Justice for All*, pp. 425–26.

35. For a liberationist analysis of this pervasively American ideology, see Rubem Alves, "Christian Realism: Ideology of the Establishment," in *Christianity and Crisis* 33 (September, 1973): 173–76.

36. See McCann, *New Experiment in Democracy*, pp. 91–121.

37. See "Joint Communique Following Meeting of U.S. and Central American Bishops," *Origins: N.C. Documentary Service* 17 (August 13, 1987): 149, 151; "Congressional Testimony on Central America" by Archbishop John J. O'Connor, *Origins: N.C. Documentary Ser-*

vice 14 (April 15, 1985): 731, 733–37; "Toward a Diplomatic Non-Military Solution in Central America" by Archbishop John Roach, *Origins: N.C. Documentary Service* 13 (August 4, 1983): 165, 167.

38. "Joint Communique."

39. McCann, *Christian Realism and Liberation Theology*, p. 5.

13

Liberation Theology, Human Rights, and U.S. Security

John W. Cooper

Neither the security of the United States and other free societies in the Americas nor the protection of human rights is threatened by the type of liberation theology that seeks genuine justice, peace, freedom, and prosperity. However, many if not most liberation theologians reject democracy and just-market economies in favor of Soviet-style communism. The theological, political, and economic ideas of liberation theologians deserve careful consideration. The *theological* insights are perhaps the most fruitful. The *political* and *economic* ideas of many liberation theologians are less appealing; insofar as they approximate communist ideology they will likely result in less, rather than more, true liberation for people, whether they are poor, middle class, or rich.

United States policy planners ought to pay careful attention to liberation theology. Its "social democratic" expressions represent no security threat to the United States. But, where liberation theology is the ideological foundation for communist revolution or subversion in Latin America, it does constitute a threat to United States security and human rights, and it should be opposed. The best response to both types of liberation theology is serious debate over the fundamental questions of justice, peace, freedom, and prosperity in the Americas.

A THEOLOGICAL THREAT?

How could the security of a nation possibly be affected by a theology? The obvious answer is the following: When any theology becomes an ideological justification for aggressive attack against a nation's territory, subversion of that nation's political system, or abuses against the human rights of its citizens—or when it becomes a justification for similar threats against its allies or other nonaggressive states—then and only then does that theology become a legitimate security concern.

Is, then, Latin American liberation theology a threat to the security interests of the United States? In general, no. In certain specific situations, as in the alliance of some liberation theologians with the self-proclaimed "vanguard of revolutionary internationalism" in Cuba and Nicaragua or their affiliated terrorist arms in other countries, yes. In other situations, as in the contributions of theologians to the developing ideas of democracy in Latin America, liberation theology may make legitimate contributions to the quest for peace, security, freedom, and justice.

LIBERATION THEOLOGY IN TRANSITION?

There are many ways of expressing the relationship between religion and politics, many ways of "doing" political theology. In modern Protestantism, one thinks of several major theologians who have contributed to this discipline: Ernst Troeltsch, Walter Rauschenbusch, Reinhold Niebuhr, Paul Tillich, and others. In modern Roman Catholicism, one thinks first of the popes—from Leo XIII to John Paul II—and also of Heinrich Pesch, Franz Mueller, John A. Ryan, Yves Simon, John Courtney Murray, Jacques Maritain, and others.

In recent years, a distinctive challenge to traditional political theology has arisen both from Protestants (for example, Jürgen Moltmann) and from Roman Catholics (for example, Johannes Metz, Gustavo Gutiérrez, Juan Luis Segundo, Jon Sobrino). It is liberation theology. Liberation theology is not monolithic. A few liberation theologians advocate democracy; most favor a left-wing authoritarianism or totalitarianism, a one-party state. Some liberation theologians endorse a regulated form of the market economy; most advocate socialist or communist economic policies. Some liberation theologians model their ideas of political economy after Cuba or the Soviet Union. A few admire the social democracies of Western Europe. It is impossible to speak in detail about the ideological significance or the

United States security implications of liberation theology without drawing such distinctions among the ideas and persons associated with liberation theology.

Paul Sigmund, an astute North American observer of Latin American liberation theology, has argued that there are really *two* liberation theologies: (1) "an anti-capitalist structuralism that has used Marxism as one of the ways to identify the causes of oppression" and (2) "a grass-roots populism that wishes to relate the Scripture and the teachings of the church to the lived experience of the poor."[1] Sigmund focuses our attention on the latter, namely on the basic Christian communities that have emerged in recent decades in the Latin American churches and primarily within Roman Catholicism. He believes that the concept of justice and the ideas about political structures that emerge from these grassroots communities are quite varied and often represent positive contributions to the societies of Latin America. He also believes, perhaps too optimistically, that "the liberation theologians have largely abandoned the crude Marxist rhetoric of the early 1970s."[2]

I believe that Sigmund is basically correct, although the degree of the movement away from Marxism in the thinking of most liberation theologians seems meager. Liberation theology may be entering a transition phase in which it will deemphasize communist revolution and pursue the laborious but essential task of creating political and economic institutions that truly help the poor. If this reality unfolds, one might expect to see the emergence of more basic Christian communities with a decidedly middle-class or bourgeois flavor. There are a few such communities already. These new grassroots communities might pioneer in the discovery of Latin American versions of the liberal society, with its distinctive democratic structures, market economies, private property rights, and cultural pluralism. As Michael Novak has argued, "The logic of history will lead liberation theologians increasingly in the direction of recreating in their own way the liberal society."[3]

Yet Sigmund notes that liberation theologians "have not abandoned...their readiness to blame 'sinful structures,' i.e., capitalism and multinational corporations, for the poverty and oppression in Latin America."[4] So, one is left with the question, Whither liberation theology? That version of liberation theology which frees itself from "crude Marxism," while still perhaps utilizing certain Marxist concepts that do not fundamentally conflict with free society, may significantly contribute to the cause of justice in Latin America. Such efforts would present no threat to United States security and might, in fact, enhance it by helping to create more stable, more democratic countries in the region. That version of liberation theology which sets itself up as the archenemy of democratic capitalism and allies itself with the Soviet Union, its client states, and its front organizations does constitute a security threat to the United States and to every country that cherishes freedom.

It is not the "social democrats" among the liberation theologians but the proponents of communism who ought to worry United States policy planners. There are legitimate differences within the free societies concerning the procedures of democracy, the appropriate level of government involvement in economic matters, the degree of cultural diversity which is desirable in a society. These are the debates between friends that are illustrated, for example, by the differences between the United States and France. Some liberation theologians have chosen to enter this ongoing debate about the nature of the free society. Occasionally, liberation theologians make statements that demonstrate a critical turn of mind and an honest grappling with the problems of social order in a free society. For example, José Comblin writes:

> In Marxist revolution there is no freedom for the people, only
> for the party. The same science that expels freedom from his-
> tory and revolution expels God from humankind and history.
> The party is supposed to be sufficient to create a new world,
> but it ends by creating a new power.[5]

This statement by a liberation theologian ought to be emblazoned on posters throughout the Third World. But far too often liberation theologians present the opposite view. For example, they express "a growing awareness that revolutionary Christians must form a strategic alliance with Marxists."[6]

One may not always be able to distinguish between the two types of liberation theology. Thus, I will attempt to trace some of the more common themes found in the literature of liberation theology and, rather than seek to discern whether they are intended to yield a democratic or totalitarian result, I will simply discuss them in relation to the concept of democratic capitalism and respect for human rights which is the philosophical basis of the free societies. The outcome of this hypothetical dialogue between liberation theology and the philosophy of democratic capitalism may, perhaps, provide some clues along the path toward greater justice for Latin America and may suggest what are and what are not legitimate concerns vis-à-vis United States security.

LIBERATION THEOLOGY AND DEMOCRATIC CAPITALISM

Adam Smith and other eighteenth-century observers of the New World noted that two radically different experiments in political economy were being carried out, one in Latin America and one in North America. The North American model employed an evolving concept of political freedom for the individual alongside the instruments of economic freedom: markets, incentives, private property rights, and limited government interference in commerce. The Latin American model employed the old aristocratic-feudal-mercantilist principles which had been the norm in the Holy Roman Empire. Political power was distributed according to class status. The nobles and the serfs had specifically defined political and economic prerogatives. Economic activism, especially entrepreneurial activity, was suspect and government restrictions were imposed on all aspects of commerce.

Adam Smith predicted that the North American model of political economy would prove superior to the Latin American model. And, indeed, it has. By an objective measure, North Americans generally enjoy significantly more political freedom and greater economic opportunity than their Latin American counterparts.

At the end of World War II, most of Latin America entered a period of steady economic growth. As the global economy expanded, Latin America began to create wealth. Yet, while a portion of the postwar boom benefited the masses in Latin America, too much of the newly created wealth ended up in the pockets of the old aristocracy, the military dictators, and the owners of monopoly businesses. While this system was commonly known as "capitalism," it was much closer in structure to the aristocratic-feudal-mercantilist economic system that had been the norm in Latin America for centuries. The intellectuals blamed their "capitalist" leaders and harbored resentment for the economic successes of their North American neighbors. North America had capitalism, too. But it was a very different type of capitalism, a *democratic* capitalism.

Onto this scene in the 1960s and 1970s came the liberation theologians. They were intellectuals with powerful, creative minds and strong aristocratic tendencies. They studied in the great theological centers in Europe, there imbibing mildly socialist ideas that some would later transform into a straightforwardly Latin American ideology blending Marxism and Christianity.[7]

In 1971, Gustavo Gutiérrez published *A Theology of Liberation,* in which he called for a new way of doing theology.[8] First, said Gutiérrez, theology must begin in *praxis* not *theoria*—it must begin in the *praxis* of revolutionary action on behalf of the oppressed poor. Second, theologians must recognize their own social location and be aware of the ways in which it affects their theology. Third, the church should guard against too close an alliance with the political and economic status quo. In other words, the church should rethink the history of Christianity as a two-stage process, primitive Christianity followed by "Constantinian Christianity." Fourth, a new emphasis on eschatology, the inbreaking of the kingdom of God into the world, ought to characterize twentieth-century Christianity.

Much of the *theological* insight of Gutiérrez and many other liberation theologians is of lasting significance. At least the issues which they raise ought to be taken seriously and debated within the Christian church. The real issue, however, is the application of theological insights to specific historical circumstances. Why, for example, should the "capitalism versus socialism" debate be elevated to eschatological proportions? Has not the identification of the kingdom of God with particular social and political revolutions resulted in the past in tremendous abuses of human rights and frightful consequences for the church? These theological issues deserve prayerful attention on the part of all Christians.

Gutiérrez and many other liberation theologians often make questionable applications of theological insights to sociopolitical realities. They frequently "baptize" specific social and political arrangements and attempt to impart to them the aura of the kingdom of God.

The deep disaffection of liberation theology from the traditional political economy of Latin America is illustrated by a seminal passage in Gutiérrez's *A Theology of Liberation:*

> The poor countries are becoming ever more clearly aware that
> their underdevelopment is only the by-product of the

development of other countries.... Development must attack
the root causes of the problems and among them the deepest
is economic, social, political and cultural dependence of some
countries upon others—an expression of the domination of
some social classes over others. Attempts to bring about changes within the existing order have proven futile. This analysis
of the situation is at the level of scientific rationality. Only a
radical break from the status quo, that is, a profound transformation of the private property system, access to power of the
exploited class, and a social revolution that would break this
dependence would allow for the change to a new society, a
socialist society—or at least allow that such a society might
be possible.[9]

In recent years, some liberation theologians, including Gutiérrez, have
begun to question the validity of dependency theory—the idea that Third
World poverty has been caused by the relative prosperity of the industrialized democracies. Yet, the dependency myth is still widespread, and alternative theories of economic development are almost absent in the
liberationist literature.

While it is true that some liberation theologians have rejected "crude
Marxism," it is still legitimate to question the basic assumptions of many
liberation theologians, especially their political and economic assumptions.
While their theological insights may prove somewhat useful, their political and economic judgments seem sadly lacking. Their advocacy of
"socialism" and their opposition to "capitalism," although these terms may
be defined in a number of different ways, have implications in both the
political and economic spheres. Some liberation theologians apparently
prefer "democratic socialist" societies, perhaps like those of contemporary
Spain or France, and would like to see Latin American equivalents
throughout the continent. Yet, Spain and France have essentially capitalist
economies and Socialist party governments. Obviously, there is a wide
variety of definitions of capitalism and socialism. For other liberation
theologians, the model seems to be Cuba, a communist state with a dictator
at its head, a one-party system, and a thoroughly socialist economy. Some
clarification, then, is necessary concerning the differences between the
democratic capitalist system, which includes the "social democratic" or

"democratic socialist" countries of Western Europe, and the communist system.

How do we define capitalism, and what is the particular form of capitalism known as "democratic capitalism"? Max Weber, the father of modern sociology, published his classic text, *The Protestant Ethic and the Spirit of Capitalism,* in 1904–05.[10] He notes that certain forms of capitalism, adventurer's capitalism, for example, have existed since time immemorial. He defines adventurer's capitalism as a system based on mere acquisitiveness and notes that all societies of all times have had their share of acquisitive individuals. Indeed, acquisitiveness as national policy is most fully expressed in the philosophy of mercantilism. But, Weber says, acquisitiveness is not the basic feature of the modern type of capitalism that he wants to examine. The idea that modern capitalism is based on greed should, said Weber, be permanently consigned to the kindergarten of the mind.

What, then, does Weber mean by capitalism? He means the division of labor, the rational organization of formally voluntary labor (that is, workers enjoying a free and fair labor market in which they can bargain for the best wages and conditions as they themselves define such things), a strict adherence to contracts and time schedules, an open and fair market for venture capital, and the cultural preconditions ("Protestantism," in this case) that make such a system viable. One "Protestant" trait that Weber sees as critical is the ability to practice delayed gratification, the key to successful long-term investment growth. Obviously, the cultural traits necessary for the successful implementation of capitalism are not limited to "Protestant" nations. The rise of capitalism in Europe owes as much to the Catholic trading cities of Italy as to the northern European cities. Confucianism in the Far East, to take another example, can also provide a strong cultural base for the development of democratic capitalism.

Democratic capitalism as we understand it in the United States today has evolved through a long series of changes and has adopted many reforms that in their day were considered "socialistic." For example, we have the social security system, unemployment insurance, minimum-wage legislation, antitrust legislation, and the welfare system. Some of these reforms are good, some may need to be revamped or even eliminated. The beauty of democratic capitalism is its self-reforming nature. It makes sense to speak of the American economy *not* in terms of "unbridled" or "laissez-faire" capitalism but as a system of "reformed capitalism" or "democratic capitalism."

Democratic capitalist countries have not achieved their level of prosperity because they have kept other countries, such as those in Latin America, in a state of dependency. The idea that the affluent countries have systematically "stolen" from the poor cannot be sustained by the facts. This is not to say that instances of unjust wealth transfer from one country to another have never occurred. Nor can one deny that acts of war, intervention, or imperialism have been carried out; the United States has a sad history of unjust interference in Latin America, although certain interventions have been justified.

Dependency theory has been thoroughly discredited by many economists. P. T. Bauer, for example, has shown that the poorest countries in the Third World today are those that were never colonized and that were relatively isolated from world trade. He notes that the most significant factor in successful Third World development has been the transfer of organizational techniques and product innovation from the developed countries to the Third World.[11]

The successful capitalist economies of the Far East—many of which have developed in conjunction with democratic or proto-democratic political structures—offer further proof of Bauer's point. They show that (1) capitalism is not a uniquely Western phenomenon, and (2) poor nations are not kept poor because the system of international trade exploits them.[12] American capitalism today is not the capitalism of the past. Yet with all its "socialistic" reforms, democratic capitalism is not communism, either.

Communism, by contrast, is that economic system that is based on the belief that (1) government ownership/control of the means of production is preferable to private ownership/control, (2) politically determined and commanded production goals and consumption patterns ("planning") are preferable to the operation of free and fair markets, (3) propaganda campaigns, threats, and intimidation will better motivate people to produce wealth than material incentives, and (4) government responsibility for the total welfare of all citizens from "cradle to grave" is preferable to a system that requires able-bodied adults to be self-reliant.

Democratic capitalism, as an economic system, is based on quite different presuppositions—private property, markets, incentives, self-reliance, and government regulations. Indeed, democratic capitalist societies not only produce more wealth and encourage more innovation, they also do a better job of fostering altruism, cooperation, and community spirit than do communist societies.

The United States, for example, does not lack a sense of community. For community spirit to exist it is not necessary for government to control all collective activities. On the contrary, the existence of a vast array of voluntary associations free from the control of the government makes the United States one of the most community-spirited countries on earth. Alexis de Tocqueville said as much in the late 1830s, and it is still true today.

What, then, about the oft-heard charge of some liberation theologians that capitalism is based on greed? There may certainly be individuals under any form of political economy who are consumed by greed. There may even be countries whose policies, like those of the earlier mercantilist states, are based on greed. But democratic capitalism as we know it today in Western Europe, North America, the Far East, and many other parts of the world is not based on greed. It is the system and the philosophy that recognizes the difference between selfishness and self-interest, that accepts the unchangeable reality of human self-interest, and that harnesses this human drive to the common good. Democratic capitalism sees self-interested activity for what it is: a drive to be individually self-reliant, an effort to provide for the material needs of a family, and, for many, an urge to participate in an occupation or profession that contributes to the common good.

Democratic capitalism is not the *Christian* form of political economy. As Reinhold Niebuhr observed, "There is no 'Christian' economic or political system."[13] But democratic capitalism is the political economy in our world that is most compatible with the Christian moral vision and the ethical teachings of the other great world religions. Some liberation theologians would do well to reevaluate their basic economic presuppositions. If they did, they would find that democratic capitalism is the most viable method known for the true liberation of all people, especially the poor and powerless.

Liberation theology stands today at a crossroads. It will either pursue an essentially Marxist theory and advocacy of communist revolution or choose the less ideologically captive task of developing the ideas of justice, freedom, and human rights within the framework of multi-party, democratic states and market economies.

LIBERATION THEOLOGY AND UNITED STATES SECURITY

Threats to a nation's security are always specific threats. Each country has its own heritage and ideals. There may be ideologies in the world that are indifferent or hostile to those ideals, but the existence of such ideologies is not in itself a security threat to the nation. Thus, the United States has nothing to fear from liberation theology unless and until it issues in actions that directly threaten the interests of the United States, its allies, or other nonaggressive countries.

The foundation of the system of international law is the prohibition of aggressive attack across international borders. The reciprocal right of the invaded country to exercise an effective defense is equally crucial to modern world order. These principles are incorporated in the United Nations charter and in the charter of the Organization of American States. Many historical examples of aggression and threats to a nation's security can be examined for insights concerning these principles. One instance of aggression in Latin America ought to be of particular interest to liberation theologians and is especially pertinent to the theme of this chapter.

In a lengthy discussion in *The American Journal of International Law,* John Norton Moore has documented the "secret war" carried on by the Sandinista regime in Nicaragua against its Central American neighbors.[14] Moore's story is chilling. Following the 1979 Nicaraguan revolution, a revolution with broad-based support, the United States provided $118 million in economic assistance to Nicaragua. The United States supported $292 million in loans to Nicaragua from the World Bank and the Inter-American Development Bank. The Sandinistas proclaimed themselves democratic and said their political system would be pluralistic. Yet the Sandinistas sought close ties with the Soviet Union and its clients. Moore writes, "The United States offered Peace Corps teachers, but the Sandinistas refused to accept a single one, although they welcomed thousands of Cuban and assorted Soviet-bloc and other radical advisers."[15] The Sandinistas rebuffed offers of military assistance from Panama and technical assistance from Costa Rica in favor of Cuban and Soviet-bloc assistance. Within Nicaragua the originally pluralistic government structure was rapidly brought under the control of the Sandinista party. Perhaps the decisive turn came when, on April 16, 1980, Decree No. 374 dramatically increased the number of seats in the legislative council and Sandinista party members were appointed to fill all but one of the new seats. This gave the party a substantial legislative majority for the first time.

By themselves, these and similar acts by the Sandinista regime, although alarming, did not constitute a threat to United States security interests. However, simultaneously with their cooptation of the Nicaraguan Revolution, the Sandinistas, with Cuban support, launched a secret guerrilla war against El Salvador and Guatemala and sponsored armed subversion against Costa Rica and Honduras.[16] These thoroughly documented actions provoked the current crisis in Central America. The real "secret war" is not the insurgency carried on by the "contra" freedom fighters in Nicaragua. It is the aggression of Nicaragua against its Central American neighbors.

Will the Nicaraguan regime fulfill the conditions of the Arias Peace Plan and negotiate with the United States? Will the Sandinistas allow elections in which opposition parties have a legitimate chance of winning? Will Nicaragua adopt a social democratic system rather than communism? These matters are far from settled. These are the questions that all the peoples of the Americas are asking, and they should be questions foremost in the minds of liberation theologians.

The links between liberation theologians and the Sandinistas are numerous and notable. The Brazilian liberation theologian Clodovis Boff, for example, calls the Sandinista regime a "model" for other Latin American countries. The most prominent theological-clerical spokesmen for the Sandinistas are two priests, Miguel D'Escoto, foreign minister, and Ernesto Cardenal, minister of culture, in Nicaragua. These high government officials of the Sandinista regime have received considerable praise in books and periodicals promoting liberation theology. I believe they represent that branch of liberation theology which adheres to a communist philosophy and pursues a deep alliance with the Soviet Union and "revolutionary internationalism."

Tennent C. Wright interviewed Cardenal for the magazine *America* shortly after the revolution in 1979. He writes: "Father Cardenal's mind was clear: There need be no separation between Christianity and communism."[17] The Catholic bishops of Nicaragua and Pope John Paul II, both personally and through his Vatican deputies, have criticized this type of liberation theology and encouraged a more genuine concept of "liberation" based on democratic pluralism and respect for human rights. Too few liberation theologians seem to be committed to this task, though perhaps more will join the effort in the future.

After carefully documenting—for fifty-six pages—the abuses of the Sandinistas, John Norton Moore sums up the "security" aspect of the Central American situation:

> Aggressive attack—particularly in its more frequent contemporary manifestation of secret guerrilla war, terrorism and low-intensity conflict—is a grave threat to world order wherever undertaken. That threat is intensified, however, when it is a form of cross-bloc attack in an area of traditional concern to an opposing alliance system. That is exactly the kind of threat presented by an activist Soviet-bloc intervention in the OAS area.[18]

What other threats to United States security manifest themselves in Latin America and what are the linkages with liberation theology? The Soviet client-state of Cuba has been a security concern to the United States for twenty-five years. The military power of Cuba should not be underestimated. During any major conventional hostilities between the Soviet Union and the United States, Cuba would present a significant obstacle to United States actions. Furthermore, as we have noted, the Cuban regime has been actively involved in the attempted subversion of Central America just as in earlier decades it tried to subvert South American countries.

Most liberation theologians are relatively silent about Cuba. After all, Latin Americans generally do not imagine Cuba to be a kind of utopia. Cuba has one of the largest populations of political prisoners in the world. Once one of the richest nations in Latin America, it is today one of the poorest. Yet, although they do not generally praise the Cuban regime, most liberation theologians fail to criticize the lack of political freedom or the economic stagnation in the island nation. They do not see that communist political and economic policies have stifled a proud, productive, and innovative people. At best, liberation theologians tend to ignore the Cuban regime. At worst, they admire it.

PROSPECTS FOR THE FUTURE

Generally in the region, communism and procommunist liberation theology are only minor phenomena. The major story in Latin America today is the growth of democratic institutions throughout much of the continent and the replacement of several military dictatorships by democratically elected governments. Economic conditions are still at a critical point. The debt crisis looms on the horizon. Yet, with appropriate governmental policies, expansion of democratic institutions, and reliance on markets, incentives, and private property rights, Latin America can repay its debts and become more prosperous and more free.

This is the "best case" scenario. What is the "worst case" scenario? It would be absolutely devastating to the interests of the poor in Latin America if there were a revival of "crude Marxism," a repetitious evocation of the discredited dependency theory, a preference for communist political and economic policies over the policies of democratic capitalism. In short, these developments would represent a victory for the ideological forces of communism, including those liberation theologians who advocate and defend communist totalitarianism in Latin America.

Perhaps Nicaragua will step back from the brink of communism, and perhaps Cuba will remain only an isolated and pathetic puppet of the Soviets. On the other hand, suppose the Sandinistas continue to imitate Cuba. Suppose both regimes then proceed to foment communist revolutions in other Central American countries. In such a case, Mexico would come under increased pressure to radicalize its politics and to placate or align with the Soviet bloc. Other Latin American countries could become communist allies of the Soviets, and the United States would face serious regional opposition to its interests.

Furthermore, imagine the toll of suffering that communism would bring to Latin America—the concentration camps, the refugees, the lost traditions of Latin American democracy. Would liberation theologians speak out against such a holocaust? One wants to answer with a resounding "Yes!" In fact, however, most liberation theologians see no dangers on the "extreme Left"; they worry not at all about Soviet intentions or the abuses of human rights under communism. Richard Rubenstein has described how these liberation theologians could someday find themselves advocating genocide:

One can with considerable justice speculate that the silence of the liberation theologians on the subject of the mass murder and the homelessness instigated by Communist regimes may be due to a certain reluctance to regard such violence as altogether criminal. By insisting that faith in Christ mandates identification with the cause of the poor, by rejecting any possible reform of capitalism, and by denying any connection between the God of the rich and the God of the poor, liberation theology offers, perhaps unwittingly, a powerful theological legitimation for the merciless elimination of those who obstruct a classless society. Atheistic Communism legitimated its elimination of "objective enemies" in the name of an unrealized secular future. Liberation theology identifies the opponents of socialism as enemies of God, a far more dangerous legitimation.[19]

Abuses of human rights are not only a crime and a tragedy, they are also a potential threat to United States security. The United States system of democratic capitalism presupposes a system of global interdependence. It is in the interest of the United States to encourage independence among its democratic friends and allies. It is also in the interest of the United States to encourage all countries, even those with socialist or communist economies, to participate in the world trade system, to support cultural exchange programs, and to have flexible policies concerning communications, travel, and immigration. Under a genuine system of democratic capitalism there is no necessary conflict between United States security and the security and independence of other countries. Those governments that forswear aggression and respect the basic human rights of their citizens need fear no opposition from the United States.

This summary of the philosophy that undergirds United States security policy ought to trouble no liberation theologian who seeks genuine justice, peace, freedom, and prosperity. It will trouble the liberation theologian who believes that the United States is the great oppressor of the world's poor, the "bastion of imperialist capitalism," and an expansionist threat to other nations.

United States policymakers should respond to liberation theology by developing a keen eye for the differences between those individuals and groups who, while they have political differences with the United States, nevertheless support democracy, human rights, and a just-market economy, and those individuals and groups who ally themselves with the Soviet Union and who promote its philosophy of "revolutionary internationalism" that seeks to subordinate all other systems and philosophies to its own.

CONCLUSION

Michael Novak has asked the most pertinent question concerning liberation theology, "Will it liberate?"[20] The *theological* concerns of liberation theology are interesting and potentially constructive, and it is appropriate for Christians to discuss them openly. But many of the *political* and *economic* assumptions of liberation theology are unclear or highly dubious. Furthermore, in a number of cases, liberation theology has become an accomplice in the suppression of democratic or proto-democratic ideas and institutions. Even worse, liberation theology sometimes aligns itself with the worst forms of communist totalitarianism and the worst abuses of human rights. Liberation theologians should be cautious. After the fact, the confession, "I was naive!" would be of little comfort to the victims of oppression, and it would not likely help to overthrow a system of power-concentration as self-righteous and disingenuous as communism.

Does liberation theology today pose a threat to United States security, to the security of other countries, or to the human rights of people? Not generally. But there is clear concern that liberation theology is an ideology that can be used to encourage and justify acts that are fundamentally inimical to the interests of the United States and other independent countries in the Americas.

NOTES

1. Paul E. Sigmund, "Epistle from a Democratic Capitalist," *Commonweal,* March 27, 1987, p. 186. Review of Michael Novak, *Will It Liberate?*

2. Ibid.

3. *"Christianity Today* Talks to Michael Novak," *Christianity Today,* July 10, 1987, pp. 54–55. Interview with Michael Novak by David Neff.

4. Sigmund, "Epistle from a Democratic Capitalist," p. 186.

5. José Comblin, *The Church and the National Security State* (Maryknoll, N.Y.: Orbis Books, 1979), p. 220.

6. From the "Christians for Socialism" document issued in Chile in 1972. See John Eagleson, ed., *Christians and Socialism: Documentation of the Christians for Socialism Movement in Latin America* (Maryknoll, N.Y.: Orbis Books, 1975), pp. 168–69.

7. Dale Vree has discussed the blending of Marxism and Christianity in a context unrelated to Latin America—namely, the Christian-Marxist dialogue in Europe. He concludes that, in order to fully participate in the dialogue, *both* Marxists and Christians had to become heretics vis-à-vis their own traditions. In other words, Marxism and Christianity are philosophically incompatible. See Dale Vree, *On Synthesizing Marxism and Christianity* (New York: John Wiley and Sons, 1976).

8. Gustavo Gutiérrez, *A Theology of Liberation,* trans. Sister Caridad Inda and John Eagleson (Maryknoll, N.Y.: Orbis Books, 1973).

9. Ibid., pp. 26–27.

10. Max Weber, *The Protestant Ethic and the Spirit of Capitalism,* trans. Talcott Parsons (New York: Charles Scribner's Sons, 1958).

11. See P. T. Bauer, *Equality, the Third World and Economic Delusion* (Cambridge, Mass.: Harvard University Press, 1981).

12. On the case of the East Asian capitalism, see Peter L. Berger, *The Capitalist Revolution: Fifty Propositions about Prosperity, Equality, and Liberty* (New York: Basic Books, 1986), chap. 7.

13. Reinhold Niebuhr, *Faith and Politics: A Commentary on Religions, Social and Political Thought in a Technological Age,* ed. Ronald H. Stone (New York: George Braziller, 1968), p. 56.

14. John Norton Moore, "The Secret War in Central America and the Future of World Order," *The American Journal of International Law* 80 (January 1986), reprinted in *World Affairs* 148 (Fall 1985): 75–130.

15. Ibid., p. 77.

16. Ibid., p. 78.

17. Tennent C. Wright, S. J., "Ernesto Cardenal and the Humane Revolution in Nicaragua," *America,* December 15, 1979, pp. 387–88.

18. Moore, "The Secret War in Central America and the Future of World Order," p. 114.

19. Richard L. Rubenstein, *The Political Significance of Latin American Liberation Theology* (Washington, D.C.: The Washington Institute for Values in Public Policy, 1986), p. 10.

20. See Michael Novak, *Will It Liberate? Questions about Liberation Theology* (New York: Paulist Press, 1986).

The Labyrinth of Liberation

John K. Roth

God give us grace to accept with serenity the things that cannot be changed, courage to change the things that should be changed, and the wisdom to distinguish the one from the other.

—Reinhold Niebuhr (1943)

abyrinths contains brilliant examples of the metaphysical *ficciones* composed by the Argentine master, Jorge Luis Borges. One of them suggests that the universe is a Library. Although no two of its volumes are the same, the Library contains every possible book. This means that "for every sensible line of straightforward statement, there are leagues of senseless cacophonies, verbal jumbles and incoherences…, but not a single example of absolute nonsense."[1]

People dwell within this Library's "indefinite and perhaps infinite number of hexagonal galleries."[2] Among these librarians, as they are called, are some who say: if the Library contains all possible books, then "on some shelf in some hexagon…there must exist a book which is the formula and perfect compendium *of all the rest*."[3] Presumably this book would clarify and justify everything. Tradition says that such a book not only exists but has even been read at least once. By this time, however, nobody can identify either the reader or the book.

Those who worked on *The Politics of Latin American Liberation Theology* trust that its views from Latin America and the United States do not put their readers in the same predicament faced by Borges's librarians. Nevertheless, as one concludes these essays, there is a sense of being in liberation's labyrinth. To finish the book by putting public policy concerns in a philosophical context, this postscript explores labyrinthine terrain by reviewing what has gone before.

GRACE, COURAGE, AND WISDOM

Suffering unmerited, injustice unrectified, basic needs unmet—these are only a few of life's tragic ways. They make the yearning to be free as contemporary and new as it is ancient and perennial. The conviction that existence is not as it ought to be, that it can be different and better, makes beings human. So does the awareness that we are not isolated, independent spirits. Instead we are finite persons who live and move and have our worldly being embodied in specific situations that connect us and in concrete circumstances that cause us to collide. Events entrap us because we do not—and perhaps cannot— know well enough what is true, discern well enough what is just, and enact well enough what both truth and justice enjoin. Formed by factors such as these, the labyrinth of liberation is where human existence is lost and found.

The now-famous prayer by Reinhold Niebuhr that serves as an epigraph for this postscript was composed on the back of an envelope and offered first in a village church in Heath, Massachusetts. According to Robert McAfee Brown, its author was a man who tilted "in the direction of courageous change rather than serene acceptance."[4] Likewise, a world in which Latin American liberation theology has become a formidable player can hardly be one in which serene acceptance predominates. Courageous change will be required on many fronts. While that fact will not eliminate the need for serenity and acceptance, it does make wisdom all the more important. The requisite wisdom must not only continue to differentiate between what can and cannot be changed, it must also confront responsibly a question that can be even more perplexing: What means can best reach the ends that should be achieved in liberation's labyrinth?

Grace, courage, and wisdom—all three are needed abundantly where the changes propounded by Latin American liberation theology are concerned. That judgment is true for those who are trying to decide what the proper responses to this movement should be. It may be even more fundamental, though more difficult, for those who have already made up their minds to accept or reject the basic challenges of this movement, which is at once religiously political and politically religious.

Neither *The Politics of Latin American Liberation Theology* nor even Niebuhr's noble prayer can be an adequate analog for that elusive Book of books in Borges's Library. There is no formula or compendium to appraise completely what Latin American liberation theology means, intends, and foreshadows. On the contrary, in this book alone there is enough diversity of outlook about Latin American liberation theology to constitute a mini-labyrinth. That diversity, however, should not be discouraging. If we are to locate the necessary grace, courage, and wisdom, the sense of being in a labyrinth ought to leave its mark. Thus, if these essays properly provide no formula, collectively they do take a stand that should guide public policy. It is consonant with the critical insight expressed in Niebuhr's prayer: *About the issues posed by Latin American liberation theology, no one should decide too soon or too late.*

SELF-DELUSION AND EVASION

The first of this book's three main parts concentrated on "Liberation Theology and History." No sooner was it under way than Paul E. Sigmund made the following observation: "Mention liberation theology to the average educated person, and you are likely to get one of two reactions, either strongly positive or equally strongly negative."

These reactions arise from fundamental feelings. First, there is the sense that there are millions of people who do not deserve to be the wretched of the earth and that liberation theology can help to improve their lot. Second, there is the sense that the politics of liberation theology poses a fundamental threat to interests that more privileged persons and communities are loath to relinquish—not least of all because many have worked long and hard to acquire and sustain them.

Latin American liberation theology entails a power struggle. If there is a path that leads toward the most desirable resolution of that conflict, it may be in a recognition that right and wrong can be found on both sides of the reactions that Paul Sigmund identifies. Therefore, unless grace, courage, and wisdom become less scarce, living within the labyrinth of liberation will be grim indeed.

"Latin American liberation theology," contends Marc H. Ellis, "is part of a worldwide theological response to the multifaceted crisis facing a troubled world." Noting that ours is an age of triage and holocaust, Ellis suggests that history has made human life worth less than ever before.

Children, women, and men are wasted, but in the midst of the destruction, religion's potency emerges once more. It provides a form of judgment that can rightly inspire protest and rebellion against powers that crush even the most modest human hopes. But the question is, What will be religion's judgment?

Those who perpetrate injustice need to feel judgment's sting. Everyone belongs in that category to some degree. If the worldwide theological response discerned by Ellis can incorporate such insight, life in the labyrinth of liberation will not end but it may become better.

Richard L. Rubenstein points out that "a principal function of theology, especially in modern times, has been *dissonance-reduction*." Particularly concerned with religion's proclivity to announce that God is on this or that group's side, Rubenstein shows how volatile such claims can be.

Eventually claims of God's favor must reckon with historical evidence, whose ambiguity, to say nothing of sometimes disconfirming judgment, threatens their credibility. History never seems to vindicate completely the claims of any human person or community. The pretentiousness that inclines any of us to think too readily that "God is on our side" can be a delusion that adds to the already vast accumulation of human waste.

"Everywhere," asserted Reinhold Niebuhr, "life is delivered unto death because it is ensnared in self-delusion and practices every evasion rather than meet the true God."[5] Echoing Niebuhr, Rubenstein suggests that all too often theology, including Latin American liberation theology, fails to discern what Niebuhr called "the true God," the One who paradoxically may be on everyone's and on no one's side at once. If recognition of that kind could occur, theology might produce a self-critical dissonance amplification that could make liberation greater.

Frederick Sontag helpfully amplifies dissonance when he warns that "Christians cannot appeal to Jesus or to religious principles to justify their political/public activity." Time and again, he realizes, such appeals have been made; doubtlessly they will continue, too. But Sontag's point is that liberation may be more awesome than is usually understood.

Liberation means that human beings are thoroughly responsible for their actions, for themselves, and also for one another. Hence, Sontag cares especially about the place of violence in the movements of Latin American liberation theology. What that place shall be, he contends, is not a decision that can be placed on Jesus' shoulders. It belongs instead on those of people everywhere who live and act here and now.

The familiar song, "He's Got the Whole World in His Hands," requires augmented lyrics. Apparently the world is in human hands, perhaps even more than we should like. Even if history is not molded completely by the desires of human hearts, it is nevertheless determined decisively by our visions and collisions concerning what is right and good. This condition keeps human life in the labyrinth of liberation. It will be to our sorrow if we fail to muster grace, courage, and wisdom in coping with that reality.

SOBER HOPE

Reflections on "Liberation Theology and History" suggest that humankind is caught inextricably in a condition that reflects what Reinhold Niebuhr saw when he wrote:

> There is an element of truth in...every sober hope. Some of the chaos of human existence can be overcome. It is possible to have a society in which there will be security for every one rather than insecurity for the many....[But] an optimism which depends upon the hope of the complete realization of our highest ideals in history is bound to suffer ultimate disillusionment.[6]

With that predicament in mind, what has followed with respect to "Liberation Theology and Socioeconomic Problems," the subject of the second major part of this book?

Although Roland Robertson argues that the general political significance of Latin American liberation theology "has been greatly exaggerated," he does emphasize that "meaning and power—primordially united, but 'officially' disconnected in much of the world during the present century—are, whether we like it or not, being reunited, particularly in the Third World." What Robertson calls the uniting of meaning and power is precisely what governs the politics of liberation theology.

Latin American liberation theology stresses that meaning is lost to the extent that meaning's credibility depends on hopes directed toward other-worldly or transhistorical dimensions of reality. Thus, if God is on the side of the oppressed, that claim either must find fulfillment in a transformed socioeconomic order or be rendered largely incredible.

Liberation theology is not going to make the world a more comfortable place, especially for the already comfortable, precisely because it is fundamentally committed to socioeconomic change. If this theology's drive is nurtured by and met with grace, courage, and wisdom, the result could be favorable. To the extent that those virtues are lacking as the thirsts for meaning and power unite, the outcome can hardly be welcome.

W. E. Hewitt sees signs for hope in this area. The base communities that liberation theology has nourished in Latin America, he says, may be less homogeneously focused on radical social change than many interpreters assume. Concentrating on Brazil, Hewitt reports that "recent research reveals…a much more heterogeneous CEB phenomenon."

Social change still sets the agenda. Yet how that change occurs and where the effort concentrates may depend more on local need than on ideological commitment. Hewitt finds a pragmatic element that reflects critical aspects of the grace, courage, and wisdom that Niebuhr envisioned. From all sides that element warrants encouragement.

While Michael Fleet is also hopeful, he acknowledges that "at the core of Christian radicalization in virtually all instances have been improved relations between Christian and Marxist groups." These improved relations produce some of the most confusing tracks in the labyrinth of liberation.

Is Christianity used and abused by Marxists, or is its message in keeping with much that Marxism teaches? Variations on that theme in the controversies over Latin American liberation theology can yield cacophonies aplenty as the advocates for and against stake out their turf. Thus, one lesson offered by *The Politics of Latin American Liberation Theology* is as follows: It is as mistaken to heed too readily any one of the voices in the controversy over liberation theology as it is to allow oneself to be deafened by their collective din. Within liberation's labyrinth, the lucidity that brings release depends on nothing so much as honest criticism and dialogue.

Important steps in that direction are taken by William R. Garrett, especially when he says that one must take Latin American liberation theology seriously and ask, "Liberation from what?" In a word, he thinks the standard answer to that question is "dependence," by which the major liberationists mean, "in the shorthand of contemporary religiopolitical parlance, the economic, political, and cultural repression and exploitation of Latin America by First World countries, and primarily the United States."

Assessing the extent of this dependence, Garrett argues that the problem is less one of external control of Latin America than one of mismanagement from within. His intent is not to wash First World hands of all responsibility for Latin American woes but to insist that responsibility must be apportioned critically, which is to say, equitably. Otherwise the predicament's nature will be misunderstood, and the odds against progress will grow. Again, liberation's labyrinth will not be sized up well apart from grace, courage, and wisdom. Shouldering the responsibility that is ours, as Garrett urges, moves in that direction.

Labyrinths come in at least two kinds. The mythical maze Daedalus built to house the Minotaur for King Minos presumably had a way in and a way out. Borges's Library of Babel, on the other hand, is a labyrinth without entrance or exit. It constitutes not a place but a condition, one in which things can change but from which there is no ultimate escape short of death. As all the contributors to this book imply, the labyrinth of liberation is closer to the second kind than to the first. It is therefore important that Humberto Belli concentrates specifically on the revolutionary motifs in Latin American liberation theology.

Revolutions, violent ones included, may change things for the better. They also may do the opposite, particularly when they are violent and occur in a labyrinth with neither entrance nor exit. The degree to which Latin American liberation theology is prepared to embrace or eschew violence is arguable, but Belli hits the mark when he says, "Although allowance should be made for a certain diversity of positions among the liberationists, the centrality of revolution (the belief that revolutionary political action against the ruling socioeconomic order is the way to make Christian love for the poor truly effective) became the distinguishing mark of the theologians who are either identified or who identify themselves with this perspective."

For the most part, Belli demonstrates, the centrality of revolution in Latin American liberation theology causes that movement, however inadvertently, to aid and abet the interests of the Marxist Left, Cuba, and the Soviet

Union. Moreover, it is hardly crystal-clear that movements supporting those interests yield a high return in human liberation.

Belli's article sounds salient notes of caution. Just as the critics of liberation theology must be careful to avoid putting selfish interest ahead of honesty and responsibility, so must liberationists be cautious about aligning and allying themselves with interests contrary to the human dignity that their theology professes to defend.

INTERSECTIONS AND CROSSROADS

Believing that "the powers of human self-deception are seemingly endless," Reinhold Niebuhr also claimed that the Christian doctrine of original sin was empirically verifiable.[7] "This doctrine," said Niebuhr, "asserts the obvious fact that all men are persistently inclined to regard themselves more highly and are more assiduously concerned with their own interests than any 'objective' view of their importance would warrant."[8] That judgment is well taken as one looks back at "Liberation Theology and Public Policy in the United States," the third major part of *The Politics of Latin American Liberation Theology*.

John K. Roth shows that Latin American liberation theology tends to see the United States as the great enemy. Remembering Niebuhr's wisdom, United States citizens need to examine that Latin American indictment seriously. Seasoned by Niebuhr's sense that nothing human is entirely free from sin, part of such a consideration will involve awareness that the labyrinth of liberation is far more complex than the liberationists' indictment suggests.

Unless Latin American liberation theology "substantially recasts its identity," Roth points out, "little that the United States can do, short of scrapping our capitalist ways altogether, is likely to win full favor from those quarters." Capitalism has its dark side, a fact that its most zealous supporters too conveniently disregard. But capitalism's ways, particularly in the democratic form that they take at their best in the United States, have brought much that is good as well.

The dismantling of capitalism is neither sufficient nor even necessary for the liberation that is possible in human existence. On the contrary, if it is genuinely and self-critically democratic, capitalism is more likely than any other candidate to provide the best available—though ever-imperfect—economic system. Therefore, the challenge for United States public policy is to make democratic capitalism work as well as possible. What that means, however, is not self-evident. Insightful determination of such meaning requires the reflection that Niebuhr urged in his realistically hopeful prayer.

Recent public policy debates in the United States have been enlivened by the nation's Roman Catholic bishops, who have issued statements critical of the United States economy. Although those bishops are less radical than the liberation theologians of Latin America, Phillip Berryman stresses what the two groups share in their respective outlooks. The intersections he finds map part of what ought to be meant when one speaks of making democratic capitalism work as well as possible.

Berryman cites the bishops' call for "a U.S. international economic policy designed to empower people everywhere and enable them to continue to develop a sense of their own worth, improve the quality of their lives, and ensure that the benefits of economic growth are shared equitably." To design such a policy, let alone to implement it, is a tall order. Nonetheless, Berryman makes a crucial statement when he suggests that an economic policy that lacks altogether a "preferential option for the poor" can hardly be deemed successful in the full and best senses of that term.

If Berryman looks for intersections between United States Catholic teaching and Latin American liberation theology, Dennis P. McCann prefers to put some distance between the two. He wants "a practical or public theology that is liberating without being liberationist." What makes the difference is the degree to which theology is circumspect in its relations with the philosophy of Karl Marx and its legacy.

Few thinkers can match Marx's incisiveness in identifying the dark side of capitalism. McCann rightly argues, however, that clarity blurs when Marxist lenses dominate vision. While any uncritical rejection of Marxist analysis is myopic, the need is to employ that analysis so that it incorporates self-referential criticism. Specifically, that criticism needs to include both Marx's insight that human ideals are rationalizations of human interests and Niebuhr's warning that sin is to some degree a factor in every human affair. If thinking of that kind plays a part in public policy, the labyrinth of liberation can include paths that are liberating without being liberationist.

According to John W. Cooper, "Liberation theology stands today at a crossroads. It will either pursue an essentially Marxist theory and advocacy of communist revolution or choose the less ideologically captive task of developing the ideas of justice, freedom, and human rights within the framework of multi-party, democratic states and market economies." Cooper implies that those who have produced and been affected by Latin American liberation theology can still have open minds. Time will tell, but even if those minds are open, United States policymakers must be vigilant to see which of the tendencies identified by Cooper will gain the upper hand.

Cooper believes that liberation theology does not generally threaten United States security. Yet he concludes that "liberation theology is an ideology that can be used to encourage and justify acts that are fundamentally inimical to the interests of the United States and other independent countries in the Americas." Hence, it behooves the United States to be watchful wherever the liberation theology of Latin America is a player.

Cooper's essay suggests how important it is that United States watchfulness should be a two-way street. There is a need to look within as well as without. To ask self-critically, "What are and what should be the interests of the United States?" is no less necessary than to discern how the aims and consequences of Latin American liberation theology will continue to develop.

The labyrinth of liberation, shows Cooper, may lack an entrance or an exit and yet not be a closed system. Because of conflict, those who dwell within it may change, individually and together, and do so for mutual benefit. At least they may do so if there is vigilance to encourage that outcome and not its opposite. Such vigilance and encouragement depend on the grace, courage, and wisdom for which Niebuhr asked.

WHAT IS AND WHAT OUGHT TO BE

This postscript began with a prayer. At first glance that may have seemed an odd way to start some last words on public policy and Latin American liberation theology. Exploration in liberation's labyrinth, however, may lead to a different conclusion—at least with respect to Reinhold Niebuhr's specific supplication.

In the Library of Babel, reports Borges, there are "official searchers, *inquisitors*" who have hoped to find "a clarification of humanity's basic mysteries." Failure's accumulation, however, has worn them down. They keep at their work, but "obviously, no one expects to discover anything."[9]

Fortunately, existence in the labyrinth of liberation may have a different outcome. Niebuhr's perspicuity sensed as much:

> Let man stand at any point in history, even in a society which has realized his present dreams of justice, and if he surveys the human problem profoundly he will see that every perfection which he has achieved points beyond itself to a greater perfection, and that this greater perfection throws light upon his sins and imperfections. He will feel in that tension between what is and what ought to be the very glory of life, and will come to know that the perfection which eludes him is not only a human possibility and impossibility, but a divine fact.[10]

If *The Politics of Latin American Liberation Theology* succeeds in driving home that judgment even a little, the efforts of its contributors and readers alike will prove worthwhile.

NOTES

1. Jorge Luis Borges, "The Library of Babel," trans. James E. Irby, in *Labyrinths: Selected Stories & Other Writings,* ed. Donald A. Yates and James E. Irby (New York: New Directions, 1964), pp. 53, 57. Incidentally, Borges served as director of the National Library of Argentina.

2. Ibid., p. 51.

3. Ibid., p. 56.

4. Robert McAfee Brown, ed., *The Essential Reinhold Niebuhr: Selected Essays and Addresses* (New Haven: Yale University Press, 1986), p. xxiv. On the same page, Brown quotes Niebuhr's prayer.

5. Reinhold Niebuhr, "The Christian Witness in the Social and National Order," in ibid., p. 98. This essay is from Niebuhr's *Christian Realism and Political Problems* (New York: Charles Scribner's Sons, 1953).

6. Reinhold Niebuhr, "Optimism, Pessimism, and Religious Faith," in *The Essential Reinhold Niebuhr,* p. 12. This essay was published originally in Niebuhr's *Christianity and Power Politics* (New York: Charles Scribner's Sons, 1940).

7. Reinhold Niebuhr, *The Irony of American History* (New York: Charles Scribner's Sons, 1952), p. 21. See also *The Essential Reinhold Niebuhr,* p. xii.

8. Niebuhr, *The Irony of American History,* p. 17.

9. Borges, "The Library of Babel," in *Labyrinths,* p. 55.

10. Niebuhr, "Optimism, Pessimism, and Religious Faith," in *The Essential Reinhold Niebuhr,* p. 16.

Glossary

Alliance for Progress. Program of United States aid to Latin America initiated by President John F. Kennedy in 1961.

ATC. *Asociación de Trabajadores del Campo* (Field Workers Association). Mass organization of landless rural laborers founded in 1977 in Nicaragua through the FSLN and CEPA.

Authoritarianism. A theory of society based on the control of all effective means of political power in conjunction with some degree of economic and cultural freedom; a societal policy commonly adopted by military dictatorships.

BPR. *Bloque Popular Revolucionario* (Revolutionary People's Bloc). Salvadoran guerrilla organization which absorbed FECCAS once it had been radicalized by liberationists.

Catholic social teaching. Initially a body of teaching on labor, property, human dignity, and human rights contained in papal encyclicals beginning with Leo XIII's *Rerum Novarum* (1891); since Vatican Council II such teaching is also expressed by episcopal conferences and is seen as part of a longer tradition reaching back through church history.

CEB. Acronym for Spanish or Portuguese *comunidad eclesial* or *eclesiais de base*, basic Christian community.

CELAM. Acronym for the Spanish title of the Latin American Bishops Conference. Its most important meetings took place at Medellín, Colombia (1968), and Puebla, Mexico (1979).

Celebracões. Popular form of the mass performed in the Brazilian community, usually by a lay minister.

CEPA. *Centro de Educación y Promoción Agraria* (Agrarian Education and Promotion Center). Nicaraguan rural development agency founded by the Jesuits in 1969.

Christian base communities (CEBs). Small-scale (30- to 50-members) and frequently lay-directed alternatives to conventional parish communities whose religious life often spills over into social and political involvement, particularly in times of crisis. More active in poorer neighborhoods and locales, they are under the jurisdiction of the institutional church, although they are more likely to be influenced by local-level personnel (priests, nuns, and lay activists). Particularly important in Brazil, though relatively little solid empirical evidence exists for Latin America as a whole as to the range of base community activities.

Christians for Socialism. A group formed in 1971 by a number of Chilean priests and theologians for the purpose of providing Christian support for the Allende government. Beginning with some eighty members, it grew to more than two hundred and spread to other Latin American countries, though it never developed a mass base or constituency. Its adherents advocated socialist ideals generally and the most radical interpretations of liberation theology, namely, that Christian teaching necessarily implies the establishment of socialism.

CNBB. *Conferencia Nacional dos Bishops do Brasil* (National Conference of Brazilian Bishops).

Conscientização or *conscientización*. Political consciousness-raising, in particular a method intiated by the Brazilian educator Paolo Freire in conducting programs that relate literacy texts to the daily experience of the poor and oppressed in a way that develops a critical attitude to the status quo.

Conselho. The directing body of a Brazilian CEB, usually containing five to ten members.

Contextualization. Making explicit the sociocultural and historical circumstances under which religions have developed.

Cortico. Resident of an inner-city slum.

Cultural hegemony. The dominant values, beliefs, and symbolic modes of communication in a society or civilization. Often used to indicate the way in which the poor and deprived are prevented from recognizing their condition of exploitation.

Democratic capitalism. A theory of society based on the diffusion of power among three separate institutional sectors, the political, the economic, and the cultural. The resulting model is a threefold blend of political democracy, economic capitalism, and cultural pluralism. This theory places special emphasis on the morality of private property, incentives, and markets.

Dependency theory. A wide range of social, economic, and political theories derived ultimately from Marxist analyses which stress the exploitation of less developed societies by First World nations through their transmission of capital to establish dependent economic orders among vulnerable second and Third World nations.

Dependencia. A socioeconomic theory developed in Latin America during the late 1960s that argued that the underdevelopment of Latin America is causally related to its dependence on the developed countries.

Developmentalism. A broad range of theories deriving from structural functionalism and other sociopolitical schools of thought popular among scholars in developed nations in the West and accentuating factors which appeared to have prompted modernization, including economic structures, political patterns, valuational commitments, and individual freedoms.

Favela. "Temporary" urban or suburban slum area in Brazil.

Favelado. Resident of a *favela*.

FECCAS. *Federación de Campesinos Cristianos de El Salvador* (Federation of Christian Peasants of El Salvador). League of Christian peasants radicalized by liberationist activists in the early eighties.

FSLN. *Frente Sandinista de Liberación Nacional* (Sandinista National Liberation Front). Nicaraguan guerrilla organization founded in 1961 and in power since July 19, 1979.

Fundamentalism. A religious tendency rooted in a literal interpretation of the Bible. Typically fundamentalists are distrustful of all forms of mediation and/or contextualization (and hence of pluralism, politics, bureaucratic processes, and reformulations of traditional teachings in the light of new challenges and discoveries).

Hermeneutics of Praxis. A method of interpretation, especially of the Bible, that relates Scripture to experience, especially that of the poor and oppressed.

IC. *Izquierda Cristiana*, a radical Christian movement (and later party) formed in 1971 by former members of the *tercerista* ("third road") faction of the Chilean Christian Democratic party.

Inculturation. Process of accommodating Christianity (or, in principle, any world religion) to local, indigenous religions.

Imperialism. A strategy employed by powerful nations to subdue less developed societies by means of military conquest, subsequently followed up by political domination and economic exploitation, where raw materials are extracted from the dominated society and manufactured goods are marketed under protective arrangements.

Izquierda Unida (IU). A coalition of small Marxist parties and independent Christian groups formed in 1980 in Peru. Currently the second leading political force in the country, with the bulk of its support coming from workers, slum dwellers, and peasants.

Liberation theology. A theological tendency originating in Latin America that has inspired and legitimated Christian involvement in radical social and political movements. Its various formulations concur in insisting that faith and the good Christian life be informed by a prior commitment to the liberation of oppressed peoples and by the findings of contemporary social science.

Magisterium. Latin for teaching of the Roman Catholic church.

MAPU. *Movimiento para la Acción Popular Unitaria*, a Christian-Marxist party formed in 1969 by former members of the *rebelde* (rebel) faction of the Chilean Christian Democratic party.

Mercantilism. An economic theory based on the assumptions that (1) there is a fixed amount of wealth in the world, usually represented by gold, and (2) governments should attempt to control as much of that wealth as possible through trade and economic policy.

Metropolitan Center. A term coined by neocolonial dependency theorists to designate the concentration of economic-political power in a First World nation, especially as this power is manifested toward less-developed societies.

Modernization. A complex social process whereby traditional societies are transformed into social orders characterized by greater industrialization, popular political participation, higher levels of education, individualism, increased urbanization, and usually more rational procedures in law and administration.

Modernization theory. Sometimes also known as developmentalism by its critics, it refers to a set of ideas developed mainly by North American social scientists in the late 1950s and early 1960s concerning the terms in which Third World societies can change so as to improve their economic, political, and other circumstances.

Mutirão. Brazilian self-help, joint-labor project.

Neocolonial dependency theory. A specific school of neo-Marxist theory developed by Paul Baran, Andre Gunder Frank, and Paul Sweezy which contends that metropolitan centers of capital concentration in the First World dominate less-developed societies through the export of excess capital, which is administered by coopted elites in Third World countries. The result is the development of underdevelopment, wherein First World corporations make substantial profits while third world producers are reduced to ever-increasing poverty.

Orthopraxis. A term used by Gutiérrez and other liberationists to refer to the importance of correct action, especially in Christian life. Often constrasted with *orthodoxy* (correct belief).

Pastoral agent. Priest, nun, or layperson designated by the church to aid in the formation and activation of CEBs.

Popular church. The term used for the elements of the Roman Catholic church that claim to speak for the people, against the hierarchy. In Nicaragua, the "popular church" has the support of the Sandinista government. The term is no longer used by its proponents because it has been strongly condemned by the Vatican and by the local hierarchies.

Popular Unity. The coalition of Marxists, Christians, and secularists that supported the Allende government in Chile between 1970 and 1973.

Praxis. A term used by Gutiérrez and other liberationists to refer to the importance of concrete behavior, deeds, action, especially in Christian life. Often contrasted with *theoria* (theory).

Preconciliar. Adjective indicating anything that took place before Vatican Council II. In the usage of Latin American liberals and radicals it is often used as a derogatory term when applied to church people or theologians, meaning obsolete, reactionary, outmoded.

Protestant ethic thesis. An hypothesis developed by the German sociologist Max Weber that the Calvinist emphasis on the Christian's duty to work for the glory of God contributed significantly to the take-off of modern, rational capitalism in Western societies.

Renovated Marxism. An openly revisionist brand of Marxism coming out of Europe in the 1970s, rejecting Leninist conceptions of party and of state-society relations. It is a point of view highly critical of historical socialist experiences, giving greater attention to cultural and political factors, and valuing democratic institutions and practices for their own sake.

Revindicacão. Complaint or action taken to resolve some complaint.

Revolutionary Christians. Generic term used by those Christians in Nicaragua who support the Sandinista government. They consider themselves followers of liberation theology.

Revolutionary focus. Strategy advocated by some Latin American Marxist guerrillas based on the creation of "liberated" insurgent regions in the remote countryside, from which guerrillas would gradually engage the government and army, using hit-and-run tactics.

Sandinistas. The Sandinista Front of National Liberation (FSLN), which is the ruling group in Nicaragua. Its principal leaders are Marxist-Leninist, but it takes its name from an anticommunist nationalist leader, Augusto César Sandino, who fought a guerrilla war against the United States occupation of Nicaragua between 1927 and 1933.

Socialism. An economic theory based on government ownership of the means of production, centralized economic planning, egalitarian distribution of income and wealth, and government responsibility for the total welfare of all citizens.

Structural-functional theory. A sociological theory pioneered by Talcott Parsons and others which focuses research on organizational patterns and the activities flowing from these institutional structures.

Synod. A meeting of bishops. Since Vatican II, worldwide synods of Roman Catholic bishops are held in Rome at three-year intervals.

Totalitarianism. A theory of society based on the control of political, economic, and cultural activities in order to concentrate power in the hands of a ruling elite; a societal policy commonly adopted by ruling Communist parties.

Tupamaros. Name of notorious Uruguayan urban guerrillas who became active in the mid-sixties and were defeated by 1971.

Bibliography

Abbott, Walter M., ed. *The Documents of Vatican II*. New York: The America Press, 1966.

Adorno, Theodor W. *Negative Dialectics*. New York: Seabury Press, 1973.

Adriance, Madeleine. *Opting for the Poor: Brazilian Catholicism in Transition*. Kansas City: Sheed and Ward, 1986.

Alexander, Jeffrey C. *The Antinomies of Classical Thought: Marx and Durkheim*. Vol. 2 of *Theoretical Logic in Sociology*. Berkeley: University of California Press, 1982.

_____. *The Modern Reconstruction of Classical Thought: Talcott Parsons*. Vol. 4 of *Theoretical Logic in Sociology*. Berkeley: University of California Press, 1982.

Altamirano, Carlos. *Dialéctica de una derrota*. México: Siglo XXI, 1977.

Althuser, Louis. *For Marx*. New York: Random House, 1970.

_____, and Etienne Balibar. *Reading Capital*. New York: Pantheon Books, 1970.

Altizer, Thomas J. J., and William Hamilton. *Radical Theology and the Death of God*. Indianapolis: Bobbs-Merrill, 1966.

Alves, Rubem. "Christian Realism: Ideology of the Establishment." *Christianity and Crisis* 33 (September, 1973).

Ames, Rolando. "Movimiento popular y construcción de la democracia." (más comentarios). In *América Latina 80: Democracia y movimiento popular*. Lima: DESCO, 1981.

Antoncich, Ricardo. *Christians in the Face of Injustice: A Latin American Reading of Catholic Social Teaching*. Maryknoll, N.Y.: Orbis Books, 1987.

Apter, David E. *The Politics of Modernization*. Chicago: University of Chicago Press, 1965.

Araya, Victorio G. "The God of the Strategic Covenant." In Pablo Richard et al., *The Idols of Death and the God of Life: A Theology.* Translated by Barbara E. Campbell and Bonnie Shepard. Maryknoll, N.Y.: Orbis Books, 1983.

Arendt, Hannah. *The Origins of Totalitarianism.* New York: Harcourt, Brace, 1951.

Arrate, J. *Iglesia, mundo cristiano, y acción política: Algunas reflexiones políticas desde la izquierda no cristiana.* Rotterdam: Instituto para un Nuevo Chile. Documento 146, mimeo.

Arriagada, Genaro. *Diez años: Visión crítica.* Santiago: Aconcagua, 1983.

Assmann, Hugo. *Theology for a Nomad Church.* Translated by Paul Burns. Maryknoll, N.Y.: Orbis Books, 1976.

_____, and Nicholas Eberstadt. "Democracy and the Debt Crisis." *This World* 16 (Spring/Summer, 1986).

Azevedo, Marcello de C. *Basic Ecclesial Communities.* Washington,D.C.: Georgetown University Press, 1987.

Ballon, Eduardo, ed. *Movimientos sociales y democracia: La fundación de un nuevo orden.* Lima: DESCO, 1986.

Baraglia, Mariano. *Evolução das comunidades eclesiais de base.* Petrópolis: Vozes, 1974.

Baran, Paul A. *The Political Economy of Growth.* New York: Monthly Review Press, 1968.

Barreiro, Alvaro. *Basic Ecclesial Communities.* Translated by Barbara Campbell. Maryknoll, N.Y.: Orbis Books, 1982.

Barth, Karl. *The Epistle to the Romans.* Translated by Edwyn C. Hoskyns. Oxford: Oxford University Press, 1933.

_____. *The Humanity of God.* Translated by Thomas Weiser and John Newton Thomas. Richmond: John Knox Press, 1960.

_____. *Protestant Thought: From Rousseau to Ritschl.* Translated by Brian Cozens. London: SCM Press, 1959.

Bauer, P.T. *Equality, the Third World and Economic Delusion.* Cambridge, Mass.: Harvard University Press, 1981.

Bell, Daniel. *The Cultural Contradictions of Capitalism.* New York: Harper and Row, 1978.

Bellah, Robert N. *Tokugawa Religion.* Boston: Beacon Press, 1957.

Belli, Humberto. *Breaking Faith: The Sandinista Revolution and Its Impact on Freedom and Christian Faith in Nicaragua.* Westchester, Ill.: Crossway Books, 1985.

_____. *Nicaragua: Christians under Fire.* Garden City, Mich.: Puebla Institute, 1984.

Bendix, Reinhard. *Nation-Building and Citizenship.* Garden City, N.Y.: Doubleday and Co., 1964.

Berger, Peter L. *The Capitalist Revolution: Fifty Propositions about Prosperity, Equality, and Liberty.* New York: Basic Books, 1986.

_____. *Pyramids of Sacrifice.* Garden City, N.Y.: Doubleday and Co., 1976.

_____. *The Sacred Canopy.* Garden City, N.Y.: Doubleday Anchor Books, 1966.

_____, and Hansfried Kellner. *Sociology Reinterpreted.* Garden City, N.Y.: Doubleday and Co., 1981.

_____, and Michael Novak. *Speaking to the Third World.* Washington, D.C.: American Enterprise Institute, 1985.

Bergesen, Albert, ed. *Crisis in the World-System.* Beverly Hills, Calif.: Sage Publications, 1983.

Bernstein, Richard. J. *Praxis and Action: Contemporary Philosophies of Human Activity.* Philadelphia: University of Pennsylvania Press, 1971.

Berryman, Phillip. "Basic Christian Communities and the Future of Latin America." *Monthly Review* 36 (July-August 1984).

_____. *Liberation Theology.* New York: Pantheon Books, 1987.

_____. *The Religious Roots of Rebellion*. Maryknoll, N.Y.: Orbis Books, 1984.

Betto, Frei. "As comunidades eclesiais de base como potencial de transformção da sociedade brasileira." *Revista Eclesiástica Brasileira (REB)* 43 (1983): 494–503.

_____. *Fidel Castro y la religión*. La Habana, Cuba: Oficina de Publicaciones del Consejo de Estado, 1985.

_____. *O que é comunidade eclesial de base?* São Paulo: Brasiliense, 1981.

Binder, Leonard, et al. *Crises and Sequences in Political Development*. Princeton: Princeton University Press, 1971.

Black, Cyril E. *The Dynamics of Modernization*. Champaign: University of Illinois Press, 1967.

Boff, Clodovis. "Agente de pastoral e povo." *Revista Eclesiástica Brasileira (REB)* 40 (1980): 216–41.

_____. "Society and the Kingdom: A Dialogue between a Theologian, a Christian Activist, and a Parish Priest." In Leonardo Boff and Clodovis Boff, *Salvation and Liberation*. Translated by Robert R. Barr. Maryknoll, N.Y.: Orbis Books, 1984.

_____, and Leonardo Boff. "Good News of Bishops' Economics Pastoral and Bad News Left Unmentioned." *National Catholic Reporter,* August 28, 1987.

Boff, Leonardo. "CEBs: A igreja inteira na base." *Revista Eclesiástica Brasileira (REB)* 43 (1983): 459–69.

_____. *Church: Charism and Power*. Translated by John W. Diercksmeier. New York: Crossroads, 1985.

_____. *Ecclesiogenesis: The Base Communities Reinvent the Church*. Translated by Robert Barr. Maryknoll, N.Y.: Orbis Books, 1986.

_____. *Jesus Christ: Liberator*. Translated by Patrick Hughes. Maryknoll, N.Y.: Orbis Books, 1978.

_____. *Kirche als Sakrament*. Paderborn: Verlag Bonifacius- Druckerei, 1972.

_____. *Liberating Grace*. Maryknoll, N.Y.: Orbis Books, 1979.

_____. "Theological Characteristics of a Grassroots Church." In *The Challenge of Basic Christian Communities,* translated by John Drury and edited by Sergio Torres and John Eagleson. Mayrknoll, N.Y.: Orbis Books, 1981.

_____, and Clodovis Boff. *Liberation Theology: From Dialogue to Confrontation*. Translated by Robert R. Barr. San Francisco: Harper and Row, 1986.

Bollen, Kenneth. "World System Position, Dependency, and Democracy: The Cross-National Evidence." *American Sociological Review* 48 (1983): 468–79.

Bonino, José Míguez. *Christians and Marxists: The Mutual Challenge to Revolution*. London: Hodder and Stoughton, 1976.

_____. *Doing Theology in a Revolutionary Situation*. Philadelphia: Fortress Press, 1975.

Borges, Jorge Luis. *Labyrinths: Selected Stories and Other Writings*. Edited by Donald A. Yates and James E. Irby. New York: New Directions, 1964.

Bourricaud, Francois. *The Sociology of Talcott Parsons*. Chicago: University of Chicago Press, 1981.

Bradshaw, York W. "Dependent Development in Black Africa: A Cross National Study." *American Sociological Review* 50 (1985): 195–207.

Braudel, Fernand. *Civilization and Capitalism: 15th—18th Century*. 3 vols. New York: Harper and Row, 1981, 1982, 1984.

Brown, Robert McAfee, ed. *The Essential Reinhold Niebuhr: Selected Essays and Addresses*. New Haven: Yale University Press, 1986.

_____. *Theology in a New Key: Responding to Liberation Themes*. Philadelphia: Westminster Press, 1978.

Bruneau, Thomas C. "Basic Christian Communities in Latin America." In *Churches and Politics in Latin America*. Edited by Daniel H. Levine. Beverly Hills, Calif.: Sage Publications, 1980.

_____. "Church and Politics in Brazil: The Genesis of Change." *Journal of Latin America* 17 (1985): 271–93.

_____. *The Church in Brazil*. Austin: University of Texas Press, 1982.

_____. *The Political Transformation of the Brazilian Catholic Church*. London: Cambridge University Press, 1974.

Cardenal, Ernesto. *The Gospel in Solentiname*. 4 vols. Translated by Donald Walsh. Maryknoll, N.Y.: Orbis Books, 1976–82.

_____. "Is Liberation Theology Marxist?" *Crisis* (June 1987).

Castillo, Fernando. *Iglesia liberadora y política*. Santiago: ECO, 1984.

Castillo-Cardenas, Gonzalo. *Liberation Theology from Below: The Life and Thought of Manuel Quintin Lame*. Maryknoll, N.Y.: Orbis Books, 1987.

Castro, Fidel. *Fidel and Religion*. Translated by The Cuban Center for Translation and Interpretation. New York: Simon and Schuster, 1987.

Cavanaugh, Michael A. "Liberalism and Rationalism in Modern Theology: The Socioligical Hypothesis." *Review of Religious Research* 29 (September 1987): 25–43.

Chambre, Henri. *Christianity and Communism*. Translated by R.F. Trevett. New York: Hawthorn, 1960.

Chang-Rodríquez, Eugenio. *Opciones políticas peruanas 1985*. Lima: Centro de Documentación Andina, 1985.

Chase-Dunn, Christopher. "The Effects of International Economic Dependence on Development and Inequality: A Cross-National Analysis." *American Sociological Review* 40 (1975): 720–38.

Chirot, Daniel. "The Rise of the West." *American Sociological Review* 50 (1985): 181–95.

Chodak, Szymon. *Societal Development.* New York: Oxford University Press, 1973.

Cleary, Edward L. *Crisis, Change, and the Church in Latin America.* Maryknoll, N.Y.: Orbis Books, 1985.

Coleman, John A., S.J. "Civil Religion and Liberation Theology in North America." In *Theology in the Americas,* edited by Sergio Torres and John Eagleson. Maryknoll, N.Y.: Orbis Books, 1976.

Comblin, José. *The Church and the National Security State.* Maryknoll, N.Y.: Orbis Books, 1979.

Cone, James. *Black Theology and Black Power.* New York: Seabury Press, 1969.

_____. *A Black Theology of Liberation.* Philadelphia: J. B. Lippencott Co., 1970.

_____. *For My People: Black Theology and the Black Church.* Maryknoll, N.Y.: Orbis Books, 1984.

_____. *God of the Oppressed.* New York: Seabury Press, 1980.

Conferéncia Nacional dos Bispos do Brasil. *Comunidades eclesiais de base na igreja no Brasil.* Sáo Paulo: Paulinas, 1983.

_____. *Comunidades: Igreja na base.* São Paulo: Paulinas, 1977.

Coser, Lewis, et al. *Introduction to Sociology.* 2nd ed. San Diego: Harcourt Brace Jovanovich, 1987.

Cotler, Julio. *Clases, estado, y nación en el Perú.* Lima: Instituto de Estudios Peruanos, 1978.

Cox, Harvey. *Religion in the Secular City: Toward a Postmodern Theology.* New York: Simon and Schuster, 1984.

Cullmann, Oscar. *Jesus and the Revolutionaries.* New York: Harper and Row, 1976.

Day, Dorothy. *On Pilgrimage.* New York: Curtis Publishing Co., 1972.

Debray, Régis. *Revolution in the Revolution?* New York: Monthly Review Press, 1967.

Delacroix, Jacques, and Charles C. Ragin. "Structural Blockage: A Cross-National Study of Economic Dependency, State Efficacy, and Underdevelopment." *American Journal of Sociology* 86 (1981): 1311–47.

Digan, Prigan. *Churches in Contestation: Asian Christian Social Protest.* Maryknoll, N.Y.: Orbis Books, 1984.

Dupré, Louis. *Marx's Social Critique of Culture.* New Haven: Yale University Press, 1983.

Durkheim, Emile. *Socialism.* Translated by Charlotte Sattler and edited by Alvin W. Gouldner. New York: Collier Books, 1962.

Dussel, Enrique. "Current Events in Latin America." In *The Challenge of Basic Christian Communities,* translated by John Drury and edited by Sergio Torres and John Eagleson. Maryknoll, N.Y.: Orbis Books, 1981.

_____. "Historical and Philosophical Presuppositions for Latin American Theology." In *Frontiers of Theology in Latin America,* edited by Rosino Gibellini. Maryknoll, N.Y.: Orbis Books, 1979.

_____. *History and the Theology of Liberation.* Translated by John Drury. Maryknoll, N.Y.: Orbis Books, 1976.

Eagleson, John, ed. *Christians for Socialism: Documentation of the Christians for Socialism Movement in Latin America.* Maryknoll, N.Y.: Orbis Books, 1975.

_____, and Philip Scharper, eds. *Puebla and Beyond: Documentation and Commentary.* Translated by John Drury. Maryknoll, N.Y.: Orbis Books, 1979.

Eisenstadt, S. N., "Reflections on a Theory of Modernization." In *Nations by Design,* edited by Arnold Rivkin. Garden City, N.Y.: Doubleday and Co..

_____, ed. *The Protestant Ethic and Modernization.* New York: Basic Books, 1968.

Elliot, Gil. *Twentieth Century Book of the Dead.* New York: Charles Scribner's Sons, 1972.

Ellis, Marc. H. *Faithfulness in an Age of Holocaust.* New York: Amity House, 1986.

_____. *Toward a Jewish Theology of Liberation.* Maryknoll, N.Y.: Orbis Books, 1987.

Evans, Peter B., and Michael Timberlake. "Dependence, Inequality, and the Growth of the Tertiary: A Comparative Analysis of Less Developed Countries." *American Sociological Review* 45 (1980): 531–52.

Fabella, Virginia, ed. *Asia's Struggle for Full Humanity: Towards a Relevant Theology.* Maryknoll, N.Y.: Orbis Books, 1980.

_____. "An Introduction." In *Asia's Struggle for Full Humanity: Towards a Relevant Theology,* edited by Virginia Fabella. Maryknoll, N.Y.: Orbis Books, 1980

_____, and Sergio Torres, eds. *Irruption of the Third World: Challenge to Theology.* Maryknoll, N.Y.: Orbis Books, 1982.

Ferm, Deane William. *Third World Liberation Theologies: An Introductory Survey.* Maryknoll, N.Y.: Orbis Books, 1986.

_____ ed. *Third World Liberation Theologies: A Reader.* Maryknoll, N.Y.: Orbis Books, 1986.

Festinger, Leon A. "Cognitive Dissonance." *Scientific American* 207 (October 1972): 93–102.

Fiala, Robert. "Inequality and the Service Sector in Less Developed Countries: A Reanalysis and Respecification." *American Sociological Review* 48 (1983): 421–28.

Fischer, Fritz. *War of Illusions: German Policies from 1911 to 1914.* New York: W. W. Norton, 1975.

Francis, Michael J. "Dependency: Ideology, Fad, and Fact." In *Latin America: Dependency or Interdependence,* edited by Michael Novak and Michael P. Jackson. Washington, D.C.: American Enterprise Institute, 1985.

Frank, Andre Gunder. *Capitalism and Underdevelopment in Latin America.* New York: Monthly Review Press, 1969.

_____. *Latin America: Underdevelopment or Revolution?* New York: Monthly Review Press, 1969.

Freire, Paulo. *Pedagogy of the Oppressed.* Translated by Myra B. Ramos. New York: Herder and Herder, 1970.

Frente Sandinista de Liberación Nacional. "Comunicado oficial de la dirección nacional del FSLN sobre la religión." *Barricada* (Managua), October 7, 1980.

Friedlander, Saul. *Pius XII and the Third Reich.* Translated by Charles Fullmann. New York: Alfred A. Knopf, 1966.

Friedman, Milton. "Good Ends, Bad Means." In *The Catholic Challenge to the American Economy: Reflections on the U.S. Bishops' Pastoral Letter on Catholic Social Teaching and the U.S. Economy,* edited by Thomas M. Gannon. New York: Macmillan, 1987.

Furci, Carmelo. *The Chilean Communist Party and the Road to Socialism.* London: Zed Press, 1985.

Galilea, Segundo. "Liberation Theology and New Tasks Facing Christians." In *Frontiers of Theology in Latin America,* edited by Rosino Gibellini. Maryknoll, N.Y.: Orbis Books, 1979.

Galindo Flores, Alberto. *El pensamiento comunista.* Lima: Mosca Azul Editores, 1982.

Garcia, John Alvarez, and Christian Restrepo Calle, eds. *Camilo Torres: His Life and His Message.* Translated by Virginia O'Grady. Springfield, Ill.: Templegate, 1968.

Garretón, Manuel Antonio. *El proceso político chileno.* Santiago: Flacso, 1983.

_____. "La transición bloqueada." *Mensaje* (Enero- Febrero 1985).

Garrett, William R. "Religion and the Legitimation of Violence." In *Prophetic Religions and Politics,* edited by Jeffrey K. Hadden and Anson Shupe. New York: Paragon House, 1986.

Gerth, H. H., and C. Wright Mills, eds. *From Max Weber: Essays in Sociology*. New York: Oxford University Press, 1946.

Gibellini, Rossino, ed. *Frontiers of Theology in Latin America*. Maryknoll, N.Y.: Orbis Books, 1979.

Gouldner, Alvin W. *The Coming Crisis in Western Sociology*. New York: Avon Books, 1970.

_____. *The Dialectic of Ideology and Technology*. New York: Seabury Press, 1976.

Gramsci, Antonio. *The Modern Prince and Other Writings*. New York: International Publishers, 1970.

Gregory, Afonso. "Dados préliminares sòbre experiêcias de comunidades eclesias de base no Brasil." In *Comunidades eclesiais de base: Utopia ou realidade?* Edited by Afonso Gregory. Petrópolis: Vozes, 1973.

Greider, William. *Secrets of the Temple: How the Federal Reserve Runs the Country*. New York: Simon and Schuster, 1987.

Gudorf, Christine E. *Catholic Social Teaching on Liberation Themes*. Washington, D.C.: University Press of America, 1981.

Guerra Garcia, Francisco. *Velasco: Del estado oligárquico al capitalismo de estado*. Lima: Ediciones CEDEP, 1983.

Gutiérrez, Gustavo. "The Irruption of the Poor in Latin America and the Christian Communities of the Common People" In *The Challenge of Basic Christian Communities,* translated by John Drury and edited by Sergio Torres and John Eagleson. Maryknoll, N.Y.: Orbis Books, 1981.

_____. "Liberation Praxis and Christian Faith." In *Frontiers of Theology in Latin America,* edited by Rosino Gibellini and translated by John Drury. Maryknoll, N.Y.: Orbis Books, 1979.

_____. *On Job: God-Talk and the Suffering of the Innocent*. Translated by Matthew O'Connell. Maryknoll, N.Y.: Orbis Books, 1987.

_____. *The Power of the Poor in History*. Translated by Robert Barr. Maryknoll, N.Y.: Orbis Books, 1983.

_____. *A Theology of Liberation*. Translated and edited by Sister Caridad Inda and John Eagleson. Maryknoll, N.Y.: Orbis Books, 1973.

Habermas, Jürgen. *Knowledge and Human Interests*. Translated by Jeremy J. Shapiro. Boston: Beacon Press, 1971.

_____. *Theory and Practice*. Translated by John Viertel. Boston: Beacon Press, 1974.

_____. *The Theory of Communicative Action*. Vol.1. Boston: Beacon Press, 1981.

Hamilton, Kenneth. *God Is Dead: The Anatomy of a Slogan*. Grand Rapids: William B. Eerdmans, 1966.

Harvey, Van A. *The Historian and the Believer*. New York: Macmillan, 1969.

Hewitt, W. E. "Basic Christian Communities (CEBs): Structure, Orientation and Sociopolitical Thrust." *Thought,* Special Edition, forthcoming.

_____. "Strategies for Social Change Employed by Comunidades Eclesiais de Base (CEBs) in the Archdiocese of São Paulo." *Journal for the Scientific Study of Religion* 25 (1986).

Hodges, Donald C. *Intellectual Foundations of the Nicaraguan Revolution*. Austin: University of Texas Press, 1986.

Horkheimer, Max. *Critical Theory*. New York: Herder and Herder, 1972.

_____. *Critique of Instrumental Reason*. New York: Seabury Press, 1974.

_____, and Theodor Adorno. *Dialectic of Enlightenment*. New York: Herder and Herder, 1972.

Horowitz, Irving Louis, et al., eds. *Latin American Radicalism: A Documentary Report on Left and Nationalist Movements*. New York: Random House, 1969.

Hughes, Robert. *The Fatal Shore*. New York: Alfred A. Knopf, 1987.

Hunter, Guy. *Modernizing Peasant Societies.* New York: Oxford University Press, 1969.

Jiménez, Roberto, et al. *Teologia de la liberación.* Caracas: CEDIAL, 1986.

Joint Communique Following Meeting of U.S. and Central American Bishops. In *Origins: N.C. Documentary Service,* 17 (August 13, 1987).

Jüngel, Eberhard. *Karl Barth: A Theological Legacy.* Translated by Garrett E. Paul. Philadelphia: Westminster Press, 1986.

Kilborn, Peter T. "Already, a New Look." *New York Times,* January 24, 1984, p. 25.

Korean Theologians. "Reflections by Korean Theologians on the Final Statement of the Asian Theological Conference." In *Asia's Struggle for Full Humanity,* edited by Virginia Fabella. Maryknoll, N.Y.: Orbis Books, 1980.

Kruger, Gustav. "The 'Theology of Crisis.'" In *European Intellectual History Since Darwin and Marx,* edited by W. Warren Wagar. New York: Harper and Row, 1967.

Lagos, Gustavo. *International Stratification and Underdeveloped Countries.* Chapel Hill: University of North Carolina Press, 1963.

Lamb, Matthew L. *Solidarity with Victims.* Maryknoll, N.Y.: Orbis Books, 1982.

Lay Commission on Catholic Social Teaching and the U.S. Economy (Michael Novak and William Simon, Co-chairmen). *Toward the Future: Catholic Social Thought and the U.S. Economy—A Lay Letter.* North Tarrytown, N.Y.: Lay Commission, 1984.

_____. "Liberty and Justice for All." A report on the U.S. Catholic Bishops' Pastoral Letter on the American Economy. North Tarrytown, N.Y.: Lay Commission, 1986.

Lenin, V. I. *The Essential Works of Lenin.* New York: Bantam Books, 1966.

Lerner, Daniel. *The Passing of Traditional Society.* New York: Free Press, 1958.

338 The Politics of Latin American Liberation Theology

Lernoux, Penny. *Cry of the People: United States Involvement in the Rise of Fascism, Torture, Murder and the Persecution of the Catholic Church in Latin America*. Garden City, N.Y.: Doubleday and Co., 1980.

_____. *In Banks We Trust*. Garden City, N.Y.: Anchor Press/Doubleday, 1984.

Levine, Daniel, ed. *Religion and Political Conflict in Latin America*. Chapel Hill: University of North Carolina Press, 1986.

_____. "Religion and Politics: Drawing Lines and Understanding Change." *Latin American Research Review* 20 (1985).

_____. "Religion, Society, and Politics: States of the Art." *Latin American Research Review* 16 (1981).

Levy, Guenther. *The Catholic Church and Nazi Germany*. New York: McGraw-Hill, 1964.

Levy, Marion J., Jr. *Modernization and the Structure of Societies*. Princeton: Princeton University Press, 1966.

Lipset, Seymour Martin. *The First New Nation: The United States in Historical and Comparative Perspective*. London: Heinemann, 1963.

_____. *Revolution and Counter-Revolution*. Garden City, N.Y.: Doubleday and Co., 1970.

Liss, Sheldon B. *Marxist Thought in Latin America*. Berkeley: University of California Press, 1984.

López Trujillo, Alfonso. *Liberación marxista y liberación cristiana*. Madrid: Biblioteca de Autores Cristianos, 1974.

McCann, Dennis P. *Christian Realism and Liberation Theology*. Maryknoll, N.Y.: Orbis Books, 1981.

_____. *New Experiment in Democracy: The Challenge for American Catholicism*. Kansas City: Sheed and Ward, 1987.

_____, and Charles R. Strain. *Polity and Praxis: A Program for American Practical Theology*. Minneapolis: Winston Press/Seabury Press, 1985.

McClelland, David. *The Achieving Society*. New York: Free Press, 1961.

McKenzie, John L. "Poor, Poverty." In *Dictionary of the Bible*. Milwaukee: Bruce Publishing, 1965.

McLelland, David. *Marxism after Marx*. New York: Harper and Row, 1979.

Mainwaring, Scott. *The Catholic Church and Politics in Brazil, 1916–1985*. Stanford: Stanford University Press, 1986.

Mandel, Ernest. *Late Capitalism*. London: NLB, 1975.

Marcuse, Herbert. *One-Dimensional Man*. Boston: Beacon Books, 1964.

Mariátegui, José Carlos. *Seven Interpretative Essays on Peruvian Reality*. Austin: University of Texas Press, 1974.

Marins, José, et al., eds. *Praxis de los padres de América Latina: Los documentos de las Conferencias Episcopales de Medellín a Puebla (1968–1978)*. Bogotá: Ediciones Paulinas, 1978.

Marx, Karl. *Capital*. New York: Random House, 1906.

Mehden, Fred R. von der. *Politics in the Developing Nations*. Englewood Cliffs, N.J.: Prentice-Hall, 1964.

Metz, Johann Baptist. *Faith in History and Society: Toward a Practical Fundamental Theology*. Translated by David Smith. New York: Seabury Press, 1980.

Michel, Irmâo. "Comunidades católicas de base são o fruto de colaboração entre duas classes sociais, a pobre e a média." *Revista Eclesiástica Brasileira (REB)* 42 (1982): 120–28.

Míguez Bonino, José. *Christians and Marxists: The Mutual Challenge to Revolution*. London: Hodder and Stoughton, 1976.

_____. *Doing Theology in a Revolutionary Situation*. Philadelphia: Fortress Press, 1975.

Mills, C. Wright. *The Sociological Imagination*. New York: Oxford University Press, 1959.

Miranda, José. "Christianity and Communism." In *Third World Liberation Theologies: A Reader,* edited by Deane William Ferm. Maryknoll, N.Y.: Orbis Books, 1986.

_____. *Communism in the Bible.* Maryknoll, N.Y.: Orbis Books, 1982.

_____. *Marx against the Marxists.* Maryknoll, N.Y.: Orbis Books, 1980.

Molina, Uriel. "El sendero de una experiencia." *Nicarauac* 5 (1981). Managua: Ministerio de Educación.

Mommsen, Wolfgang J. *The Age of Bureaucracy: Perspectives on the Political Sociology of Max Weber.* Oxford: Basil Blackwell, 1974.

_____. *Theories of Imperialism: A Critical Assessment of Various Interpretations of Modern Imperialism.* Translated by P. S. Falla. New York: Random House, 1980.

Moore, John Norton. "The Secret War in Central America and the Future of World Order." *The American Journal of International Law* 80 (January 1986). Reprinted in *World Affairs* 148 (Fall 1985): 75–130.

Mott, Michael. *The Seven Mountains of Thomas Merton.* Boston: Houghton Mifflin, 1984.

Moulian, Tomás. "Crítica a la crítica marxista de las democracias burguesas." In *América Latina 80: Democracia y movimiento popular.* Lima: DESCO, 1981.

_____. "Evolucíon de la izquierda chilena: La influencia del marxismo." In *Qué signífica hacer política?* edited by N. Lechner. Lima: DESCO, 1982.

National Conference of Catholic Bishops/United States Catholic Conference. *The Challenge of Peace: God's Promise and Our Response.* Washington, D.C.: USCC Office of Publishing and Promotion Services, 1983.

_____. *Economic Justice for All: Pastoral Letter on Catholic Social Teaching and the U.S. Economy.* Washington, D.C.: USCC Office of Publishing and Promotion Services, 1986.

Neely, Alan. "Liberation Theology in Latin America: Antecedents and Autochthony." *Missiology: An International Review:* 6 (3), 1978.

Nettl, J.P., and Roland Robertson. *International Systems and the Modernization of Societies: The Formation of National Goals and Attitudes.* New York: Basic Books, 1968.

Neuhaus, Richard John. "Liberation Theology and the Cultural Captivity of the Gospel." In *Liberation Theology,* edited by Ronald Nash. Milford, Mich.: Mott Media, Inc., 1984.

Niebuhr, H. Richard. *Christ and Culture.* New York: Harper and Row, 1951.

Niebuhr, Reinhold. *Faith and Politics: A Commentary on Religious, Social and Political Thought in a Technological Age.* Edited by Ronald H. Stone. New York: George Braziller, 1968.

Nieto, Jorge. *Izquierda y democracia en el Perú,* 1975–1980. Lima: DESCO, 1983.

Nisbet, Robert A. *Social Change and History.* New York: Oxford University Press.

Norman, Edward. *Christianity in the Southern Hemisphere.* Oxford: Clarendon Press, 1981.

Novak, Michael. "*Christianity Today* talks to Michael Novak." *Christianity Today,* July 10, 1987. Interview with Michael Novak by David Neff.

_____. *Freedom with Justice: Catholic Social Thought and Liberal Institutions.* San Francisco: Harper and Row, 1984.

_____, ed. *Liberation South, Liberation North.* Washington, D.C.: American Enterprise Institute, 1981.

_____. "Moral Clarity in the Nuclear Age." *National Review,* April 1, 1983.

_____. *The Spirit of Democratic Capitalism.* New York: Simon and Schuster, 1982.

_____. *Will It Liberate? Questions about Liberation Theology.* New York: Paulist Press, 1987.

O'Connor, John J. "Congressional Testimony on Central America." In *Origins: N.C. Documentary Service* 14 (April 15, 1985).

_____. "The Meaning of Economic Imperialism." In *Readings in U.S. Imperialism,* edited by K. T. Fann and D. C. Hodges. Boston: Porter Sargent, 1971.

Palmer, Spencer J. *Korea and Christianity: The Problem of Identification with Tradition.* Seoul: Royal Asiatic Society, 1986.

Panoso Loero, Teresa. *Los cristianos por el socialismo.* Santiago: El Mercurio, 1975.

Parsons, Talcott. *The Structure of Social Action.* New York: Free Press, 1949.

_____. *The Social System.* New York: Free Press, 1951.

_____, et al. *Working Papers in a Theory of Action.* New York: Free Press, 1953.

Pásara, Luis. *Radicalización y conflicto en la iglesia peruana.* Lima: Ediciones El Virrey, 1986.

Pennock, J. Roland, ed. *Self-Government in Modernizing Nations.* Englewood Cliffs, N.J.: Prentice-Hall, 1964.

Pius IX. "On Atheistic Communism." In *Seven Great Encyclicals.* Glen Rock, N.J.: Paulist Press, 1963.

Pye, Lucian W. *Politics, Personality, and Nation Building.* New Haven: Yale University Press, 1962.

Quade, Quentin L., ed. *The Pope and Revolution.* Washington, D.C.: Center for Ethics and Public Policy, 1982.

Rahner, Karl. "The Fundamental Option." In *A Rahner Reader,* edited by Gerald A. McCool. New York: Seabury Press, 1975.

Ramos, Joseph. "Dependency and Development: An Attempt to Clarify the Issues." In *Liberation South, Liberation North,* edited by Michael Novak. Washington, D.C.: American Enterprise Institute, 1981.

Ramsay, William M. *Four Modern Prophets: Walter Rauschenbusch, Martin Luther King, Jr., Gustavo Gutiérrez, Rosemary Radford Ruether.* Atlanta: John Knox Press, 1986.

Ratzinger, Joseph Cardinal, and Vittorio Messori. *The Ratzinger Report.* San Francisco: Ignatius Press, 1986.

Rau, William, and D. W. Roncek. "Industrialization and World Inequality: The Transformation of the Division of Labor in 59 Nations, 1960–1981." *American Sociological Review* 52 (1987): 359–69.

Richard, Pablo. "Biblical Theology of Confrontation with Idols." In Pablo Richard et al. *The Idols of Death and the God of Life: A Theology.* Translated by Barbara E. Campbell and Bonnie Shepard. Maryknoll, N.Y.: Orbis Books, 1983.

_____. "The Experience of Christians in Chile during the Popular Unity Period." In *Cristianos Revolucionarios II* 4 (1980). Managua: Instituto Histórico Centro Americano.

_____, et al. *The Idols of Death and the God of Life: A Theology.* Translated by Barbara E. Campbell and Bonnie Shepard. Maryknoll, N.Y.: Orbis Books, 1983.

Riding, Alan. "The Sword and the Cross." *New York Times,* May 28, 1981.

Ritschl, Albrecht. *The Christian Doctrine of Justification and Reconciliation.* Translated and edited by H. R. Mackintosh and A. B. Macauley. Edinburgh: T. and T. Clark, 1900.

Roach, John. "Toward a Diplomatic Non-Military Solution in Central America." In *Origins: N.C. Documentary Service* 13 (August 4, 1983).

Robertson, Roland. "The Development and Modern Implications of the Classical Sociological Perspective on Religion and Revolution." In *Religion, Rebellion, Revolution,* edited by Bruce Lincoln. New York: St. Martin's Press, 1985.

_____. "Global Aspects of the Politicization of Religion." In *The Changing Face of Religion,* edited by James Beckford and Thomas Luckmann. Beverly Hills: Sage Publications, 1988.

_____. "Latin America and Liberation Theology." In *Church-State Relations: Tensions and Transitions,* edited by Thomas Robbins and Roland Robertson. New Brunswick, N.J.: Transaction Books, 1987.

_____. "Liberation Theology in Latin America: Sociological Problems of Interpretation and Explanation." *In Prophetic Religions and Politics,* edited by Jeffrey K. Hadden and Anson Shupe. New York: Paragon House, 1986.

_____, and JoAnn Chirico. "Humanity, Globalization and Worldwide Religious Resurgence: A Theoretical Exploration," *Sociological Analysis* 46 (3), 1985.

_____, and Andrew Tudor. "The Third World and International Stratification: Theoretical Considerations and Research Findings." *Sociology* 2 (2),1968.

Rohter, Larry. "Southern Summit Rekindles Old Dreams of Latin Unity." *New York Times,* November 29, E, 1987.

Rubenstein, Richard L. *The Age of Triage: Fear and Hope in an Over-crowded World.* Boston: Beacon Press, 1983.

_____. *The Cunning of History: Mass Death and the American Future.* New York: Harper and Row, 1975.

_____. *The Political Significance of Latin America Liberation Theology.* Washington, D.C.: The Washington Institute for Values in Public Policy, 1986.

_____, and John K. Roth. *Approaches to Auschwitz: The Holocaust and Its Legacy.* Atlanta: John Knox Press, 1987.

Rubison, Richard. "The World-Economy and the Distribution of Income Within States: A Cross-National Study." *American Sociological Review* 41 (1976): 638–59.

Sacred Congregation for the Doctrine of the Faith. *Instructions on Certain Aspects of the Theology of Liberation.* In *Origins: N.C. Documentary Service* 13 (September 1984)..

_____. *Instruction on Christian Freedom and Liberation.* Vatican City: Vatican Polyglot Press, 1986.

Sanders, Thomas G. "The Catholic Church in Brazil's Political Transition." *American Universities Field Staff Reports* 48 (1980).

Schleiermacher, Friedrich. *On Religion: Speeches to Its Cultural Despisers.* New York: Harper Torch Books, 1958.

Schumpeter, Joseph A. *Capitalism, Socialism, and Democracy.* New York: Harper and Row, 1962.

Schüssler Fiorenza, Elisabeth. *In Memory of Her: A Feminist Theological Reconstruction of Christian Origins.* New York: Crossroads, 1983.

_____. "Toward a Feminist Biblical Hermeneutics: Biblical Interpretation and Liberation Theology." In *The Challenge of Liberation Theology: A First World Response,* edited by Brian Mahan and L. Dale Richesin. Maryknoll, N.Y.: Orbis Books, 1981.

Second General Conference of Latin American Bishops. *The Church in the Present-Day Transformation of Latin America.* 2 vols. Washington, D.C.: U.S. Catholic Conference, 1970.

Segundo, Juan Luis. *The Liberation of Theology.* Translated by John Drury. Maryknoll, N.Y.: Orbis Books, 1976.

_____. "Capitalism—Socialism: A Theological Crux." In *Liberation South, Liberation North,* edited by Michael Novak. Washington, D.C.: American Enterprise Institute, 1981.

_____. "Capitalism and Socialism, The Theological Crux." In *The Mystical and Political Dimension of the Christian Faith,* edited by Claude Geffré and Gustavo Gutiérrez. New York: Herder and Herder, 1974.

Sigmund, Paul E. "Epistle from a Democratic Capitalist." *Commonweal,* March 27, 1987, p. 186. Review of Michael Novak, *Will It Liberate?*

Sinai, I. Robert. *The Challenge of Modernization.* New York: W. W. Norton, 1964.

Smith, Brian. *The Church and Politics in Chile.* Princeton: Princeton University Press, 1982.

Sobrino, Jon. *Christology at the Crossroads.* Translated by John Drury. Maryknoll, N.Y.: Orbis Books, 1978.

Stackhouse, Max. *Public Theology and Political Economy.* Grand Rapids: William B. Eerdmans, 1987.

Tabb, William, ed. *Churches in Struggle: Liberation Theologies and Social Change in North America.* New York: Monthly Review Press, 1986.

Tamez, Elsa. *Bible of the Oppressed.* Maryknoll, N.Y.: Orbis Books, 1982.

_____. "Good News for the Poor." In *Third World Liberation Theologies: A Reader,* edited by Deane William Ferm. Maryknoll, N.Y.: Orbis Books, 1986.

Tironi, Eugenio. *La torre de Babel: Ensayos de crítica y renovación política.* Santiago: Ediciones Sur, 1984.

Tocqueville, Alexis de. *Democracy in America.* Edited by J. P. Mayer and translated by George Lawrence. Garden City, N.Y.: Doubleday Anchor Books, 1969.

Torres, Sergio, and John Eagleson, eds. *Theology in the Americas.* Maryknoll, N.Y.: Orbis Books, 1976.

Tovar, Teresa. *Velasquismo y movimiento popular, otra historia prohibida.* Lima: DESCO, 1985.

Tucker, Robert C., ed. *The Marx-Engels Reader.* 2d ed. New York: W. W. Norton, 1978.

_____. *Philosophy and Myth in Karl Marx.* New York: Cambridge University Press, 1961.

Valenzuela, Arturo, and J. Samuel Valenzuela, eds. *Military Rule in Chile.* Baltimore: Johns Hopkins University Press, 1986.

Vallier, Ivan. *Catholicism, Social Control, and Modernization in Latin America.* Englewood Cliffs, N.J.: Prentice-Hall, 1970.

Vega Centeno, Imelda. *Aprismo popular: Mito, cultura e historia*. Lima: Tarea, 1986.

_____. *Ideología y cultura en el aprismo popular.* Lima: Tarea, 1986.

Vidales, Raul. "Methodological Issues in Liberation Theology." In *Frontiers of Theology in Latin America,* edited by Rosino Gibellini. Maryknoll, N.Y.: Orbis Books, 1979.

Vree, Dale. "A Critique of Christian Marxism." In *Liberation Theology,* edited by Ronald Nash. Milford, Mich.: Mott Media, Inc., 1984.

Vree, Dale. *On Synthesizing Marxism and Christianity.* New York: John Wiley and Sons, 1976.

Vuskovic, Pedro. *La religión: Opio del pueblo y protesta contra la miserio real.* Rotterdam: Instituto para un Nuevo Chile, 1982.

Wallerstein, Immanuel. *The Capitalist World-Economy.* Cambridge: Cambridge University Press, 1979.

_____. *The Modern World-System.* New York: Academic Press, 1974.

_____. *The Modern World-System II.* New York: Academic Press, 1980.

Walzer, Michael. *Exodus and Revolution.* New York: Basic Books, 1985.

Watson, Adam. "New States in the Americas." In *The Expansion of International Society,* edited by Hedley Bull and Adam Watson. Oxford: Clarendon Press, 1985.

Weber, Max. "'Objectivity' in Social Science and Social Policy." In *The Methodology of the Social Sciences,* translated and edited by Edward A. Shils and Henry A. Finch. New York: Free Press, 1949.

_____. *The Protestant Ethic and the Spirit of Capitalism.* Translated by Talcott Parsons. New York: Charles Scribner's Sons, 1958.

Weigel, George. *Tranquillitas Ordinis: The Present Failure and Future Promise of American Catholic Thought on War and Peace.* New York: Oxford University Press, 1987.

Welsh, John R. "Comunidades Eclesiais de Base: A New Way to be Church." *America* 8 (1986): 85–88.

West, Cornel. *Prophesy Deliverance: An Afro-American Revolutionary Christianity.* Philadelphia: Westminster Press, 1982.

Willis, Robert E. *The Ethics of Karl Barth.* Leiden: E. J. Brill, 1971.

Wilson, Bryan R. *Magic and the Millennium: A Sociological Study of Religious Movements of Protest Among Tribal and Third-World Peoples.* New York: Harper and Row, 1973.

Wright, Tennent C., S.J. "Ernesto Cardenal and the Humane Revolution in Nicaragua." *America,* December 15, 1979, pp. 387–88.

Index